The New Black Politician

Andra Gillespie

The New Black Politician

Cory Booker, Newark, and Post-Racial America

New York University Press • *New York and London*

NEW YORK UNIVERSITY PRESS
New York and London
www.nyupress.org

References to Internet websites (URLs) were accurate at the time of writing.
Neither the author nor New York University Press is responsible for URLs
that may have expired or changed since the manuscript was prepared.

Library of Congress Cataloging-in-Publication Data
Gillespie, Andra.
The new Black politician : Cory Booker, Newark, and post-racial America /
Andra Gillespie.
p.   cm.
Includes bibliographical references and index.
ISBN 978-0-8147-3244-1 (cloth : alk. paper) — ISBN 978-0-8147-3868-9
(ebook) — ISBN 978-0-8147-3869-6 (ebook)
1. Booker, Cory. 2. African American mayors—New Jersey—Newark—
Biography. 3. Mayors—New Jersey—Newark—Election. 4. Newark (N.J.)
—Politics and government—21st century. 5. Newark (N.J.)—Race relations
—Political aspects—History—21st century. 6. African Americans—Politics
and government—Case studies. 7. Post-racialism—United States—Case
studies. 8. Elite (Social sciences)—United States—Case studies. 9. Political
entrepreneurship—United States—Case studies. 10. United States—Race
relations—Political aspects—Case studies.   I. Title.
F144.N653B664 2012
974.9'044092—dc23   2011051072
[B]

New York University Press books are printed on acid-free paper,
and their binding materials are chosen for strength and durability.
We strive to use environmentally responsible suppliers and materials
to the greatest extent possible in publishing our books.

Manufactured in the United States of America

10 9 8 7 6 5 4 3 2 1

To God be the glory,
and to the people of Newark, who embraced my research and
inspired me with their transparency and indomitable spirit.

Contents

Acknowledgments

It is hard to believe that after nearly a decade of being in the field, this project has finally produced a full book! I am grateful to many people for helping me reach this point. First, I give honor to my Lord and Savior, Jesus Christ, for bringing me to this point in my career. I know that the completion of this project is nothing short of miraculous. There were times when landing certain interviews or getting access to certain types of data seemed hopeless. It was only after prayer that I saw those doors open. I am forever humbled and grateful.

A number of people assisted me in invaluable ways. First and foremost, I am eternally indebted to Kimberly McMillon, the most wonderful friend a researcher could ever have. Since 2003, she has opened her home to me nearly every time I needed to travel to Newark for work. She let me stay at her house when she was on vacation. She even let me stay, rent free, at her house for months on end. She single-handedly saved me at least $20,000 in hotel costs. If it were not for her, this book would not have been written. She asked only that I mention her in the acknowledgments, and I am happy to make good on the promise that she would be the first person after Jesus that I thanked!

Countless others provided help and succor along the way. On those rare occasions when Kim's guest room was not available, I could always count on Jerusha Schulze, Ronald Rice Jr., Karen Henderson Knight, and James Gillespie Jr. (my dad) to lend me their couches. Thank you so much for letting me crash! I also am grateful to the friends and family (especially my mother, Celestine Gillespie) who encouraged me, prayed for me, and put up with my incessant stories about Newark.

Many academics also played a significant role in the development of this project. When I first started doing research in Newark, the National Science Foundation generously supported my graduate education. As I completed this project, I had the privilege of serving as a Ford Foundation Diversity Fellow at Princeton University. I had the opportunity to present parts of this book at the Emory Political Science Department Brown Bag

Colloquium Series, the annual meeting of National Conference of Black Political Scientists, the annual meeting of the American Political Science Association, the Kirwan Institute Conference at the Ohio State University, and the Faculty-Graduate Seminar at the Center for African American Studies at Princeton University. I am grateful to all those who provided feedback in those forums, especially Maurice Magnum, Eddie Glaude Jr., Jim Steichen, William Nelson, Robert Smith, Lorenzo Morris, Joseph McCormick II, and Steve Erie. I am grateful, too, to my friends and colleagues who provided feedback in other venues: Nadia Brown, Carrie Wickham, Beth Reingold, Elizabeth Griffiths, Karyn Lacy, Adia Harvey Wingfield, and Isabel Wilkerson. I am especially grateful to Amy Benson Brown of Emory's Manuscript Development Program for her helpful comments on an earlier draft of this manuscript. In addition, I thank all the anonymous reviewers who read drafts of this book. I pray that my revisions do justice to your critiques.

I have been blessed to have had a number of wonderful research assistants over the course of this project. Jennifer Cooper, Kelly Hill, Joshua Strayhorn, Joshua Bridwell, Elizabeth Janszky, Olivia Young, Rumbidzai Mufuka, and James Ragland all helped with coding, transcribing, and/or keeping my schedule straight. I could not have finished this project without their help, and I thank them immensely. And while he is not a research assistant, I must publicly thank Dominique Tremblay, the academic services coordinator for the political science department at Emory University. He had the thankless task of scanning almost all the images in this book. Downloading and formatting those images took a long time, so I can only imagine how long it took him to scan them. I thank him from the bottom of my heart.

I am grateful as well to the editorial staff at NYU Press. Ilene Kalish believed in this project from the moment I suggested it to her. I thank her for her patience and for helping me bring this project to fruition. I would also like to thank Aiden Amos for all her assistance.

I would like to extend a heartfelt thanks to all those who gave me the privilege of interviewing them. I am grateful to those who gave me leads, even if they could not speak on the record. In short, I am touched by how helpful most people were to me, and I pray that I have done justice to your collective story.

I would be remiss to not thank the entire Booker family for all their help. I never imagined that when I met Cory Booker in 2001 that he would become an integral part of my research agenda. He graciously humored most of my research ideas, and I am grateful to him and his staffers (past and present) for giving me access to his campaigns and administration.

I am especially grateful to Cory's parents, Cary and Carolyn Booker, who helped me gain access to their son. And over the course of this project, they have been personally encouraging to me. Thank you so much for all your help.

Finally, I would like to acknowledge a pioneer in the study of African American leadership. Ron Walters was a role model to many students of black politics. So many of us are privileged to have our careers today because of his trailblazing. I know he had a chance to read my manuscript, and his support of this project was overwhelming. Sadly, Professor Walters passed away on September 10, 2010. I am heartbroken that he did not get to see the final product, but I am grateful to him for supporting and affirming this project while he lived.

Portions of chapters 3 and 4 appeared earlier in Andra Gillespie, "Losing and Winning: Cory Booker's Ascent to Newark's Mayoralty," in *Whose Black Politics? Cases in Post-racial Black Leadership*, ed. Andra Gillespie (New York: Routledge, 2010), 67–84. Used with permission.

Introduction

UNDERSTANDING BLACK POLITICS in Newark, New Jersey, at the dawn of the twenty-first century is a complex task with many moving parts. It is the story of a generational clash on the electoral front, the story of a clash of political styles (deracialized versus racialized), the story of the relationship between political brand development and electoral viability, and the story of the evolution of middle-class black representation of poor black constituents.

Kenneth Gibson, Newark's first black mayor, famously said that "wherever America's cities are going, Newark will get there first."[1] While Newark's story may seem unique to Newark, in reality it figures broadly into larger discussions of African American politics. To many, the city is synonymous with urban unrest, having been the site, in 1967, of one of the worst urban riots in American history. In the aftermath of those riots, Newark was also the site of the first National Black Power Conference, which sought nationalist solutions to the systemic problems made painfully apparent by the 1967 rebellion.[2] In 1970, Newark became the first major northeastern city (and only the third large city in the United States) to elect a black mayor.[3] The city has long been a barometer in discussions about the vitality of urban centers and the viability of creating and achieving an African American political agenda.

Given Newark's recent history of being in the vanguard with respect to black politics, it should not be surprising that it would also be on the front lines of further political innovation. With the election of the nation's first black president, the end of the first decade of the twenty-first century ushered in what journalists commonly referred to as a "post-racial" era of American politics. The election of Barack Obama supposedly proved that America had finally atoned for centuries of slavery and codified segregation. Black candidates now would be free to run as candidates, judged only by the soundness of their racially transcendent policy proposals and not by the color of their skin.[4] Featured prominently among the first wave of this latest group of black political innovators was Cory Booker, Newark's third black mayor.

To be sure, the idea of a post-racial body politic is a farcical idea to most people who study race and American politics. Although our nation has indeed improved race relations and reduced inequality, it is in no position to rest on its laurels and proclaim that Dr. Martin Luther King Jr.'s dream has been fulfilled. Cities like Newark bear witness to the reality of persistent poverty and racial inequality that belies the claim of having entered a post-racial age. In 2000 (the most recent census at the start of this project), Newark's population was 53.5% black and 29.5% Latino. Only 58% of the city's residents over age twenty-five had completed high school, compared with just over 80% of similarly aged adults nationally. Only 9% of the population over age twenty-five had a bachelor's degree or higher, compared with nearly 24.5% of all Americans in the same age bracket. Fewer than one in four residents (23.8%) owned their own homes, compared with more than 66% of all Americans, and 28.4% of residents lived below the federal poverty line in 1999. While blacks made up more than half of Newark's population, they owned only 23% of the city's businesses in 2002. Latinos were also underrepresented, owning 23% of the city's businesses. And while Newark's population accounted for just over 3% of New Jersey's population throughout the first decade of the twenty-first century, the city's business activity represented only 1% of the state's retail sales in 2002, 1% of the state's wholesale sales in 2002, and just under 2.5% of the state's hotel and food service sales in 2002.[5]

These statistics indicate that black rule did not necessarily translate into a higher standard of living for Newarkers in general and black Newarkers in particular. As scholars like William Nelson and Linda Williams pointed out in the 1980s, black mayors across the United States assumed control in cities just as federal support started to disappear and the effects of recession and deindustrialization started to sink in. As a result, the black politicians who won election to mayoralties in the 1970s and 1980s were largely hamstrung in their well-meaning attempts to use electoral power to ameliorate poverty in black communities.[6]

In this context, the rise of young "post-racial" politicians takes on new meaning. The failures of previous generations of black elected officials to address entrenched inequality and poverty created opportunities for new politicians to emerge and critique their elders' approach. It is these critiques that led to the acrimonious intraracial debates that frame a number of high-profile electoral contests featuring older and younger black politicians.

Infighting is common in politics, including black politics. What is interesting here is the tone of the infighting. Should black politicians emphasize racial issues or frame their platform as race neutral? Should candidates focus on traditional civil rights issues or broad-based economic issues? Is the failure of black elder statesmen to improve the quality of life of their communities an artifact of larger systemic inequality or the result of poor leadership? The subtext of these important debates includes discussions of moral rectitude and technocratic competence. To be sure, black civil rights leaders have long been preoccupied with the moral uplift of poor black urban dwellers.[7] Today, though, the intraracial public discussion is just as likely to focus on the moral lapses and lack of preparation of black leaders as a source of urban decay just as much as on the individual failings of black citizens.

In her book *The Boundaries of Blackness*, Cathy Cohen introduced the theory of secondary marginalization to explain how black legislative and civil rights leaders were able to separate HIV/AIDS from the mainstream black agenda for the first decade of the crisis. She argued that black leaders had an incentive to concentrate on racial justice issues that were not so clearly identified with the most socially marginal members of the black community (i.e., gays and intravenous drug users). By centering on issues on which all blacks could agree and by publicly condemning the behaviors of some blacks as being pathologically indefensible, black leaders were able to maintain an air of social respectability and thus gain access to mainstream governmental institutions.[8]

My book extends Cohen's argument into the electoral realm. I contend that the same forces that discouraged black leaders from addressing controversial problems in black communities also created opportunities for deracialized political candidates to gain political currency. Cohen focused on the relationship between black elites and the black masses, demonstrating that black elites stake their claim as legitimate black leaders by publicly upbraiding marginal blacks for bad behavior.[9] In this book, I hope to show that the forces of secondary marginalization govern relationships in the cadre of blacks vying for leadership positions in the African American community. I call this form of secondary marginalization *elite displacement*. In elite displacement, black political challengers seize on both the moral and the policy failings of incumbent black leaders to challenge them for political office. That is, insurgent candidates use the shortcomings of their predecessors to marginalize them, and they present themselves to the general public as being better positioned to assume a role of political leadership within the black community.

To some, the strategy of elite displacement seems like a shrewd strategy that is part of everyday political maneuvering. However, elite displacement has serious normative implications. It rarely occurs in a vacuum. In the United States, stereotypes that questioned blacks' fitness to hold political office have existed since Reconstruction.[10] When one black candidate employs elite displacement against another black candidate, we have to consider whether he or she may be reinforcing and perpetuating negative stereotypes about black leadership generally. We also must ponder if such attacks will affect the challenger's public persona as well. Ironically, the candidate who is perceived as doing the most to abolish stereotypes about blacks could be the one who is in fact perpetuating them.

Perpetuating these stereotypes hurts both the challenger and the incumbent. The incumbent may eventually (and deservedly) lose her job, but as a result of his hard-nosed campaign tactics, the challenger may find it difficult to create lasting political coalitions in the community that he serves. This difficulty in creating political coalitions in turn hampers his ability to deliver on his key campaign promise—to do more than his predecessors to improve black communities—even if he maintains outside political support.

Finally, the story of Newark, and the story of elite displacement generally, shows how race continues to permeate our political lives in subtle yet insidious ways. I hope that by pointing out the processes that continue to reinforce racial stereotypes, I can contribute to a wider debate about creating an empowering agenda that eliminates stereotypes and inequality while affirming the dignity and political efficacy of Americans of all walks of life.

With this in mind, I use the case study of Newark to illuminate a larger theory. Relying on a single case study has both advantages and disadvantages. I was able to observe Newark's politics as a participant observer for about eight years, and the depth and richness of my information about this city are unparalleled. I recognize, however, that critics may have some concerns about its generalizability. I direct them to Mayor Gibson's pronouncement, that "wherever America's cities are going, Newark will get there first." I also point out that political science in general and urban politics in particular has benefited from the work of scholars who developed broad political science theories using single-city case studies. Robert Dahl's *Who Governs?* and Clarence Stone's *Regime Politics* are two, formidable, single-city case studies (of New Haven and Atlanta, respectively) that generated years of robust scholarly debate.[11] More recently, Todd Shaw used Detroit to study the effectiveness of grassroots activism on housing policy outcomes.[12] To be sure, some comparative analysis is helpful. Accordingly, I draw comparative parallels where appropriate (particularly in chapter 1) to demonstrate that the phenomena I witnessed in Newark have analogues in other campaigns in other parts of the country.

In chapter 1, I outline the theory of elite displacement to explain how ambitious black politicians like Cory Booker strategize to defeat popular, often entrenched, black incumbents.

In chapter 2, I trace the evolution of black political power in Newark from the 1967 riots through the ascendance of the black and Puerto Rican conventions that led to the election of Kenneth Gibson as the city's first black mayor. The chapter then charts the political successes and failures of both Kenneth Gibson and his successor, Sharpe James. It was in this environment that young black leaders like Cory Booker emerged to try to challenge the black establishment. I offer basic biographical information about Booker and use interviews with his peers to explain how he was able to ascend to power starting in 1998.

Chapter 3 covers the 2002 mayoral election. This election is notable because election theories predicted that a moderate like Booker would be able to beat an embattled, racialized incumbent like Sharpe James. Booker, however, lost this election because the black community refused to embrace him. This chapter explains why Booker lost, using content analysis, campaign literature analysis, and focus-group data. Essentially, although Booker had a huge media advantage, James was able to leverage that media advantage to position Booker as an outsider. Furthermore, Booker's camp reinforced his outsider status through a series of campaign missteps. In the end, black Newarkers remained skeptical of Booker and thus chose to continue to support Sharpe James.

Chapter 4 explains why Booker won the 2006 mayoral election. Although to some people, it may seem fortuitous that James dropped out of the race, Booker's campaign planned for years to either run against him or push him out of the race. In any case, they made deliberate, strategic decisions to neutralize the racial and outsider attacks. These efforts contributed to James's decision to drop out of the race, and they positioned Booker to be able to score a resounding victory over Deputy Mayor Ronald Rice Sr. As the district-level data indicate, however, Booker still had relatively weaker support among black voters, which did not portend well for him going into his first term in office.

In the second half of the book, I analyze Booker's first term in office. In chapter 5, I study his progress on two key campaign initiatives, improving public safety and promoting economic development.

Chapter 6 explores how Cory Booker is perceived as a mayor. Perceptions are extremely important when voters judge candidates. How do voters and elites see Booker's policy successes and failures, and how do they view him as a politician and mayor?

In chapter 7, I discuss Booker's role in local and state politics. Using election return data from a number of 2007 state and local races, I examine the length of Booker's political coattails and the implications of those coattails for Booker's relationship with other officials and to run for higher political office.

I look at Booker's 2010 reelection campaign in chapter 8. Even though Booker was able to win handily, the political vulnerabilities that became apparent in 2007 were still present in 2010 and had long-standing consequences for Booker's ability to govern.

Finally, in chapter 9 I conclude with some closing thoughts and applications for future black politicians, and in the epilogue I offer a brief synopsis of the first month of Booker's second term in office.

PART I

The Clash of Two Black Americas

1

Black Political Entrepreneurship, Twenty-First-Century Style

The Theory of Elite Displacement

That which has been is that which will be, And that which has been done
is that which will be done. So there is nothing new under the sun.

—Ecclesiastes 1:9

IN THE OLD TESTAMENT, King Solomon reminded the faithful that the
more things change, the more they stay the same. This is certainly true in
politics. Times, techniques, and contexts may change, but certain aspects
of politics stay the same. One of the longest-lasting continuities in American politics is the invocation of negative racial issues and imagery to help a
political actor gain a comparative advantage over his or her opponents. For
instance, journalist James Callender reported the allegations of Thomas
Jefferson's sexual relationship with Sally Hemings in an attempt to destroy
his presidency. Lee Atwater produced the infamous Willie Horton ad to
derail Michael Dukakis's 1988 presidential candidacy. And the Republican National Committee primed voters' fears of interracial romance when
they developed the infamous "bimbo ad" featuring a winking, scantily
clad blonde asking the Tennessee U.S. Senate candidate Harold Ford Jr. to
"call me."[1]

Another continuity in American politics is the struggle that black candidates face in projecting a strong, competent, and ethical image. Charlton
McIlwain points out that one of the factors dooming Jesse Jackson's 1988
presidential candidacy was white voters' perception that Jackson was not
a strong leader. Even Barack Obama struggled with this perception, scor-
ing lower on the leadership dimension than Hillary Clinton during the
2008 Democratic primaries. (In 2008, voters wanted change, and Obama

outscored Clinton on this dimension).[2] Indeed, blacks aspiring for political office today encounter many of the same challenges that their predecessors faced in the 1870s and 1920s. They still face the reasonable expectation that they have to be twice as good as whites in order to be considered adequate, and they continually face the stereotype of being corrupt or not quite ready for prime time. For instance, in his 1935 preface to Harold Gosnell's *Negro Politicians*, the University of Chicago sociologist Robert Park defended the black congressmen and senators from the Reconstruction era as neither "as ignorant or as incompetent as they have been represented to be."[3] He went on to highlight their elite educational pedigrees and—if he could be critical—contended that as a whole, the Reconstruction-era congressmen "were disposed to take themselves seriously and to be, if anything, a little too conscious of their responsibilities."[4] Thus, for as long as they have been holding office, black American politicians have had to contend with being perceived as too incompetent, too uppity, or too corrupt.

For black politicians, the history of racially polarized voting, glass ceilings, and intraracial voting consensus have distorted, even minimized, the impact of these stereotypes. Times are changing, though, as blacks have broken glass ceilings and sometimes run against one another for prominent offices. How will stereotypes affect black candidates' strategic choices in this changing environment? Will historic stereotypes have a lesser or a greater impact on blacks' ability to win elections, to legislate, or to govern?

I argue that—at least in the short term—the conditions that enable post-racial or "breakthrough" black candidates[5] to emerge onto the national political stage actually help amplify and reify the negative stereotypes that have plagued black politicians (racially transcendent or otherwise) for more than a century.

It is important to consider the racial context in which we base this discussion. There has been tremendous change for blacks in the past half century. Some of these changes are positive. Since the civil rights movement, racial minority groups have gained greater access to America's most elite educational, social, and professional institutions. Until the late 1960s and early 1970s, most of the nation's most selective colleges and universities accepted only a few black students. By 2008, blacks made up at least 10% of the freshman classes at five elite universities (Columbia, the University of North Carolina at Chapel Hill, Stanford, Duke, and Yale).[6] Although no Fortune 500 companies had black CEOs in 1995, five had black CEOs in 2008.[7] Much progress is still to be made in these areas, as blacks make up more than 12% of the U.S. population and thus still are underrepresented. But arguably now, a critical mass of middle-aged black professionals have been able to spend their entire work lives in the same elite institutions as their white counterparts.

Nonetheless, other things remain the same. While it is not unheard of for blacks to win political office in majority-white jurisdictions,[8] black officeholders usually serve constituencies in which the majority of the residents are minorities or in which blacks make up the critical swing vote. For instance, in 2001 (the year before the start of this study), of the forty-seven black mayors of cities with a population of 50,000 or more, twenty led cities in which 50% or more of the population was black, and twenty-eight led cities in which blacks made up 35% or more of the population. The results are even more dramatic at the congressional level. Of the thirty-seven full-voting black members serving in the 107th Congress, twenty-four were from districts whose population was more than 50% black. All but five black members were from districts that were at least 35% black.[9] Even prominent younger black politicians—those born after the civil rights movement who have been the best positioned to benefit personally from integration—tend to start their careers in majority-black districts.[10] Therefore, despite the progress the United States has made in racial integration—and even though we know that blacks can effectively represent white constituents[11]—black politicians still are likely to at least start their careers largely representing other black people.

Combining the increasing integration of our country's most elite institutions with the constraint of blacks still beginning their political careers in black enclaves creates a dynamic, if sometimes volatile, electoral climate. Black candidates who might be naturally inclined to use deracialized political tactics to seek political office in more multiracial or majority-white districts end up using the strategy to seek office in majority-black jurisdictions, where they have to compete against a more racially conscious black political establishment and against black incumbents who, owing to previous constraints on black political mobility, cannot seek higher political office. As a result, black politicians who might be complementary allies find themselves embroiled in bitter battles over political style and generational succession.

I call this dynamic *elite displacement*. The ambitious political newcomers who use the strategy accentuate their sterling credentials and social assimilation in an attempt to unseat entrenched, racialized incumbents who are determined to retain power.

As theorized, elite displacement improves upon existing theories about candidate selection and strategy, which do a poor job explaining office seeking in the black community. To illustrate my point, I present two case studies which explain how and when black candidates use elite displacement. I then outline the positive and negative externalities of the strategy.

Political Succession and the Need for Elite Displacement

In his classic study of political succession in urban regimes, Robert Dahl tracks the transitions of power in New Haven, Connecticut, where he distinguishes four groups of people who controlled the city government from 1784 to 1960. The Puritan patricians who first dominated local politics were succeeded by white entrepreneurs who were succeeded by white ethnic politicians. The white ethnic politicians were then replaced by ethnically transcendent members of the same groups. Dahl used New Haven's electoral history to develop his theory of pluralism, or "dispersed inequalities."[12] According to this theory, Puritan oligarchs gradually ceded political power to new groups as they increased in population and economic influence. As power spread throughout New Haven, different groups could leverage their resources to sway elected officials to support policies that would benefit them. Dahl noted that no one group won every political battle. For this reason, New Haven fundamentally embraced the norm of equality and distributed political resources with rough parity.[13]

Dahl's theory has been criticized in the past fifty years, most notably by students of race and politics who believe that pluralism does not adequately explain the relationship between racial minorities and the majority-white political and economic system.[14] For example, Lucius Barker, Mack Jones, and Katherine Tate note that historic racial discrimination and persistent economic inequality in black communities have made blacks less able to translate the resources that they do have (e.g., population density in key metropolitan areas) into proportional political power.[15]

For this study, the bigger criticism of pluralism is the tacit assertion that the transition from one regime to the next is smooth and organic. In describing the political demise of New Haven's patrician class, for instance, Dahl writes, "Thereafter, the old Federalists whose memories carried them back to the days of unchallenged dominion grew feeble and died off one by one, leaving younger conservatives with different memories and traditions."[16] While he acknowledges that ethnic politics emerged in New

Haven because its ethnic residents organized around the fact that they were victims of discrimination, he argues that ethnic politicians took over largely because of the sheer size of their communities. Thus, white ethnics outnumbered the white entrepreneurs, and white entrepreneurs stepped aside in a spirit of democratic fairness. Moreover, when he describes the transition from ethnic politics to transcendent politics, Dahl argues that the new politicians were a reflection of larger changes in the ethnic community. As members of ethnic communities assimilated into the mainstream, the need for ethnic politicians subsided. Dahl does recognize that ethnic politicians still held onto office in some areas but considers these politicians as mere relics of a bygone era.[17]

The literature on candidate recruitment and strategy seems to tacitly accept Dahl's notion of organic transitions in elected leadership. Incumbents enjoy a high reelection rate. More than a quarter century ago, Gary Jacobsen and Samuel Kernell argued that potential challengers modified their behavior in response to their diminished odds of defeating an incumbent. Instead of engaging in what could be perceived as a quixotic, David-versus-Goliath run for office, challengers often wait for incumbents to retire (either for personal reasons or to run for higher office) before mounting a campaign. Moreover, vulnerable incumbents often see the handwriting on the wall and bow out of a race before engaging in a bloody electoral battle.[18]

Unfortunately, neither of these theories adequately explains the dynamics of electoral politics in black communities. In the United States, the elections of the first blacks to win elective office, particularly at the municipal level, were far from the velvet revolutions that Dahl described. Zoltan Hajnal studied major mayoral elections in the post–civil rights era and found that those first elections in which blacks were elected were marked by rancor and racially polarized voting. Although this subsided after the first election—black incumbents enjoyed far greater support from white voters in their reelection campaigns— the outcomes of those first elections were far from inevitable, and whites were not willing to give up power without a fight.[19]

Historically, blacks have had difficulty winning statewide or national office. To date, only five blacks have won election to statewide office (either U.S. Senate or governor) since Reconstruction (Edward Brooke, Douglas Wilder, Carol Moseley-Braun, Barack Obama, and Deval Patrick), and of course, only one black, Barack Obama, has been elected president. Thus, many blacks with progressive political ambitions may have chosen to remain in congressional or mayoral seats for exceptionally long periods of time because their chances of winning higher office were severely circumscribed. For instance, Alan Gerber found that blacks had some of the highest seniority rates of all members of the House of Representatives because they were less likely to risk their seats for dubious senatorial or gubernatorial bids.[20]

In addition, it is not uncommon for black elected officials at the municipal or congressional level to face only nominal competition. In a previous work, I discussed the competitiveness of congressional races featuring Congressional Black Caucus members from 1945 to 1994. Of the 239 races during this period, nearly two-thirds of those races (154) were won by at least a sixty percentage point margin. An additional sixth of the races were completely uncontested. Only fifteen races in this period were decided by margins of twenty or fewer percentage points.[21] To be sure, all congressional incumbents enjoy a huge advantage. Incumbent U.S. House members have had reelection rates of 85% or greater since 1964, and incumbent U.S. senators have had reelection rates of 75% or higher since 1982, a rate that includes incumbents who retired or chose not to run for office.[22]

Black Political Entrepreneurship

Given the special inertia that black elected officials face (especially in the absence of term limits), it is not surprising that some would eschew traditional norms of strategy and take the foolhardy step of challenging incumbents who appear to be unbeatable. A person could spend an entire career waiting for a black incumbent to die, retire, or succumb to scandal. Accordingly, ambitious challengers may consider drastic measures in order to fulfill their political career goals. The people who take huge risks and run apparently ill-considered campaigns are known as *black political entrepreneurs.*

Some black political challengers appear more likely than others to attempt to jump the queue. In my work on young black elected officials (i.e., those born after 1960),[23] I found that many viable candidates differed on an important dimension: their ties to the black political establishment. On the one hand, many prominent national figures (e.g., members of Congress or big-city mayors) are the children of prominent black politicians or activists. These officials either succeeded their parents in office (as in the case of former Congressmen Harold Ford Jr. or Kendrick

Meek) or used their family name to run for open seats (as in the case of Congressman Jesse Jackson Jr.). They did not have to challenge incumbents for their seats. On the other hand, those without strong ties to the black establishment (because they lacked the familial connections or were not mentored by prominent older black elected officials and activists) have so far been the candidates most likely to challenge strong incumbents for power, emphasizing their impressive credentials in the process. President Barack Obama, Congressman Artur Davis, and Newark Mayor Cory Booker are among those who fall into this category of black political entrepreneurs.[24]

The fact that these challengers emphasize their stellar credentials provides clues to the strategies that black political entrepreneurs often employ to mount a credible political campaign. Every competitive campaign needs to find some way to distinguish itself from the also-rans and the perennial losers. Clearly, the traditional attention-grabbers, such as raising large sums of money and hiring fancy consultants are part of that strategy, but how do black political entrepreneurs acquire the resources to raise the money and hire the consultants in the first place? Simply put, black political entrepreneurs must market themselves as qualitatively different from their predecessors.

This differentiation is difficult. In earlier times, there were clear class differences between older and new black leadership. Gunnar Myrdal, for instance, noted that while white civic leaders preferred an uneducated, supplicant black leadership cadre, middle-class blacks were clearly becoming leaders in the 1930s and 1940s.[25] The middle-class dominance of black leadership solidified later in the twentieth century, causing Robert Smith to write that "leadership in the black community has passed to the solid middle class."[26] Katherine Tate's work on black members of Congress reinforces this point. She finds that most black members of Congress are college educated and come from professional backgrounds.[27] Indeed, even some members of the older cohort of leadership graduated from elite universities. Virginia Congressman Bobby Scott, for instance, is a Harvard graduate. The late Chicago mayor Harold Washington graduated from Northwestern University Law School, and former Philadelphia mayor Wilson Goode earned a master's degree in public administration from the University of Pennsylvania.[28]

In light of this information, we must conclude that there are no substantive class or professional differences between the old and the aspiring cohorts of black leadership. This is not a scenario of college-educated people trying to seize power from illiterate establishment incumbents. Instead, black political entrepreneurs must take other steps to establish themselves as different from, and better than, their predecessors. In short, entrepreneurs must figure out a way to marginalize relatively powerful peers in order to gain clout.

It may seem oxymoronic to use the terms *marginalize* and *powerful* in the same sentence. After all, the word *marginalize* implies a certain powerlessness on the part of its subject that one does not usually associate with people who enjoy the prestige of having been elected to some of the country's highest political offices. However, Cathy Cohen taught us that power is not the either/or concept that others had previously envisioned. In her study of the black community's response to the AIDS crisis, she notes that even though they have fewer political and economic resources, blacks are not powerless. In the face of discrimination, blacks created subaltern institutions and networks that are influential both inside and outside the black community. The leaders of these organizations enjoy a prominence within the black community and become the spokespeople of black interests to people outside the community. Some people and interests are not represented by the traditional subaltern networks. In Cohen's study, for instance, black gays, lesbians, and drug users are not part of the mainstream civil rights network. Because these constituencies are underrepresented and because their policy interests are controversial, mainstream black leaders choose to ignore their concerns—that is, marginalize their interests— for the sake of group unity and to achieve the civil rights goals on which everyone agrees.[29]

In explaining how marginalization occurs, Cohen notes that the process is multifaceted. First, a group must be easily labeled as peripheral, and then the powerful group must create a narrative that serves to stigmatize the peripheral group. In her AIDS example, gays, lesbians, and drug users were clearly peripheral members of society. Thus the narrative of deviant sexuality and illegal behavior could easily justify ignoring AIDS as a policy issue, because addressing the issue would serve to legitimize what was perceived to be pathological behavior.[30]

Is it possible to apply the same logic to political battles between two groups of elites vying for prestigious offices? There is much to be learned from Cohen's model of marginalization. In particular, the idea that stories justify the relegation of certain groups to the periphery is a powerful concept. If one can create a compelling narrative that resonates in the right places, one may be able to use that narrative to supplant an elder in a position of power. Although that elder may not be relegated to the extreme margins of society (we are talking about relegating people to comfortable early retirements with government pensions, not to lives of penury), the most compelling narratives can cost an established politician influence and prestige if the challenger is able to gain support and elective office as a result.

Narratives are important because candidates and the media can easily manipulate them to help generate buzz. This becomes especially important to black political entrepreneurs because they need to circumvent black communities' traditional bases of support. For example, if the black incumbent has the explicit or tacit endorsement of traditional figures such as other black elected officials, civil rights and labor organizations, and political party leaders, then the black political entrepreneur must look for support in other places. Often, he looks beyond the black community for support, particularly financial support. To gain the attention of this outside network, he relies on the media to portray him in a sympathetic light. Becoming a media favorite not only helps fund-raising but also may convince volunteers to work for his campaign. In short, a black political entrepreneur tries to become a media darling in order to circumvent traditional black information networks and appeal directly to constituents and potential donors and volunteers.

It may be easier to bypass traditional black subaltern networks than previously believed. During the civil rights movement, black institutions such as churches, civil rights organizations, and historically black colleges played a critical role in mobilizing blacks to participate in protests.[31] But since the civil rights movement, fewer blacks have connections to these institutions. While nearly one in ten blacks belonged to the NAACP in 1950, only 1% of blacks were members of this organization in 2000. And while blacks were still more likely to attend church than whites, black religious attendance declined at nearly the same rate as white church attendance in the latter part of the twentieth century.[32]

There is substantial evidence, moreover, that political machines in black cities have undergone serious, even crippling, decline. William Nelson notes that after Carl Stokes stepped down as Cleveland's first black mayor, the political organization that propelled him to office fell apart.[33] Indiana Congresswoman Katie Hall relied on Gary Mayor Richard Hatcher's crumbling election machine to aid her reelection bid in 1984 and lost her seat.[34] In Birmingham, Alabama, former mayor Richard Arrington's Jefferson County Citizen's Coalition lost political clout in the late 1990s, and as a result, Bernard Kincaid, an Arrington opponent, was able to win the mayoralty in 1999.[35]

If black political entrepreneurs bypass traditional black information networks by harnessing the power of modern mainstream media, do they retain full control of their candidacy's narrative? To answer this question, we must understand the process by which narratives are created. Marjorie Hershey explains that journalists have their own interests in creating an overarching narrative for electoral contests. For them, the contest must be narrowed down to one archetype versus another. These archetypes are called *media frames*. Once the media assign one of these tropes to a candidate, they filter their coverage of the candidate through that lens and thus will find it harder to publish or air stories of candidates when they deviate from their type. If a black political entrepreneur benefits from the press's defining his opponent as corrupt or incompetent—and from being personally cast in saintly terms—he can use that positive media coverage to recruit campaign volunteers and to raise campaign funds. This becomes especially important for fund-raising, because if an incumbent has already locked up the political and financial support of the local and/or black political establishment, positive media coverage can help entrepreneurs identify new sources of human and financial capital.[36]

How do candidates of similar class status and credentials distinguish themselves from one another? At first glance, incumbents would seem to have an advantage because of their longer record of service. Morris Fiorina explained that an incumbent's record made him a known quantity; that is, when voters voted for him, they knew what kinds of policies they could expect based on his past performance. Thus, voters engage in what Fiorina calls *retrospective voting*. Challengers, in contrast, want voters to engage in *prospective voting*. Newcomers have a harder time invoking their record, since they rarely have already served in the office to which they aspire. Consequently, they try to convince voters that they are capable of doing what they promise to do in their campaign platforms and that the incumbent has not done much. Because the promise of the future is often riskier than the inertia of the present, incumbents generally retain the advantage because they are a known quantity. A successful challenger, however, can sometimes convince voters that he is worth the electoral risk because anything is better than another term of paltry accomplishments by the incumbent.[37]

When black political entrepreneurs create strategies to upset black incumbents, they employ a two-pronged strategy. First, entrepreneurs try to cast doubt on the incumbent's substantive record. Second, they imply that subtle social differences between them and the incumbents influence the incumbent's professionalism and effectiveness.

Many newer black politicians have logical reasons for using substantive critiques to try to gain an electoral foothold. Despite the more than six-fold increase in the number of black elected officials in the United States between 1970 and 2001,[38] material benefits for blacks have been slow to follow. Regardless of what one thinks about old or new leadership, few can argue that black communities are still grappling with the same issues that beset them at the end of the civil rights movement. Blacks have consistently been about twice as likely to be unemployed as whites. Blacks make about two-thirds the income of whites. Blacks' median net worth was about one-tenth of the median net worth of whites in 2005; by 2009, that gap widened to one-twentieth of the median net worth of whites. On most leading measures, such as high school graduation rates, life expectancy, and infant mortality, blacks continue to lag behind whites, despite some improvement. In addition, approximately 70% of black children are born out of wedlock, putting these children at a greater risk to be raised in poverty, to have health problems, and to be poorly educated.[39]

To be sure, there are structural explanations for these observed differences. The first wave of African American elected officials came to office in the late 1960s and 1970s hoping to turn the tide on inequality in black communities. Unfortunately, their efforts were hampered by either a lack of incorporation or recessionary pressures on city governments in the 1970s, which reduced city budgets, thereby preventing the expansion of certain services intended to lift poor people out of poverty.[40]

Explaining away a generation of entrenched inequality with a structural arguments does not create compelling narratives, though. Seizing on this fact, black political entrepreneurs assess the conditions of their communities and make the case to voters that black incumbents not only have failed in their efforts to lead these communities but also have violated the trust of their communities with this failure and do not deserve to stay in office. When these issues are framed for public consumption, the black political entrepreneur minimizes the structural explanations and tacitly questions the incumbent's competence or will to solve these problems.

Often, the substantive failures of black elected officials are framed not just as policy failures but as moral failings as well. It helps that some of the deficits just mentioned, such as joblessness, illegitimacy, and welfare dependency, carry with them the additional baggage of being stereotypically associated with blacks.[41] That black leaders have failed to solve these issues suggests that they have failed in their task to improve the moral fiber—and, by extension, the overall social standing—of the black community.[42]

Black incumbents are especially vulnerable to facing elite displacement when their personal shortcomings are widely known. Even if the incumbent herself was not directly involved in a scandal, her mere association with someone who was involved in wrongdoing may be enough to convince a black political entrepreneur that he can use such a vulnerability to win an election.

Calling attention to scandal is a risky move, though. If done improperly, the black incumbent can rally sympathy from black voters to stay in office. Melissa Harris-Lacewell points out that embattled blacks can take a defiant position toward the white political establishment that some blacks find refreshing.[43] In an electoral context, some black candidates can use this posture to win votes. Recent history provides examples of this. In 1990, when Washington, DC, mayor Marion Barry was caught on tape smoking crack cocaine with a prostitute, many blacks defended him, charging that he had been unfairly entrapped by white police officers. Not only did blacks support Barry in his criminal case, but they also reelected him to Washington's city council in 1992 and as mayor in 1994.[44] In 2003, Philadelphia mayor John Street was up for reelection. At the time, his administration was being investigated in a corruption probe, and the FBI secretly bugged Street's office, looking for evidence against the mayor. When Street publicly disclosed the wiretap, his lead in the mayoral race grew to a decisive margin, with blacks largely supporting Street and whites largely supporting Sam Katz, Street's white opponent. Local analysts surmised that voters sympathized with Street as a victim of unfair police surveillance. (Incidentally, Street was not indicted, but the former Philadelphia city treasurer, Corey Kemp, was convicted of running a pay-to-play scheme.).[45]

The upside of exposing the moral shortcomings of an entrenched black incumbent is that the black political entrepreneur often uses those failings to generate support outside his constituency. Even though this group of supporters cannot vote for him, they can provide positive media coverage and needed campaign donations. And if he loses a first election, the black political entrepreneur, with the help of these outside supporters, can often rebound and win his desired office on the second try.

The ease with which black political entrepreneurs can take advantage of the frame that the incumbent is a bad guy exposes black establishment elites' tenuous relationships in mainstream circles. While this depiction might be true in some cases, the ease of characterization suggests that despite the power and prestige that older blacks may have acquired in public office, they may not be fully integrated into the mainstream elite. Louis Hartz noted that equality is not just legal equality. Social equality also is important.[46] When differentiating between aspiring and established black elected leaders, if established black leaders have strained relationships with both the mainstream media and mainstream leaders, this could help solidify the characterization that they are ineffective in their jobs.

It is important to consider, then, whether social mobility, or the ability to integrate and navigate elite social circles with ease, helps make distinctions among different kinds of black politicians. In the late 1960s, William Domhoff used the concept of social mobility to identify America's ruling elite. To Domhoff, having money, status, or political power did not automatically give a person entrée into America's ruling elite. Rather, Domhoff argued, social mobility also was important to identifying America's true elite.[47]

Popular culture provides two different analogies to help explain the concept. In the 1960s, the United States created enforceable codified legislation that asserted the equality of everyone, regardless of race. But this legislation did not require Americans of different races to befriend one another. The film *Guess Who's Coming to Dinner?* epitomizes this paradox.[48] Just because blacks won the legal right to equal treatment on buses and at lunch counters did not mean that blacks were dining with whites and marrying into white families with ease.

Consider also the contrast between playwright and filmmaker Tyler Perry and actor Will Smith. Both of them are Hollywood success stories in their own right. Perry's films have huge profit margins (he specializes in low-budget films), demonstrating the huge, untapped market for black-themed films. In 2008, Smith was the highest-paid actor in Hollywood. Despite both these men's success, only Smith is fully mainstreamed. Perry, whose work is well received by black audiences, is not a traditional Hollywood insider. Rather, he operates out of Atlanta, and his original work is regularly panned[49] by the mainstream media.[50]

Politically speaking, then, black political entrepreneurs are like Will Smith, and members of the "old guard," regardless of their age, are like Tyler Perry. The idea that a prominent black can be loved within his racial community and reviled outside it is not new. This idea of social mobility and which black elite can claim it figures prominently in the theory of elite displacement. One segment of the black elite emerged from the civil rights movement (or embraces the mantle of the movement). Many in this group literally fought for access to the nation's corridors of power, whether that was entry into the nation's elite educational institutions, representation in corporate offices, or electoral office. When people in this cohort broke barriers, they often had to deal with chilly receptions in their new environs. Some of these chilly receptions are well documented. The late Congressman Adam Clayton Powell noted, for instance, that his black colleague, Congressman William Dawson of Illinois, could not find lodging in Washington when he came to serve in Congress. He also was not welcome in the Capitol dining room because of his race. When Douglas Wilder served as a Virginia state senator in the 1980s, white colleagues refused to invite him to have lunch with them at the exclusive (and all-white) Commonwealth Club.[51] Even though these people had acquired power, they were still treated like outsiders.

Public opinion data provide further evidence of the social marginalization of prominent African Americans. Comparisons of white and black favorability ratings of well-known blacks reveal a racial chasm of perception. The Joint Center for Political and Economic Studies regularly queries white and black sentiments toward key political figures and has found marked differences in black and white perceptions of prominent African American political figures (see table 1.1). For example, in 1997, 87% of the blacks surveyed rated Jesse Jackson Sr. favorably, compared with only 30% of whites. Even worse, whereas 40% of blacks viewed Nation of Islam

Table 1.1

Favorability Ratings, by Race, for Selected Black Public Figures

		Blacks (%)		Whites (%)[a]	
		Favorable	Unfavorable	Favorable	Unfavorable
1997	Jesse Jackson	87	8	30	50
	Louis Farrakhan	40	37	4	59
	Colin Powell	70	11	78	8
1999	Jesse Jackson	88	8	57	29
	Colin Powell	78	8	79	7
2004	Jesse Jackson	58	29	33	53
	Colin Powell	69	23	74	17

Sources: David Bositis, "1997 National Opinion Poll: Politics" (Washington, DC: Joint Center for Political and Economic Studies, 1997), available at www.jointcenter.org/databank/NOP/reports/1997_politics_reports (accessed January 16, 2009); David Bositis, "1999 National Opinion Poll: Politics" (Washington, DC: Joint Center for Political and Economic Studies, 1999), 20–21; and David Bositis, "2004 National Opinion Poll: Politics" (Washington, DC: Joint Center for Political and Economic Studies, 2004), 6–7.

[a] The 2004 favorability ratings for whites are general population estimates.

leader Louis Farrakhan favorably, only 4% of whites viewed him favorably. In contrast, 78% of whites had a favorable impression of Colin Powell, compared with 70% of blacks.[52]

The general finding—that compared with blacks, nonblacks embrace some, but not all, black political figures—has remained consistent over time. The Joint Center revisited the same questions in 1999 and 2004 (Louis Farrakhan was omitted from later polls, so I am excluding him from my analysis). In 1999, a majority of whites gave Jesse Jackson Sr. favorable marks. But the 57% white favorability rating that Jackson received was still substantially lower than the 88% favorability rating that blacks gave him. Whites continued to have a favorable impression of Colin Powell in 1999, and black favorability ratings increased. In 2004, the old pattern of racial polarization emerged again. Blacks viewed Jesse Jackson Sr. as more favorable than unfavorable by a two-to-one margin, whereas the overall sample viewed Jackson more unfavorably than favorably, 53% to 33%. Again, survey participants generally viewed Colin Powell very favorably, with 74% of respondents having a favorable impression of the then secretary of state, compared with 17%, who had an unfavorable opinion.[53]

The public opinion data thus reveal whites' preferences for less-threatening black leaders. Black leaders who are too racialized or associated with the Black Nationalist or civil rights movements do not win the esteem of whites. In contrast, more racially moderate blacks are in a position to curry favor outside the black community.

The social slights and stigma that racialized black political figures face are significant. Even though elected officials were able to break barriers and be elected to office; even though these officials were able to win over and work with their white constituents and win greater support from whites in subsequent elections;[54] and even though some of these black leaders were ensconced enough in their offices to have real political power, they still had limited access to all the perks of political office. They still were viewed with suspicion and held in relatively lower esteem among whites, and they were not fully accepted socially even if they were tolerated as political colleagues.

Being tolerated makes officials susceptible to being targeted for elite displacement. If a black elected official is not fully embraced by his white colleagues, he will enjoy a modicum of influence as long as he has a clear monopoly on leadership or appears to be the designated spokesperson for his particular black constituency. When an elected official runs unopposed in multiple elections or with minimal challenges, he therefore is largely left alone. But when a credible challenger emerges and appeals to outside support from mainstream sources, the challenger can amplify his opponent's weaknesses by tapping into mainstream biases against the incumbent or against black leaders generally. By pointing out the incumbent's character flaws, the challenger reminds his mainstream supporters that the incumbent is pesky or not very likeable. By presenting himself in a less confrontational style, he then seeks to make mainstream supporters comfortable with him. And when a challenger highlights his similarities with mainstream supporters (whether that is education, speech patterns, etc.), he signals to mainstream supporters that he has a social mobility, even a cachet, that the incumbent lacks.

In a 1996 *Journal of Politics* article, David Canon, Matthew Schousen, and Patrick Sellers studied the impact of black candidates' styles on the outcome of 1992 House races in majority-black districts. They coded the candidates according to whether they presented themselves as traditional or new race leaders. The old-style candidates were more likely to run racialized campaigns and don the mantle of the civil rights movement, and the new-style candidates were more likely to employ deracialized techniques in which they emphasized universal issues and eschewed overt racial language.[55] Deracialized candidates are also, in the words of Joseph McCormick and Charles Jones, more likely to present a racially nonthreatening image in order to put white voters at ease.[56] Canon and his colleagues hypothesized and found that when old- and new-style blacks competed against each other in Democratic primaries, the new-style candidate won. The candidates split the black vote, and the less-threatening, new-style candidate won the majority of the white vote to secure victory. Based on Canon and his colleagues' findings, it would appear that if given a choice, white voters prefer black candidates who do not appear to be threatening or prone to play the race card.[57]

The Consequences of Elite Displacement

The strategy of running as a racial moderate against a more racialized incumbent is certainly shrewd, but it can have negative externalities, especially if it in any way frames a racialized opponent in a negative light. While the black political entrepreneur employing the strategy benefits immensely from painting a caricature of his opponent, such a frame may help reinforce negative stereotypes about blacks, particularly poor blacks.

There is ample evidence to suggest that a significant number of whites still view blacks negatively. In their landmark study *Racial Attitudes in America*, Howard Schumann and his colleagues tracked public opinion on race for more than a generation. As late as 1996, a slim majority of white survey respondents believed that blacks were in a subordinate social and economic position because they were not motivated to improve their lot. The authors noted that while few whites endorsed the idea that blacks were innately inferior, whites were less likely over time to cite discrimination as a source for persistent racial inequality.[58]

More recent survey data seem to corroborate the persistence of stereotypes within a substantial portion of the population, as well as diverging opinions about poor and affluent blacks. In November 2007, the Pew Research Center found that a majority of both whites and blacks believed that poor blacks were different from middle-class blacks.[59] In September 2008, the Associated Press and Yahoo News released an election-related survey, conducted by Stanford University, which asked likely voters about their perceptions of blacks and race relations. Noticeable minorities of white respondents reported harboring less than flattering images of blacks. For instance, 20% of white respondents believed that "violent" described blacks extremely or very well. If we expand the category to include those who believed that "violent" described blacks moderately well, that number swells to 48% of white respondents. Twenty-nine percent of whites believed that "complaining" described blacks extremely or very well, and 57% of whites thought the term described blacks very or moderately well. Thirteen percent of whites agreed that "lazy" described blacks extremely or very well, and 38% thought the term described blacks at least moderately well. Finally, 11% of whites thought that "irresponsible" described blacks extremely or very well, with 40% believing that the term described blacks at least moderately well.[60]

The Stanford study probed more deeply into questions of race to ask what explained the inequality of blacks and whites. Fifty-four percent of respondents strongly or somewhat agreed with the idea that if white ethnic immigrants could overcome prejudice, then blacks could do so, too —"without special favors."[61] Forty-eight percent of white respondents strongly or somewhat believed that blacks could attain the same status as whites if they just tried harder. Forty-six percent of white respondents believed that black welfare recipients could survive without welfare, and 24% of white respondents believed that blacks received more economic benefits than they deserved.[62]

Both historical and contemporary public opinion data indicate that large portions of the white American population still subscribe to negative stereotypes about and racial resentment of blacks. Consequently, even if a black political entrepreneur has no desire to reify stereotypes, being framed as the saint vis-à-vis the buffoonish black establishment opponent can have long-term consequences for the social status of blacks in this country and for general perceptions of black leadership. Black political entrepreneurs may be unwittingly framing themselves as the "exception that proves the rule" about black pathology even while they make reasonable, impassioned, and convincing arguments for being allowed the privilege to serve the public. In an earlier, era, such people were called "credits to their race," which is, at best, a backhanded compliment.

There is sufficient evidence that mainstream opinion leaders look to black political entrepreneurs to supplant older black civil rights leaders in order to mute the discussion of race in public discourse. Right after Barack Obama won the Iowa caucus in 2008, the panel on *The McLaughlin Group* debated the impact of the rise of young black leaders on the future of black politics. Here is what they said:

MR. MCLAUGHLIN: OK, listen to this. "Transcending race. Transrace politicians. Obama represents a new era of powerful black politicians. They are above race and beyond race." According to *The American Prospect*, these new leaders are not what they used to be, called "race men." They argue that they don't need to concern themselves primarily with the uplift of their race. They appeal to black voters, to be sure, but to white ones as well. They don't want to be just mayors or congressmen from majority-black districts; they want to be governors, senators, and presidents. Black leaders today include Massachusetts Governor Deval Patrick, Washington, D.C., Mayor Adrian Fenty, former congressman Harold Ford Jr., Congressman Arthur Davis of Alabama. Here's how *The Nation* describes them: "They have been hailed not just as a development in black American politics, but as a repudiation of black American politics. Not just as different from Jesse Jackson, but the epitome of the anti-Jesse. Ivy League professionals, heirs to the civil rights movement who are determined to move beyond both the mood and the message of their forebears."

QUESTION: There's more to Obama's win than Obama. There is also the political evolution of black America. That's what this piece says. Is it true?

MR. PAGE: Well, we always remember Jesse back in the early eighties said, "I'm a tree shaker, not a jelly maker." And indeed that was true. He and Al Sharpton are the tree shakers. But you've got the inside players, like the Barack Obamas, and this political generation now who are the jelly makers. They're inside the system. They're crossing over, outside the black community, because you can't depend just on black votes if you want to have any expansion of power, and that's what you're . . .

MR. MCLAUGHLIN: Isn't there a cultural distinction between the two?

MR. PAGE: This goes back to an earlier session we had on this show, John.

MR. MCLAUGHLIN: Yes.

MR. PAGE: With a growing black middle class, you've got growing black middle-class values. So you might see a reflection of that.

MR. BUCHANAN: John.

MR. MCLAUGHLIN : Isn't this phenomenon bigger than Obama?

MS. CLIFT (?): Yes.

MR. MCLAUGHLIN: So we have now a context in America that will accept what it would not accept in the era of Jesse . . .

MS. CLIFT: Well, he's a biracial . . .

MR. MCLAUGHLIN: Jesse had to do what Jesse did.

MS. CLIFT: He's a . . .

MR. PAGE: But you can see by that crowd there in Iowa, look behind Obama's head [inaudible] crowd there.

MR. BUCHANAN: John . . .

MR. MCLAUGHLIN: Is it a true phenomenon? Is it a true . . .

MR. PAGE: I'd call it evolution, really. It's a political evolution. Iowa [inaudible].

MR. BUCHANAN: Hey, John, John . . . let me look, John . . .

MR. MCLAUGHLIN: We're talking about Harvard. We're talking about Yale.

MR. BUCHANAN: John, the comparison is . . .

MR. MCLAUGHLIN: We're talking about Duke. Go ahead.

MR. BUCHANAN: The comparison is this. Take Al Smith in 1928 . . . very Irish Catholic. Joe Kennedy, Jack's dad, Irish Catholic, hard Irish versus the English. Then you get Jack Kennedy . . . smooth, WASPy, Harvard. They've moved into, in other words, the establishment and the elite, and that's what Obama has done. Jesse and Sharpton are back in race politics. This guy's getting above it, because when you get above it, that's how you get the jobs that are the highest . . .

MS. CLIFT: Well, he's also a biracial candidate who grew up in Kansas. I mean, he is comfortable in these worlds. He does not make distinctions between them, and most Americans don't want to make distinctions anymore. And when you saw that tableau of this young family before the all-white Iowa voters, that sends a message to African Americans that he can win, and I think you're going to see him do very well in South Carolina. . . .

MR. BUCHANAN: He's got the best of both worlds as of now, John. John, he's got the best of both worlds as of now. He will really make a mistake if they get into too much of the "It's our turn" and they turn it into "This is a victory for black America" rather than "He's got that." He should stay above that, stay away from [inaudible] stay away from Jena and all that stuff.[63]

A number of themes emerge from this discussion. First, it is very clear that the younger black politicians are defined in direct contrast to the older political leaders. Massachusetts Governor Deval Patrick is the polar opposite of Al Sharpton. Second, it is abundantly clear which cohort of leadership the panel prefers. Pat Buchanan hopes aloud that the election of Barack Obama permanently silences the civil rights activists.[64] It is important to note that it is not just conservatives who are making these distinctions. Even the liberals on the panel join in the conversation about how the younger generation is different from—and by implication, better than —the old guard. Clarence Page extols the middle class values that the new guard embodies, and Eleanor Clift goes to great pains to point out that Obama is biracial (and mistakenly claims that he was born in the Heartland), as though she is saying that he is not quite black enough in a good way—black enough phenotypically and culturally to be embraced by African Americans but without the political stridency of establishment civil rights leaders that threatens whites.

The emergence of a younger, more racially moderate cohort of black politicians allows us to revisit generation-old questions about the efficacy of deracialization. This strategy has been controversial since Charles Hamilton first proposed it in the 1970s. When *First World* magazine published his articulation of the strategy in 1977, his comments were juxtaposed with an interview with Julian Bond in which Bond panned the strategy because he believed that it called for black political candidates to ignore obvious racism.[65] Joseph McCormick and Charles Jones worried that blacks who deemphasized racial issues in order to win white votes might be forced to never address racial inequities once in office lest they lose those white votes. In their view, the whole point of blacks holding office is for "the purpose of using the policy tools of government to improve the material lives of constituents in a way that is sensitive to the historical role and continuing impact of white racism in American political life."[66] To these critics, deemphasizing racial issues for political gain would be a huge betrayal to blacks, who are still underrepresented in elective office and disadvantaged on most health, educational, and economic indicators.[67]

McCormick and Jones's critique of deracialization raises an interesting empirical question: Would replacing the older, more civil rights–oriented black elected officials with younger, more moderate ones lead to different substantive outcomes for blacks in the United States? The preliminary evidence suggests that this is not the case. While there has not yet been a wholesale replacement of the old guard of black elected leadership by a more deracialized cohort of post-racial leaders, the younger, more deracialized blacks who do serve take very similar positions on civil rights issues as their older, more racialized colleagues.

For example, if we look at the *National Journal*'s ideological rankings of members of the 110th Congress, we find that Congressional Black Caucus (CBC) members of all generations and political styles usually fall on the liberal end of the spectrum. Most of the more conservative CBC members come from southern districts that are more likely to be culturally conservative, although not all black members of Congress from the South are conservative. These members included such old guard representatives as Sanford Bishop and such black political entrepreneurs as Artur Davis.[68] If we look at the ratings of the Leadership Conference on Civil Rights (LCCR, the standard measure of a Congress member's support for civil rights issues), we find that all black members of Congress—both the activist-oriented and the entrepreneurial factions, the racialized and the deracialized—vote the same way on race-based civil rights issues. All the black members of the 110th Congress earned LCCR scores of 95% or higher.[69]

If black political entrepreneurs are just as likely to support civil rights as their elders were and prove to be more successful at passing policies that improve blacks' life chances (regardless of whether or not those policies are framed in racialized language), then it does call into question the tactics of the old guard. Is stridency and overt racialization necessary when moderation is just as productive? Moreover, if black political entrepreneurs end up passing more initiatives than their elders did, what does that say about the elders' effectiveness? Although reasonable people will acknowledge that the work of previous generations paved the way for newer leaders to usher in sweeping changes, they will attribute the success of black political entrepreneurs, in contrast to the old guard, to their superior diplomacy or competence.

As more and more black political entrepreneurs gain power, we will have more and more data on which to test the hypothesis of which group actually does more to improve the material well-being of blacks. Scholars clearly will need to revisit this question for years to come.

Bringing Class Tensions to the Fore

In the short term, there still are larger questions about the impact of class differences on intraracial political interactions. Sociologists have long studied the tensions facing influential middle- and upper-class blacks in many different sectors of society. Sharon Collins's study of black corporate executives showed that her subjects were genuinely concerned about pushing their employers to be socially responsible and to reach out to their black consumer bases. Accordingly, many black executives felt the need to lead community outreach offices specially designed to fulfill this mission. While these executives were typically well paid for their efforts, they also were marginalized for having engaged in community outreach. Because outreach offices do not generate revenues, their employees are not viewed as being as valuable to the organization as are employees of the income-generating divisions. In many ways, community outreach divisions represent the largess of organizations with extra money to spend. When profits shrink, corporations tend to cut back on their community commitments, demonstrating the tenuousness of some companies' commitment to social justice.[70] Critics of deracialization fear that while black political entrepreneurs may run for office with the intention of improving their communities and providing uplift for blacks, their partners in that effort (i.e., the media and their campaign donors and volunteers) may not share those values and could withdraw their support at critical junctures, especially if a political entrepreneur deviates from his post-racial persona to address a compelling racial issue.

In addition, powerful blacks are often viewed with suspicion by the lower-class blacks that they are trying to help in their new positions of influence. First Lady Michelle Obama, experienced that as an executive at the University of Chicago Hospital. Obama served as the vice president of community affairs for the hospital before her husband won the presidency. In that capacity, she tried to improve the hospital's image in the surrounding neighborhood, with which the University of Chicago has had a long-standing strained relationship. Obama's job was to serve as a bridge between the community and the hospital. Overall, she was widely praised for her work, and she clearly did some good things to protect black residents from being exploited by the hospital. For instance, the hospital wanted to recruit neighborhood girls to take part in a research trial for the cervical cancer vaccine Gardasil. When Obama learned of the plans, she intervened and prevented the hospital from proceeding as planned. Given the long history of exploiting poor blacks for the sake of science, Obama wanted to avoid the appearance of creating another Tuskegee syphilis experiment.[71]

Even though Michelle Obama's employment at the University of Chicago was a net positive for the surrounding community, her tenure was not without controversy. For example, Obama won federal grant money to set up community clinics so that residents did not have to use the emergency room for primary care. Clinics are cheaper and are designed to help provide residents, who have only sporadic access to health care, with something close to a regular physician.[72] But some local leaders criticized Obama's efforts as a slick move by the University of Chicago's health system to not have to treat poor, less profitable patients. (Since the clinics are funded with grant dollars, they are technically not part of the University of Chicago Health System.) The fact that Michelle Obama, who grew up on Chicago's South Side, was the face of this effort did not satisfy these activists.

What is worse, Obama's colleagues may not have completely understood her predicament. According to quotations in a *Washington Post* article about her work life, Obama's colleagues asserted that she was the perfect ambassador for the hospital. For instance, Joe Stephens cited Susan Sher, the hospital's general counsel and the person who recruited Michelle Obama for the job, who explained, as he put it, that because "Michelle Obama 'grew up in this community,' . . . that makes her uniquely qualified."[73] But Sher's statement betrays a subconscious assumption that as a black woman from the neighborhood, Obama was the best person to "sell" the hospital's plans to the community. Granted, these were not nefarious plans, but Sher's comment almost appears to exploit Mrs. Obama's background for the hospital's benefit, even if it does help the community. This may be enlightened self-interest, but it is not surprising that some people might take issue with the hospital's PR strategy.

No one should infer from my comments that Michelle Obama was an unwitting dupe in this process. Instead, this scenario reflects the reality that Michelle Obama, her husband, and countless blacks in positions of mainstream influence often have to strike a precarious balance between representing the interests of the mainstream institutions they have joined and the black communities from which they came.

Mary Patillo studied the gentrification of a predominantly black working-class neighborhood, North Kenwood- Oakland, which is not far from the University of Chicago Medical Center. This neighborhood witnessed postindustrial depopulation and economic decline in the 1960s, 1970s, and 1980s. But in the late 1990s, real estate developers began to invest in the area, building trendy condominiums and other owner-occupied dwellings that appealed to middle-class buyers, particularly black professionals. The middle-class blacks who moved to North Kenwood-Oakland were motivated in part by the affordability of the housing stock, but they also felt a sense of obligation to help improve a historically black community. Their idea of uplift, though, sometimes clashed with the ideals of older residents. The middle-class residents, most of whom were home owners, supported development efforts that enhanced the property values of their homes or fit their bourgeois values. Sometimes their wishes clashed with those of the black working-class residents, most of whom were renters. In addition, on some issues, the black middle-class home owners aligned with white developers and the city of Chicago against the wishes of the working-class residents who had lived in the community for years. Not surprisingly, the developers welcomed the support of black middle-class residents because it lessened the appearance of racism.[74]

Patillo contends that middle-class blacks—whether they are new home owners in North Kenwood-Oakland or aspiring young black politicians in other inner cities—play the role of middlemen. The middleman (or middlewoman) has adopted the bourgeois values of mainstream white America but still identifies with the black community. When issues arise in which the interests of the black community conflict with those of the mainstream whites in power (whether those are business or governmental interests), middle-class blacks often play the role of interpreter. They explain lower-class black grievances to the whites in power, and they try to explain white policy preferences to poor blacks. The most skilled middlemen and -women have mastered DuBoisian double consciousness and Fanonian mask wearing. Patillo writes, "The person in the middle, if she's good, speaks at least two languages in order to translate, has two sets of credentials for legitimacy, and juggles a double-booked calendar to keep all the relationships cordial, memberships current, and constituencies appeased."[75]

It is important to keep in mind that middlemen and -women are not dispassionate translators. They are self-interested, and they take sides. But because they feel cross-pressures from their racial and class peers, they try to balance their obligations within and across racial and class lines. Patillo argues, "Because they have been shaped by many worlds, middlemen have sincere interests that coincide with the groups on either side of themselves and can genuinely make bargains with each. Taking different sides in different contests is in fact how they maintain legitimacy."[76]

The middleman dynamic that Patillo is describing has direct implications for the study of black politics. First, it calls into question the notion of a unified black body politic. When Michael Dawson offered a black utility heuristic in 1994, he explained why blacks of all class backgrounds seemed to make similar political decisions pertaining to policy preferences and vote choices. This observation was paradoxical because it seemed irrational for middle-class blacks, in particular, to support social welfare policies that would raise their taxes. The black utility heuristic states, however, that many blacks base their political decisions on group, not individual, interests because they believe in *linked fate*, or the idea that what happens to other blacks affects them. Thus middle-class blacks who profess to believe in linked fate are more likely to support civil and economic rights policies even if those policies cost them money or might stigmatize their achievements, as in the case of affirmative action.[77]

The black utility heuristic helps explain a lot of idiosyncrasies in black voting behavior, starting with why blacks are the strongest Democratic voting bloc in the United States. Blacks see the Democratic Party as having a clear advantage on civil rights, even if some are sympathetic to some of the Republican Party's probusiness or socially conservative stances. Thus, supporting civil rights is more important to blacks as a whole than endorsing any Republican platform.[78]

Because it is easy to mistakenly deduce from black voting behavior that blacks' interests are uniform, it is important to keep a few things in mind. First, it is difficult to determine what "the black agenda" really is. Given the history of racial discrimination in the United States, most blacks have an interest in eradicating racial discrimination. At various points in black history, civil rights leaders and black elected officials convened to decide on their agenda, and some of those meetings ended in failure. For instance, Robert Smith discussed the 1972 Gary convention at which black leaders were supposed to create a ten-point agenda to guide protest and legislative efforts. While the convention did produce a list of goals, only two of which were even partly achieved, and the meetings fell apart because the stakeholders vehemently disagreed about substance and strategy. The interests of the leftist activists could not be reconciled with the interests of elected officials, and the elected officials withdrew from the convention in order to protect their reputations in Washington.[79]

More recent public opinion data reveal that not all blacks give priority to the same issues. Besides generational differences are the differences between black elites and ordinary black people. Reporting the results of the Joint Center's 2002 National Opinion Poll, David Bositis found that a majority of blacks were in favor of vouchers;[80] that younger blacks identified less with the Democratic Party; and that blacks were far more concerned about the economy, foreign affairs, and education than they were about racism.[81] What is more, when the Joint Center compared the political attitudes of black elected officials with the black electorate, it found that generational differences in blacks' attitudes generally paralleled the generational differences among black elected officials.[82]

Although we are more aware of intraracial difference in black communities, we should remember that intraracial difference and linked fate are not mutually exclusive. Black people can disagree on issues and still acknowledge that what happens to other blacks will affect them. Moreover, black people from disparate backgrounds can profess a sense of linked fate. This question of linked fate is important because it looms large in popular assessments of black political entrepreneurs who challenge established black politicians for power. Some believe that young black political entrepreneurs' ambitious political stunts evince more self-interested hubris than linked fate. For example, in 2003, thirty-two-year-old congressman Harold Ford Jr. ran against Nancy Pelosi for House Minority Leader. Ford, who was then entering his fourth term in Congress, had been a telegenic keynote speaker at the 2000 Democratic National Convention. To the elders who witnessed this spectacle, including his CBC colleagues who voted against him, Ford was an arrogant kid pulling a stunt. Ronald Walters, for instance, essentially implied that Ford thought he was cute and that he deserved to lose: "To step out there because you've got a pretty face and no agenda, you're going to lose every time."[83]

Furthermore, some people are suspicious that the personal backgrounds of these young black political entrepreneurs may inhibit rather than enhance their linked fate. Dawson argued that persistent discrimination has helped blacks of all stripes to develop linked fate. While it was very clear to some persons that race influences the lives of poor people, Dawson helped articulate how racism affected middle-class blacks and contributed to their political outlook. He contended that middle-class blacks have historically been the targets of racial violence. In addition, because of income and wealth inequalities, middle-class blacks often lead precarious economic existences, which make them more supportive of social welfare policies. Finally, middle-class blacks often maintain ties to black social and cultural institutions, such as churches, black fraternities and sororities, and barbershops, which help reinforce a sense of group identity.[84]

Critics are concerned that certain black political entrepreneurs may not have linked fate because they never had to develop it. To these naysayers, those entrepreneurs who grew up in white communities and were largely accepted by their white peers are automatically suspect. How will this person be able to lead if he has no intimate understanding of the struggles that other blacks face daily? Can she be an honest broker of black interests when meeting with powerful whites, or will she capitulate to the prejudiced interests of the majority (when applicable) because she does not know when to spot and challenge racist behavior? Indeed, critics of black political entrepreneurs, particularly those who have had an exotic upbringing, crudely express these fears when they label these entrepreneurs as "not black enough." In actuality, they worry that because of their youth and inexperience with racism, this group is more susceptible to manipulation than are other sectors of the black elite. Indeed, Ronald Walters contended that the reason that black political entrepreneurs curry so much favor in elite white circles is because the white power structure "would rather supplant [the old guard] with a far more accommodating leadership. They are going to pit them against the so-called old leadership because they have been threatened by the interests and power of the black leadership who really have the influence and control of black people."[85]

To be sure, Patillo's data show that while middle-class blacks are certainly shaped by their socialization into mainstream institutions, they do express a strong sense of linked fate to black communities and seek to balance their class interests with their sense of racial-group identity. From a normative perspective, Tommie Shelby observed that while not all blacks have personally experienced racism, they can choose to identify with the antiracist struggle and should be embraced.[86] For skeptics, however, black political entrepreneurs are guilty of lacking linked fate until proved otherwise.

To quell concerns that someone is racially clueless or is merely using black communities to promote his or her own self-interest, black political entrepreneurs and their peers have a few options. These men and women can seek to draw legitimacy from familial connections. Earlier I mentioned that some young black politicians inherit their offices from their parents. These politicians rarely face challenges to their bona fides because it is assumed that their politician or activist parents instilled in them a sense of linked fate. In contrast, black political entrepreneurs who lack these connections can join black organizations to signal to their black audiences that they have a sense of linked fate. For instance, a black political entrepreneur who belongs to Alpha Phi Alpha Fraternity, Inc., or Delta Sigma Theta Sorority, Inc., will be more warmly embraced than a black political entrepreneur who is a member of Kappa Sigma Fraternity or Delta Delta Delta Sorority. Likewise, people assume that a Howard graduate has linked fate but may require further evidence from a Harvard graduate.

Black political entrepreneurs can also demonstrate linked fate through their record of service. Barack Obama famously had to endure the "black enough" test when he announced his candidacy for the presidency in 2007. In honor of his candidacy, the *Journal of Black Studies* commissioned a special edition devoted entirely to studying him and his campaign. In that issue, Ronald Walters studied Obama's record of racial advocacy in both the Illinois legislature and the U.S. Senate. He concluded that nothing in Obama's advocacy background and state legislative record suggested that he would oppose civil rights and economic justice legislation in the future.[87]

Black political entrepreneurs adopting this approach must take care to avoid the appearance of instrumentalism. If an entrepreneur is suspected of embracing black voters and supporting civil rights as a means to an end, then his efforts may be viewed with suspicion. This, then, begs the questions of whether a black political entrepreneur can lose his racial bona fides after convincing constituents that he has a sense of linked fate and whether black political entrepreneurs always have the burden of proving their racial solidarity. The reality is that this very well may be the case, especially if the entrepreneur is an outsider in the community he wants to serve. An entrepreneur may be able to convince a constituency that he is the best person to lead them, and he may be able to allay concerns about whether or not he can empathize with residents who may have different racial experiences from his. Once the issue of racial bona fides is raised, however, any slipup can reopen old wounds and resurrect old suspicions.

Thus, some black political entrepreneurs (particularly those with fewer demonstrable ties to black institutions) walk a delicate tightrope, balancing their desire to affirm their multicultural dispositions while having to cater to the demands of black constituents to show their racial solidarity. Given these demands, some people may wonder why black political entrepreneurs would even want to represent blacks. Why not represent more racially diverse, even majority-white, jurisdictions? First, some black political entrepreneurs feel a genuine call to give back to black communities. This in itself is arguably evidence of the racial-group consciousness that leads to linked fate. More important, blacks still are seldom elected in jurisdictions that do not have large black populations. Thus, even the most deracialized black candidates often need to cultivate a base of black support to launch their careers. Even with the obstacles of having to beat deeply entrenched incumbents, black candidates have a better chance of being elected, especially to that critical first office, in places with many black voters.

But in the end, some intraracial political differences may be insurmountable. Adolph Reed famously dismissed the notion of a unified black body politic in *Class Notes* when he asserted that black politics is merely middle-class black politics.[88] Michael Dawson predicted that black politics could fracture on class lines if racism persisted but intraracial income inequality worsened. In this scenario, Dawson argued that we would end up with "two black Americas," a lower- and middle-class subset, each vying for resources and political influence to counter the class-tinged racial discrimination that they still faced.[89]

Two black Americas may not be the worst compromise, although it certainly would upend popular assumptions about black politics. If we could ensure that both lower and upper class blacks had ample resources and access to decision makers, then it could be manageable, though not ideal. Such a political situation might even be tolerable if lower- and middle-class blacks occupied different physical spaces and required separate representation (because they were in different towns or different congressional districts). Unfortunately, blacks of all classes are more likely to live among other blacks because of historic patterns of residential segregation. Middle-class black suburbs have historically been located close to poor black communities, and lower-middle-class urban neighborhoods, in particular, confront many of the same social challenges with crime and poverty as inner-city communities. This dynamic could be further compounded by the presence of upper-middle-class blacks, who also are more likely than their upper-middle-class white counterparts to live in cities.[90] If two or more groups of black residents with diverse interests live within the same political boundaries, tensions are likely to emerge. And when these political disputes arise, the poorer blacks will be more disadvantaged than their more affluent counterparts, who have more resources and more social access to decision makers.[91] Thus, structural forces conspire to force blacks with disparate interests into political conditions in which only one position will be privileged, perpetuating the specious idea of a monolithic black political agenda when only one faction of blacks dominates the discourse.[92]

To be sure, older black elites represent the same affluent interests as do black political entrepreneurs, so nothing about black elite displacement really alters the power dynamic between poor and affluent blacks. But because of their connections to the civil rights movement, older black elites were able to cultivate populist images that helped them curry favor among rank-and-file blacks. As a result, black voters may have certain expectations about how black elected officials will relate to them, based on the behavior of previous politicians. Black elected officials correctly interpreted that the political landscape would allow them to consolidate their own limited political power as a result of black social isolation.[93] When black political entrepreneurs act differently from their predecessors, black voters may not respond similarly, even if the entrepreneurs' position papers are brilliant and the older black politicians' political influence is really a chimera.[94] Black political entrepreneurs must find their own way of ingratiating themselves to black voters. One way to do this is to appear to be more accessible than the older black elites are. Former Washington, DC, Mayor Adrian Fenty famously did this in a 2006 primary campaign ad, in which he ran around neighborhood with not one but two Blackberries. Fenty hoped to convey to voters that he was always working on behalf of citizens and always accessible.[95]

On the surface, promising greater accountability and accessibility seems like a good way to allay concerns about inexperience or limited linked fate. But Mary Patillo cautions that middlemen or -women cannot retain their status if they appear to be biased toward one side or the other. She argues that "the role of the middleman emphasizes compromise, negotiation, and cunning."[96] A black political entrepreneur may make all the claims he wants to about accountability and accessibility. Those claims may even win him an elected office. In order to maintain the goodwill of his constituents, though, he must continue being accountable and accessible. And he will have to demonstrate to rank-and-file blacks that he gives the same consideration to their policy preferences as he does to the preferences of other stakeholders, whether they are members of other constituent groups, the private sector, or political colleagues.

Examples of Elite Displacement

Earlier I suggested that the candidates most disposed to engaging in elite displacement were ambitious politicians without access to traditional political networks in black communities. As a result, their political entrepreneurship reflects their need to create political opportunities for themselves. To illustrate this, I present two short case studies of black-on-black electoral contests featuring embattled incumbents. In one case, the black political entrepreneur clearly used elite displacement, but in the other case, the entrepreneur did not have to do so.

The Absence of Elite Displacement: Harlem 1970

To explain elite displacement, it is helpful to understand what it is not. Elite displacement is not a general term for all negative campaigning, for it is possible to engage in a negative campaign without engaging in elite displacement. A black challenger may campaign against an incumbent, for example, and not engage in elite displacement.

In 2010, many looked at Representative Charles Rangel as an object of derision and pity. As a result of financial improprieties, the once powerful chairman of the House Ways and Means Committee had to abdicate his committee chairmanship and was censured by the House of Representatives. Forty years earlier, though, Rangel was a political breath of fresh air in New York's Eighteenth Congressional District.

A series of appointments set off a chain of events that jump-started Charles Rangel's elective political career. When President Lyndon Johnson named Constance Baker Motley to the federal court of appeals, Assemblyman Percy Sutton, Rangel's longtime political mentor, replaced her as Manhattan Borough president. Someone would have to replace Sutton in the New York State Assembly, and the New York Democratic establishment unanimously endorsed Charles Rangel, a former high school dropout who, after graduating from New York University and St. Johns University Law School, went on to become an assistant U.S. attorney. As a state legislator, Rangel became a tireless advocate for his black Harlem constituency. He proposed legalizing the numbers trade to make lotteries the moral equivalent of bingo and off-track betting. He advocated forcing Columbia University to open its athletic facilities to neighborhood children. He sponsored legislation that would eventually allow Harlem to gain local control of its schools within the New York City Public School System.[97]

Rangel was a staunch supporter of the legendary Congressman Adam

Clayton Powell Jr., who by the late 1960s was fighting for his political survival. A Harlem resident had won a lawsuit against him for defamation of character, and Congress had investigated him for using public funds to pay for personal junkets to the Caribbean. To avoid prosecution, Powell spent most of his time living off the coast of Bimini, in the Bahamas. In 1967, Congress formally expelled Powell from the House, even though Harlem residents voted him back into office. The U.S. Supreme Court eventually ruled that as a duly elected member of Congress, Powell had to be seated, but the congressional leadership took away his committee chairmanship, essentially rendering him powerless.[98]

Many Harlem residents supported Powell through this scandal because they believed that the attack against him was racially motivated. In a 1967 *New York Times* article, entitled "Powell Absence Felt by His 'Real People,' Who Resent 'Whitey,'" black Harlemites expressed disgust at the perceived unfair treatment of their congressman.[99] Rangel is quoted in the article defending Powell and those residents. Then in a *New York Times Magazine* article published a couple of months later, Paul Good depicted Rangel as riding Powell's electoral coattails. He cited the following message emanating from a sound truck on Rangel's behalf: "Keep the best. We ask you to reject the rest. Vote for the leadership of Adam Clayton Powell, Percy Sutton and Charles Rangel."[100]

In 1970, Rangel chose to enter a five-way primary contest to defeat Powell. He did not announce his candidacy until February because he wanted to make sure that he could finance a successful challenge. When he did enter the race, not only was he confident of his financing, but he also had the backing of New York's political establishment. Rangel won the endorsement of the Republican and Liberal parties, and by the end of the primary campaign season, he had earned the endorsement of Mayor John Lindsay, Congresswoman Shirley Chisholm, and Howard Samuels, a Democratic gubernatorial candidate that year.[101]

With this support, Rangel could campaign on the moral high ground. He pledged not to personally attack Powell. Instead, he contended that he would

> base his campaign on the "tragedies of the '60's, the disastrous results we've had without a congressman and what we have to do to meet the problems of the '70's . . . we'll base our campaign on the fear in the streets, the apartments without heat and hot water, and the fact there has been a stepped up war in Vietnam while there has been a retreat in the war on poverty."[102]

This does not mean that Rangel did not attack Powell. Indeed, Rangel used Powell's own words to attack him for his absenteeism from Congress. For example, he printed an advertisement in the *New York Amsterdam News* that started out with a quotation from Congressman Powell: "I Am a Part-Time Congressman," which referenced Powell's threat to not return to Congress if they continued to pay him only half his salary. It ends with the declarative statement "Rangel Is Ready." In the ad, Rangel notes that because of Powell's absenteeism, he missed votes on issues related to poverty that would be of critical interest to his Harlem constituency.[103]

Rangel narrowly won the election, beating Powell by about two hundred votes. In an analysis of his victory, the *Los Angeles Times* observed that Rangel's strong performance among young people, newly redistricted whites from the Upper West Side, and Powell's lack of campaigning (he had recently undergone treatment for cancer) likely contributed to the outcome of the election.[104]

Rangel did not use elite displacement in his attack on Adam Clayton Powell, even though Powell provided more than enough fodder to enable such an attack. Rangel did not have to. With the support of much of the local political establishment, he could easily assume the front-runner position and stay above the fray. In fact, the rhetoric of some of Powell's other, less well-connected opponents shows that they were more prone to attack both Powell and Rangel on personal and moral grounds.

For example, John Young was a local community activist who ran unsuccessfully against Powell in 1968 after he had been expelled from Congress. When he announced his candidacy in 1970, Young claimed that Powell was "irrelevant" and "unfit to run for office."[105] When Vincent Baker, a Republican, announced his candidacy, he attacked Powell for his hubris, saying,

> Who can forget the stomach-turning arrogance of his boast that if he were to die, the people of Harlem would prop him up in a chair and vote for him? Here it must be admitted that so far as his usefulness to the community is concerned, he has been dead for some years, and the people have propped him up, and voted for him.[106]

Jesse Gray, a leading advocate of tenants' rights, implicitly attacked both Powell and Rangel for being inauthentically black when he asserted that "the day is over for pretty boys and just talk."[107]

By virtue of his connections to other powerful political figures, Rangel had the luxury of being able to circumscribe his attacks against Powell. In contrast, his opponents with fewer resources appear to have used attacks at least in part because they did not have another way to gain an electoral advantage.

Just because Rangel did not engage in elite displacement does not mean that he did not attack Powell. Any rational candidate seeks to contrast himself with his opponent. In practice, political strategists often distinguish between attack pieces and contrast pieces. The "I Am a Part-Time Politician" ad qualifies as a contrast piece, as it is decidedly negative but wholly substantive. Moreover, since Rangel used the ad to frame himself as a populist crusader against poverty, a racialized issue, he would not earn any points with the mainstream media. In fact, the mainstream media largely remained silent on this race. The *New York Times*, for instance, did not cover the primary contest until after the election and then, it only discussed Adam Clayton Powell's request for a recount.[108]

Elite Displacement in Action: Alabama's Seventh Congressional District, 2000 and 2002

Rangel's case contrasts with that of former Congressman Artur Davis. In 2000, the then thirty-two-year-old Davis, a Harvard-educated, former assistant U.S. attorney, challenged the six-term incumbent Earl Hilliard in Alabama's Seventh Congressional District. Although Hilliard had been a long-term player in Alabama politics, Davis was highly dissatisfied with his performance and believed that he could do a better job. Hilliard himself recalled that he had first met Davis at a community meeting where Davis publicly upbraided him for not doing his job. Hilliard said that at that moment, he knew Davis was probably setting himself up to run against him.[109]

In 2000, Davis was outmatched financially, had no real support from the black political establishment, and had low name recognition. Hilliard easily beat him by a nearly two-to-one margin. Determined to win in 2002, Davis continued to campaign and started doing local television commentary to boost his name identification. He also enlisted the help of professional consultants and friends who helped him plan his attack and raise money. In the wake of the September 11 attacks, Davis was able to use Hilliard's controversial trips to Libya to raise money from outside Alabama. Davis found that by publicly criticizing Hilliard on Libya in Alabama (including airing a television ad that featured Hilliard and Osama bin Laden in the same frame), he could generate funds in faraway places like Washington and New York. Thus, while Hilliard may have had the home-team advantage in fund-raising, Davis cleverly found a way around that obstacle. Davis also availed himself of redistricting changes, which brought in to the district new voters who were unfamiliar with Hilliard as well as more white voters. In this way, Davis was able to overcome his previous deficits and post a solid victory against Hilliard in 2002.[110]

The Hilliard-Davis contests are clear examples of elite displacement. Davis had little regard for Hilliard's leadership and ran against him. But as a political outsider, Davis initially faced obstacles to victory. After losing his first election, he regrouped and found a moral issue on which to attack Hilliard. By portraying his opponent as soft on terrorism, he found not only an issue that resonated with voters but also a way to generate political resources when most black Alabama political insiders opposed him. Davis thus was able to use both that opening and more favorable demographics to seal his victory.

Analysis

Even though Charlie Rangel and Artur Davis are very different political figures, they do share some similarities. Both had to beat incumbents in order to be elected to their seats, and both incumbents in these cases had made personal and professional decisions that made them politically vulnerable, with Powell's being the more obvious. Rangel and Davis thus had to craft a strategy to take advantage of this. Rangel had a number of resources at his disposal: he had an established record of advocating for blacks and poor people; he was mentored by an established black politician; and he had the endorsement of the political machine. Consequently, when he pointed out Powell's obvious flaws (it is hard to represent Harlem in Congress when you are in the Bahamas all the time), he could do so without his constituents reading racist or classist undertones in his actions.

In contrast, Artur Davis entered the 2000 congressional primary with little more than a belief in his own ability to be a more effective member of Congress. He therefore had to compensate for his deficits by finding a way around the fact that most political insiders backed Hilliard. He did this by using districting changes to his advantage and the ancillary issue of terrorism to tap new donation sources outside Alabama. Davis engaged in elite displacement.

Many younger, Third Wave black politicians find themselves in the same position as Charlie Rangel. Based on different familial connections, political opponents, and life experiences, some candidates are less disposed to using elite displacement. For instance, when Jesse Jackson Jr. ran against Emil Jones to replace Mel Reynolds in the House of Representatives in 1995, he did not use elite displacement because his name was a greater asset, and, besides, he was running for an open seat.[111] Harold Ford Jr., as the heir to his congressional seat, never had to face a strong black incumbent.

In fact, his greatest challengers (real and hypothetical) had always been white, which is an entirely different electoral dynamic.

Conclusion

Intraracial class divisions have long been a feature of black politics. The history of status-blind discrimination in the United States has minimized the public expression of such conflict and has united blacks around what appeared to be a common agenda for racial equality. In the aftermath of the civil rights movement, some blacks have had the opportunity to flourish while others have been left behind. This suggests that blacks should organize individually around their different status interests. Because of tradition, inertia, and the vestiges of systemic racism, though, many blacks feel the need to maintain a patina of racial unity.

Ambition, however, sometimes makes that veneer of unity hard to maintain. Although black political entrepreneurs often come from the same class stratum as the black elites they challenge for power, the fact that they are mounting such a challenge reopens old questions about which black interests actually are represented in policy and legislation. Because black political entrepreneurs assume a moderate posture and often cast aspersions on the comportment and competence of the older leaders, they are implicitly sparking old debates about the politics of respectability in the black community.

Implying that older black leaders are uncouth, incompetent, or corrupt may have positive short-term benefits but serious long-term implications. Black political entrepreneurs may unwittingly play to the prejudices of mainstream audiences and reinforce old stereotypes about the general social desirability of blacks. Those stereotypes can easily be turned against a black political entrepreneur during a moment of moral weakness or when he is forced to address a racial issue in ways that upset mainstream audiences. But more important, making such implications may alienate black political entrepreneurs from the constituents they may genuinely aspire to help. Moreover, by attacking seasoned political veterans, black political entrepreneurs may alienate a lot of institutional memory and wisdom that may prove helpful during a crisis or other unanticipated situation. Perhaps the greatest irony of all this is that it is not known whether the interests of poor blacks are better represented by black political entrepreneurs or by the older black elite.

2

Prelude

The Rise of Cory Booker

A BRIEF HISTORICAL examination of recent politics in Newark shows that conditions were ripe for a black political entrepreneur like Cory Booker to win elective office through elite displacement. When Booker moved to Newark in 1996, the city's black political establishment had not sufficiently cultivated a younger generation of leadership to assume office once they retired. This left an opening that allowed Booker to contest power. He began small, challenging an amiable incumbent for a ward council seat. His victory on the ward level would enable him to stage a bigger challenge later on.

People typically think of the 1967 Newark riots as the springboard for blacks to take over Newark's city government. The riots were a direct response to the police beating of a black taxi driver, but Komozi Woodard shows that a panoply of factors contributed to the unrest ignited by that beating. In particular, black residents had grown weary with only token political representation. They were being exploited by shopkeepers who charged them exorbitant prices for substandard goods and services, and parts of Newark's black community in the Central Ward were being razed, without consultation, to make room for the construction of the University of Medicine and Dentistry of New Jersey (UMDNJ).[1]

The 1967 riots hastened white and black middle-class flight out of the city of Newark.[2] While their flight had a negative economic impact on the city, it did serve to increase the proportion of the city's black population. Now, with blacks as the city's clear majority, they were in a position to challenge the white political establishment.[3]

In the wake of the riots, the city's black and Puerto Rican residents united in the 1969 Black and Puerto Rican Political Convention, at which they outlined a political strategy to take control of city government. They also named a slate of candidates to run for political office in 1970. At the top of the ticket was Kenneth Gibson, a city engineer who in 1966 had run unsuccessfully for mayor against incumbent Hugh Addonizio. Gibson was soft spoken and far from militant, and convention leaders hoped that he would calm white fears of a radical black taking over at city hall. The slate for municipal council also included a young gym teacher named Sharpe James, who had become well known for trying to calm the unrest during the 1967 rebellion.[4]

The 1970 elections were marked by extremely racially polarized voting. In his study of white attitudes toward black mayoral candidates, Zoltan Hajnal estimated that in the cities he studied, the first black mayors, elected between 1967 and 1993, won an average of 30% of the white vote. If we limit our analysis to mayors elected between 1967 and 1980, the average falls to about 21%. Gibson was elected with only 10% of white support, the second-lowest proportion of white support of all the elections that Hajnal studied and the lowest proportion in the elections between 1967 and 1980. This means that of the first wave of historic elections that put black mayors in office, Gibson's election was arguably the most racially polarized.[5]

Gibson's election was also important because black nationalists played a key role in helping get him elected. For instance, poet and activist Amiri Baraka was a leader in the Black and Puerto Rican Political Convention that nominated Gibson to run for mayor. Indeed, black nationalists hoped that Newark would become the model for electing blacks to office in urban centers with large minority populations.[6]

The cordial relationship between Gibson and the black nationalists soon ended, however, and several years later, black nationalists in Newark bitterly recalled how Gibson sold them out. At a rally commemorating the fortieth anniversary of the Newark riots, speaker after speaker railed against political leaders who ignored community interests in favor of corporate interests. To the untrained ear, one would think that these activists were referring to Cory Booker, but they also were talking about Sharpe James and Kenneth Gibson.

Not long after that rally, Amiri and Amina Baraka explained that they naively thought in 1970 that blacks were so heavily represented in Newark's poor communities because they were being oppressed by white politicians. They reasoned that if they organized against Addonizio and his political machine and replaced the white politicians with black ones, conditions in the city's black wards would improve. In their interviews, they both confessed that their thinking was overly simplistic. They said that they learned that black politicians also could be beholden to corporate interests and could not be trusted to make decisions that would benefit blacks just because they shared the same racial identity.[7]

Although the rift between Gibson and black nationalists probably was inevitable, this does not negate the shrewdness of placing Gibson at the top of the ticket. His moderation worked to his electoral advantage, and his calm demeanor also helped him once he was in office. Gibson easily earned the trust of the business community and was widely seen as an honest power broker with an even temperament, which was just what the city needed after the riots.[8]

The Newark of 1970 presented Gibson with daunting odds. People were fleeing the city en masse; housing stock was crumbling or destroyed; the city had one of the country's highest infant mortality rates; and deindustrialization was costing the city thousands of jobs. Yet according to Gibson, he was able to make some tremendous gains. He started rebuilding the city's housing stock; he improved the city's infant mortality rates; and he restored city services.[9]

Despite the gains and Gibson's calming presence, many people felt that he did not provide visionary leadership. Business leaders contended that he was a good functionary—someone who could help return the city to a sense of normalcy and make sure that the trash was collected on time and potholes were fixed. Gibson was not, however, a big-picture person who engaged in long-term planning or inspired residents.[10]

People close to Gibson also contended that fatigue got the best of him toward the end of his sixteen-year tenure as mayor.[11] Gibson's legal troubles may have contributed to that fatigue. In 1982, he was implicated in a corruption scandal in which he and the president of the city council, Earl Harris, were indicted for giving a no-show job to a former council member.[12] Both Gibson and Harris were acquitted of all charges in that case.

In addition, the city experienced notable declines during Gibson's tenure as mayor. The city's lost about 68,000 residents from 1970 to 1986. Unemployment jumped from 8.4% in 1970 to 12.2% in 1986. In addition, the number of hotels and retail businesses in the city fell by half; the number of restaurants in the city decreased 75%, and all the city's bowling alleys closed. These losses were exacerbated by the fact by 1986, the federal government had slashed Community Development Block Grant and Comprehensive Employment and Training Act funding by about 75%. Indeed, federal support for Newark started to decline as early as 1978.[13]

Gibson faced two electoral challenges during his tenure as mayor. Earl Harris, Gibson's alleged co-conspirator in the 1982 scandal and the last

Republican to serve on Newark's municipal council, challenged him for the mayoralty in 1982. He forced Gibson into a runoff election. (Newark conducts nonpartisan municipal elections, so candidates have to win an outright majority of the vote in order to win on the first ballot.) Even though Gibson won, having to compete in a runoff after one's third term was clear evidence of his vulnerability.

Harris did not challenge Gibson again, but in 1986, Councilman Sharpe James emerged as Gibson's leading challenger for the mayoralty. James had served on the council since 1970, when he won the South Ward council seat. He then graduated to an at-large council seat in 1982, thus demonstrating his ability to win a citywide election.

James ran on a platform of "Sharpe Change" (Amiri Baraka takes credit for coining the phrase),[14] arguing that Kenneth Gibson had been in power too long and needed to be replaced. In particular, James cited high crime and a dearth of recreation options for children as evidence of Gibson's complacency. The crime issue hit close to home for James, as his oldest son, John, had survived a mugging and shooting in December 1985. James publicly criticized Gibson's decision to reduce the number of police officers in the city. James also contended that Newark had fallen behind other cities under Gibson's leadership. Making light of Gibson's claim that "wherever America's cities are going, Newark will get there first," James quipped, "He was wrong. Other cities, like Atlanta, Boston and Baltimore, have gotten there first."[15]

Despite James's bluster and the negative statistics, he was an underdog in this race. Kenneth Gibson's fund-raising outpaced James's by a margin of more than two to one. James could not secure the explicit endorsement of white business leaders, despite their dissatisfaction with Gibson. Moreover, Gibson won the endorsement of the *Star-Ledger* (the *New York Times* argued that neither Gibson nor James could "inspire its [Newark's] growth").[16] Gibson even had the support of Anthony Imperiale, the former Newark councilman who ran against Gibson in 1974 and had earlier gained notoriety for antagonizing blacks and Puerto Ricans.[17]

James ended up beating Gibson handily on the first ballot, by about sixteen percentage points.[18] Once in office, James served as a tireless cheerleader for the city. He, along with local business leaders, successfully lobbied the state to build the New Jersey Performing Arts Center in downtown Newark. He brought minor league baseball and a stadium to the city, and toward the end of his tenure, James was one of the driving forces behind building a hockey stadium for the New Jersey Devils in downtown

Newark. Finally, he was responsible for tearing down much of the city's blighted public housing high-rises.[19]

Despite these successes, James's administration also became mired in unethical behavior. In the late 1990s, close associates of the mayor were implicated in major corruption scandals. For instance, James's chief of staff, Jackie Mattison, was convicted of accepting bribes, the money found in the floorboards of his girlfriend's house.[20]

In addition, the city's reputation suffered. In the 1990s, Newark was dubbed the "car theft capital" of the United States and the "carjacking capital of the world."[21] Although the mayor does not have direct authority over the schools, a state judge put Newark's public school system into receivership in 1995. The state of New Jersey had been monitoring students' progress in the city for ten years, and their test scores were not improving. Moreover, there were allegations that the school board had grossly mismanaged its budget, wasting money on cars and lavish trips, while a majority of students were failing.[22] In addition, in 2006, the head of the Newark Housing Authority, Harold Lucas, resigned amid allegations of nepotism and the misspending of millions of dollars of federal aid.[23]

Because of these developments, a number of prominent black leaders challenged James for mayoral control. In 1998, he survived a challenge from State Senator Ronald Rice Sr. and Councilwoman Mildred Crump, easily beating both on the first ballot.

Of particular interest, though, was Ras Baraka's 1994 challenge to the mayor. Ras Baraka, the son of Amiri and Amina Baraka, ran against the mayor in a crowded field in part because he wanted to protest James's failure to include young people in his administration. His contention was that James had failed to mentor a new generation of young leadership.[24]

Although he is loath to admit it, Ras Baraka was actually part of a generation of young, black Newarkers who had been politically socialized as youngsters and were coming of age in the early 1990s. This generation included Sharpe James's eldest son, John; Ronald Rice Sr.'s son Ronald Jr.;[25] Mildred Crump's son Larry; Grace Spencer, whose parents were active South Ward Democrats; Marjory Avant, whose parents were close friends of Sharpe James; Anton Wheeler; and Karriem Arnold; among others. Most of these young people had grown up campaigning together, sometimes on their parents' campaigns, and as teenagers, most of them had worked together in the city's summer youth employment program. Based on their connections and experiences, they could reasonably expect to be supported if they chose to run for office later in life. In the mid-1990s, many of them were in law school, and more than a few harbored dreams of running for elective office at some point in the not-too-distant future. In the meantime, many of these young people could rest comfortably, knowing that, as Marjory Avant said, they had access to mayor if they needed anything.[26]

Another group of young people in Newark were a little more restless. They had come to Newark in the mid-1990s, fresh out of college or graduate school. They were a multicultural group, most of whom had come to Newark (although some were native Newarkers) to work in the nonprofit sector. One of them was Modia Butler, who was from Philadelphia and had moved to Newark after earning a graduate degree from Rutgers. He began his career with a nonprofit called Newark Do Something. As he recalled, this group of young people met regularly to discuss their work and trade notes. He said that it was an exciting time to do nonprofit work in the city because of all the dynamic young people around, but he also remembers being frustrated that he and his friends had only limited access to the political in-crowd.[27] His recollection was markedly different from that of Gayle Chaneyfield, whose family had been operating a nonprofit day care center in the city since the early 1970s. Chaneyfield, whose family was politically well connected, was about to start her own political career in the mid-1990s as an at-large councilwoman, and she remembered the era as being the high point of government-nonprofit partnership in the city.[28]

In 1996 a former Rhodes Scholar and Yale law student named Cory Booker decided to move to Newark. Booker, who had grown up twenty miles north of Newark in Harrington Park, New Jersey, missed living in New Jersey and wanted to go home, even though his parents were now splitting their time between Washington, DC, and Atlanta. Booker planned on pursuing a career in public service (though not politics), so Newark was an attractive city. He soon found lodging in a rooming house and began commuting from Newark to New Haven to complete law school. He also started participating in a tenants' law clinic.[29] During this time, Booker met the young people who were working in the nonprofit sector, as well as the scions of the political families who were just finishing law school. They all complained that the city's political establishment was not mentoring young people, and eventually they decided that one of them should run for office and challenge the establishment.

Although many in this group of young people would have made able politicians, very few were in a position to run for office in the late 1990s. Some of the nonprofit people were planning to leave Newark for further training or other job opportunities.[30] And the recent law school graduates had to work to support themselves and pay off their student loans.[31] Booker, though, was in a different position. When he graduated from Yale Law School in May 1997, he won a fellowship from the law firm of Skadden, Arps, Meagher, Slate and Flom, LLC to practice tenants' rights law in Newark. The fellowship allowed him to burnish his activist credentials with residents and gave him free time to pursue politics if he chose. As Grace Spencer put it, Booker became the first person to run for office because he was the only person who had the luxury of time to do so in 1998.[32]

There is some dispute about how Booker decided to run for Central Ward councilman in 1998. Booker says that one of the tenant leaders he worked with on a lawsuit against a slumlord drafted him to vote. She says that Booker asked for her support (which he got) after he and others decided that he would run.[33] In any case, there is no dispute that Booker challenged the sixteen-year incumbent George Branch.

By all accounts, it was very hard not to like George Branch. A former boxer, he used his skills to help provide children with after-school activities. But Branch was not an educated man. Nonetheless, because of his work with children, he had a wide following among residents of the Central Ward.[34]

In 1998, Branch had the support of Mayor Sharpe James in his reelection bid. Cory Booker, however, was an indefatigable candidate who knocked on every door in the ward asking for votes.[35] His efforts paid off. In the municipal election, he came in second place in a three-way field, but Branch won only a plurality of the votes. According to local election laws, candidates had to win a clear majority of the votes. Thus, Booker and Branch had to face each other in a runoff election.

Booker's campaign staff set out to improve their field operation for the runoff election. In particular, they needed to make sure that every potential voter that they had identified was reminded to vote on the next Election Day. They surmised that the reason they had come in second place on the first ballot was that they had not mobilized every voter who had pledged his or her support during the campaign season. The Booker campaign rectified this in the runoff and pulled off a decisive victory.[36]

Does Elite Displacement Explain 1986? 1998?

It is important to consider the role that elite displacement did or did not play in launching Newark political candidates in general and in jump-starting Cory Booker's political career in particular.

One argument is that Sharpe James employed some, but not all, of the elements of elite displacement against Kenneth Gibson in 1986. By framing himself as the reformist candidate, he was able to draw contrasts between himself and Gibson. But many other factors prevent considering this election as a displacement election. It would be very difficult for Sharpe James to argue that Kenneth Gibson, with his more temperate personality, was the more socially unacceptable of the two to mainstream audiences. Indeed, he had been selected to run for mayor specifically in the hopes that he would have a great crossover appeal. When Gibson ran for reelection in 1986, the white business establishment did not forcefully oppose him, and he earned the endorsement of the local newspaper. More important, as a sixteen-year municipal council incumbent, Sharpe James was hardly a political outsider; he was a former running mate of Kenneth Gibson.

There is evidence, however, to support the idea that Booker began to hone parts of an elite displacement strategy in 1998. At that time, he did not need to create class distinctions between himself and George Branch, as Booker clearly came from a higher echelon. But Booker did use his pedigree to justify his candidacy, in part because at age twenty-nine and only a year out of law school, he had a very thin record on which to run. Booker often recounted a story about a woman who asked him if his being a Rhodes Scholar meant that he had problems keeping his pants zipped. She was clearly referring to Bill Clinton and the Monica Lewinsky scandal that captivated the nation that year. Booker's story, however, also suggests that he accentuated rather than downplayed his credentials.

From the outset of his career, Booker also used his contacts outside Newark to help bankroll his campaigns. For instance, Booker returned to New Haven on at least one occasion to raise money among his friends from Yale. In fact, his bypassing the traditional Newark establishment for support helped deter challenges from other potentially credible opponents.[37]

Conclusion

Booker's elite pedigree gave him access to opportunities that allowed him to pursue politics faster than his other talented peers could. He then used his social network to raise funds to launch his political career.

In chapter 1, I presented the idea that elite displacement was a logical strategic move because it gave black political entrepreneurs an opportunity to differentiate themselves from their political opponents. I also noted that this strategy is fraught with risk. The political opponent rarely accepts the black political entrepreneur's characterization of him without a fight, and that fight can leave long-term political bruises on both candidates. Indeed, elite displacement does not always propel a black political entrepreneur to elective office the first time around.

Fig. 3.1. Online magazine the *Black Commentator* published these cartoons, by Khalil Bendib, accusing Cory Booker of being a puppet of right-wing interests. Articles from the *Black Commentator* were printed and mailed anonymously throughout Newark during the 2002 campaign. *Sources:* "Newark: The First Domino?," *Black Commentator* (online source), May 8, 2002; "First of the Poisoned Tree," *Black Commentator* (online source), April 5, 2002; used with permission.

3

Losing

The 2002 Mayoral Election

ONE FEATURE OF elite displacement is that it takes time. It is not unusual for black political entrepreneurs to lose their first election for a major office. In that first election, voters are often skeptical of the black political entrepreneur's reform claims and prefer to deal with the "devil they know," so to speak.

Cory Booker was no stranger to early defeat, and his unsuccessful 2002 campaign is a good example of an elite displacement campaign. We see how a black political entrepreneur cultivates his profile to generate media attention and grassroots support. We also see how the countermobilzation to the black political entrepreneur helps identify the candidate's weakness. In Booker's case, his embrace of deracialized campaign tactics did not resonate immediately with black voters, who were more accustomed to their politicians using more racialized political frames.

What Black Political Entrepreneurs Do and Why It Does Not Always Work the First Time

Black political entrepreneurs rarely win endorsements from established black political figures when they first enter the political scene. In fact, they often are challenging these political figures for power. When a member of the black political establishment does not support a black political entrepreneur, it also blocks his access to campaign volunteers and fund-raising bases. Therefore, if the entrepreneur has any hope of mounting a credible candidacy, he must identify and cultivate alternative bases of support. Black political entrepreneurs, then, must use their own networks to create their own campaign foundations.

What black political entrepreneurs lack in connections to the black political establishment, they make up in connections to mainstream institutions. If they cannot win the support of a black political boss or high elected official, or if lieutenants in black political machines refuse to support them, black political entrepreneurs can go to other social networks to find volunteers and donors. For instance, they may approach their college friends or childhood neighbors.

It is important to keep in mind that these contacts do not necessarily have ties to the community that the black political entrepreneur is hoping to lead (although they can). Furthermore, they may not even have the same racial or ethnic background of the majority of the community's residents. But these contacts are loyal to the black political entrepreneur, and they may have access to resources that could overwhelm the resources of the black political establishment that rebuffed the political entrepreneur. These friends could come from wealthy communities that would be happy to financially support an entrepreneur's candidacy. They may also have contacts in mainstream political and intellectual circles that could be very helpful to the black political entrepreneur. These contacts could arrange for entrepreneurs to meet valuable political professionals who could provide consulting services for the entrepreneur. They could also use their relationships with journalists and opinion leaders to obtain positive media coverage. Even though the black political establishment tried to shut out the black political entrepreneur, he may be able to circumvent these obstacles to create a formidable political organization.

Just because a black political entrepreneur creates a formidable political machine, however, does not mean that it will be instantly successful. While large political apparatuses can be constructed quickly, it often takes time for them to develop credibility.

Deracialization, Its Critics and Caveats

Implicit in the idea of black political entrepreneurs' circumventing traditional centers of black political power to establish their political careers is a concern about whether they feel the need to eschew black support in their quest for political office. Ironically, this concern often arises in majority-black communities. These concerns, along with the tendency of black political entrepreneurs to employ deracialized campaign tactics, reopen old debates about the efficacy of emphasizing or deemphasizing race in political campaigns.

Questions about the best strategy to maximize the election of black elected officials have been a part of the discussion in black politics for more than a generation. In the 1970s, Charles Hamilton urged blacks to adopt a deracialized political strategy in order to maximize their political influence. He contended that civil right leaders' emphasis on racial redress had caused a backlash among white voters, thus opening the door for the election of Republican candidates who were, on the whole, predicted to be less responsive to the needs of black voters than Democrats would have been. By emphasizing universal concerns that transcend race, such as health care and job creation, Hamilton argued, blacks would be in a better position to join broad-based coalitions and to elect candidates of their choice to office.[1]

By the late 1980s, scholars observed that black candidates had internalized Hamilton's suggestions with at least a modest degree of success. The 1989 elections in particular stand out, as black candidates used deracialized or racially transcendent strategies to win office in a number of high-profile and groundbreaking elections. For example, David Dinkins urged voters to "vote your hopes and not your fears" to become New York City's first black mayor.[2] In Baltimore, Kurt Schmoke became that city's first black mayor by advocating a platform of economic development designed to benefit black and white residents alike.[3] And most notably, L. Douglas Wilder became the nation's first black elected governor in Virginia by running on a law-and-order platform.[4]

The elections of 1989 were historic for a number of reasons. First, the black candidates who won were often the first African Americans to be elected to their respective offices. Second, these candidates ran in areas where blacks were not the majority of the electorate. Finally, they won those offices with substantial white support. Whereas earlier black candidates typically earned about 25% of the white vote, these candidates increased their share of the white vote by more than 50%.[5]

To be sure, there was some evidence of deracialization in majority-black jurisdictions or in areas where blacks had a history of holding elective office. In 1989, Maynard Jackson, Atlanta's first black mayor, sought a third mayoral term to succeed Mayor Andrew Young. Jackson's first bids for office had been marked by racial polarization, and Jackson was elected despite white opposition. In his third bid for office, however, there was much less racial polarization. In 1989, Jackson faced two separate challenges from black opponents. The first challenger, Fulton County Commissioner Michael Lomax, had considerable support among whites and middle- and upper-class blacks. But Jackson, who ran on a neighborhood improvement platform, had strong support among these groups as well as among some lower-class blacks. Lomax eventually decided that he could not beat

Jackson and dropped out of the race. He was replaced by Rev. Hosea Williams, a poverty and civil rights activist. Williams had a natural base of support among poor blacks, but in Lomax's absence, Jackson consolidated his support among middle-class blacks and whites, which guaranteed his victory.[6]

Cleveland provides another example of deracialization at work in a city with a relatively long history of black electoral success. In 1989, Michael White became that city's second black mayor in a surprising upset over George Forbes, the powerful president of the city council and a protégé of Carl Stokes, Cleveland's first black mayor. White, who won a key endorsement from the *Cleveland Plain-Dealer*, was the surprising second-place finisher in the city's nonpartisan primary, earning him a spot in the general runoff election. In that election, White, who had campaigned in both the black and white sections of town, consolidated his support among white voters and won just enough black votes (20%) to win 54% of the overall vote.[7]

These two examples demonstrate at the local level what David Canon, Matthew Schousen, and Patrick Sellers modeled at the congressional level. They examined the proliferation of black congressional candidates in newly created black majority districts in 1992. Given that these races often pitted two black candidates against each other at the primary level, they could no longer assume that black voters would vote for the black candidate. So how would black voters distinguish among multiple black candidates?[8]

Canon and his colleagues classified the candidates according to their level of deracialization. Deracialized, or "new-style," candidates ran moderate campaigns and tried to appeal to voters outside their racial group, whereas "traditional" candidates ran on a traditional civil rights agenda and appealed mostly to a black base. Based on this classification, Canon and his colleagues then made a number of hypotheses about the electoral outcomes. Three of those hypotheses are noteworthy. First, they predicted that if only one black candidate ran for office, that person would likely be a traditional candidate. Second, they hypothesized that if a white candidate ran against both a new-style and a traditional black candidate, it was possible for the white candidate to win. Under those circumstances, the black candidates might split the black vote, leaving the white candidate to consolidate the white vote and eke out a plurality win. But if there was no white candidate, the race featured both new-style and traditional black candidates, and the district was at least 30% white, the new-style candidate would probably win by splitting the black vote and consolidating the white vote.[9]

Canon, Schousen, and Sellers then tested their hypotheses using the 1992 congressional elections. Nearly 90% of the races they studied fit one of their hypothesized models. In particular, the new-style candidate won all but one of the races in contests pitting new-style candidates against traditional candidates.[10]

Canon, Schousen, and Sellers's findings show an empirical endorsement of deracialized strategies in black-on-black elections, even after controlling for incumbency and candidate quality. But they failed to consider the normative implications of using deracialized strategies. Many scholars have questioned the utility of such strategies in advancing an African American political agenda. Specifically, they have expressed concerns about the ability of deracialized elected officials to address specific racialized concerns once in office. Could a deracialized official publicly denigrate overt and structural racism and maintain a rainbow electoral coalition, or did they make an implicit compact with white voters to not discuss race in exchange for descriptive representation?[11]

Another risk is that black political entrepreneurs who bypassed traditional black cultural and political centers might be accused of a certain obtuseness or insensitivity with respect to racial issues. Yes, political circumstances forced them to bypass black communities to develop their political organizations, but some people may wonder whether black political entrepreneurs bypassed those communities in part because of a greater comfort level in mainstream communities, especially when a black political entrepreneur is not from the community he wants to represent. That suspicion leads some to speculate about an entrepreneur's motives for trying to seek office in the first place.

These kinds of suspicions thus amplify the need for black political entrepreneurs to cultivate an image to which their constituents can easily relate. Simply put, it is not enough to be the new-style candidate running against a traditional candidate. The other aspects of campaigning, such as demonstrating empathy and personal proximity, still are important and can spell the difference between winning and losing elections.

Richard Fenno captured the essence of this idea in his travels with congressional candidates over the last forty years. In *Home Style*, he argues that "qualification, identification and empathy" are at the foundation of any relationship between a candidate and his potential constituent.[12] He has to prove that he is capable of doing a good job if elected, especially if he is not an incumbent. He has to prove how similar he is to his constituents. Finally, he must demonstrate that he can easily place himself in his constituents' shoes. If he fails to convey these qualities to the electorate, or if the qualities conveyed are somehow out of sync with or offensive to the electorate, then he risks losing the election, especially if his opponent seems to have a better personal fit with the community. Fenno's point is probably best summed up in his account of Congressman A, who represented a southern, rural, conservative district. He compared himself with a liberal colleague from central Pennsylvania who had a penchant for purple shirts. The congressman recalled being asked about the probability that "a man like that would have of getting elected in our district. . . . And I said, 'Exactly the same chance as I would have of getting elected in Wilkes-Barre, Pennsylvania.' "[13]

Fenno observed that candidates cultivate their reputations by managing how they present themselves to others. In Congressman A's case, he interpreted his community's conservative culture to mean that he needed to pay attention to his wardrobe. Others also play a key role in helping define candidates, which can help or hinder a person's electoral chances. Marjorie Hershey noted that the media often use the raw material of candidates and their campaigns to create media frames, or contexts, in which they interpret the stories of the election season. A media frame is much like the plot in a novel or a movie: it helps identify the overarching themes and key archetypes. In short, frames provide heuristics to help voters process the onslaught of campaign information.[14]

To illustrate her point, Hershey used the 2000 presidential election as her case study. A couple of frames dominated the 2000 presidential election. Clearly, there was a lot of interest in the horse race, but reporters also helped reinforce certain stereotypes of the candidates. Al Gore was often portrayed as dour, stiff, and prone to exaggeration, and George W. Bush developed the reputation for being affable and unintelligent. When the candidates played according to their characterization, the media reinforced the stereotype, and when the candidates played against type, the media often ignored them. So when Bush overestimated the extent to which he was being outspent by the Gore campaign, no one noticed. But when Gore misstated the cost of his dog's arthritis medication relative to his mother's, it reinforced the frame that Gore was dishonest. Similarly, when Gore made verbal gaffes, it got very little media attention, but when Bush mangled words, it received considerable press.[15]

Hershey believes that media frames are important because next to the candidate's outreach to voters, media reports are one of the principal ways that voters gather information about candidates.[16] Constantly hearing that a candidate lies or is not smart could have a serious impact on a voter's desire to support him.

In a black politics context, media frames can convey a tremendous amount of information about whether black political entrepreneurs possess or lack empathy or relate well to black voters. For historical reasons, mainstream media support can be a mixed blessing. For generations, blacks have had an antagonistic relationship with the mainstream media and society at large. Carolyn Martindale and Lilian Rae Dunlap provide an overview of the tension between blacks and the media. The history of journalists' coverage of black issues generally is either nonexistent or presents a dysfunctional view of black life and culture. Given the media's poor track record in covering black issues, then, Martindale and Dunlap argue that it is logical for blacks to mistrust them.[17]

Blacks' mistrust of the media explains some of the skepticism when traditional black public figures are cast in a negative light. Martindale and Dunlap write that "the backlash includes an unwillingness of many African Americans to believe the worst, despite the evidence, about a black hero, because they feel the evidence was obtained through racist motives."[18] This explains why blacks continued to support Marion Barry after he was caught on tape smoking crack cocaine, and it explains why blacks supported O.J. Simpson even when he was on trial for murder.[19]

Martindale and Dunlap's analysis complements the work of Melissa Harris-Lacewell, who argues that the defiant posture is a common trope in everyday black political communication:

> Scholars of black political culture have regularly noted the bad man as a recurring icon in African American culture. . . . The "bad nigger" is about the power of the powerless. Black bad men are cathartic because they represent a kind of direct resistance that is not realistically available to most African Americans.[20]

If blacks have a historically antagonistic relationship with the mainstream media, then this puts black candidates with extensive mainstream media support at a disadvantage in some black communities. Adolph Reed observed this phenomenon during Jesse Jackson's first presidential bid in 1984.[21] In that race, Jackson did not have the complete support of the black community, as poorer blacks were less likely to support his candidacy.[22] However, Reed pointed out that Jackson received an inordinate amount of media attention for someone with such low poll numbers. Accordingly,

Reed decried the Jackson of 1984 as being a white media construction who used the media to impose himself as a leader on black Americans.[23]

Ronald Walters and Robert Smith underscored the importance of legitimacy to determining who is a black leader. They acknowledged that legitimacy in an African American context can come from both inside and outside black communities. That is, blacks and whites can perceive different people as leaders in the black community. Black constituents can select their own leaders internally and not have those leaders recognized by whites. Or a presumed leader can derive his legitimacy from whites, thus making him an external leader. If both blacks and whites recognize a particular leader, she is a consensus leader. Finally, if no one recognizes a leader as legitimate, then that person is an "autoselected" leader.[24]

Walters and Smith's deconstruction of legitimacy provides an important context for judging the black political entrepreneur's first forays into major political contests. He may gain notoriety by obtaining mainstream support. Although having mainstream media support is evidence of having external legitimacy, it does not automatically confer internal legitimacy. Therefore, the black political entrepreneur may have to work especially hard to cultivate internal legitimacy in order to offset the suspicions of some blacks about too much positive media attention.

Hypothesis

How does this help us explain the 2002 Newark election? This election pitted a black political entrepreneur (Cory Booker) against a more traditional black politician (Sharpe James). If we apply Canon, Schousen, and Seller's hypothesis to this election, Booker should have won by creating a coalition of some blacks, who made up 52% of the population, and the rest of Newark. But he lost because he did not capture enough of the black vote to win. Whereas Booker won in predominantly white (62% to 37%) and Latino (57% to 42%) precincts, he lost in predominantly black (40% to 59%) precincts.[25]

The 2002 Newark mayoral election suggests that the black political entrepreneur's moderation is not enough to ensure victory, even in a majority-black city with a sufficient nonblack population. Black votes still are important to the moderate black candidate's rainbow coalition, and moderate blacks must actively campaign for black votes, even if they are destined to win only part of the black community. In campaigning for those black voters, black political entrepreneurs still have to be mindful of how they present themselves to voters. In short, home style still matters, and black political entrepreneurs still must earn the trust and admiration of all their potential constituents, including black voters.

A Brief History of the 2002 Newark Mayoral Election

Until 2002, Sharpe James appeared to be an invincible political figure. Since first winning elective office in 1970, he had never lost an election. After serving sixteen years on Newark's municipal council, he successfully challenged incumbent Mayor Kenneth Gibson in 1986. Indeed, James was such a popular mayor that he ran unopposed for reelection in 1990. And although he faced multiple challenges in 1994 and 1998, he easily beat all of his opponents (including Ras Baraka in 1994 and State Senator Ronald Rice Sr. and Councilwoman Mildred Crump in 1998) on the first ballot. James was so assured of victory that he had the luxury of running his own campaigns and did not have to rely on scientific polling to gauge the pulse of his community.[26]

Something changed in 2002. James started the campaign season as usual, running his own campaign and ignoring modern campaign technologies. Given his opponent's youth and inexperience, this should have been an easy race. But advisers close to James began to worry that he might be in trouble. So they invited Washington pollster Ron Lester to work on the campaign. Lester quickly fielded a poll that revealed an incumbent politician's worst fear: vulnerability.

RON LESTER: So, I designed a poll real quick, put the poll in the field. Talked to [Steve] DeMicco and Brad Lawrence, the message guys, and the poll came back. It was 45–45, 10% undecided. And Sharpe's theme —and he already had literature up and signs up around the city—was like "Let's keep a good thing going.

ANDRA GILLESPIE [*correcting him*]: Let's continue the progress?

RON LESTER: Continue the Progress. And people weren't, like, feeling the progress. It was high unemployment. But [James] was quite popular among blacks. And he was in a net favorable position among Latinos. He was in a net negative position among whites. So the only way for him to win was really to maximize the black vote, consolidate the black vote. Because he was getting, maybe, 53%. Cory was getting, like, 20%. And that was just too much. . . . But Cory was leading among whites and Hispanics and overall, the numbers were 45–45. . . . So, what happened was, we did the poll and then we had a retreat. . . . And I was the first presenter, and I basically said that it was an election that usually an incumbent would lose. Because [the] reelect number was 41%. Usually, when they go below 40[%], they lose. And just the fact that he was below 50[%] against, you know, a first-time challenger, didn't look very good, in terms of the prospects.[27]

Lester's comments reveal that Cory Booker was not the typical, weak, opponent. Challenging a sixteen-year incumbent may strike some as a quixotic enterprise,[28] but a number of factors suggest that Booker's run in 2002 could be classified as strategic. Booker maintained that conditions in the city (i.e., high unemployment, low home ownership, and low high school graduation rates) had not improved since James had taken office. Moreover, James's administration had been implicated in corruption scandals. Even though he was a long-term incumbent, he had vulnerabilities on which Booker, a savvy, experienced, and better-financed candidate, hoped to capitalize.[29]

In order to win this election, the James campaign would have to shore up support in the black community. In order to do that, they would have to exploit Booker's weaknesses among blacks. At the outset of the campaign, however, Booker was not that weak among blacks. Lester noted:

Cory's numbers were pretty solid among blacks. I mean, he didn't really have a net unfavorable, you know. But he didn't have that 65% favorable among blacks that Sharpe had. So, we knew . . . if we consolidated the black vote and maximized black turnout, that he could win. . . . And that's where "The Real Deal" came in. . . . So we decided to develop that and to do a concentrated direct mail program and cable television buy for three weeks and then track again. And we did. And we had gone from 45[%] to 51[%], and Cory had gone from 45[%] to 41[%]. So, 51[%]–41[%]. And that's pretty much where it stayed until Election Day. And it ended up being, Cory got, like 46[%]. We got, like, 53[%].[30]

Lester's comments, which were corroborated by media consultant Steve DeMicco, show that Sharpe James responded to Cory Booker's candidacy by making the election a contest of racial authenticity. Because James realized that he was losing among whites and Latinos, he knew he had to consolidate the black vote. His campaign responded by using racial solidarity among blacks, calling James the "real deal."[31]

Cory Booker challenged Sharpe James in 2002 on a general reformist platform, with a campaign slogan proclaiming him "the change we want;

the leadership we need." Throughout the campaign, Booker made light of the statistics, which he believed proved that James had not done enough to improve Newark residents' quality of life. In a campaign video distributed to undecided voters the week before the election, Booker cites high unemployment and high school dropout rates as some of the key reasons that James did not deserve a fifth term in office.[32] The Booker campaign also charged that James was an entrenched and corrupt politician. Direct-mail ads, like those shown in figures 3.2–3.3, noted that James had been in office all of most young adults' lives and that he had profited from his time in office, being able to buy a Rolls Royce and a yacht on a public servant's paycheck.

The 2002 campaign was the most contentious mayoral race since Kenneth Gibson's historic mayoral victory in 1970, if not in the city's history. Both sides raised a combined total of $5 million, making it the most expensive mayoral race to date in New Jersey history.[33] The race also was marked by surprising rancor, including allegations of sign vandalism and campaign office break-ins. Supporters of Sharpe James and even James himself alleged that Booker was not really black and was a tool of outside interests who wanted to take over the city. The situation was so tense that the U.S. attorney's office sent in observers to monitor the election.[34] I myself witnessed some of the racial rancor and was cursed at and accused of carpet-bagging while working with and for Booker's campaign.

Content Analysis

As my content analysis demonstrates, Booker also had an advantage in his mainstream media support. For this analysis, I created a database of 169 articles published from January 1, 2002, to May 14, 2002, that discuss the Newark mayoral election.[35] Because of their publication dates, voters could have been exposed to the content of these articles before they voted. This database includes all the full-text English-language articles I could find that were stored in such Internet databases as LexisNexis Academic Universe, nj.com's online archive of the *Newark Star-Ledger* and other New Jersey publications, and Ethnic Newswatch that mention either Cory Booker or Sharpe James. I searched LexisNexis and nj.com in 2003, as well as Ethnic Newswatch, periodically from 2005 to 2007[36] to ensure that minority periodicals were adequately represented in the database. I also included articles from salon.com and BlackCommentator.com, which are online magazines. The *Black Commentator* was particularly important because its articles were distributed in Newark during the 2002 election

First elected in 1970...and he's still holding on 32 years later.

Sharpe James has
been holding office
All Of Your Life.

His act is getting old.

It's time for a change.

Fig. 3.2. Booker Team ally Citi Pac released this ad asserting that Sharpe James had been in office too long, along with the accompanying photo reinforcing the idea that James is a buffoon.

32
YEARS
Of Sharpe James
IS ENOUGH.

Sharpe James has been neglecting Newark since 1970. That's 32 years. 32 years of drug dealing, car theft and mismanaged schools.

Only 4 out of 10 Newark students graduate High School.

You are twice as likely to get murdered in Newark than in Brooklyn or the Bronx.

30 to 50% of the State's childhood lead poisoning cases are in Newark.

It's way past time for a change.
Let's retire Sharpe James on May 14.

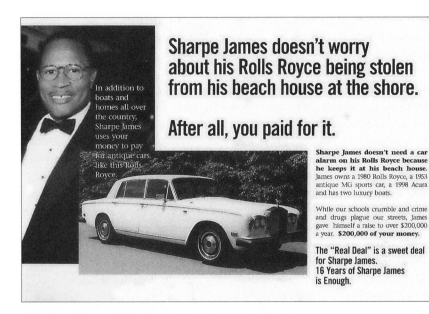

Sharpe James doesn't worry about his Rolls Royce being stolen from his beach house at the shore.

After all, you paid for it.

In addition to boats and homes all over the country, Sharpe James uses your money to pay for antique cars like this Rolls Royce.

Sharpe James doesn't need a car alarm on his Rolls Royce because he keeps it at his beach house. James owns a 1980 Rolls Royce, a 1953 antique MG sports car, a 1998 Acura and has two luxury boats.

While our schools crumble and crime and drugs plague our streets, James gave himself a raise to over $200,000 a year. **$200,000 of your money.**

The "Real Deal" is a sweet deal for Sharpe James. 16 Years of Sharpe James is Enough.

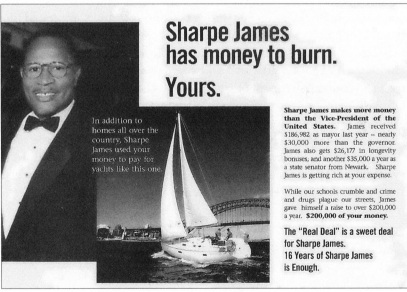

Sharpe James has money to burn. Yours.

In addition to homes all over the country, Sharpe James used your money to pay for yachts like this one.

Sharpe James makes more money than the Vice-President of the United States. James received $186,982 as mayor last year -- nearly $30,000 more than the governor. James also gets $26,177 in longevity bonuses, and another $35,000 a year as a state senator from Newark. Sharpe James is getting rich at your expense.

While our schools crumble and crime and drugs plague our streets, James gave himself a raise to over $200,000 a year. **$200,000 of your money.**

The "Real Deal" is a sweet deal for Sharpe James. 16 Years of Sharpe James is Enough.

Fig. 3.3. The Booker campaign charged that Sharpe James was living off the largesse of voters. In the two ads shown here, the campaign notes that James, a public servant, has enough money to own a boat and a Rolls Royce.

season. In fact, I first heard about the magazine after receiving a flyer that included photocopied excerpts from it. Moreover, its inclusion in the database further ensured adequate minority press representation. The data set contains articles from twenty-one news sources as varied as *Jet* magazine and the *Financial Times*. But the vast majority (71%) of the articles come the [Newark] *Star-Ledger* (120 articles). The *New York Times* came in second with twenty-three articles (nearly 14% of the database), plus four articles from the *Times of Trenton* and three from the *Black Commentator*. Of the articles I studied, only eight (or 4.7% of the total), came from black periodicals like the *Amsterdam News*. Twelve articles came from minority news sources, which include African American publications and other periodicals targeted to religious minorities or with an explicit mission to target communities of color generally or to promote interracial dialogue. No doubt, some articles related to this election were not included in one of these databases, but I nonetheless compiled an exhaustive collection.

An outside coder performed the content analysis of the articles,[37] which offered certain advantages to the research. In addition to providing a consistent coding measure, she was unfamiliar with Newark and its politics before undertaking this coding project. Consequently, she viewed the articles with a fresh and objective eye and was not unduly influenced by preconceived evaluations of the candidates. To ensure reliability, I coded a random subset of the articles[38] and compared my codes with those of the outside coder. We agreed on 77%[39] of the coding decisions, which is a good agreement[40] rate for subjective[41] coding decisions.

We first classified the articles according to their genre: feature/human interest story, general news article, news analysis, or editorial (see table 3.1).[42] More than half were general news articles, and about one-fifth were news analyses. Approximately one-tenth of the articles were editorials, and one in seven were feature or human interest articles.

Table 3.1
Breakdown of Newark Mayoral Coverage by Genre

Genre	Number of articles (%)
General News	93 (55.0%)
Editorial	18 (10.7%)
Analysis	35 (20.7%)
Feature/Human Interest	23 (13.6%)
N	169

Source: Author's compilation.

Table 3.2

Classification of Articles by Tone

Theme	All articles (%)	Number of mainstream media articles (%)[a]	Number of mainstream national media articles (%)[b]	Number of New Jersey articles (%)[c]	Number of black press articles (%)
Pro-James	4 (2.4%)	4 (2.5%)	2 (6.1%)	2 (1.6%)	0 (0.0%)
Anti-James	25 (14.8%)	24 (15.3%)	9 (27.3%)	15 (11.7%)	1 (12.5%)
Pro-Booker	15 (8.9%)	12 (7.6%)	6 (18.2%)	7 (5.5%)	0 (0.0%)
Anti-Booker	4 (2.4%)	1 (0.6%)	0 (0.0%)	4 (3.1%)	3 (37.5%)
Neutral	121 (71.6%)	116 (73.9%)	16 (48.5%)	100 (78.1%)	4 (50.0%)
N	169	157	33	128	8

Source: Author's compilation.

[a] Mainstream media articles are all those that did not appear in minority (i.e., black, Jewish, or multicultural) or religious press sources.

[b] Mainstream national media sources exclude mainstream articles that appeared in the New Jersey press.

[c] New Jersey press articles include articles that appeared in minority media sources based in New Jersey.

We then coded the articles for content, for their positive and negative portrayals[43] of each candidate, as well as for discussions of key election themes that could help construct media frames. In particular, I was looking for discussions of the generational divide, race, the insider/outsider contrast (i.e., that James was from Newark and/or Booker was not and was supported by outsiders), the cost of this election, and education (i.e., Booker's pedigree). Table 3.2 presents the results. Here, we found that most articles (72%) were neutral and did not lean one way or the other for either candidate. There was a clear bias, however, in the remaining articles. Approximately one-quarter either presented Booker in a positive light (9%) or cast James in a negative light (15%).

It was important to know whether tone varied by local or national coverage. With this in mind, table 3.2 also breaks down the coding for both New Jersey and mainstream national coverage and includes statistics for all mainstream coverage, both inside and outside New Jersey. Mainstream coverage is defined as any coverage appearing in the nonethnic or non-ethno-religious press. The New Jersey coverage (which was mostly from the *Star-Ledger* but also from the *Black Commentator*,[44] and others) was the most neutral (78%). The remaining national mainstream articles were far less neutral. Almost one-quarter (27%) of the national mainstream coverage cast James in a negative light, as did about 12% of the New Jersey coverage. Eighteen percent of the mainstream national mainstream media coverage was favorable to Booker, as was 6% of the New Jersey coverage.

This amount of favorable press coverage seems small in comparison to the number of neutral articles included in the data set. The descriptive statistics indicate that James received very little positive coverage and Booker received little negative coverage. Only two national mainstream media articles (6%) and two New Jersey articles (2%) were favorable to James. No articles in the mainstream national press were negative overall toward Cory Booker. Three percent of the New Jersey coverage, or four articles, were coded as unfavorable to Booker. Three of those articles appeared in one publication, the *Black Commentator*, which was heavily biased against Booker.

The key frames that emerged in the coverage of the 2002 Newark mayoral race centered on the issues of race and racial authenticity; the candidates' (particularly Booker's) educational background; the generation gap that this race exposed; the insider/outsider dichotomy (i.e., the allegations that James was a real Newarker and Booker was a carpetbagger); the level of fund-raising and campaign spending; and the type of politicking (i.e., campaign strategy, who was pulling down whose signs, and so forth). The coder coded the articles for both these frames and substantive policy discussions, just as she coded articles for their tone. The classification is presented in table 3.3.

With the exception of the coverage of politicking, each of the frames just listed was mentioned in approximately 20% to 40% of the articles. A little more than one-quarter of the articles mentioned the generation gap, and approximately 30% mentioned race or Booker's educational credentials. Nearly a third of the articles discussed the insider/outsider dichotomy, and around 40% addressed campaign finance or policy issues.

It is clear, though, that the media devoted much more attention to the campaign hoopla than to any other aspect of this election. Overall, nearly 80% of the articles in the database addressed an aspect of politicking: what strategies the campaigns were adopting, who was taking whom to court over campaign signs, and the like. The national mainstream media coverage of the 2002 race was most preoccupied with various aspects of campaigning. Almost 94% of the national mainstream media coverage mentioned politicking, compared with only 80% of the New Jersey coverage. In contrast, only 38% of the black press's articles mentioned politicking, although my sample admittedly was small.

Race and class figured less prominently in New Jersey coverage of the mayoral race, but they did play a significant role in the national mainstream and black media coverage of this election. For instance, while only 23% of the New Jersey coverage of the Newark mayoral election discussed

Table 3.3

Classification of Articles by Theme

Theme	Total number of articles (%)	Number of mainstream media articles (%)[a]	Number of mainstream national media articles (%)[b]	Number of New Jersey articles (%)[c]	Number of black press articles (%)
Race	49 (29.0%)	42 (26.8%)	16 (48.5%)	30 (23.4%)	4 (50.0%)
Education/pedigree	52 (30.8%)	45 (28.7%)	20 (60.6%)	28 (21.9%)	4 (50.0%)
Generation	45 (26.6%)	40 (25.5%)	15 (45.5%)	27 (21.1%)	3 (37.5%)
Insider/outsider	55 (32.5%)	50 (31.8%)	17 (51.5%)	35 (27.3%)	3 (37.5%)
Campaign finance	65 (38.5%)	61 (38.9%)	17 (51.5%)	46 (35.9%)	2 (25.0%)
Politicking	134 (79.3%)	130 (82.8%)	31 (93.9%)	102 (79.7%)	3 (37.5%)
Policy	69 (40.8%)	63 (40.1%)	22 (66.7%)	44 (34.4%)	5 (62.5%)
N	169	157	33	128	8

Source: Author's compilation.

[a] Mainstream media articles are all those that did not appear in minority (i.e., black, Jewish, or multicultural) or religious press sources.

[b] Mainstream national media sources exclude mainstream articles that appeared in the New Jersey press.

[c] New Jersey press articles include articles that appeared in minority media sources based in New Jersey.

race and intraracial differences, 49% of the national mainstream media articles and 50% of black press articles discussed race. Many of these articles addressed James's raising the concern that Booker was not an authentically black candidate or that the two candidates represented two different forms of black politics. Whereas 22% of the articles in New Jersey periodicals talked about the candidates' educational background, 61% of the national press articles and 50% of the black press articles considered the candidates' pedigree (e.g., that Booker was a Rhodes Scholar and/or was Ivy League educated).

This descriptive breakdown was not surprising. Given the volume of news coverage devoted to the mayoral race in New Jersey, finding that local newspaper coverage focused more on the minutiae of the race is to be expected. Also, given what we know about media framing,[45] it is not surprising that the national mainstream media coverage would be so favorable to Booker and that race and class would be examined to the extent that they were. The national press would have a large incentive to create a narrative and to place it in a larger context. Framing a story about a contest between a young Ivy Leaguer and an old stalwart of the civil rights era over whose version of black politics would prevail created a compelling narrative that reporters could use to justify covering another locale's metro news. This story became even more compelling when one of the candidates was portrayed as the good guy and the other candidate played the villain.

While most of the coverage was neutral, the coverage that did favor or oppose one candidate was definitely skewed in favor of Booker and against James. There were more negative articles about James than there were positive articles about him (a ratio of more than 6 to 1). In contrast, there were almost quadruple the number of positive articles about Booker as there were negative articles about him.

Given that the national media coverage appeared to be biased in favor of Booker, it is helpful to determine which issues were correlated with positive or negative press coverage. Since the descriptive analysis shows that the national mainstream coverage took a particular interest in examining issues of race and class (i.e., educational achievement) and that Booker might have been more appealing to the mainstream media because of his background, it is very likely that the discussions of these issues biased the tone of the articles in which they appeared. Those issues changed the tone differently depending on the source of that article. Given the evidence, it seems that discussions of race and class in national press articles were correlated with a tonal bias in Booker's favor.

To test this theory, I developed the following model:

$$\text{Tone of coverage} = \alpha + \beta(\text{race}) + \beta(\text{education}) + \beta(\text{in/outsider}) + \beta(\text{campaign finance}) + \beta(\text{generation}) + \beta(\text{policy}) + \beta(\text{politicking}) + \beta(\text{New Jersey periodical}) + \beta(\text{feature}) + \beta(\text{editorial}) + \beta(\text{analysis}) + \mu.$$

In this model, I coded the tone of coverage from –1 to 1, coding articles that were pro-James or anti-Booker as –1, articles that were pro-Booker or anti-James as 1, and neutral articles as 0. All other variables were coded as dummy variables.

Table 3.4 presents the regression coefficients for the full model, which includes all the articles in the dataset. In model 1, the general model, only one of the election's themes is significantly correlated with the tone of article coverage at the .05 level of significance. When the articles looked at the candidates' policy proposals, they were less favorable to Booker or veered toward neutrality. As expected, the New Jersey press articles produced a significantly higher number of neutral-to-negative articles about Booker than the mainstream national press did, but the editorials were significantly more favorable to him.

The regression results from the general model suggest that the themes of style or pedigree or identity politics had little relationship to the tone of the article. Policy articles were less biased toward Booker, and

Table 3.4

OLS Model of the Relationship between Media Content and Tone of Media Coverage

Variable	Model 1		Model 2	
Constant	.406	$(.117)^{**}$	.258	(.173)
Race	−.024	(.100)	−.334	(.229)
Age/generation	−.115	(.114)	−.274	(.178)
Education*insider-outsider			.399	$(.208)^*$
Insider-outsider	.187	(.120)		
Education	−.166	(.138)		
Campaign finance	.097	(.085)	.613	$(.200)^{**}$
Policy	−.197	$(.082)^{**}$	−.412	$(.163)^{**}$
Politicking	.082	(.092)	.228	(.187)
New Jersey press	−.312	$(.093)^{**}$	−.033	(.195)
Editorial	.456	$(.131)^{**}$	.359	$(.131)^{**}$
Analysis	−.127	(.104)	−.091	(.099)
Feature	.023	(.135)	−.088	(.132)
NJ press*race			.232	(.251)
NJ press*age			.251	(.226)
NJ press*insider-outsider*education			−.328	(.255)
NJ press*campaign finance			−.643	$(.217)^{**}$
New Jersey press*policy			.209	(.185)
New Jersey press*politicking			−.241	(.211)
R^2	.213		.287	
MSE	.812		.752	
N	169		169	

$^{**}p < .05;$ $^* p < .1$, both two-tailed tests
Note: Standard errors are in parentheses.

editorials were more likely to praise him. In addition, New Jersey media sources tended to be less favorably disposed to Booker than the national press was.

It was necessary to dig further to determine whether the themes of this election had any relationship at all to the tone of the coverage. To that end, I created a series of interaction terms to see whether the discussion of the campaign themes in the New Jersey media was correlated with positive or negative media coverage of Booker.

Model 2 focuses on articles appearing in the New Jersey press. To avoid extreme multicollinearity,[46] I created an interaction term using the education and insider/outsider variables. All but twelve of the articles with those frames used both. I then interacted that term with the New Jersey press variable. When I added the interaction terms to the model, articles that mentioned both Booker's educational background and his outsider status now were predicted to be positively disposed to Booker at the $p < .1$ level of significance. In addition, articles discussing campaign finance were

Table 3.5

OLS Model of the Relationship between Media Content and Tone of Media Coverage
(mainstream media only)

Variable	Model 3		Model 4	
Constant	.357	$(.137)^{**}$	.225	(.170)
Race	−.048	(.099)	−.254	(.220)
Age/generation	−.081	(.114)	−.243	(.195)
Education*insider-outsider			.428	$(.205)^{**}$
Insider-outsider	.124	(.121)		
Education	−.046	(.143)		
Campaign finance	.077	(.082)	.452	$(.136)^{**}$
Policy	−.163	$(.083)^{**}$	−.397	$(.185)^{**}$
Politicking	.100	(.099)	.232	$(.103)^{**}$
New Jersey press	−.286	$(.097)^{**}$	−.249	$(.145)^{*}$
Editorial	.468	$(.128)^{**}$	.364	$(.128)^{**}$
Analysis	−.079	(.103)	−.047	(.096)
Feature	−.067	(.139)	−.111	(.132)
NJ Press*race			.189	(.243)
NJ Press*age			.215	(.237)
NJ Press*insider-outsider*education			−.348	(.249)
New Jersey press*policy			.314	(.206)
New Jersey press*campaign finance*politicking			−.542	$(.163)^{**}$
R^2	.205		.282	
MSE	.649		.657	
N	157		157	

$^{**}p < .05$; $^{*}p < .1$, both two-tailed tests
Note: Standard errors are in parentheses.

significantly more likely to be favorable to Booker. Editorials remained
pro-Booker.

The interesting finding in this model is that the New Jersey press articles discussing campaign finance were significantly less likely to biased in
Booker's favor. The first two statistical models suggest that the local (New
Jersey) press and articles that considered policy tended to be more even-
toned (or even critical of Booker) than those that focused only on race,
pedigree, or age. Moreover, the fact that New Jersey articles focused on
money were less favorable to Booker indicates that they were less inclined
to give Booker credit for his prodigious fund-raising skills.

At this point, it is helpful to look at the mainstream media coverage in
isolation, to ensure that the tone of minority media sources (particularly
the biased *Black Commentator*) did not influence our findings, which appear in table 3.5. The first model in that table, model 3, essentially replicates
model 1, but this time excludes minority press sources. Here, the coefficients indicate that articles appearing in New Jersey media sources were

associated with more neutral-to-negative coverage of Booker and that the editorials were associated with more positive coverage of Booker.

Model 4 replicates model 2 with just the mainstream media articles. To avoid extreme multicollinearity, I combined the New Jersey discussion of campaign finance and politicking into a single interaction term. The removal of the ethnic press articles actually revealed some interesting correlations. Those articles about Booker's pedigree and his outsider status were now significantly and positively associated with pro-Booker coverage at the .05 level of significance. Articles mentioning campaign finance were still significantly associated with positive coverage of Booker. Articles discussing policy were less likely to be pro-Booker, a relationship that got stronger. Editorials were still positively associated with pro-Booker coverage, although less so than in model 3. New Jersey press articles talking about both campaign finance and politicking were significantly less likely to be biased toward Booker.

The preceding analysis helps explain why the mainstream media supported Cory Booker in their coverage of the 2002 mayoral election in Newark. In the New Jersey press, Booker's press support suffered when reporters considered the cost of the election and all the politicking surrounding the race. All the press articles that discussed policy tended to be more neutral to critical. However, mainstream coverage that mentioned both Booker's pedigree and his outsider status were more favorable to him, and editorial coverage was clearly supportive of Booker.

The mainstream media's sympathy for Booker unwittingly allowed Sharpe James to make political hay out of a perceived disadvantage and activate suspicion among black voters about Booker's motives. James used his relatively weak position in the mainstream press to elicit sympathy among Newark voters and to define Booker as an external media construction. James's position was further enhanced by a series of tactical mistakes that Booker supporters made during the campaign. These errors served to reinforce black mistrust of mainstream media and to reinforce Booker's image as being culturally separate from ordinary Newarkers.

Playing the Race Frame: Campaign Literature Analysis

Sharpe James and his supporters played the race card both explicitly and implicitly in the direct-mail flyers they distributed during the mayoral campaign.[47] By calling himself "The Real Deal,"[48] James implied his own street credibility. He also was able to parlay that credibility into a discussion of his qualifications as a genuine Newarker. His campaign literature

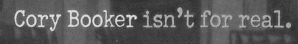

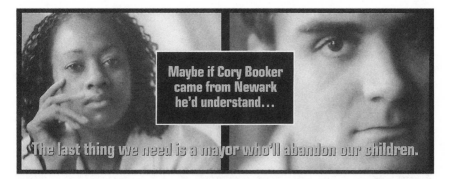

Maybe if Cory Booker
came from Newark
he'd understand...

The last thing we need is a mayor who'll abandon our children.

Facing page: Fig. 3.5. Sharpe James's campaign reinforces the idea that Booker was a media construction who shirked his responsibilities as councilman and was not as ethical as he claimed.

Above: Fig. 3.6. Sharpe James uses Booker's support of vouchers to highlight his inauthenticity to lead Newark. In this ad, James emphasizes that Booker is from out of town, and he questions Booker's empathy by drawing class distinctions. He says Booker was educated in private schools, but in fact, he attended public school from kindergarten through the twelfth grade.

highlights his long residency in Newark. In contrast, his negative campaign literature highlights Booker's recent arrival and thus his inability to understand the city. Furthermore, it characterizes Booker as being a jet setter more concerned about his future political career than about tending to Newark business.[49]

In the ads in figure 3.5, Sharpe James's campaign reinforces the idea that Booker was a media construction who shirked his responsibilities as councilman and was not as ethical as he claimed. James also made substantive policy attacks that had implicit racial and class ramifications. In a piece criticizing Booker's support of school vouchers, James calls him a Republican, highlights the fact that he's a privileged child of the suburbs, and labels him a hypocrite. He then concludes by saying that "Booker can't be for real."[50] Clearly, the James campaign was using a substantive issue to imply that Booker's policies were incongruent with the interests of urban blacks, thus creating a chasm between Booker and the rest of Newark.

What James did implicitly, some of his tacit supporters did very explicitly. In a letter to Urban League official Lee Daniels, Professor Emeritus Martin Kilson of Harvard University referred to Booker "an errand boy Black politician for conservative Republican power-class penetration of governing control of Black Newark."[51] For Kilson, anyone that conservative columnist

Fig. 3.4. Sharpe James touted himself as "the real deal" on the opposite side of this ad
(not shown) and disingenuously suggested that he had Bill Clinton's endorsement
in 2002.

George Will liked could not have the best interests of the black community at heart.[52] This letter was published on BlackCommentator.com and
mailed anonymously to some residents in Newark.

Booker and his supporters did try to address the race issue. For instance, allies in the organization CitiPac (which was headed by the Booker
campaign's chief strategist, Carl Sharif) produced a leaflet that compared
voter intimidation on the part of James's political machine to racism in Birmingham in the 1960s. Thus, Sharpe James became analogous to Bull Connor. The intent was clear: James was promoting regress and not progress
for black Newark.[53]

This illustration may not have been the most effective metaphor for
Newarkers. By selecting an analogy from the nonviolent struggle phase of
the southern civil rights movement, CitiPac invoked imagery that may not
have resonated with northern or younger voters. Resurrecting the image
of Bull Connor also failed to address Newark's history as a hotbed of black
cultural nationalism. Komozi Woodard noted that by the 1960s, black and
white Newark were in a violent struggle for control of the city and that the
fight for black political power became a "life or death struggle against white
racism and internal colonialism."[54] It is under these circumstances, then,
that black self-determination understandably became of the utmost.[55]

Leaders that Woodard discusses in his book from the 1960s and 1970s still figured prominently in Newark politics in 2002. Besides Amiri Baraka, Father (later Monsignor) William Linder one of Newark's largest social service agencies. Donald Tucker, who had to be convinced to not campaign for city council in a dashiki in 1970, sat on Newark's municipal council from 1974 until his death in 2005.[56] Thus, to go back to the marches and ignore the cultural nationalism that followed is to ignore a key facet of Newark's political culture.

Furthermore, Booker's literature did not adequately respond to James's charge that he was a closet Republican. Unfortunately, some zealous supporters may have helped corroborate this pejorative image of Booker. An organization called Citizens for a Better Essex County, which was independent of the Booker campaign, mailed literature to some Newark residents in support of Booker's candidacy. One piece highlighted Booker's fiscal conservatism. Another piece positively compared Booker's efforts as a city councilman to make government more efficient with Rudolph Giuliani's efforts to do the same as mayor of New York City.[57]

Given the tenor of the attacks against Booker and Newark's cultural nationalist past, these surrogate mail pieces were more of a hindrance than a help to Booker's campaign. Of course, not every black person in Newark is a cultural nationalist, nor do all Newarkers really understand the importance of the black and Puerto Rican conventions of the 1960s and 1970s. Unfortunately, when James and his supporters claimed that Booker was a tool of conservatives and Booker's supporters then called him a conservative and suggested he would implement policies associated with Republicans, perhaps blacks believed James's charges, thus hurting Booker's chances to win in 2002.

Focus-Group Data

Other reasons might explain Booker's loss. Voters could have perceived Booker as too young and inexperienced, or they could have been suspicious of his campaign contributors and thus of him. Maybe they just liked Sharpe James and were satisfied with his leadership. To test additional suppositions about why Booker lost his election, I conducted a focus group for two and a half hours in March 2003 in the West Ward of Newark.

I spoke with ten African American residents who were active members of a West Ward community organization. Their ages ranged from thirty to seventy-one, with a median age of fifty-two. While two of the respondents were recent arrivals to the city (having moved to Newark within five years of our conversation), most were long-term or lifelong residents of the city; the median length of residency was 43.5 years. Six women and four men participated in the group. Three were active in local politics as workers and candidates.[58] One respondent was a consultant who had interacted with both James and Booker. This person demonstrated a sought-after technical expertise and thus should not be considered a political consultant. Two of the respondents were married to each other. In an anonymous, introductory questionnaire, I asked the respondents to reveal their vote choices in 2002. Four had voted for Booker, and three had voted for James. One respondent confessed to not having voted in the mayoral election. Another indicated having voted in the council race, which I assume means that this person abstained from voting in the mayoral race. One respondent refused to reveal a vote choice.

The group was recruited largely by snowball sampling. I contacted one of the respondents, who then recruited the other respondents, so this was clearly a convenience sample, but given their civic involvement and length of residence in the city, this was an extremely well-informed convenience sample. The respondents gave their informed consent to participate in this group, were aware of my connection to Booker, and were given dinner for their time.

In particular, I was interested in understanding how the respondents perceived the candidates and their relative strengths and weaknesses. They reported that the 2002 race was the most contentious they remembered. They argued that James won because he retained the common touch that Booker never seemed to grasp. The respondents appreciated that James seemed to relate easily to them. In contrast, Booker always seemed to be campaigning, and this irritated voters. One woman said:

When the two [Booker and James] showed up, I know Cory was there, I mean, he used the ball, he came in, he was campaigning down on his knees, you know, old people at the table, you know what I mean, umm, you know, trying to solicit votes. You know, the mayor, however, came and just dances with all the women all night [laughter]. He never said anything about the campaign or you know, or getting out and vote, coming out to vote, or anything like that. He stayed and he did socially with the residents, you know, who were out. And I think that really worked for him.

A male respondent echoed the same sentiment:

Cory did that even after the election. I went to the speech . . . in the North
Ward and he was running from table to table to table. Even then he was
. . . [laughter]. The mayor, like, he was a people person. He came over to
you, he chatted with me and that was it.

This concern with Booker's sincerity also led the respondents to be
suspicious of him, given the fact that he was a relative newcomer who financed his campaign with outside money. One man remarked, "I don't
believe in those outside people. They don't truly know what you need because they've never been here to experience the day-to-day to see what this
community that they want to represent really needs." A female respondent
put it this way:

I think, uh, people who have worked within the community and built that
trust are the ones who are going to be supported. People from the outside
are going to be looked at just like that. You're outside. You're outside the
loop. How are you going to know what's best for us? So we don't, I mean,
being able to determine our own destiny is an important thing that we've
been fighting [for] years and so now because that person is black or white
or green or whatever, you know, for them to come from outside and try to
tell us what's best for us, I think it's a slap in the face and I don't think the
community and the inhabitants of Newark buy it.

Another female response was "But what you also have to have [is] a track
record. You can't build a track and have nothing to show for it. And one
of the things about Sharpe is a lot of folks knew him before he became
mayor, before he got out on the political trail."

Clearly, the issue of experience tempered the respondents' impression
of Booker's credentials. I asked how important education was to evaluating
the candidates. One man said:

OK. I'm saying, Cory Booker has a very important résumé. That's great.
However, he doesn't have the experience. He has a lot of book knowledge,
but he doesn't have the experience. Sharpe has a lot of experience, and
. . . educated too, but he also works in the community and has a lot of
experience. He knows the community very well and he's from this area.
. . . There's a reason why older people are wiser and younger people are
more energetic. And that's the way it is. The other thing is Sharpe James
can relate to a lot of people, the older folks as well as the younger folks.

He has the ability to do that. Cory did both, however, when we wanted to sit down one-to-one and talk about issues, it was very hard for him to talk about direct issues. I would say experience with education.

I probed the issue of race in the election, asking whether the voters were influenced by the notion that Booker was not authentically black. This charge did resonate with the voters, but in varied and complex ways. One man understood the slogan "The Real Deal" to be explicitly racial: "Yeah, he [Sharpe] meant he was the 'real deal' that he was the real black man." Other respondents tied the slogan and the issue of race more closely to the insider/outsider dichotomy, to substantive policy, and to campaign finance. One male respondent said:

> I thought "The Real Deal" was "look at what I've done." This is the real, this is my track record. To me, that's how I looked at it when I looked at "The Real Deal." Not really at race. They were both black, and to me, black is black. He was saying he was the real deal, born and raised in Newark, doing his thing.

Other comments, also coming from men, reflected the suspicion that Booker had been bought by outside interests. One man observed, "I thought you knew who was backing him. That's why you considered him as an oreo. The power of the white dollar was backing his whole campaign." Another remarked, "You see what I'm saying. I thought that ultimately he would be doing things to benefit others. And not the people of Newark [murmurs of agreement]."

The focus-group data indicate that these voters were very suspicious of Booker. Although they admired his achievements, they thought he was too much of a politician and not genuine. Moreover, they seriously mistrusted the intentions of his campaign donors and believed that if elected, he would have to cater to their interests and not to the needs of residents. But the respondents did indicate that they would be willing to consider Booker as a viable candidate in the future, after he had established roots and built a bigger track record of achievement.

Conclusion

Booker's experience in Newark approximates the experience of other black elected officials who initially were unsuccessful in winning the offices to which they aspired in majority-black jurisdictions. For instance, Barack Obama recalled to William Finnegan of the *New Yorker* that in his failed congressional bid in 2000, people would tell him "he seemed like a nice fellow, with some good ideas. 'But Bobby [Rush] ain't done nothing wrong.' "[59] Similarly, Artur Davis, a racially moderate, Harvard-educated lawyer who challenged Congressman Earl Hilliard for the Democratic nomination in the Seventh Congressional District in Alabama, needed two attempts to beat him. When we look at their experiences together, it is clear that being a smart, racially moderate candidate is insufficient to beat aging civil rights stalwarts. Racially moderate candidates still have to reach out to their base of black voters, even if that base is not the entire black community. And enough of those black voters need to identify with the racially moderate candidate to ensure his or her success.

Richard Fenno perhaps put it best when he explained the importance of personal campaigning, albeit with a caveat: *"Presentation of self enhances trust; enhancing trust takes time; therefore, presentation of self takes time"*[60] (italics in original). The lesson of 2002, then, is clear: racially moderate aspirants to elective office in majority-black jurisdictions must take time to learn about their communities and to cultivate a following in those communities in order to increase their chances of electoral success. Their crossover appeal, fancy credentials, large war chests, and well-reasoned policy proposals alone will not guarantee victory.

4

Winning

The 2006 Election

CLEARLY, 2002 WAS a challenging year politically for Cory Booker. Despite his use of elite displacement to try to unseat Sharpe James, Booker suffered a narrow but nationally publicized defeat in his quest to become Newark's mayor. Booker's loss to the then-sixteen year incumbent Sharpe James was particularly devastating given the racial vitriol of the campaign. James attacked Booker's racial authenticity, labeling him a "faggot white boy" and claiming that he had received campaign donations from Jews, the Ku Klux Klan and the Taliban. James went on to win the election by soundly beating Booker in all three of Newark's predominately black wards, including Booker's own Central Ward.

In January 2006, it appeared that there would be a rematch between Booker and James. Booker announced his candidacy, and many expected that James would attempt to run for an unprecedented sixth term. Some assumed that should a rematch take place, the race, at best, would be close. The Associated Press quoted political scientist David Rebovich, who predicted that "it will be an uphill battle for Booker if James runs."[1]

A Booker-James rematch was not to be, though. On March 27, ten days after filing for his candidacy in a very public spectacle, James pulled out of the race, leaving Booker to face State Senator and Deputy Mayor Ronald Rice Sr. and two minor candidates in the May 9 municipal election. Booker soundly defeated his opponents, winning more than 72% of the vote. By June 13, Booker's running mates or supporters had managed to secure every seat on Newark's municipal council, beating longtime incumbents and even Sharpe James's own son, who was running for an open seat in the South Ward.

Why were Booker's fortunes so different in 2006 than in 2002? Clearly James's decision not to run had a positive impact on the magnitude of Booker's victory. But that outcome was not just good fortune. Booker may have lost in 2002, but his campaign put Newark's old black political guard on notice and set the stage for his subsequent victory. In 2006, Booker and his team were able to build on their 2002 efforts to make certain tactical decisions and take advantage of the deteriorating quality of life in Newark that worked in his favor, especially against an unorganized and underfunded candidate.

That being said, the ghost of Sharpe James did loom over the 2006 campaign. James's personal racial attacks against Booker in 2002, while far less effective in 2006, did not disappear completely. Booker's opponent in 2006 was far less capable of levying such attacks, and Booker's campaign also became more adept at neutralizing them. By 2006, even though the voters had grown comfortable enough with Booker to elect him to office, the data show that Booker's opposition had already begun to take shape in his landslide 2006 victory.

The Interim Period, 2002–2005: Settling In and Building Bridges

After losing in 2002, Booker affirmed his commitment to Newark. He continued to live in Brick Towers, a housing project in the Central Ward. He became partner in a West Orange–based law firm, opening an office in Newark, and founded a nonprofit organization called Newark Now, which provides training and assistance to local community organizations and sponsored high-profile activities such as an annual Easter egg hunt, a Thanksgiving turkey giveaway, and a holiday toy drive.

Political Maneuverings

Booker also vowed to fight again for his seat. The day after losing to James, Booker promised to try again for the mayoralty.[2] This time, though, Booker would run as a little less of a maverick. Between 2002 and 2005, Booker reached out to selected members of Newark's old guard in a series of key tactical decisions that solidified his position as a force to be reckoned with in Newark politics.

Sharpe James's choke hold on the municipal council loosened to some degree during his last term as mayor. In 2003, he proposed turning over the management of Newark's water system to a nonprofit corporation, arguing that the arrangement would be similar to one in Passaic County and would benefit the community. Opponents, including the future West Ward councilman Ronald Rice Jr., contended that the plan was merely another way for James and his cronies to benefit financially at the expense of taxpayers.

James and members of the municipal council would serve on the board of the nonprofit water board (for which they would be paid) and would likely be able to set their terms so that they would guarantee themselves seats on the board after they retired from elective office.

It was during the water optimization debate that Councilman-at-Large Luis Quintana and East Ward Councilman Augusto Amador emerged as critics of Sharpe James. Actually, the water optimization proposal was one of many issues that pitted Quintana and Amador against Sharpe James in the first part of his last term. James had offended Quintana and North Ward Councilman Hector Corchado by making insensitive comments about the role of Latinos in Newark's power structure. Furthermore, just before James proposed the water optimization plan, the city of Newark adjusted property taxes. According to Luis Quintana, taxes in the predominately Latino and Portuguese North and East Wards tripled, while property taxes in the predominately black South Ward sometimes decreased.[3]

In this climate, Booker was able to forge an alliance with Quintana, Amador, and Councilman-at-Large Donald Tucker (Corchado decided to remain independent). With Booker's support, Quintana challenged Sharpe James for the Democratic nomination for the state senate (James also was a state senator) in 2003. Donald Tucker's endorsement of Quintana signaled his public support of Booker. Carl Sharif, Booker's campaign manager, pointed out that Tucker, who died in 2005, was no fan of James and had never publicly rebuked Booker nor opposed anything he had proposed while representing the Central Ward.[4]

Booker's staff also tried to appeal to others aligned with James, with mixed success. In 2004, Carl Sharif approached Oscar James Sr. (no relation to Sharpe James), who had worked for Sharpe James or his administration since 1979—most recently as the field director for his 2002 campaign—to coordinate the Booker team's field activities for the Central, South, and West Wards. I asked Mr. Sharif about that decision; why would Booker hire someone who had worked against him in the last election? Sharif explained that he and Oscar James had always had a good working relationship and that he trusted James to be loyal and work hard to elect Booker. Moreover, Sharif was strategic. He figured that as long as Oscar James was working for Cory Booker, he would not be working for anyone else. Apart from any consideration of his skills as a field operative, this was reason enough to invite James to be part of the team.[5]

When I asked Oscar James why he switched sides between 2002 and 2006, he told me that he had always admired Cory Booker but did not think that he was a viable candidate in 2002. By 2004, however, he believed that Booker could beat Sharpe James in a head-to-head match. Oscar James added that in early 2004 he had had a meeting with Sharpe James about Booker's electoral prospects, in which Sharpe James stated that he truly believed he could still beat Cory Booker. Oscar James indicated to me that Sharpe James's delusional conviction was what compelled him to join the Booker team.[6]

Another event may have also helped influence Oscar James to join the Booker team. Oscar James's son Sidney (Oscar S. James II) ran with Booker as the candidate for South Ward Council. Sidney had graduated from Villanova University in 2004 with a degree in political science. While at Villanova, an African American politics professor had challenged him to think critically about the failed political agendas of the civil rights generation of leadership. In separate accounts, both Oscar and Sidney James recalled a conversation in which Sidney announced that he could never support Sharpe James again, presumably because he represented failed leadership. After graduating from college and returning to Newark, Sidney started driving for Booker[7] and eventually became the South Ward councilman.[8]

Booker's campaign also tried to recruit West Ward Councilwoman Mamie Bridgeforth. Carl Sharif had helped Bridgeforth, a social work professor at Essex County College, get elected to her seat in 1998. But once on the municipal council, she supported most of Sharpe James's agenda. Many in the Booker camp assumed that Bridgeforth had just succumbed to the pressure of James's power and had been overwhelmed by the number of James's supporters on the municipal council. Consequently, they believed that if progressive, reformist politicians made up a majority of the council, she would support them.[9]

Booker's pursuit of Mamie Bridgeforth was significant because her presence on the Booker team would have strategic consequences for Ronald Rice Jr., the son of Booker's eventual opponent in 2006 and a longtime Booker supporter. In 2002, Rice Jr. ran and lost on the Booker team for an at-large council seat. Given the difficulty of running citywide, he considered running for the West Ward seat in 2006. His father had held that seat from 1982 to 1998, so he thought he had a better chance of winning that seat. But Booker wanted Rice Jr. to run for an at-large seat again so that Bridgeforth could run as an incumbent on the Booker team. There was some friendly tension between Rice Jr. and Booker over this matter. Rice Jr. was determined to run for the ward seat and made it clear that he would run as an independent if Booker chose Bridgeforth as his teammate. Meanwhile, Bridgeforth was debating whether to join the Booker team. Understanding that Rice Jr.'s threats were serious, the Booker campaign gave Bridgeforth a deadline to decide whether to join the ticket. When she did not meet the deadline, they invited Rice Jr. to the ticket as the West Ward candidate.[10]

Booker's political dealings between the 2002 and 2006 elections show a level of political sophistication and realism that observers had not seen previously. Sharif, Booker's longtime political mentor, noted that Booker had become more realistic in the intervening four years and now understood that he could not dismiss everyone in the established power structure in order to achieve political change. Indeed, Booker's political rapprochement with some members of the municipal council reflected this realism.

Booker's political maturity may have come at a price, however. Embracing some members of the old guard as teammates shut out longtime Booker supporters and 2002 teammates. For example, Ronald Rice Jr. was almost pushed off the ticket in favor of Mamie Bridgeforth. In addition, Sharif acknowledged that deciding to make peace with some of the old guard did alienate Booker from some of his young, politically progressive black peers in the city. He also admitted that Booker's new alliances may have contributed to Karriem Arnold's independent run for South Ward councilman and to former Booker team member Marjory Avant's largely dropping out of politics.[11]

The 2006 Election

Booker officially announced his candidacy in January 2006. For this election, he ran on a crime, kids, economic development, and efficient government services platform. Carl Sharif stated that their focus-group data indicated that crime was the residents' foremost concern.[12] This information, coupled with a rash of teenaged homicide victims in the previous year, strongly influenced the Booker campaign to run on an anticrime platform. They then linked crime to children and family issues by arguing that addressing crime would make it safer for kids to walk home from school. Booker also proposed increasing recreation funds for the city as a deterrent to gang recruitment.

Booker took a populist stance on economic development, one that would appeal to local residents and perhaps cast the James administration as being so corrupt as to be economically damaging to the city. Booker often brought up the explosion in new housing construction in the city. But he also pointed out that the developers who received these contracts (1) did not live in the city of Newark, (2) were friends and supporters of Sharpe James, and (3) received heavy discounts for the lots they purchased. A common refrain throughout the campaign was that these developers bought the property for $4 a square foot when the market value was substantially higher. Moreover, Booker noted that often the construction workers were not from Newark, which was unacceptable, given the discounts the developers received and Newark's high unemployment rate.

Booker's embrace of populism on the housing issue as it related to economic development served a couple of purposes, intentionally and unintentionally. The housing kickbacks clearly demonstrated that corruption in the James administration was hurting Newark financially. Furthermore, by embracing a Newark-first policy in hiring, Booker was able to demonstrate his commitment to the city, potentially neutralizing the accusation that he was a carpetbagger who would invite New Yorkers to take over the city.

My conversations with voters indicate that some of them may have had a different view. They clearly were concerned about the rate of housing growth, particularly that the new housing was overpriced and substandard. In 2006, the new three-family houses reportedly ranged in price from $400,000 to $750,000, and rents could run from $1,000 to $1,500, depending on the size of the apartment. At a March 15 municipal council meeting, residents complained about the new, substandard, housing, especially the exposed live wires and thin walls. There was a genuine concern in the community that the new houses were destined to fall apart in a couple of years.

Many black residents also worried that they were being shut out of the new housing on account of race. Black voters, particularly in the Central and South Wards, complained that Latinos were shutting them out of the new housing. On one afternoon in the South Ward, residents were complaining that Hasidic Jews from New York were flipping properties and driving up the values of houses in their neighborhood so that blacks could not purchase homes in these communities. So while Booker may have embraced housing as an issue to burnish his credentials as being concerned about Newarkers first and foremost, some residents may have cast their concerns in more bigoted or ethnocentric terms.

Government services also became a primary component of the Booker platform. In 2002, Booker tried to run on the same plank, noting that none of his then council colleagues could read spreadsheets (so he put Carlos

Gonzalez, a CPA, on his team as an at-large candidate), thus making it difficult for them to do their main job of passing the city's budget (which never was passed on time). Booker also observed that in 2002, residents should be able to pay their bills and fines online, in an effort to streamline government services and make them easy to use.

Booker shifted the focus of his government proposals in 2006 from process to customer service. Marilyn Gaynor, the West Ward's field director, constantly referred to city hall under the James administration as "silly hall" because of the poor quality of customer service. The platform was probably best articulated by Terrance Bankston, the South Ward's field director. At a mid-March rally in the South Ward, Bankston urged supporters to vote for Booker if they wanted to call city hall and actually have someone answer the phone, or, if someone did answer the phone, to ensure that he or she would not be rude.

Staffing Decisions

In addition to modifying the platform to make it more personally relevant to everyday voters, the Booker campaign made staffing decisions that were more sensitive to the residents' racial concerns. The demographic makeup of Booker's staff was noticeably different in 2006. Many of Booker's young, white, just-out-of-college and not-from-Newark staff were absent in 2006, although he still had whites, non-Newarkers, and young people on his staff. Instead, blacks and/or Newarkers had key positions. In particular, his press secretary was Sakina Cole, an African American woman, whereas Booker's 2002 press secretary was white. The campaign took care to send white and out-of-town volunteers to work in the North and East Ward, where they would be less conspicuous.[13] Both Carl Sharif and Oscar James Sr. contended that this racial matching was necessary in order to avoid the negative perceptions of the Booker campaign that pervaded the 2002 race.[14]

More Subtle Racial Cues

The campaign team even discussed how to make Booker more "hip." Voters and some of the people I spoke with acknowledged that Sharpe James's style fit Newark residents better than did Booker's style. Voters and elites remembered James dancing at parties and relating to people on a personal level. According to the focus-group findings cited in chapter 3, voters negatively perceived Booker as always campaigning. Even Carl Sharif admitted that Booker's love of incessant policy discussion could be off-putting at times but that after becoming better acquainted with him, residents had started to warm up to him.[15]

The Booker campaign avoided obvious attempts to make Booker more urban, more hip. Sharif noted that someone had proposed hiring an image consultant, but everyone agreed that this would be too extreme a move. Nonetheless, there were some subtle changes in 2006. I, for one, noticed that Booker's wardrobe changed. Instead of wearing the same black suit, blue shirt, and red tie, he now had a more extensive and colorful wardrobe. On the day before the election, I asked a friend of Sharif's if the wardrobe change was deliberate. He started laughing and said that Elnardo Webster, the campaign treasurer, had pulled Booker aside and told him that he dressed like "a goddamned white Republican." Webster apparently had helped Booker put more variety into his wardrobe. Although Webster denied that he had been that emphatic in his critique of Booker's wardrobe, he did intimate that Booker's rumpled 2002 look did not convey the confidence that black constituents wanted to see in their leaders. He also took credit for introducing him to a tailor who made clothes that fit Booker better. For his part, Booker also denied that anyone ever told him he looked like a Republican. Rather, he credited another staffer, Bari Mattes, with "introducing [him] to Barneys [New York]."[16]

Booker's famous black friends also moved into the spotlight during this campaign in ways they had not done before. In 2002, white celebrities such as Barbara Streisand and Bobbi Brown were highlighted as strong Booker supporters. In 2006, Oprah Winfrey was the booster of choice. Moreover, Winfrey's friend Gayle King appeared in Newark on Booker's behalf, fueling speculation that she and Booker were dating. Such rumors helped deflect criticism that Booker did not identify with black people.[17]

Why Sharpe James Dropped Out

In addition to all these changes in campaign strategy between 2002 and 2006, the Booker team was determined to run an offensive campaign. To do that, they seized on a proposal by Sharpe James about how to spend part of a $460 million settlement from a dispute over rents from the Port Authority for Newark Liberty International Airport. James proposed privatizing $80 million of the settlement for redevelopment. Fifty million dollars would go into a fund for core/downtown development, and each ward would receive $6 million for neighborhood redevelopment. The structure of the private corporation overseeing the funds would be similar to that proposed for the failed water optimization board. James and the members of the municipal council all would have seats on the board, and their terms would outlast their terms in elective office.

The Booker campaign quickly attacked the core downtown redevelopment proposal[18] as another scheme by Sharpe James to make money off taxpayers. The campaign issued a mailer entitled "Scheme Machine," which was tailored for the Central, South, and West Wards. The mailer attacked James and the appropriate ward member of the municipal council for trying to fund their retirement, and it included photos of the at-large members of the municipal council accused of being a part of this scheme. The mailer also showed members of the Booker team expressing their indignation and calling for a change in leadership.[19] This strategy contributed to a sense of outrage in the local community, and at the March 15 municipal council meeting, residents spoke out against the redevelopment fund.

The mailer drew criticism from council members and their supporters. From the dais, Councilwoman Mamie Bridgeforth threatened to seek $25 million in libel damages from the Booker team for this mailer, and she also mentioned that she had been given photos of Booker and Ronald Rice Jr. in compromising positions. Other council members said that they would join the suit as well. Poet Amiri Baraka, father of Councilman at-Large Ras Baraka, protested that the mailer attacked only black officials. "They're trying to divide us [blacks and Hispanics]," Amiri Baraka contended. He went on to assert that Newark did not need any "buppies, yuppies, puppies, or closet Republicans" in power, implying his disdain for Booker and his teammates. (Because the Booker team was not fielding a candidate in the North Ward, the mailer did not criticize Hector Corchado, who also had voted for the plan.)

The Port Authority settlement privatization proposal clearly elicited a viscerally negative response in the community. Sharpe James then suffered another defeat when he lost the endorsement of SEIU Local 617 on or about March 18. Local 617 represented many city workers, and the union had been a longtime supporter of James. By 2006, though, the union leaders believed that James had become greedy and power hungry at the expense of being a good leader, and so they decided to endorse Booker instead. This endorsement, according to Rahman Muhammad, president of Local 617, meant that James would lose a significant number of his

Facing page: Fig. 4.1. The Booker team released a mailer in the Central, South, and West Wards, which alleges that the James administration and allied city council members planned to use Port Authority money to maintain control over part of the city's budget. The Central Ward mailer is shown here.

The Sharpe James and Charlie Bell
SCHEME MACHINE

$50,000,000
CASH LIMIT

NEWARK
TAXPAYER MONEY

They're using $50 Million of your money to fund their retirement account.

On May 9, election day, remember how they voted:

Charlie Bell

VOTED YES

Donald Bradley

VOTED YES

Mamie Bridgeforth

VOTED YES

Bessie Walker

VOTED YES

Ras Baraka

VOTED YES

Newark City Councilmembers Charlie Bell, Donald Bradley, Mamie Bridgeforth, Bessie Walker, and Ras Baraka all chose to play politics with Sharpe James instead of doing the right thing.

Behind closed doors, this scheme to take control of $50 Million was Sharpe James idea - but it was these council members who signed off on the plan to take our money for there own secret agenda.

They will come up with all kinds of excuses to explain why they joined Sharpe James in this scheme. But this money could have been used for police protection. Instead, our money is being used to feed their greed for power. Remember their vote on May 9 - and then vote for leadership that believes in cleaner, safer neighborhoods for all of us.

Election Day workers. This, in Muhammad's estimation, was the proverbial nail in the coffin of Sharpe James's municipal career. Muhammad argued that until Local 617 refused to endorse James, everyone had been afraid to defy him for fear of retribution. But once one group was willing to stand up to James, other groups felt safe in not going along with him as well.[20]

Despite the controversy surrounding the Port Authority settlement money and the loss of a crucial union endorsement, Sharpe James made a very public entry into the mayoral race on March 17. Donning a track-suit and straw hat and riding a bike hitched to a wheelbarrow filled with petitions, James made the deadline to appear on the ballot. Ten days later, however, he quietly withdrew from the race, stating that he wanted to concentrate on being a state senator.

James's exit from the race left State Senator and Deputy Mayor Ronald Rice Sr. as Booker's main competitor. Rice Sr., the first black councilman from Newark's West Ward, had more than twenty years of experience in elective office. He also had run for mayor before, against Sharpe James in 1998. By all accounts, Rice Sr. had expected for years to be James's heir apparent, and as his son told me during the ethnographic portion of my project, James had all but promised to step down as mayor and endorse him in 1998. Consequently, after losing to James that year, Rice Sr. became his campaign chairman in 2002, in the hopes of securing his endorsement to run for mayor in 2006.

Unfortunately, Rice Sr.'s strategy did not work out as planned. He was hesitant to begin his 2006 campaign in earnest until Sharpe James made his final decision about whether to run. James's late departure from the race meant that Rice had only six weeks to organize a campaign. Moreover, James's support of Rice was lukewarm at best. It was assumed that James would endorse Rice and offer him financial and personnel support. But James did not endorse him until the last week of the campaign, having skipped the event at which he was to formally endorse him because he had allegedly heard that there would be no photographers there.[21]

Rice also suffered from an extreme disadvantage in fund-raising. Whereas Booker amassed more than $6 million in campaign contributions for himself and his council teammates, Rice Sr. raised only about $150,000.[22]

Despite these obvious disadvantages, Rice Sr. joined forces with incumbents Ras Baraka, Mamie Bridgeforth, Charlie Bell, Bessie Walker, civil servant Norma Gonzalez, and John Sharpe James, the mayor's son, to run as the "Home Team." As the Home Team, they and their surrogates attempted to paint Booker as an inexperienced outsider who was being funded by outside interests. Rice Sr. attacked Booker for having no record, maintaining that his only claim to fame was that "he attended college on a scholarship."[23] A flyer distributed by Activists Concerned for Newark noted that approximately ten of Booker's contributors, including former Circuit City chairman Richard Sharp, had also contributed to George W. Bush in 2004 (see figure 4.2).[24]

The Home Team's attacks on Booker were to no avail. Despite their efforts, they could not make up for the disparity in resources. On May 9, Booker won in a landslide, securing more than 72% of the vote (see figures 4.2, 4.3, and 4.4).

Fig. 4.2. In an attempt to besmirch Booker as a Republican, his opponents noted that some of his donors had also donated to George W. Bush.

Fig. 4.3. Booker formed an alliance with the Payne family in 2006, adding Donald Payne Jr. to his ticket as an at-large candidate during the 2006 runoff elections. Booker is pictured here with the candidate's father, Congressman Donald Payne Sr.

On the surface, it seemed that Booker had effectively neutralized the attacks on him as being a carpetbagger who did not understand the plight of poor people of color, particularly blacks. I asked Carl Sharif whether the 2006 campaign had settled those issues in the voters' minds. Sharif doubted that these issues were entirely dead, but he firmly believed that

Fig. 4.4. An anonymous group, calling itself "Concerned Citizens for Newark," distributed this flyer, attacking Booker for his pro-voucher policy position. They also accused Booker of taking money from poor, black, inner-city residents and giving it to affluent, white suburban residents. On the flip side of the flyer, the group tried to paint Booker as a Republican, alleging that he had ties to former Jersey City Mayor Bret Schundler, former U.S. Supreme Court nominee Robert Bork, and the late President Ronald Reagan.

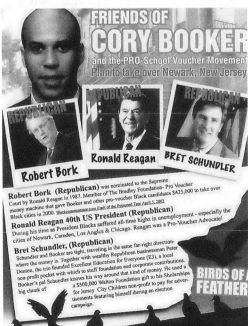

Table 4.1

Turnout Rates by Ward, 2006 Municipal Election

Composition of non-Hispanic black precincts (%)	Number of precincts	2006 turnout (%)	Booker (all candidates) (%)	Booker (Booker vs. Rice only) (%)
Less than 25% black	47	38.98	88.90	93.04
25% to 75% black	37	33.35	75.45	78.92
More than 75% black	84	37.88	60.24	63.29
Citywide	168	37.20	72.02	75.51

Source: Compiled by the author, using 2000 U.S. census data and 2006 election returns from the Newark city clerk's office.

the voters, particularly blacks, had begun to warm to Booker, although he acknowledged that there was still some skepticism about him. In his estimation, they were willing to give Booker a chance but might be quick to crucify him, so to speak, if he did not deliver change quickly.[25] Sharif's comments echo the analysis by a personal friend of mine, whom I will call Corinne Smith. Smith is a longtime friend of Ronald Rice Jr. and worked on his 2002 and 2006 campaigns. When I first arrived in Newark, I asked her to update me on what had happened. She told me that there was definitely a desire for change in the city. From her perspective and in her conversations with voters, she sensed that people interpreted Sharpe James's request for four more years in 2002 to be a desire to finish what he had started. In her view, the voters indeed meant to give him only four more years. By 2006, they were clearly ready for a change in leadership. When I asked her to assess the mood of voters she canvassed, she interpreted it as being pro-change, not necessarily pro-Booker.

A basic analysis of the turnout data suggests that both Smith and Carl Sharif may have correctly interpreted the voters' mood, particularly among black voters. Booker's support was weakest among black voters. Table 4.1 maps the results according to 2000 census demographic precinct data. While the data do not show a correlation between the proportion of blacks in a precinct and voter turnout, there does appear to be a correlation between the concentration of blacks in the precinct and Booker's average share of the vote in those precincts. Booker's performance was strongest in those precincts where fewer than 25% of the residents were black, and weakest in precincts where more than 75% of the residents were black.

To further examine this issue, I conducted a district- or precinct-level linear regression analysis of the 2006 electoral results. New Jersey does not collect racial information from voters because it is not covered under the Voting Rights Act. I thus was unable to conduct ecological inference analysis and so will not speculate about how individuals voted in this election. But I was able to use the available data to make inferences about how districts with certain demographics voted.

I regressed Booker's share of the two major candidates' votes—excluding the small share of the vote that went to the two minor candidates—on the percentage of the district that was black and Latino. In other models, I included the district's percentage of vacant housing and the percentage of owner-occupied housing (proxies for class) and the district's turnout rate as control variables.[26] All of these variables were coded as interval variables on a scale of 1% to 100%. I compiled this data set using election returns supplied by the Newark city clerk's office and demographic and housing data available at the precinct level in the 2000 census.

The regression results are listed in table 4.2. A district's concentration of black residents was significantly and inversely correlated with that district's final vote tally for Cory Booker. Simply put, the Booker-Rice race was more competitive in those districts with higher concentrations of black residents. This relationship holds even after controlling for district voter turnout and class. In the more fully elaborated model, other district characteristics can be used to help explain the election results. Booker seems to have gained an advantage in districts with a higher turnout, for instance, reflecting an improvement from 2002 (see table 4.3). In 2002, districts with a higher voter turnout were slightly, but significantly, less likely to support Booker, but in 2006, high-turnout districts were more likely to support Booker.

Table 4.2
OLS Model of District-Level Support for Cory Booker, 2006

Variable	Model 1		Model 2	
Constant	95.391	$(2.477)^*$	90.678	$(4.767)^*$
Percentage black	−35.943	$(2.628)^*$	−34.197	$(2.858)^*$
Percentage Latino	1.306	(3.688)	3.098	(3.959)
Percentage turnout			.175	$(0.79)^*$
Percentage vacant housing			−1.247	(8.145)
Percentage owner-occupied housing			−13.593	$(3.669)^*$
R^2	.820		.833	
N	168		168	

$^*p < .05.$
Note: Standard errors are in parentheses.

Table 4.3

OLS Model of District-Level Support for Cory Booker, 2002

Variable	Model 1		Model 2	
Constant	61.217	$(2.724)^*$	68.528	$(6.081)^*$
Percentage black	−24.769	$(2.891)^*$	−25.151	$(3.064)^*$
Percentage Latino	1.494	(4.056)	−1.621	(4.717)
Percentage turnout			−.201	$(.094)^*$
Percentage vacant housing			−8.513	(9.544)
Percentage owner-occupied housing			14.106	$(4.098)^*$
R^2	.647		.669	
N	168		168	

$^*p < .05.$

Notes: Districts were consolidated after 2002, and the sample size reflects the 2006 districts. Standard errors are in parentheses.

The most surprising finding was the relationship between a district's concentration of owner-occupied housing and its support for Cory Booker. In 2002, districts with a higher concentration of owner-occupied housing were significantly more likely to support Booker (see table 4.3), but in 2006, the opposite was true. Districts with higher concentrations of owner-occupied housing were predicted to give Booker less support. This is a somewhat counterintuitive finding. We would assume that Booker's appeal would be especially great among middle-class residents, who presumably would be the bulk of the city's home owners.

A deeper analysis of the districts with the highest concentration of homeowners may help shed some light on these findings. I looked at the forty-five districts with the highest concentration of owner-occupied housing (i.e., districts where 30% to 70% of the housing stock was owner occupied in 2000). Of the forty-five districts, eighteen were in the West Ward, and twelve were in the South Ward. In particular, the West Ward districts were in the Vailsburg section of the ward, which (anecdotally) is the home of many longtime city employees. Its also happens to be the home of Ronald Rice Sr. and, currently, Kenneth Gibson. Thus, it is very likely that many residents in this neighborhood (1) wanted to support their neighbor and (2) had a vested interest in maintaining the status quo, which would guarantee job security for some of them. The South Ward is the political base of Newark's traditional black political elite, most of whom are, presumably, home owners. Thus, it should not be surprising that districts like Sharpe James's, which has a high concentration of home owners, voted against Booker.

Analysis and Conclusion

In many ways, the election returns from Newark's recent mayoral election reflect David Canon, Matthew Schousen, and Patrick Sellers's predictions of what happens when moderate and more civil rights–oriented or militant black candidates face each other in congressional elections. In their article, Canon and his colleagues predicted that the moderate black candidate would win a majority of the nonblack vote and split the black vote, thereby creating enough of a rainbow coalition to win.[27] This strategy clearly did not work for Booker in 2002, when he did not win enough of Newark's large black electorate to win. By 2006, however, Booker had become enough of a known player in Newark politics that he was able to attract enough black support to be able to win the election decisively.

Larger questions loomed for the Booker administration. His support was the softest in the city's black sections, particularly in middle-class black areas with ties to the old black political establishment. Would Booker be able to maintain his coalition, or would small slights cause black voters to withdraw their support?

PART II

It's Not Easy Being Elite

Governing Challenges in Post-Racial Black America

5

Policy Is Politics

IN MARCH 2008, I had the opportunity to interview the then Washington, DC, mayor Adrian Fenty for a different, but related, project. I spoke with him to learn more about why he ran for office and about the challenges he faced during his first year as mayor. At one point, I drew a comparison with Cory Booker by asking if he saw Newark's mayor as a kindred spirit. Fenty indicated that while he did view Booker as a comrade-in-arms, he also shared a bond with young, white mayors like Gavin Newsom of San Francisco and John Hickenlooper of Denver. The link that bonded all these men together, Fenty argued, was their commitment to reform.[1]

Despite critics' charges that black political entrepreneurs are nothing but craven opportunists prone to media stunts, many genuinely feel a call to help the communities that they lead. Indeed, their tendency to formulate a media image of themselves as highly educated, technocratic do-gooders often stems from this desire to use their education to improve their community.

In this chapter, I explore the policy implications of electing a black political entrepreneur. Using Cory Booker's election in Newark as my case study, I study the changes that his administration made in two key policy areas during his first term: public safety and economic development. Booker made these two issues a priority in his 2006 mayoral campaign, and many people, both inside and outside Newark, watched eagerly to see whether he could deliver on his campaign promises to reduce crime and create development within the city.

To explore these questions in depth, I collected the relevant aggregate data on crime and economic issues[2] and conducted interviews on these issues with key stakeholders: law enforcement officials, political leaders, and business leaders. Political leaders, particularly those from the James administration, provided institutional memory, while the leaders in the Booker administration could explain the rationale for the current policy. Many of the business leaders to whom I spoke have had relationships with the last three mayors, and they were incredibly useful in placing Newark's economic development in a historical context.

Elite Displacement Mandates Results

When black political entrepreneurs run against entrenched black politicians, they try to cultivate an image that is diametrically opposed to that
of their political opponents. Because they share the racial and class status
of their entrenched black political opponents, they have to use other issues to help voters and political contributors make distinctions. In particular, these candidates emphasize their elite background, assume a reformist
posture, and imply that because they are better trained and more comfortable in integrated settings, they will be better equipped than their predecessors to navigate the corridors of power and work with white politicians
to deliver needed resources and policy innovations.

Black political entrepreneurs target black incumbents that they think
are politically vulnerable. Although many of these incumbents have enjoyed only marginal electoral challenges during their careers, black political entrepreneurs hope that ethical lapses or lackluster performance in office will provide an opening to allow them to make an electoral beachhead.

Students of African American politics and urban politics have different
metrics for judging mayors. For example, black politics scholars tend to
look at mayors alongside members of Congress, and they judge success by
whether or not these elected officials can deliver the resources needed to
help improve black communities. These scholars found that earlier cohorts
of black elected leaders did have some difficulty delivering vital resources
and improvements to their communities. Linda Williams attributed this in
part to economic conditions, pointing out that the first black politicians
elected as mayors and members of Congress in the late 1960s and early
1970s came to power during a period of national economic decline. A stag-
nant economy led to decreased federal aid to cities, a pattern that persisted
into the 1980s. Early black mayors thus could do little to address the issues
of poor blacks. Instead, they focused on ameliorative policies such as affirmative action and set-asides, which disproportionately benefited black
middle-class residents.[3] Robert Smith echoed Williams's observation, contending that black mayors had largely failed in their objective to provide
uplift to black communities. He argued that in addition to affirmative action, black mayors tended to focus on developing the city center and re-
sponding to police brutality.[4]

Black political entrepreneurs often are outsiders to the communities
they aspire to lead, both literally and figuratively. They typically have few
ties to the black political establishment, and they may also be newcomers

to these communities. Being an outsider and challenging established black politicians, particularly cherished politicians, puts black political entrepreneurs in a precarious political situation. Established black politicians can counterframe their entrepreneurial opponents as opportunistic interlopers and charge that black political entrepreneurs lack the racial bona fides to govern black people. Although these charges are not insurmountable, they may never disappear completely. Even if a black political entrepreneur succeeds in convincing voters that he deserves a chance to demonstrate his technical competence in elective office, voters may still be suspicious of his motives for wanting to acquire political power.

The reality of potential latent suspicions amplifies the need for black political entrepreneurs to deliver policy innovations and other needed improvements to their constituents. Whereas voters may have been willing to accept the lackluster performance of the black political entrepreneur's predecessor because they knew and liked him, they will likely be less forgiving of someone who wins office by charging the beloved opposition with incompetence and malfeasance. Since black political entrepreneurs ask to be judged by whether they can deliver on promised policy innovations, they risk being quickly booted out of office if keeping campaign promises turns out to be more difficult than they thought.

Melvin Holli contends that one of the best ways to measure a mayor's effectiveness is to gauge how effective he is at using finite resources to achieve measurable goals (e.g., did he maximize the resources at his disposal to achieve a measurable policy end?) and to determine whether he initiated or innovated policy.[5] The best mayors are credited with creating new institutions or policies and with making the best use of their resources to improve their communities.

In a seminal piece on mayoral leadership, Clarence Stone uses the biographies of four twentieth-century mayors to compare and contrast effective versus ineffective city leadership. In many ways, he echoes Holli's contingency theory. Although Boston's mayor Thomas Curley was a skillful politician and orator, his penchant for corrupt patronage impeded any attempt at successful institution building or even the creation of a viable economic development plan. In contrast, Fiorello LaGuardia rallied New Yorkers around patronage reform and in the end created or fortified some of the city's lasting institutions, such as the park system, City College, and the airport named in his honor. In Chicago, Mayor Richard Daley Sr. was widely credited with being able to work with all the city's stakeholders, but he was tone-deaf to the needs of the rapidly growing black community.

In contrast, Harold Washington, albeit less politically nimble than Daley, was more successful at integrating community organizations into city government, thereby giving a voice to the voiceless. Thus, in Stone's estimation, a mayor's success is a function not just of his ability to win reelection or amass political power. He also has to create institutions or governing norms that outlast his tenure in office.[6]

In some ways, black political entrepreneurs who become mayors are uniquely positioned to be effective. Assuming that their reformist rhetoric is genuine, the natural impulse of black political entrepreneurs to shake up existing patronage systems puts them on the path to policy innovation. Unfortunately, they must guard against structural factors that may impede the realization of their policy goals. As Clarence Stone pointed out more than two decades ago, local government is bigger than city hall, and mayors, along with public and private stakeholders, are part of governing regimes.[7]

Adapting Stephen Skowronek's theory of executive power to the local level, Richard Flanagan maintains, much as Holli and Stone do, that the most effective mayors are those who innovate, observing that timing is everything to a mayorship. Those mayors best positioned to innovate (Flanagan calls them "reconstructive mayors") are those who replace weak incumbent regimes.[8] Beating an incumbent does not necessarily mean that one has defeated a regime. One can replace a mayor, but if the rest of the regime remains intact, the new mayor will have difficulty creating a transformative order. Flanagan says of these "preemptive mayors":

> Political executives brought to power in such situations face particular leadership challenges. Unable to conquer adversaries, they attempt to co-opt them. The litmus test of leadership turns on their individual performance as politicians instead of the policies that they produce. The great disadvantage of the preemptive leadership stance is that it limits the leader's warrant to transform the polity in an enduring fashion.[9]

To prove his point, Flanagan uses a revisionist case study of Fiorello LaGuardia. LaGuardia rose to power as the opponent of the infamous Tammany Hall machine. As the mayor of New York City, he railed against patronage and professionalized the city's workforce. Where he could not count on support from the local and state Democratic Party, he relied on support from President Franklin D. Roosevelt. Over time, though, LaGuardia's running against the establishment became untenable. Not only was he now the establishment, but he also had made critical alliances that belied the cultivation of an outsider posture. Opponents began to point out the hypocrisy of LaGuardia's claiming to not be entrenched, and LaGuardia stopped pushing for reform.[10]

Flanagan believes that the neoliberal mayors of the 1990s—who are in many ways the forbears of the black political entrepreneurs who began seeking political power in the 2000s—are the prototypical preemptive executives.[11] By promising technocratic skill, improved customer service, and a flexible commitment to ideas over ideology, these mayors set themselves up to have a limited impact on the direction in which their cities were headed. Using Rudolph Giuliani (New York City), Ed Rendell (Philadelphia), and Dennis Archer (Detroit) as examples, Flanagan notes that for all their bombast coming into office, they did not change much. Ed Rendell extracted concessions from Philadelphia city workers but did not eliminate patronage in government contracts. Initially, Dennis Archer opposed gambling, but then he supported it. Unfortunately, he was unable to build a major casino because of infighting with Detroit's city council. And while Rudolph Giuliani famously took credit for reducing crime in the city and cutting social services, he did not demand concessions from the city's labor unions.[12] In the end, Flanagan concludes that these mayors' efforts were largely hollow:

> All three mayors oversold their transformative powers and vision . . . they had a difficult time enacting changes across a wide range of policies. When they pushed, they polarized, unable to build the bridges necessary for sweeping reform. When they relaxed, their administrations drifted. Thus, they spent an ordinate [sic] amount of time consumed with public relations. The relentless concern with media and image added a cynical veneer to their governance, and tarnished some of their real, although modest, accomplishments.[13]

In some ways, Cory Booker fits the profile of a preemptive mayor, but in other ways, he does not. While he was able to displace Sharpe James and his allies on Newark's municipal council, much of Newark's political machine, which was opposed to Booker, remained intact. Will having a cooperative legislative branch help him pass certain policy initiatives? Realize certain goals? Will the opposition have a beachhead from which to organize? To help answer these questions, I examined Booker's achievements in regard to public safety and economic development.

Newark has a strong mayor system, which gives the mayor responsibility for initiating policy. In May 2006, Cory Booker and his team were well aware that he would likely have a short honeymoon period once he was elected mayor. Thus, they quickly set out to get busy and set the stage to improve the quality of life in the city. Before even taking office, Booker held community meetings to ask voters how they wanted to see the city improve, and they cited public safety and economic development (including job creation) as priorities.

Public Safety Policy

Since the 1967 riots, Newark has been stigmatized as a blighted and unsafe city. Those riots, in part a reaction to police brutality of blacks, hastened the white flight out of the city already under way and sent the city spiraling into a period of urban decay, decreased city investment, a shrinking tax base, and urban crime. These problems only got worse in the 1980s, as many Newarkers succumbed to selling or becoming addicted to crack cocaine. In a study of the impact of crack cocaine in large American cities, Roland Fryer and his colleagues found that between 1985 and 2000, Newark had been affected the most by crack cocaine.[14]

After the riots, the city of Newark did institute some measures to try to address its problems, such as improving relations between the mostly white police force and the majority-black and Latino community. The unspoken policy was that either the city's police chief or the police director had to be black or Latino, a policy established in hopes of building better relationships with the minority community. But there still were racial disparities in the police force. Even as late as 2007, all but three of the police captains were white, on a force that was nearly half minority.[15] So even though a minority might be in one of the top positions, in reality the police precincts were still disproportionately being run by whites.

Despite these changes, the city still had a reputation for being unsafe. In 1996, for example, *Money* magazine rated Newark as the least safe city in the United States. According to the magazine, Newark's rates of violent crime and car theft were six times the national average, and 4% of Newarkers had been victims of violent crime.[16] In 2005, the city still was regarded as being unsafe. Even though Newark had a lower crime rate (total crimes per 1,000 population) than did other New Jersey cities, such as Irvington, Orange, and Camden, its crime rate was more than twice the statewide average.[17]

Newark's overall crime rate did drop in the late 1990s and early 2000s, and Sharpe James would often boast about this in his public comments. This lower crime rate coincided with a nationwide reduction in violent crime from 1992 to 2004.[18] Nonetheless, Cory Booker learned from his internal public opinion research that Newark residents still were very concerned about public safety.[19] This was a particularly salient issue for residents because in the eighteen months leading up to the May 2006 election, more than a dozen teenagers were murdered in the city. Booker ascertained from his door-to-door campaigning that parents were too scared to let their children participate in after-school activities because they had real concerns about their safety on the way home from school. Consequently, Booker made public safety the centerpiece of his campaign, even promising to walk kids home from school himself if that is what it would take to ensure their safety.

Many people in Newark's old political establishment disagreed with Booker's concentration on crime control. To them, Booker was making a promise that he might not be able to keep. By placing so much emphasis on eradicating crime in the city, they believed that he might be opening himself up to unfair criticism whenever a high-profile crime was committed.[20]

There was some evidence to corroborate their concerns. Right after Booker was inaugurated in 2006, he started the Safe Summer Initiative with his former nonprofit, Newark Now. Newark Now worked with the administration and the ward council members to hold weekly block parties in rough neighborhoods throughout the city. On any given weekend, at least five block parties were held, one in each ward. In addition, in the summer of 2006, Booker played midnight basketball in one of the city's public housing projects every Saturday that he was in town. That summer, the Safe Summer Initiative also held outdoor slumber parties in three housing projects in the Central, South and West Wards, at which children could sleep on the playground, watch movies, play games, and receive free meals.

In the first two months of the Booker administration, the mayor's office announced that the city's July and August 2006 crime rates had fallen from those of the same period the year before, which they attributed in part to Safe Summer. Safe Summer was a terrific public relations introduction for the Booker administration, and it did help bring residents out of their houses and provide a fun family activity for residents of high-crime communities. But crimes continued to be committed in the communities where these gatherings were held, and overall, homicides and shootings were up during this time period in 2006.[21] For instance, in the summer of 2006, I attended most of the West Ward's Safe Summer events between my interviews, including that ward's sleepover in Bradley Court. Although the events were wonderful, Councilman Rice's staff was not sure that they deterred crime. Indeed, two of those block parties were followed the next day by shootings in the same vicinity. The night before I arrived in Newark for the Bradley Court sleepover (the first night of a two-night party), someone fired a gun in the air right outside the complex. Despite the Booker administration's quantitative data on their side about crime reduction, it might have been difficult to convince residents that Safe Summer had anything to do with it.

As evidence of why mayors should not promise to eliminate crime, many critics cited the 2007 Mount Vernon School shootings, where gang impostors killed four innocent college students. Immediately after the shootings, activists held protests on the steps of city hall demanding Booker's resignation because he had not delivered on his public safety promises (these activists already had begun a recall movement several months before the shootings).[22]

Nonetheless, Booker remained steadfast in his commitment to reduce crime in the city. He believed that if he could reduce the city's crime rate, not only would the existing residents' quality of life improve, but he would be in a better position to promote the city to businesses and tourists.[23]

Booker has been a long-term believer in the "broken windows" theory, which was made popular by William Bratton, New York's police commissioner under Mayor Rudolph Giuliani. Booker spoke glowingly about this theory to voters during his 2002 campaign, at great political risk. The theory—which was developed by Professors George Kelling and James Q. Wilson in a 1982 article in the *Atlantic Monthly*[24]—holds that if police officers enforce community standards of decorum (e.g., no loitering, panhandling, littering, squeegee window washing, and the like), criminals will get the message that residents care about their community and will not tolerate crime. This idea led to the belief that police officers can reduce the number of major crimes by enforcing the laws regarding even minor infractions.[25]

When Booker was elected mayor, he embarked on a national search to find law enforcement administrators who shared his broken windows philosophy. He ended up finding Garry McCarthy, a former deputy of Bratton's, in Brooklyn, New York. McCarthy implemented the broken windows principle in his district, instituted high-tech data collection on the geographic dispersion of crime, and used this information to pinpoint areas of high crime and offer additional police support. As a result, his district experienced a precipitous drop in violent crime.[26] Booker hoped that McCarthy would be able to replicate those results in Newark.

McCarthy's selection was not without controversy. He is white and not from Newark, which was a huge red flag to people both inside and outside the administration. Since Booker had opted to make the interim police director Anthony Campos[27] the police chief, Newark's top two law enforcement officers would be white, which, to some people, smacked of racial insensitivity. For instance, Charles Bell, Booker's successor as Central Ward councilman, accused the mayor of not even considering blacks' opinions when he made the decision to hire McCarthy, and he called the hiring "a major misstep."[28]

McCarthy also had had his own run-ins with the law. He had been accused of abusing his badge when he defended his daughter, who, he believed, had been unfairly pulled over by the police on the Palisades Parkway. McCarthy was later acquitted of all charges, and he defended his actions to help his daughter, who, he asserted, had been harassed by rogue cops.[29]

When McCarthy assumed his position as Newark's police director, he immediately set about to restructure the department. The police department was working with a low morale, a politicized force, and a crumbling infrastructure. For example, before Cory Booker took office, Corinne Smith attended a citizens' meeting with a public information officer from the police department in Newark's West Ward. She returned from the meeting quite troubled. The police officer had acknowledged that the ward was perpetually underpoliced, particularly during the overnight hours. This officer confessed that on a good night, ten police officers patrolled the ward. On a bad night (i.e., when everyone called in sick), only four officers were assigned to patrol the ward. According to the 2000 census, the West Ward had more than 50,000 residents.

Councilman Ronald Rice Jr. recounted Booker's first visits to police precincts as mayor. On Booker's first weekday in office, he attended the police precincts' roll calls to introduce himself to the force. While there, he toured the stations with council members and was appalled at what he saw. The precinct buildings were infested with rats and reeked of urine. The officers' locker rooms were falling apart, and the officers themselves reported low morale. They were still typing arrest reports on typewriters.[30]

Moreover, the department's structure was wildly inefficient. In early 2007, Councilman Rice casually mentioned in a phone call that the municipal council had just approved the creation of a narcotics division for the police department. I actually thought he was joking. I could not imagine that that Newark's police department had not had a formal narcotics division sooner. Rice, however, confirmed this later in my formal interview with him.[31]

Members of Sharpe James's administration dispute this characterization of the police department. Calvin West, one of James's senior aides and a former chief of staff, insisted that the police department did have a narcotics division.[32] Councilman Augusto Amador, who has served on the municipal council since 1998, corroborated both stories and provided some context. Although the Police Department had a narcotics division in the James administration, he told me, it was heavily politicized and lacked authority. He explained,

> One of the most difficult jobs police officers have is narcotics, in the fight, in confronting narcotics and the narcotics trade. So, it would be very appropriate not to have a narcotics division because you don't want to give the perception that a problem exists, first of all. Second, you, you, you lose that sense of professionalism where everyone is treated the same way, by putting people in a particular division that is a very dangerous division, therefore putting in danger the rest of society. What I'm trying to say is this, their not . . . developing a narcotics division in the past was more used as a, as a sign of punishment in the police department. . . . Well, you're not behaving too well . . . you're not following our guidelines, therefore, I'm going to put you in the narcotics division. That's like punishment to you.[33]

When Campos and McCarthy came into the police department, they started to correct the most readily apparent problems. Campos bought computers for the department to allow police reports to be submitted electronically.[34] When McCarthy was hired in the fall of 2006, he immediately began depoliticizing personnel decisions, to create a force whose work assignments reflected their mission to serve the public. To that end, McCarthy moved uniformed officers out of clerical positions where possible, and he hired civilians to perform those duties. This put more officers on the street. He also prevented seasoned officers from abusing their seniority to get out of patrolling duties. When McCarthy came to the police department, 40% of officers worked Monday to Friday from 9 A.M. to 5 P.M. only, even though most crimes took place during the overnight and weekend hours. This staffing abuse explains why so few officers were assigned to overnight and weekend duty in the West Ward. McCarthy required police officers to return to street patrols and to work nights and weekends. He also reconstituted the narcotics division so that it was not the place where enemies of the mayor were exiled, and he also created a major case squad.[35]

McCarthy revamped the department's data collection process by instituting a new program, called Compstat, to keep track of where crimes were being committed, at what times they were being committed, and who was committing them. Precinct commanders could then aggregate these data to find crime waves or clusters. McCarthy gave his commanders the flexibility to reassign officers to address pressing concerns in their jurisdiction. For instance, if the data showed an uptick in car burglaries between midnight and 3 A.M. in the Ironbound Section, the commander in that region had the flexibility to reassign officers to patrol that area during those times with the express purpose of catching the perpetrators.[36]

McCarthy argued that the old data collection system was confusing and not terribly helpful to fighting crime. Under the old system, shootings were categorized in creative ways that made little sense to the layperson. For instance, the department distinguished between "shootings" and "shooting hits." Shootings were any time a gun was fired, and shooting hits were any time a bullet actually hit someone. There was also little to no geographic mapping of crime. Moreover, precinct commanders did not have the flexibility to modify their crime-fighting strategies to address surges in crime in their precincts because all strategic changes had to be approved at the top. By revamping the data collection process and giving the precinct commanders greater ownership of their precincts, the hope was that precincts would become leaner, more effective crime-fighting organizations.[37]

The first evidence suggested that McCarthy's reforms paid off. Violent crime fell dramatically in the city in 2007, and the staffing changes seemed to have had the immediate impact of helping deter crime.[38] Increasing the number of police patrols at night, when most violent crime happens, had the effect of either deterring the crime or catching the criminals before they were able to act. The most notable decline was in the city's homicide rate. On the day that I interviewed Director McCarthy, we were interrupted with a phone call from the mayor. McCarthy reported to Mayor Booker that the city was on track to post its lowest homicide rate in eleven years.[39] The city also experienced two homicide droughts in 2008. For six weeks in January and February and for three weeks in July, the city had no homicides, and by the end of the year, Newark had recorded only sixty-seven homicides, which was 32% fewer than the ninety-nine murders in 2007.[40]

These improvements have not come without controversies and additional challenges. In particular, grassroots activists were convinced that McCarthy's changes in data collection were a conspiracy to hide a growing crime rate.[41] The Booker administration stands by its policies.

Ultimately, the true test of the Booker administration's efforts to reduce crime is whether the actual statistics indicate a decrease over time.
To make that determination, I looked at longitudinal crime statistics data.
By studying Newark's crime rate over time and in context, I was able to test
the Booker administration's claim that it reduced crime using commonsense procedural changes. Furthermore, by comparing Newark's crime
rate with the national crime rate, I could determine whether alternative hypotheses may explain any changes in Newark's crime rate.

To that end, I compiled data from the FBI's Uniform Crime Reports
from 2000 to 2009.[42] The Uniform Crime Reports collect data from local police departments on the number of reported[43] murders, rapes, aggravated assaults, robberies, burglaries, larcenies (petty thefts), and automobile thefts[44] that took place in a particular geographic jurisdiction in a
given year. The FBI aggregates the violent (murder, rape, assault, and robbery) and property (burglary, larceny, and automobile theft) crime numbers to create composite violent and property crime rates.

My purpose in presenting this information is twofold. First, by looking
at Newark's crime rate over time, I can determine whether the city's crime
rate fell during the Booker administration and whether any decline from
2006 to 2009 was part of a larger trend that predates the Booker administration. If crime fell precipitously after 2006, this would lend credence
to the Booker administration's claim that its policy reforms helped reduce
the overall crime rate. Second, comparing Newark's crime rate with the
national crime rate helps put Newark's crime into context. If the rate of
change in Newark's crime statistics is comparable to changes in the national crime rate, then local policy reforms are likely not the reason for
the observed reduction or increase in crime. Rather, changes in Newark's
crime rate are a reflection of national changes.

Graph 5.1 compares the violent and property crime rates for Newark
and the United States from 2000 to 2009. As we can see, during much
of the 2000s Newark did have a higher crime rate than the United States
as a whole. But when we compare Newark's property and violent crime
rates with national trends, we find two distinct patterns. Overall, both
the national and Newark's violent crime rate remained relatively constant throughout the first decade of the twenty-first century. Ironically,
though, Newark enjoyed the biggest reduction in the overall violent crime
rate between 2000 and 2003, when Sharpe James was mayor. During that
time, Newark's violent crime rate fell an average of 13.2% a year, compared
with an average annual reduction of 2.1% nationally. During the Booker

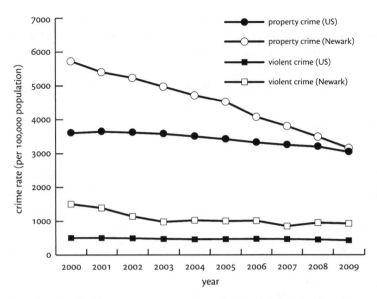

Graph 5.1. Violent and property crime rates for Newark and the United States, 2000–2009

administration, violent crime fell 15.6% between 2006 and 2007, compared with a 1.4% reduction nationally, and increased 11.7% between 2007 and 2008, compared with a 2.7% reduction nationally.[45]

Although the national property crime rate fell slightly during the 2000s, Newark's property crime rate decreased dramatically throughout the decade, dropping 44.8% from 2000 to 2009, compared with 15.6% nationally. It is important to note that the rate of change in Newark differed between the first and second half of the decade. Property crime rates fell an average of 4.6% annually from 2000 to 2005, but 8.6% annually from 2005 to 2009. From 2007 to 2009, the middle of Booker's first term, property crime rates in Newark fell an average of 8.9% annually.

It is helpful to disaggregate the national crime rates to compare Newark's individual crime rates with those of similar cities. I used the Uniform Crime Reports' comprehensive data on cities' crime rates from 2006 to 2009 to compile a database of average crime rates for Newark's so-called peer cities. To compare the different types of peer cities, I looked at all those of comparable size (i.e., populations of 100,000 to 500,000),[46] New Jersey cities with populations of more than 100,000 (Elizabeth, Jersey City, and Paterson), and majority-black New Jersey cities (Irvington, East Orange, Orange, and Camden).[47] To find out Mayor Booker's effectiveness on crime relative to that of other black mayors, I also compared Newark's crime rate with that of other large cities (with populations of 100,000 or more) led by black mayors. I identified these black-led cities using the Joint Center for Political and Economic Studies 2007 data on black elected officials.[48]

Murder

Newark's homicide rate receives the most attention. In fact, much of Cory Booker's popularity nationally stems from the dramatic reduction in the city's homicide rate during his first term as mayor.[49] Graph 5.2 charts the changes in Newark's murder rate relative to national trends from 2000 to 2009. During that period, Newark's homicide rate was approximately four to seven times higher than the national murder rate. During that decade, the national homicide rate stayed relatively constant, dropping slightly in the last two years of the decade. In contrast, Newark's homicide rate fluctuated. With the exception of a decline in homicides from

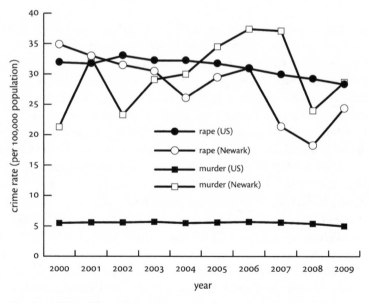

Graph 5.2. Newark's murder and rape rates, in comparison to national trends, 2000–2009

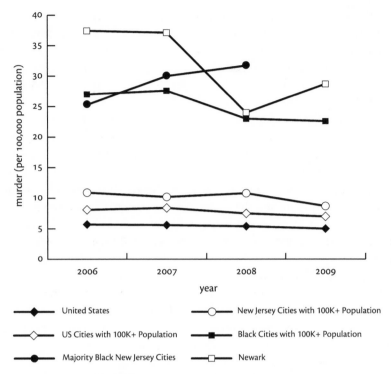

Graph 5.3. Newark's murder rate in comparison with peer cities, 2006–2009

2001 to 2002, Newark's homicide rate increased through the first half of the decade, peaking in 2006. It then fell precipitously, particularly in 2008, and increased in 2009.

Graph 5.3 shows the murder rate data from 2006 to 2009, a period covering the last six months of Sharpe James's administration and the first three and a half years of Booker's first term as mayor. During this time, the city's murder rate fell about 23% overall. A closer examination of the data, though, reveals that the decline in murders was inconsistent during this period. For instance, the murder rate fell less than 1% in 2007 but decreased dramatically (35%) in 2008. Then in 2009, Newark's murder rate started to creep up, by nearly 20% over the previous year. In 2010, the number of homicides in the city increased 23% from the previous year.[50]

Graph 5.3 also presents data from Newark's various peer cities. In general, cities of comparable size to Newark have a slightly higher murder rate than the national average, and the murder rate in New Jersey's big cities is slightly higher than the murder rate in comparably sized cities in the United States. Despite the higher murder rates, the longitudinal patterns in the comparably sized cities nationally and New Jersey's large cities largely mirror national trends, although New Jersey's cities experienced a steeper decline in murders in 2009.

Even though Newark's murder rate is generally higher than any of the comparison groups, it more closely approximates the murder rate in cities led by black mayors. Much like Newark, the murder rates of "black peer" cities remained steady between 2006 and 2007. The black peer cities' murder rate declined steeply in 2008, but Newark's murder rate declined even more sharply during the same period. The greatest divergence came in 2009. Murder rates continued to fall, but not as sharply, in the black peer cities while Newark's murder rate increased nearly 20% during the same period.

Despite the fluctuation in Newark's murder rate between 2006 and 2008,[51] there are noticeable differences between the murder rate in Newark and that in New Jersey's other majority-black cities. Whereas Newark experienced a decrease in murders over that time period, New Jersey's majority-black cities had an increase in their murder rate.

Rape

Graph 5.2 also presents data on reported rape rates in Newark and nationally from 2000 to 2009. Nationally and in Newark, the number of reported rapes decreased slightly from 2002 to 2009. But the downward trend was punctuated by local spikes in rape rates from 2004 to 2006 and from 2008 to 2009. In 2010, the number of reported rapes in Newark had increased nearly 16% from the same time the year before.[52]

Graph 5.4 shows a comparison of the reported rape statistics for Newark's peer cities from 2006 to 2009. Newark's reported rape statistics were noticeably lower than those for most of the comparison groups for the period studied, and they were comparable to those of New Jersey's other large cities (i.e., Elizabeth, Jersey City, and Paterson). In fact, Newark's reported rape rate exhibits nearly the same parabolic trend as those of New Jersey's other large cities. New Jersey's other majority-black cities started to see their reported rape rates increase in 2008, whereas U.S. cities with populations between 100,000 and 500,000 and black-led cities with populations above 100,000 saw decreases in their reported rape rates for the entire period studied.

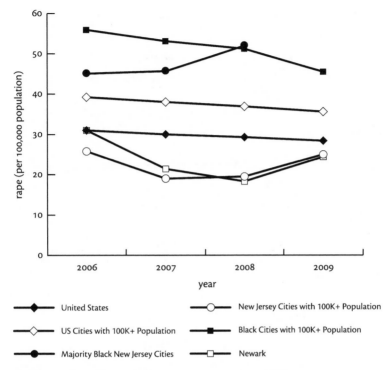

Graph 5.4. Newark's reported rape rate in comparison with peer cities, 2006–2009

Robbery and Aggravated Assault

Graph 5.5 compares Newark's robbery and aggravated assault rates with national rates from 2000 to 2009. Nationally, robbery and assault rates remained relatively constant for much of the period. Although Newark's robbery and assault rates were higher than the national average, overall the city reported lower rates of both crimes over the decade. The biggest declines were between 2000 and 2003. Between 2003 and 2006, Newark's robbery rate decreased slightly, while the assault rate increased slightly between 2003 and 2005 before falling slightly in 2006. Both the robbery and the assault rates fell in 2007. After that, the assault rate remained relatively constant, while the robbery rate increased in 2008 and decreased slightly in 2009. In 2010, the Newark police department reported a 21% increase in the number of reported robberies from the previous year, while the number of aggravated assaults decreased by 2%.

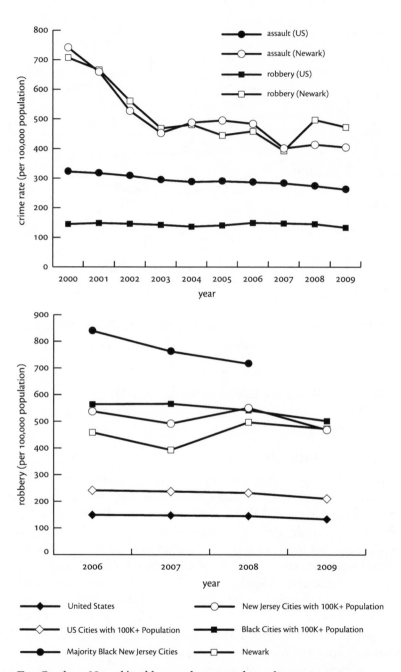

Top: Graph 5.5. Newark's robbery and aggravated assault rates, in comparison to national trends, 2000–2009. *Bottom*: Graph 5.6. Newark's robbery rate in comparison with peer cities, 2006–2009.

Graph 5.6 allows us to put Newark's robbery rate between 2006 and 2009 into local and national context. Whereas cities with populations between 100,000 and 500,000 had a higher robbery rate than the national norm, the robbery rate for these cities was similarly constant over the period studied. Although the robbery rates of black-led cities were higher than Newark's, they, too, exhibited the same constant to slightly downward trend seen in the national data. Black cities in New Jersey had the highest robbery rates—higher than Newark's—although those cities' robbery rates decreased from 2006 to 2008.

Perhaps the biggest surprise I found in the data was Newark's robbery rates and the robbery rates in comparably sized New Jersey cities. On average, Elizabeth, Jersey City, and Paterson had higher robbery rates than Newark from 2006 to 2008, and those rates fluctuated in a similar pattern. Only in 2009 was Newark's robbery rate nearly identical to the robbery rates in its sister cities, and that was because the sister cities' robbery rates fell at a faster rate in 2009 than Newark's did.

The aggravated assault data from 2006 to 2009 shown in graph 5.7 exhibit

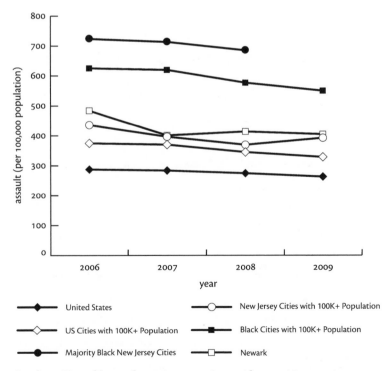

Graph 5.7. Newark's assault rate in comparison with peer cities, 2006–2009

very similar trends. Medium-sized U.S. cities had higher assault rates than the United States did overall, and black-led cities with populations of more than 100,000 had higher rates than did medium-sized cities. The rate of decrease in assault in these categories, though, is comparable. When we look at assault rates in New Jersey's other majority-black cities, we see a similarly steady to slightly downward trend between 2006 and 2008.

Newark's assault rate closely mirrors the rate for New Jersey's other large cities, decreasing from 2006 to 2007. In Newark, the assault rate remained relatively constant from 2007 to 2009, although there was a very slight increase in 2008. In New Jersey's other large cities, the assault rate also remained relatively constant but dipped in 2008 before rebounding slightly in 2009. In 2009, Newark's assault rate was nearly identical to the average rate in Elizabeth, Jersey City, and Paterson.

As graph 5.8 indicates, Newark's property crime rates generally improved during the 2000s, whereas nationally the burglary rate remained

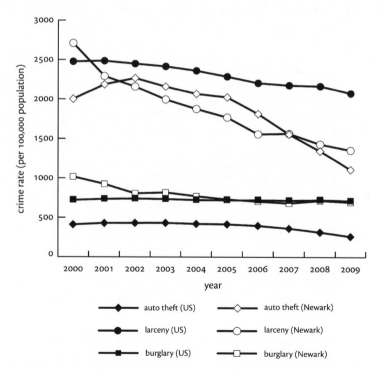

Graph 5.8. Newark's property crime rates, in comparison to national trends, 2000–2009

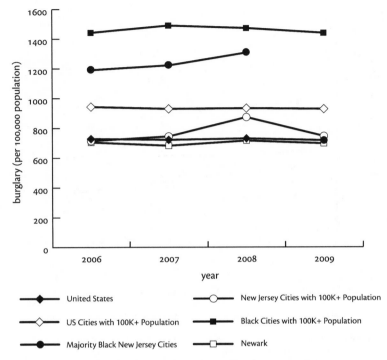

Graph 5.9. Newark's burglary rate in comparison to peer cities, 2006–2009

relatively constant over the decade. In 2000, there were nearly three hundred additional burglaries per 100,000 population in Newark than in the United States as a whole. Newark's reported burglary rate fell substantially from 2000 to 2002, and by the end of the decade, Newark's burglary rate was nearly identical to the national burglary rate. In fact, from 2006 to 2008, Newark's burglary rate was actually slightly lower than the national burglary rate. It appears that the trend of lower burglary rates continued in Newark in 2010. That year, the city reported a 1.4% reduction in its reported burglary rate.

Burglary

Graph 5.9 compares Newark's burglary rate from 2006 to 2009 with the robbery rates of its peer cities. Newark's peer cities, black peer cities, and New Jersey black peer cities all had much higher reported burglary rates. With the exception of the 2008 burglary rates (which were higher),

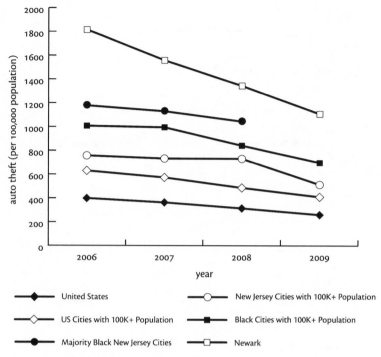

Graph 5.10. Newark's auto theft rate in comparison to peer cities, 2006–2009

Newark's burglary rate was comparable to that of other large cities in New Jersey. New Jersey's other black cities had a spike in burglaries in 2008.

Auto Theft

As graph 5.10 shows, Newark has a serious auto theft problem relative to the rest of the country. The city's auto theft rate far exceeded both the national auto theft rate and the auto theft rates of any of the comparison peer city groups I examined. But Newark made steady progress in reducing its auto theft rates from 2006 to 2009, when the annual rate of reduction hovered between 13.7% and 17.6%. To be sure, between 2008 and 2009, auto theft rates fell by double-digit margins in all the city groups I examined, but from 2006 to 2007 most of these groups had only single-digit decreases in their auto theft rates. Unfortunately, the city's auto theft rate started to creep up in 2010. That year, the city reported a 16.5% increase in car thefts from the previous year.

Larceny

Newark's reported larceny rate is one of the bright spots in the overall crime analysis, as can be seen in graph 5.11. Newark's larceny rate has been lower than the national average since 2001. The city continued to post reductions in its larceny rates in 2010, when there was a 5.4% reduction in reported larcenies from the previous year. On average, all the New Jersey cities I studied reported larceny rates that were lower than the national average. In contrast, medium-sized cities and cities led by black mayors reported larceny rates that were higher than the national average.

Analysis

It is important not to view any of the changes in Newark's crime rate in a vacuum. If changes in Newark's crime rates parallel changes in crime rates in other American cities, or if the start of those changes predate Booker's installation as mayor, it is likely that the changes are really an artifact of

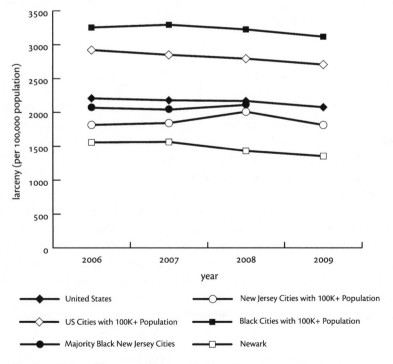

Graph 5.11. Newark's reported larceny rate in comparison to peer cities, 2006–2009

larger trends. This would mean that unfortunately the Booker administration cannot take full credit for the subsequent reduction in crime.

Overall, the data seem to suggest that the Booker administration's record on crime is mixed. In the case of property crime, the rate began to fall years before Cory Booker became mayor of Newark. Therefore, the Booker administration can take credit for continuing the progress that began in the previous administration. The changes in the violent crime rate have been inconsistent. Yes, Newark's murder rate dropped precipitously between 2007 and 2008, but it crept back up in 2009 and 2010 (although as of the fall of 2010, the murder rate had not reached the 2006 level). The rape rate also started to rise after 2008. The robbery rate increased as the murder rate decreased in 2008, although they both fell slightly in 2009, and the aggravated assault rate stayed relatively constant.

Of course, no one should begrudge the Newark police director's decision to change the department's personnel policies in order to put more police officers on the streets. That type of commonsense strategy could lower crime rates over the long term. But by the summer of 2010, those policies had not consistently yielded the desired effect.

Economic Development

Public safety and economic development are two sides of the same coin. If a city is not safe or is perceived to not be safe, that will discourage economic investment in the city that can produce jobs. The Booker administration made public safety a policy priority in part because it wanted to create an investment-friendly climate that could produce jobs for city residents.

Newark's Office of Economic Development has a broad and complex mandate. It oversees city planning and the implementation of the city's master plan. It negotiates development deals with interested business parties and assists in major construction projects like the October 2007 completion of the Prudential Center, the hockey arena for the New Jersey Devils. It runs a job placement office for city residents and a special office devoted to helping place convicted felons in full-time employment.

Economic Development under Sharpe James

As someone who was first introduced to Newark through the Booker campaign, I admit I had some misconceptions of how the previous two mayors had handled economic development. I remember one of Booker's aides telling me in 2002 on more than one occasion that Newark had not updated its master plan in forty or fifty years. According to some Booker supporters, the James administration was completely inept when it came to economic development and city planning. Indeed, they allowed developers who contributed to James's campaign free rein to put up substandard housing haphazardly throughout the city with little regard for aesthetics, land use, environmental concerns, and safety. The James administration contended that developers should not be held accountable for hiring city residents first and that most development was in the city center anyway, so it had little benefit for ward residents.

This version of events is not completely inaccurate, but what happened is more complex than it appears on the surface. Newark was not completely without planning; the city has always employed city planners.[53] Not all the plans were completely coordinated, but the city does have a land-use plan governing zoning that has been periodically updated. Until the Booker administration, though, that land-use plan had not always been coordinated with major development projects, such as the building of the hockey arena. Another set of plans was said to govern those major projects,[54] but according to local business leaders, those major project plans were largely ad hoc. Sharpe James, in particular, preferred to keep the business community at arm's length. While business leaders wanted to create a comprehensive plan for the city's economic development, James wanted to work with business leaders only on major projects (such as building the arena or the New Jersey Performing Arts Center) as they arose.[55]

Land Deals in the James and Booker Administrations

Booker also criticized the James administration for selling city land to developers for pennies on the dollar. In his 2006 campaign, he charged that the city had sold property for $4 a square foot when the market rate was at least four times that amount. He contended further that the city sold land at that rate to give preferential treatment to developers who had contributed heavily to Sharpe James's political campaigns or were his personal friends.

It is important to put this claim into context. Most people agree that the city had trouble attracting development and selling excess property in the 1990s. In order to spur development, therefore, the city was encouraged to sell property at a heavily discounted rate. In fact, during Cory Booker's term as a city councilman, the municipal council, with Booker's support, approved the "fire sale" of blighted property at $2 a square foot.[56]

To be sure, Sharpe James was involved in some questionable land deals.

In 2007, journalists uncovered evidence that Sharpe James and his sons had acquired downtown property in the vicinity of major city projects that would likely boost property values in those neighborhoods. Moreover, the James family received loans for property purchases from a bank that did business with the city.[57] James also was indicted in 2007 and convicted in 2008 for illegal land deals involving his mistress, Tamika Riley. James had approved the discounted sale of land to Ms. Riley under a program approved by the municipal council. The program mandated that purchasers of discounted land had to significantly develop their properties before they could be resold. Ms. Riley, however, was accused of flipping the properties—at a generous profit—without developing the land. Both Riley and James were convicted in this incident, but not for the fire sale. According to the presiding judge in this case, the sale was legal and actually generated higher revenues than the municipal council had mandated. The problem was that because of her relationship with James, Riley had been allowed to illegally profit from the sale of the property.[58]

The Booker administration has engaged in its own land sales as well. In the spring and summer of 2008, the city sold undeveloped parcels to interested developers at bargain prices. The administration argues, however, that its land sales were quite different from those that took place under the James administration. First, all interested buyers had to go through a competitive application process, during they had to explain how they were planning to develop the land. Those entities that promised to develop the parcels were given purchasing priority over groups or individuals that wanted, for instance, to purchase adjacent lots to build driveways. Commercial developers had to agree to certain terms and conditions, such as abiding by first-source legislation, which mandates that developers and businesses hire from a pool of interested Newark applicants before hiring outsiders. If the developers proposed developing large-scale residential properties, they had to agree to set aside a portion of their units for low- to moderate-income families.[59]

The Prudential Center Arena

Booker also was highly critical of James's focus on big projects. James was at the forefront of building a state performing arts center in Newark, which opened in 1997. He also built a minor league baseball stadium, and there was an aborted attempt at building a shopping mall in downtown Newark. The biggest plan, though, was to build a sports arena in downtown Newark. This arena was initially planned to host New Jersey

Nets basketball games,[60] in addition to New Jersey Devils hockey. James planned on paying for the arena ($210 million) using bonds that would be repaid with rent money from the Port Authority of New York and New Jersey for Newark Liberty International Airport. James made the arena the centerpiece of his 2002 mayoral campaign, intimating that he wanted one more term to see the arena come to fruition. He even got the support of then governor James McGreevey, who inadvertently pledged his support during the campaign to see the arena built (McGreevey later retracted that statement, insisting that he did not mean to use the arena as a carrot to help James get reelected).[61]

Cory Booker was an ardent critic of the arena and of most of James's development projects in 2002. He argued that James focused on downtown development at the expense of neighborhood development.[62] He also thought that the arena project was wasteful. Anticipating that the Port Authority funds might be needed to shore up a budget deficit, he felt that the money could be put to better use. Moreover, he was dubious of the claims that sports arenas generated meaningful economic growth and full-time employment.

When Booker was elected mayor in 2006, he tried to enjoin the groundbreaking for the arena. His request was denied, so he was stuck with having to make the best of what he perceived to be a bad situation. Booker's economic development office worked to try to make the arena as much of an economic boon as possible. They developed a plan to develop the Broad and Mulberry Street corridors around the arena by attracting restaurants and sporting goods stores. They also tried to market the arena as a year-round facility, not just a winter sports facility. For instance, the first event held in the arena was a Bon Jovi concert, and since its opening, the Prudential Center has hosted acts such as the Jonas Brothers, Hannah Montana, Alicia Keys, Taylor Swift, gospel extravaganzas, and Booker's fund-raisers. In addition, the arena also serves as the home court for Seton Hall University's basketball team.

The transformation of the neighborhood around the arena is ongoing, so it remains to be seen whether the arena will be the development boon that was promised. It also remains to be seen if existing businesses in the corridor will be able to survive. Right after the arena opened, reporters from he *New York Times* interviewed small shop owners who worked around the arena. Some of them, particularly the owners whose businesses did not naturally cater to arena clientele, were worried that the arena would cause rents to spike and force them out of business. I asked

Stefan Pryor, deputy mayor for economic development, how he planned to address those concerns. He commented that they were overblown, that the increased foot traffic should help most, if not all, businesses. Moreover, Pryor indicated that his office was willing to work with business owners to help them select merchandise that would cater to the arena clientele, in the hopes of generating the increased revenue that could support higher rents. If a business could not adapt to the changed climate, he maintained, his office would help it relocate to a more suitable location.[63]

Job Creation

Perhaps one of the Booker administration's biggest challenges is creating jobs for city residents. Joblessness and poverty have been an intractable problem in the city for nearly two generations, and the Booker administration seems to be only beginning to solve this problem.

The origins of Newark's joblessness problem date back to the mid-twentieth century when Newark's manufacturing sector began a slow but steady decline that was felt in the city most in the late 1960s and early 1970s. The 1967 riots only hastened this steady decline. After the riots, most of the city's middle class—both black and white—fled the city for the suburbs, taking with them not only a comfortable tax base but also businesses. With a smaller population, suburbanites afraid to come into the city to go shopping, and the lure of the suburban mall, the city could no longer sustain long-standing retail establishments like department stores and boutiques. When these businesses left, city residents were left without viable employment options.[64]

Without a thriving commercial center, the city became the employer of choice for many city residents. In fact, Sharpe James could be said to have used the city as an employment agency, and many of his supporters praised him for helping out-of-work residents by providing them with city jobs. Indeed, it was not unusual for James to help struggling young men, particularly those just out of prison, by giving them entry-level positions in the public sector.[65] Unemployment had long been a problem in the city, particularly among blacks. In 2000, the local field coordinator for the NAACP's National Voter Fund's get-out-the-vote effort estimated that black unemployment in Newark was 16%, four times the national average at the time.

When he was a councilman, Cory Booker tried to find jobs for his constituents. When I visited his council offices in 2002, I often saw flyers advertising employment opportunities or job fairs posted on the wall. Given the state of the city's budget, Booker could not resolve the unemployment problem through patronage—and he did not want to do that anyway—so his economic development office had to help residents find jobs.

Under the deputy mayor for economic development, Stefan Pryor, the Booker administration turned the Mayor's Office of Employment and Training (MOET) into a new organization called Newark One Stop. At the Newark One Stop offices, prospective employers (especially those who are required by law to hire Newarkers first) post job openings. Clients can then search the listings for jobs that match their interests and skills.[66] Pryor's office also undertook the task of looking for additional jobs for Newark residents, and in his conversation with me, Pryor boasted that he had convinced Continental Airlines to open six hundred entry-level jobs for Newark residents.[67]

One of the challenges in finding jobs for Newark residents is working around some of their limitations. Only 12% of Newark's population have a college degree, compared with about 27% of the U.S. population,[68] and many Newark residents are ex-felons, making it difficult for many of them to find well-paying jobs for which they are eligible.

Booker made it a personal priority in his administration to address issues of prisoner reentry. To him, this is the new front line in the civil rights movement. After our formal interview in August 2008, Booker and I continued our conversation. It was clear that he was passionate about this issue and understood that if he did not address it, millions of men across the country, particularly black men, could be permanently relegated to the underclass. Booker believed that it was in everyone's interest to work to provide employment opportunities for ex-prisoners, and he hoped that he could be a champion for this issue, echoing a pledge in his inaugural address to make Newark a model city for prisoner reentry.[69]

His administration's prisoner reentry plan proceeded with fits and starts. When Booker took office, a staffer was assigned to conduct research (mostly a listening tour throughout the city) on the issue. After nearly a year, this person was relieved of his duties, and the city hired Dr. Byron Price, who was then a public administration professor at Rutgers–Newark. He had published a book on prison policy and was regarded as an expert on the prison-industrial complex. But according to Price, when he started work at city hall, he was not given adequate resources, not even a desk and a phone. Most important, Stefan Pryor did not brief him on his job responsibilities. For months, Price tried to get an appointment with Pryor to pin down his role in the administration, but Pryor would not make time to meet with him. Price once threatened to quit, but Booker intervened and convinced him to stay. Although Price was under the impression that he was supposed to develop the city's master plan for prisoner reentry, he soon found out that a researcher on loan from the Manhattan Institute was developing the master plan. At that point, he did quit.[70]

For his part, Stefan Pryor acknowledged that there had been some turnover in the prisoner reentry office, but he assured me that the personnel situation had stabilized. Without any prompting from me, he also confirmed that Price had been replaced by a researcher from the Manhattan Institute.[71]

Utilizing the services of the Manhattan Institute to develop a prisoner reentry plan for a majority-minority city like Newark is incredibly risky from a public relations standpoint. In popular circles, the Manhattan Institute is known as a conservative-leaning organization. At the time, its most prominent fellows included black conservative John McWhorter and Abigail Thernstrom, a leading intellectual of the anti-affirmative-action movement. Booker was heavily criticized during the 2002 campaign for giving a lecture at the Manhattan Institute in late 2001, and that talk was used as evidence to justify the accusation that Booker was a closet Republican who was the tool of right-wing conservatives who wanted to take over the city.

Given Booker's past troubles with being labeled a conservative, it was surprising that he would accept the services of the Manhattan Institute. The symbolism of one of its analysts replacing a black academic to do policy work on a racialized issue such as prisoner reentry could be explosive. I pushed Pryor to explain why, given the political stakes, he would hire someone from the Manhattan Institute to design Newark's prisoner reentry program. Pryor responded that the Booker administration looks for the best ideas wherever they are and is not bound by ideology. Besides, he told me, he had never asked the analyst about her political views, and so she might very well be a liberal Democrat.[72]

Since my interview with Stefan Pryor, the prisoner reentry office has become a model program. In 2008, the U.S. Department of Labor gave the city a $2 million grant to fund it, and the Manhattan Institute still pays the salary of the office director, Ingrid Johnson. But young ex-felons I spoke with while canvassing in 2010 were highly critical of the office, claiming that it did not help them find jobs. I asked Ms. Johnson for detailed information about the number of felons her office has helped. But citing a need to clear any interviews with senior staffers, Ms. Johnson refused my request for data.

Impact of Booker's Economic Development Plan

As with crime, the test of Booker's economic development policies is whether they produce results. Did his policies help put more Newarkers to work? How did the 2008 recession affect unemployment, and did Newark's unemployment trends follow national trends? Since Cory Booker took office, how many projects has he started? How many projects have been completed? And how, if at all, did the 2008 economic crisis affect development?

Unemployment

Job creation was a critical plank of Cory Booker's platform. From promising to bring in new jobs to enforcing Newark's first source legislation,[73] he has been a tireless advocate of putting Newarkers to work. During his first term, Booker proudly announced each new business he had attracted to Newark and was quick to note the number of jobs that each business was supposed to bring. Continental Airlines did bring six hundred jobs to Newark, and Pitney-Bowes brought nearly two hundred jobs to the city.

The larger question is whether these new jobs have had an impact on the city's unemployment rate. To investigate this question, I looked at federal unemployment statistics. Each month, the Bureau of Labor Statistics reports national and state unemployment rates, unemployment rates by race, and unemployment rates for cities with populations over 25,000. These reports allowed me to track Newark's unemployment rate over time and to compare it with national, state, and local trends. The unemployment rate from January 2000 to June 2010 allowed me to determine whether any changes in unemployment predated Cory Booker's installation as mayor in July 2006. I also tracked unemployment before and after the start of the 2008 economic crisis (the recession officially started in December 2007).

Note first that the unemployment rate refers to the percentage of potential workers who are actively seeking work. It does not include the percentage of discouraged workers, or individuals who have stopped looking for work. Second, I report seasonally *un*adjusted unemployment rates, as the Bureau of Labor Statistics does not report seasonally adjusted unemployment rates for cities. This means that the reported unemployment rates over the course of a year are volatile. Some industries, like construction and tourism, have cyclical unemployment, so these workers report higher unemployment rates at certain times of the year.

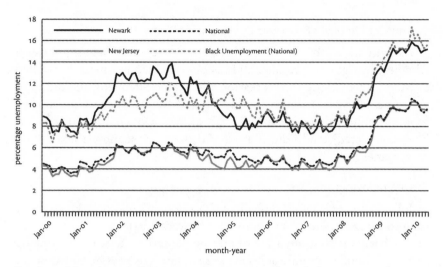

Graph 5.12. Newark unemployment rates versus national trends, January 2000–June 2010

Graph 5.12 compares Newark's unemployment rate with the national, state, and national black unemployment rates. Nationally, the unemployment rate hovered around 4% in 2000 and the first half of 2001. Unemployment started to rise in late 2001, when the country faced a small recession, and remained around 6% from 2002 to 2004. Unemployment fell slowly— though not to 2000 levels—from 2005 to 2007. Then the unemployment rate registered a sharp increase throughout 2008, particularly in the last few months of the year. Given the recession and the mortgage crisis, this is not surprising. Unemployment stayed high (at around 10%) throughout the period examined in 2009 and through the first half of 2010.

New Jersey's unemployment rate largely tracked the national unemployment rate. As graph 5.12 shows, the two lines are mostly intertwined. New Jersey had a lower unemployment rate from late 2004 to late 2005, but in general, the differences in the national and state unemployment rates were negligible.

Newark's unemployment rate was significantly higher. But because the city has a higher-than-average poverty rate and a lower proportion of college graduates than the country as a whole, this finding is not surprising.[74] In January 2000, when the nation's unemployment rate was 4.5%, Newark's unemployment rate was 8.9%, or nearly double the national rate. Newark's unemployment rate rose during the 2001 recession, fluctuating between

12% and 14% from January 2002 to January 2004 and then falling sharply in 2005. From January 2005 through the first half of 2008, the unemployment rate remained between about 7.5% and 9.5%. Not surprisingly, the unemployment rate started to increase sharply in the second half of 2008 as the mortgage crisis and recession began to affect the overall economy. The unemployment rate in Newark surpassed 15% in July 2009 and, for the next year, stayed there.

While Newark's unemployment rate was considerably higher than the national average, its ebbs and flows did correspond to national trends. Unemployment spiked during the 2001 and 2008 recessions both nationally and locally, suggesting that Newark's unemployment rate was affected more by national trends than it was by the efforts of the James or Booker administrations. If Newark's unemployment rate had decreased while the national unemployment rate increased (or vice versa), then different factors would explain each set of unemployment rates. Since the city's unemployment rate moved in the same direction and magnitude as the state and national unemployment rates, it is reasonable to assume that they all were affected by the same macrofactors.

How can we explain the difference in the gap over the years? It may help to compare Newark's unemployment rate with the black unemployment rate. Since the majority of Newark's residents in the 2000s were black, the factors affecting black unemployment nationally may also have disproportionately affected unemployment in Newark. For decades, black unemployment has been significantly higher than national unemployment. If Newark's unemployment rate is comparable to the national black unemployment rate, then the structural factors that explain black unemployment generally may apply to Newark specifically.

Graph 5.12 shows national black unemployment rates as well, which generally follow the same trends as the national, New Jersey, and Newark unemployment rates. Black unemployment tends to be one and a half to two times as high as national unemployment and rose during the 2001 and 2008 recessions. Newark's unemployment rate was noticeably higher than the black unemployment rate during the 2001 recession and noticeably lower in 2005. For the first half of 2009, Newark's unemployment rate lagged national black unemployment. In general, though, Newark's unemployment rate tracks the national black unemployment rate. This is further evidence that after accounting for the fact that Newark's unemployment rate was structurally higher, changes in Newark's jobless rate were likely the result of macrolevel and not local factors.

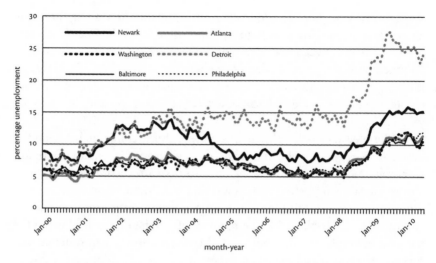

Graph 5.13. Newark unemployment rates versus unemployment in selected black-led cities, January 2000–June 2010

I also compared Newark's unemployment rate with the unemployment rates of other cities led by black mayors. For this analysis, I chose Atlanta, Baltimore, Detroit, Philadelphia, and Washington, DC. Although these cities have larger populations than Newark, they all have been led by more than one black mayor and have, at one time or another, recently been led by young, progressive, "third wave" black mayors (i.e., black political entrepreneurs).[75] Was Newark's unemployment rate comparable to that of this group of black peer–led cities?

The comparative unemployment data are presented in graph 5.13. Unemployment in all these cities rose during the 2001 recession and sharply again during the 2008 recession. Unemployment rates in Atlanta, Baltimore, Philadelphia, and Washington were roughly comparable, but Newark's unemployment rate was consistently higher than that of these black peer cities.

The comparison of Newark with Detroit yielded different findings. From January 2000 to early 2003, Newark's and Detroit's unemployment rates were similar. But when Newark's unemployment rate started to fall, Detroit's unemployment rate stayed constant and then increased sharply in 2008. Although Newark's unemployment rate rose, it never rose as sharply as it did in Detroit, which reported a nearly 28% unemployment rate in July 2009.

The differences in the unemployment rates of Newark and its black peer cities have a number of explanations. The near collapse of the automotive industry in the Detroit area is well documented, and it is not surprising that unemployment rose so sharply in that city. Similarly, Atlanta, Baltimore, Philadelphia, and Washington all have larger economies and better-educated workforces.[76] Thus, it is not surprising that unemployment in these cities was consistently lower than in Newark.

Graph 5.14 compares Newark's unemployment rates with the unemployment rates in other New Jersey cities: Elizabeth, Jersey City, and Paterson. All four of New Jersey's largest cities experienced the same cyclical changes in unemployment rates. Unemployment rose during the 2001 recession, fell from 2003 to 2006, and rose sharply as a result of the 2008 recession. The cities had different unemployment rates, however. Jersey City, for instance, which convinced the financial services giant Goldman Sachs to relocate its headquarters there after the September 11 attacks, had a consistently lower unemployment rate over the decade than did the other cities. Elizabeth also had a lower unemployment rate than Newark over the same period. Through mid-2008, Newark's and Paterson's unemployment rates were similar, but in the last two years of data studied, Paterson's unemployment rate was higher than Newark's.

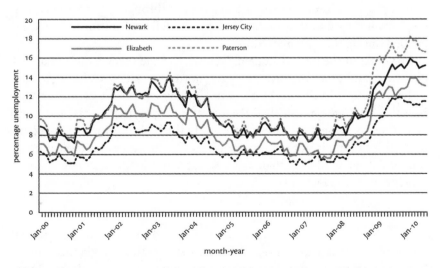

Graph 5.14. Newark unemployment rates versus unemployment in other New Jersey large cities, January 2000–June 2010

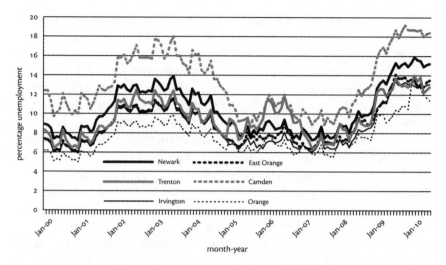

Graph 5.15. Newark unemployment rates versus unemployment in majority-black New Jersey cities, January 2000–June 2010

In addition, I compared Newark's unemployment rate with the jobless rates in New Jersey's majority-black cities. Graph 5.15 reveals that just as in the other comparison cities, black cities in New Jersey experienced the same cyclical ebbs and flows in employment throughout the 2000s. Unemployment rose during the 2001 recession, fell until 2006, and then increased during the 2008 recession.

For most of the period studied, Newark had the second-highest unemployment rate of all of New Jersey's majority-black cities, although from early 2006 to mid-2007, Trenton's unemployment rate was higher than Newark's. Orange typically had the lowest unemployment rates, and Camden's unemployment rate was consistently the highest of the cities examined. This finding is not surprising, as Camden has an even lower proportion of college graduates than Newark does, and its poverty rate is about 50% higher than Newark's.

Analysis

That Newark's unemployment rate ebbs and flows with the national economic cycle is instructive, as it means that national economic conditions are a strong predictor of Newark's unemployment rates. In good economic times, Newark's unemployment rate drops. In times of economic contraction, the city's unemployment rate increases, regardless of who is mayor.

To be sure, some structural factors contributed to Newark's higher-than-average unemployment. Newark is a majority-minority city, and the unemployment rates for black and Latino workers tend to be significantly higher. Newark's population also is poorer and less educated, groups that usually have higher unemployment rates. Newark's significantly higher unemployment rates are likely an artifact of these long-standing structural problems.

The purpose of my analysis is to determine whether Newark's unemployment patterns changed after Cory Booker became mayor. Unemployment rates fell most sharply between 2003 and 2005, when Sharpe James was still mayor, but those rates had started to creep up during James's last year in office. In 2007, Booker's first full year in office, unemployment rates did start to fall, but then the 2008 economic crisis hit, and any employment gains the city had made evaporated.

The 2008 economic crisis confounded my analysis of Cory Booker's job creation strategy in his first term in office. While he can rightfully count any new job created in his city as an accomplishment, the overall impact of his strategy was marginal given the larger economic conditions.

The Creation of Small Businesses

Other indicators reinforce the idea that the 2008 recession hurt job creation. I contacted the Newark permits office and the New Jersey Department of Labor to determine the number of businesses in the city of Newark. Although they could not provide me with all the data I requested (both offices claimed to not keep accurate records of the number of retail businesses), they were able to give me information about key business sectors. Table 5.1 lists the number of small business permits issued by the city of Newark: permits for food businesses, gas stations, dry cleaners, florists, and the like. Permits do not, however, necessarily mean that the business actually opened, and in some instances, they allowed an existing business to expand into new product lines.[77] Nonetheless, the issuance of permits does offer a sense of the robustness of Newark's entrepreneurial climate. The data in table 5.1 indicate that the national economic climate may correlate with business creation in Newark. Overall, the number of business permits issued by the city increased annually from 2005 to 2008. The city issued fewer permits in 2009, which is not surprising given the economic crisis.

Table 5.1

Permits Issued for Selected Business Sectors, City of Newark, 2005–2009

Permit type	2005	2006	2007	2008	2009
Building contractors	731	623	519	273	496
Cigar stores	194	245	307	269	202
Dance halls	21	22	5	19	52
Dry cleaners	7	4	1	1	5
Eateries	143	154	222	175	46
Florists	5	2	4	4	3
Food vendors	127	207	147	249	259
Garages/gas stations	189	195	184	174	157
Ice-cream trucks	18	116	88	146	151
Ice stores	179	189	273	247	196
Junk shops	27	31	30	30	24
Laundries/laundromats	28	26	28	32	23
Meat plants/processors	11	14	11	17	12
Merchandise vendors	135	222	133	213	237
Milk stores	197	179	225	193	160
Precious metals and gems	33	35	30	31	30
Parking lots/garages	96	101	92	88	95
Restaurants	294	335	398	456	403
Sidewalk cafés (alcoholic & not)	2	3	11	16	19
Tire shops	35	34	37	33	30
Used car lots	48	50	47	37	31
Wrecker trucks	36	45	26	41	46
Total business permits (includes sectors not cited in this table)	6,158	6,597	6,750	7,244	7,089

Source: Newark permits office.

An analysis of the permits issued in certain business sectors sheds further light on the ebbs and flows in business activity in Newark over time. For instance, the city issued only about half the number of permits for building contractors in 2008 as it had in 2007, and it issued nearly one hundred fewer permits for merchandise vendors in 2007 than it did in 2006. The number of milk store permits fell between 2007 and 2009, and the city issued fewer permits for used car lots in 2008/2009 than in previous years. Nevertheless, some sectors did grow during Mayor Booker's first term in office. For instance, six times as many sidewalk café permits were issued in Newark in 2009 than in 2006. And even though the city issued fewer restaurant permits in 2009 than in previous years, it had issued increasingly more restaurant permits in the years leading up to 2009.

The state controls the licensing of businesses that provide professional services. Table 5.2 lists the number of active licenses issued to someone at

a Newark address. Unfortunately, this information does not include businesses that may have been open at some time over the past five years but
are no longer in operation. And like the city permit data, having a license
only gives the holder permission to practice; it does not necessarily mean
that the holder is operating a business. The state also maintains information about when applicants apply for their licenses. In a separate category,
I note how many of the active licenses were issued after July 1, 2006, when
Cory Booker became mayor of Newark.

According to table 5.2, some sectors attracted many new licensees in
Newark, despite the adverse economic climate. For example, more than
70% of the active contracting licenses issued to businesses based in Newark were first issued on or after July 1, 2006. About 40% of the hair salon
licenses and more than 25% of the pharmacy licenses in Newark also were
first issued after Booker took office. So, in the midst of economic stagnation, there were signs of economic life.

Outside Evaluation of the Booker Economic Development Plan

At this point, it is difficult to project the long-term impact of Booker's
economic development plan. The administration has taken steps to enforce the mandate to hire local workers, and it has explicitly included af-
fordable housing in its development plans. Because many of these projects

Table 5.2

Business/Professional Licenses Issued for Selected Businesses/
Professionals Registered in Newark by the State of New Jersey

	Number of active licenses as of 8/2010	Number of active licenses issued since 7/2006
Architectural firms	2	2
Athletic trainers	5	3
Barber shops	8	n/a
Contractors	460	333
Electricians	33	7
Engineering firms	16	3
Funeral homes	15	3
Hair salons	250	102
Movers	2	1
Moving & storage companies	6	2
Nail salons	25	15
Pharmacies	76	20
Plumbers	22	2

Source: New Jersey Department of Labor.

are still in their nascent phases, it is too early to say whether or not they will be successful.

One question remains: if fully implemented, will Booker's economic development plans have a gentrifying effect on the city of Newark? Stefan Pryor did not seem to think so, arguing that market-rate housing and commercial development was taking over the city's abandoned spaces. Because this development was not displacing anyone, it could not be gentrification. Also, the city required developers to set aside housing units for low- to moderate-income residents.[78] On the surface, it seems that Pryor took some necessary steps to avoid gentrification, but his comments evince a certain naïveté. It is not hard to see the conversion of once abandoned buildings into trendy living and entertainment spaces driving up the cost of living on a block or in a neighborhood.

Pryor also had trouble convincing the city's stakeholders that he had done a good job. My interview data revealed that the biggest complaint about the Booker administration's first-term economic development plan was that projects had been too slow coming to fruition. A former economic development official for the city contended that the Booker administration's reluctance to continue projects begun under the James administration contributed to the appearance of stagnation. According to him, the Booker administration stopped all pending development projects so that they could be reviewed to ensure that all negotiations proceeded ethically. He argued that if the city had not held up so many of those projects, Booker could have taken credit for finishing some of Sharpe James's last development projects. Moreover, this official contended that by holding up some projects, the Booker administration may have jeopardized the start of those projects in the first place. It is a very real possibility, given the credit crisis and fragile economy, that the city would no longer receive the same financing that was available in 2006.[79]

Even Booker boosters were impatient with the city's slow economic development. Alfred Koeppe, the former chairman of PSE&G, a utility company, and president of the Newark Alliance, which created its own development plan for the city in 1999, was mildly critical of Deputy Mayor Stefan Pryor. In his view, Pryor had not done enough yet to prove that he was an effective community development officer. To Koeppe, if the economic development plan were working, there should be cranes in the sky and more people on the job rolls. By late summer 2008, that just had not materialized.[80]

I brought these issues up with Cory Booker during my interview with him. He, like Pryor before him, listed a number of pending projects that were soon to be announced. I pushed him on this point, telling him that the plans were great but that most people did not have the privilege of being able to sit down with the mayor and deputy mayor and be told about all this pending development. Booker conceded that perhaps the administration had not done a good job informing the public about its pending negotiations and plans.[81]

In the second half of Booker's first term, the administration did make some progress on major development projects. Table 5.3 lists the status (as of mid-December 2010) of major development projects that were announced during Booker's first term in office.

I drew up this list in consultation with an official in the city's planning office. Of the thirteen projects, only one of them, an apartment building, had been completed by December 2010. Six projects were past the planning phase (i.e., they had signed performance agreements with the city, had broken ground, or were under construction). Three of these projects were mixed use, incorporating residential, educational, and commercial buildings. One of these projects was the expansion of the New Jersey Institute of Technology. Two projects were hotels, and the final project was an apartment building. Four residential projects were in the planning phase as of December 2010. Three projects (residential, mixed use, and hotel space) were not active in December 2010.

The recession between 2007 and 2009 greatly affected the city's development projects. All three inactive projects listed in table 5.3 were sidelined because of the recession. One of them is for sale, and the developers of the other two projects chose to ride out the recession by focusing their attention on other projects. In addition, some unannounced projects were put on hold indefinitely as a result of the recession. For example, the city had been negotiating with a major retailer to open a store in Newark. But when the recession took hold, the corporation froze all its plans to expand its operations in North America. Similarly, the initial retail development project intended for the former Pabst Blue Ribbon factory site fell through as a result of recession.

Contrary to popular opinion, most of the major developers in Newark have established a business presence in the city. Of the twelve developers listed in table 5.3, eight have offices in Newark. Two other developers are headquartered or maintain offices in New Jersey.

There is definitely room for Newark's major developers to improve their minority representation. Only one of the twelve developers listed in table

Table 5.3

Status of Development Projects (as of December 2010) Started during First Term of Booker Administration

Project	Address (ward)	Description	Lead development company (headquarters)	Black/Latino/ Portuguese developer?	Projected completion date	Current status (as of 12/2010)	Recession victim?	Notes
2 Center St.	2 Center St. (East Ward/downtown)	Residential	Dranoff Properties (Philadelphia, PA)	No		Planning phase		The project's preliminary site plan has been approved, but the final site plan has not been submitted.
Continental Condominiums	Ferry Street (East Ward)	Residential (owner)	Vision Downtown Urban Renewal (Newark, NJ)	Yes (Emilio Farina)		Planning phase		The development plan is being retooled after the planning board rejected a plan to reduce parking to increase number of apartment units.
Courtyard by Marriott	Broad and Lafayette Streets (East Ward/ downtown)	Hotel	Tucker Development Company (Highland Park, IL; Fort Lee, NJ)	No	Mid-2011	Under construction		
Hotel Indigo Project	Broad Street and Edison Place (East Ward/ downtown)	Hotel	Hanini Group (Newark, NJ)	No	Mid- to late 2011	Between planning and construction		Developer is submitting a performance guarantee.
Lincoln Park	Central Ward/ downtown	Residential, green, and cultural space	Lincoln Park Coast cultural district (Newark, NJ)	Yes (Baye Wilson)	2011	Under construction		
NJIT Expansion	University Ave, MLK Blvd and James St. Corridors (Central Ward)	Mixed-use (dormitory, retail, conference space, etc.)	Jones Lang Lasalle (Chicago, IL)	No		Between planning and construction		

Project	Location	Type	Developer		Date	Phase		Notes
Old Science High School Project	Rector Street (East Ward/downtown)	Residential	Boraie Development Company (New Brunswick, NJ)	No		Planning phase		The project has historic preservation approval, but no further plans have been finalized. The developer is working on another project (renovating the Newark Screens Movie Theatre).
Packard Lofts	Broad and West Kinney Streets (East Ward/downtown)	Residential (rental)	Dubrow Management (Newark, NJ)	No	2010	Completed		Model apartments are being shown now.
Richardson Lofts	50 Columbia St. (East Ward/downtown)	Residential	Newwork LLC (Newark, NJ)	No		Not active	Yes	Project is unfinished and for sale.
Russbader Family Project	Ferry and Main Streets (East Ward)	Residential and retail space	Russbader family	No		Not active	Yes	The project likely suffered as a result of the recession.
Sheraton and A-Loft Project	Market and Mulberry Streets (East Ward/downtown)	Hotels	Edison Properties (Newark, NJ)	No		Not active	Yes	Developer is focusing on its primary business (parking lots) during the recession.
Studebaker/BAT District Lofts	Clay and Broad Streets (North Ward)	Residential (rental)	Associates 368, LLC (Montclair, NJ; Newark, NJ)	No		Under construction		
Teachers' Village	Halsey and Williams Streets (Central Ward/downtown)	Residential and retail space	RBH Group, LLC (New York, NY; Newark, NJ)	No	Phase I: 2012	Breaking ground		The developers did modify the design of the housing units to attract more buyers, but they probably would have had to make those changes anyway.

Source: City of Newark, Office of Planning and Development.

5.3 is black, and no developers are Latino (one developer is Portuguese). The official in the planning office noted that minority developers in Newark often focused on building houses on multiple sites dispersed throughout the city. Because these projects were not part of one neighborhood or development project, their efforts, albeit important, do not register as major development projects.

Conclusion

In his book *In a Shade of Blue*, Eddie Glaude distinguishes between younger and older black politicians. To him, younger black politicians are committed to the project of racial uplift, but they also are motivated by pragmatism and guided by the success of the civil rights movement. Because the civil rights movement was a success, younger black politicians now have the freedom to think about racial questions in a broader context and to use less orthodox methods to addressing problems that disproportionately affect blacks, such as poverty and crime. This does not absolve members of the black community from addressing these issues; rather, older blacks must acknowledge that younger blacks bring equally valid perspectives to the table when working to solve problems in black communities.[82]

Journalists observed this pragmatism when they noted younger black politicians' willingness to use unorthodox, free-market methods to try to solve problems like the achievement gap or the digital divide.[83] This sense of pragmatism also motivates these politicians' self-presentation. Young black politicians, particularly black political entrepreneurs, use their record of achievement to stay in political office.

Cory Booker is banking on his ability to deliver on key campaign promises. Voters, supporters, and skeptics all are waiting to see whether he can reduce crime and create jobs for residents. We will not have a definitive answer for a few years about Booker's ability to turn around his city, but the early signs suggest that he has been marginally successful. The commonsense changes at the police department had an almost instantaneous but short-lived effect on homicide. But when we compare Newark's crime rate with that of cities of similar size, proximity, and demographic makeup, we see that Newark's crime rate was similar to—and sometimes better than —that of New Jersey's other large cities, the state's other majority-black cities, and cities with a history of black mayoral leadership. So even though

Newark's overall outlook on crime was not as rosy as advertised in 2008, the city still is making progress.

The mayor's impact on economic development in Newark is still not yet known. The city has certainly benefited psychologically from the opening of the hockey arena, and as of 2010, new development projects were breaking ground in the city. But we will not be able to assess their full impact for years, as many of these projects have not yet been completed.

The impact of these and other projects on unemployment has been marginal at best. Newark's unemployment rate tracks black unemployment nationally, and Newarkers, like countless other Americans, were hurt by the Great Recession. It still may be too early to tell whether the rest of the mayor's economic development initiatives will have a positive impact on the city and whether Newark's economy will recover.

Of course, the most important judges are the voters.

6

Perception Is Reality

Judging Cory Booker

I PLANNED AN interview trip to Newark in April 2008 to coincide with the end of classes at Emory University. It had been nearly four months since I had made an extended trip there. In the interim, the city had enjoyed a six-week period when there were no homicides. Considering that almost every other major city in the United States was grappling with an increase in violent crime at that time, this feat was phenomenal.

Booker received wonderful press as a result of this development. Peter Boyer of the *New Yorker* praised him, and the *New York Times* provided mostly positive press coverage.[1] From my comfortable perch in Atlanta, I assumed that Booker had won the respect and admiration of his constituents for having delivered on a key campaign promise to improve public safety. I figured that such a winning streak would have silenced critics who only ten months before had started a recall effort against him. In all honesty, I was looking forward to observing a city that had every reason to be in love with its mayor.

After landing in Newark, I headed toward my night's destination. While driving, a huge billboard on McCarter Highway jolted me to attention. It said "Pay to Play Is Alive and Well at City Hall."[2]

I was not sure whether I had stepped into or out of the Twilight Zone.

In the last chapter, I began to explore the impact of Cory Booker's election on public policy outcomes in the city of Newark. In Booker's first term in office, his administration had mixed success delivering on a couple of key campaign promises, notably improving public safety and bringing jobs and economic development to the city.

Booker's successes and failures could affect his future electoral prospects. If voters' assessments of political figures were completely objective, then we could rationally predict their preferences for politicians based on their records of accomplishment. If an official proved to be a competent manager who was able to deliver goods and services, then he should win the admiration of citizens and be able to translate that esteem into votes. Unfortunately, voters do not use only rational assessments. As psychologist and neuroscientist Drew Westen put it, voters "think with their guts, too."[3]

This chapter explores the extent to which voters judged Cory Booker by his record and the extent to which they thought about him with their guts. This question is important. If Booker faced a credible opponent in a future election, any voter dissatisfaction could make him vulnerable. A shrewd challenger could then use displacement tactics against Booker to try to unseat him.

I begin the chapter with a brief overview of the significance of voters' perceptions on their evaluation of candidates. I then discuss how Booker is perceived by his various constituencies (elites, constituents, city hall employees, New Jersey political leaders, and non-Newarkers). Booker has to walk a fine line in maintaining good relationships with all these camps. Sometimes he has succeeded in maintaining this balance, but at other times, he has failed. These failures underscore latent resentments against Booker that have plagued his candidacies since the beginning of his career and, given the right political conditions, could defeat him.

What Do Voters Look For? Style or Substance?

In his book *The Political Mind*, Drew Westen challenges the rational-choice idea that voters objectively weigh political candidates' platforms and select the one whose positions on issues best approximate their own. Instead, Westen argues that voters respond to emotional judgments as much, if not more, than rational assessments of the candidates. Accordingly, those candidates who appeal to pure rationality actually place themselves at an electoral disadvantage.[4]

To illustrate his point, Westen compared the introductory political ads for Bill Clinton and John Kerry. Bill Clinton's ad ("The Man from Hope") tells the story of how he grew up poor in small-town America. Clinton spoke about his hopes and dreams and recounted meeting John F. Kennedy at the Boy's Nation summer camp. He talked about his work on behalf of working families in Arkansas, and he expressed the hope that in Washington, he would be able to expand on his good work.[5]

In contrast, John Kerry's ad began with his narration of his biography: he was born on an army base and always felt the call for military service, especially since he had had the privilege of going to Yale. His navy comrades praised his leadership; his daughter talked about his work as a prosecutor; and his wife pointed out that he was optimistic.[6] Westen deemed Clinton's ad as clearly superior:

> Clinton told his own life story, but he told it as a parable of what anyone can accomplish if just given the chance. He tied the theme of hope to the well established theme of the American dream, presenting himself not as a man of privilege descending (or condescending) to help those less fortunate but as someone no different from anyone else who grew up on Main Street in any town.[7]

In contrast, Westen judged the Kerry piece to be a disaster:

> The fact that he [Kerry] was from Massachusetts was well known . . . the phrase "Massachusetts liberal" had become so successfully branded by the Republicans in 1988 in the Bush-Dukakis campaign that either word could readily evoke the other. When Kerry added the reference to Yale, he fully activated the primary network that the conservative movement has worked for so many years to stamp into the American psyche to galvanize disdain and resentment toward Democrats: the *liberal elite.*
>
> Whatever its intended goal, that first paragraph of the Kerry ad served to convey one primary message that would stick in the neural networks of voters for the remainder of the election: *This guy isn't like me.* (italics in original)[8]

When candidates appeal to voters, they must first grab their attention and establish their affinity with their intended constituency. Westen observed that in recent memory, Democratic candidates in particular have made the mistake of trying to appeal to reason to generate votes. They marshal facts, figures, and logical arguments and expect voters to vote according to the merits of their proposals. Voters, however, are also moved by emotion, by psychologically compelling presentations of data, and they want assurances that their intended leaders are effective public servants who care about them.[9] Although brilliantly constructed policy papers appeal to the wonks who pay attention to them, voters also need to know that the wonk can put down the paper and act like a real human being, preferably using language that everyone can understand.

There is evidence in the political science literature to confirm Westen's point. In the 1960s, Phillip Converse famously pointed out that only a fraction of the American electorate made their political choices based on extensive knowledge of the issues. Most voters either used party identity as a heuristic or based their vote on other characteristics, such as a candidate's physical appearance or personality.[10]

Later work acknowledges that candidates face an interesting paradox when they challenge incumbents. In their study of the 1984 presidential election, John Sullivan, Eugene Borgida, and Wendy Rahn probe the question of whether voters like candidates who are just like them (everymen) or are morally superior (supermen). They contend that voters assess candidates on three character dimensions: whether they are selfish, exhibit self-control, and are trustworthy. Asserting that "most political analysts implicitly assume that voters prefer the candidate who is the 'most above average' on relevant characteristics,"[11] they test this idea empirically. They asked respondents to rate humans generally on these dimensions and then to rate Walter Mondale and Ronald Reagan on them. If the political analysts are correct, then voters should have expressed greater preference for the candidate who was morally superior (i.e., the person who had the better scores on these dimensions and the person whose scores were the highest relative to how the respondents judged human behavior generally).[12]

The findings of this study were somewhat surprising. Walter Mondale had a slight advantage in moral superiority, mainly because people thought Ronald Reagan was a little bit selfish. Given Mondale's advantage, political analysts would have expected people to like him (the superman) better. This was not the case. Instead, people professed to like Reagan (the everyman) better, which the authors attributed in large part to his incumbency. They argued that challengers must be exceptional supermen to get elected but that incumbents retain their office by projecting a common touch.[13]

How Elite Displacement Can Exacerbate Emotionalism

In the past when we have thought about blacks running for elective office, it was blacks running against whites for historic first seats. But nearly fifty years into the post–civil rights era, blacks often run against other blacks as well.

Black political entrepreneurs find it difficult to distinguish themselves from black incumbents. Both groups tend to be college educated and professionally employed, and while incumbents may not have kept their promises to markedly improve the quality of life of their communities, entrepreneurs often lack the experience to make voters comfortable with their claims that will do a better job if elected. Entrepreneurs buttress their promises of reform, then, by flagging subtle differences in their background in the hope that the media and outside supporters will take notice and help create a buzz around their candidacies. To that end, black political entrepreneurs are prone to emphasize their graduation from elite institutions and to signal that they enjoy greater acceptance from the mainstream community as evidence of the fact that they are serious reformers.

In light of the role that emotions play in generating positive affects for political candidates, we can see how this strategy may become a double-edged sword. On the one hand, if Sullivan, Borgida, and Rahn are right, then challengers, including black political entrepreneurs, must present themselves as supermen in order to take attention away from the incumbent.[14] To win office, they have to be exceptional supermen, but to stay in office, they have to cultivate a more ordinary appeal.

If a black political entrepreneur's persona is too exceptional, it could have far-reaching consequences. Although he may be elected, he may cultivate such a superior persona that constituents would have a hard time relating to him. Furthermore, the black political entrepreneur may burn so many bridges on the way to the top that he may have difficulty later reconciling with members of the black political establishment who could lend valuable support.

How does this work? Earlier, I noted that black political entrepreneurs are not always successful the first time they challenge an incumbent for elective office. Sometimes they lose, but in the process, they enhance their name recognition to fight another day. If entrepreneurs wage a competitive battle against incumbents who were thought to be unbeatable, then that first election can tarnish the incumbent's reputation of invincibility. If the entrepreneur wages a second challenge, more constituents may be emboldened to take risks and vote for the challenger the second time around.

Incumbents rarely go out without a fight. In that first contest, incumbents can draw on the loyalty and sympathy of their longtime constituents to stay in office. They can also make class-tinged, racial appeals to group solidarity and attempt to paint the black political entrepreneur as a traitor to the group for even suggesting that the incumbent is corrupt, incompetent, or uncouth. If the entrepreneur is particularly effective in eliciting sympathy from the mainstream media, then the incumbent can turn that disadvantage into a short-term advantage by reminding black constituents of the contentious relationship between blacks and the news media and of the media's thriving on negative, sensational depictions of blacks.[15] By invoking latent racial suspicions about mainstream institutions, incumbents try to mobilize black voters to rally to their defense at the ballot box. Those media attacks are not just attacks on one individual; rather, they are attacks on black people that warrant a collective response. Moreover, incumbents can use the opportunity to demonstrate resoluteness, or to speak truth to power, which many constituents could view as a plus.[16]

If a black incumbent succeeds in surviving an initial challenge by a black political entrepreneur with a sympathetic, compelling media persona, then he also may succeed in planting doubts about the entrepreneur. The black political entrepreneur's behavior during that initial election will help shape his media frame for much of his career. Thus, a person who wins a lot of media attention for being cast as a saint vis-à-vis his buffoon opponent could find that others perceive his motives as opportunistic, disrespectful, or pandering to long-standing media stereotypes about blacks. Such a frame could always elicit doubt about his motives in future elections, even if his initial opponent loses the next election or retires. From then on, that entrepreneur will have to prove that his behavior in that initial election did not reflect his real values but was merely strategic. Having to prove that, though, is fraught with peril, because then the entrepreneur must admit some instrumentality and duplicity, which would tarnish the pristine image he cultivated in order to distinguish himself from his opponent in the first place.

Those doubts about a black political entrepreneur will remain latent as long as he performs well in office or does not face a credible challenge. The moment trouble arises, however, those doubts may come bubbling up to the surface. Remember that the candidate ran as superman, so any deviation from the morally superior playbook is a liability, a chink in the armor, proof that he was not all that he was cracked up to be.

This is especially important because of the social distance that black political entrepreneurs place between themselves and their constituencies in their initial attacks on black incumbents. Even though black incumbents enjoy the same upper-class status as black political entrepreneurs, they cultivate a populist image that clearly resonates with voters, particularly older or poor black voters. Many of the incumbents could invoke their participation in the civil rights movement as evidence of their being men and women of the people. Accordingly, by casting himself as a better alternative to such incumbents, a black political entrepreneur may unwittingly signal to these voters that he rejects not only the political style of the incumbent but also the indigenous political culture of the people he aspires to represent. The entrepreneur may intend to attack a culture of graft and corruption in city hall or the U.S. Capitol, but some may interpret that as a more personal attack.

If black political entrepreneurs cultivate an everyman persona, they may be able to allay such an impression. They, however, have placed themselves in a difficult position to be able to develop such an identity. By distinguishing themselves through their pedigree or by suggesting that they are better at socially navigating the corridors of power, especially in jurisdictions where the majority of residents are poor or not college educated and have few occasions to have to use the correct fork, black political entrepreneurs make it difficult to reframe themselves as everymen once they are in office. Consequently, even though black political entrepreneurs may feel justified in scaring or outmuscling an incumbent from office, they still have to jump over many hurdles to be completely accepted socially by their own constituents, to be perceived as "one of the folks." It is easier for black political entrepreneurs who are from the communities they want to represent to get over this hurdle, but black political entrepreneurs who are newcomers to their communities—especially if they come from a more affluent background—will have an especially hard time.

Cory Booker certainly faced this paradox. In 2002, Sharpe James successfully branded him as an outsider beholden to white interests. Booker's fight against Sharpe James that year ended in defeat, but it eventually helped position him to scare James out of a rematch in 2006. Despite his success, some voters and political elites maintained their suspicions about Booker. At times, he was able to quell those doubts, but at other times in his first term, he made some critical public relations errors that reinforced the suspicions that Sharpe James planted years earlier.

First Impressions

Cory Booker maintains that his path to the mayoralty was accidental. When he was a college student, he felt the call to public service and assumed that he would work in either the nonprofit sector or the ministry. He says that he never considered becoming a politician because he regarded politicians as part of the problem, not the solution.[17]

Booker moved to Newark in 1996 while he was still enrolled at Yale Law School. I asked him why he made such a move then. In particular, I was curious about why he did not immerse himself in New Haven's politics, because that city has many of the same problems that Newark faces. His answer was quite simple: he never fell in love with New Haven, and he wanted to return to the state in which he grew up.[18]

When Booker moved to Newark, he immediately immersed himself in tenants' rights issues and started doing clinical work in the city.[19] He also started meeting prominent local residents. I asked them to describe their first encounters with Cory Booker and their first impressions of him. A common theme throughout their stories was that Booker was smart, impressive, and earnest but that they also perceived some insecurity and naïveté. Many people noted that he seemed overeager to move people with his intelligence. For instance, Gayle Chaneyfield-Jenkins, a former at-large councilwoman, said that Booker was always trying too hard to impress people and that he used quotations to prove how well read he was. In her view, he did not need to try so hard.[20] Clement Price, a professor at Rutgers University–Newark and the city's unofficial historian, recounted a similar story. He met Booker on a train. While Price was very impressed with Booker and instantly recognized that he had a bright future, he also remembered that he talked too much, as though he had something to prove.[21] Even those who would be naturally inclined to like Booker had similar impressions of him. George Norcross, the south Jersey political boss, said that when he met him, he thought he was "very gifted" and "extraordinarily energetic," but he also thought that Booker initially approached politics with a bit of "naïveté."[22] Similarly, Alfred Koeppe, the president of the Newark Alliance, described Booker as "long on vision, short on granularity."[23] It was this impression of Booker—visionary but too eager to please—that led many people to assume that he came to Newark with the intention of shaking up the political establishment.

Booker insists that he came to Newark without any plans to run for political office. Instead, he claims that it was through his tenant advocacy work that he was first recruited to run for public office. His parents helped corroborate part of his story. In separate conversations with both his mother and his father, they confirmed that Booker did not express political aspirations as a high school or college student. They also confirmed that he did not consult them about running for office. While only Booker knows how long he considered running, his parents' comments prove that he did not mull over these plans for decades before he made his announcement.[24]

There are conflicting versions of the story of Booker's initial political ascent. Booker claims that he was drafted to run for the Central Ward council seat by tenant leaders, particularly Virginia D. Jones, but she disputed this claim. According to her, Booker asked for her support after he collected enough signatures to get on the ballot.[25] Moreover, John James, son of the former mayor, alleges that as early as 1999, Cory Booker called him to inquire about rumors that his father planned to retire in 2002. To the younger James, Booker's interest in his father's pending retirement evinced a desire to run for the seat.[26]

In any case, from the outset, the old black establishment clearly viewed Booker as a threat. Kenneth Gibson, Newark's first black mayor, labeled Booker a "carpetbagger."[27] Others said that they knew Booker was plotting a mayoral bid as soon as he was elected Central Ward councilman.[28]

That Booker was instantly perceived as a threat no doubt hampered his building good relationships with the city's black political establishment, as they saw Booker as arrogant and condescending. The views of Ron Rice Sr., Booker's eventual opponent in 2006, are especially enlightening. In public comments, Booker referred to the fact that he initially regarded Rice as a potential mentor and reached out to him for support and advice but that Rice rebuffed his overtures. Rice Sr. addressed this claim indirectly, condemning Booker, his own son (Booker's running mate), and their peers:

> We finally [saw] your generation, coming up, like my son and them, and we [saw] where it was going when we had them in school. We said, now we are in good shape. When they come home, we can bring them in. The problem is they came home attacking us. Like, "Wow, we['re] home now, we finished college, and we should be president of the convention" . . . whoa . . . slow down, OK. Hold it . . . back up a little bit, OK. You know, "I should be the mayor of tomorrow." No, no, no . . . slow down, OK. Let's work . . . give you some experience. Give you an internship, something. They don't want it."[29]

What Rice Sr. contends, then, is not that black political entrepreneurs did not contact him. Rather, he viewed their overtures as an affront and a power grab. In later comments, Rice Sr. revealed that he really believed that Booker thought he should be given power because of his credentials and nothing else, and he indicated that he really thought Booker believed that members of the older generation were stupid.[30]

Booker's Background: Asset or Liability?

Despite the perception that Booker might have a little hubris, some members of Newark's black political establishment recognize that he is talented and has much to offer the city. They insist, however, that Booker has to improve his home style,[31] or how he relates to residents and elites. He may be black and may have grown up twenty miles north of the city, but in the minds of many residents and elites, he might as well be purple and from Mars. Whereas Booker tries to focus on what he has in common with Newark's residents, his critics focus on the differences. Surprisingly, even some of Booker's advisers recognize that the differences do cause problems.

Many of Booker's critics charge that while he is eminently well trained and brings many technical assets to the table, he does not relate well to his constituents, particularly poor black people. Mamie Bridgeforth, for instance, asked whether Booker was a good "cultural fit" for Newark:[32]

> Newark has always been a parochial kind of town, even with the other ethnic groups. But what I think happened is after . . . the rebellion, Newark turned inwards. It was almost like a dysfunctional family, it was us versus the world. We'll fight each other, but nobody better come up against us. And I think what happened with the people in Newark is that they felt that nobody is going to help them. And therefore, the only way they could survive was on their own. And so, as a result, it made them resistant and suspicious of outsiders. Having said that . . . you have someone like Cory, who has come from a privileged background, coming into the city of Newark. If he had grown up in Newark, like a Ronald Rice Jr., it would be a different thing. But he came into Newark, and he is looked at with suspicions because he is not from Newark.[33]

Bridgeforth first acknowledges what to the uninitiated appears to be a paranoid suspicion of outsiders in Newark. Considering the racial tensions revealed by the 1967 riots, this point of view becomes more understandable. Bridgeforth also refers to Ronald Rice Jr., Booker's running mate and her successor on the municipal council, who was born and raised in Newark. In sum, while people may disagree with Rice Jr.'s politics, the fact that he was a known quantity (indeed, the son of a prominent local politician) made him far less threatening than Booker, even though they both opposed the black political establishment.

Others extrapolated from Booker's outsider status that his commitment to black politics was tenuous. Former Assemblyman William Payne, the brother of Congressman Donald Payne, was especially blunt: "Booker just doesn't get black people."[34] Both Payne and Ronald Rice Sr. cited a profile of Booker in the *Star-Ledger*, in which reporters questioned both

Cory Booker and his older brother, Cary Jr., about their experiences growing up in the almost exclusively white Harrington Park, New Jersey. Cary acknowledged that it was difficult being one of the few blacks in town and that when he was a teenager, he really wanted to explore black culture and learn about his heritage. In contrast, Cory expressed few misgivings about his childhood experiences. To Payne and Rice Sr., Cory Booker seemed blissfully ignorant of racial issues, and they were convinced that he could not relate to black people if he did not understand racism. Moreover, their criticism of Booker on this dimension coincided with the criticism that he was too aligned with white interests. If he did not see the racism that his own brother saw when growing up, then perhaps he could not be trusted to know when white developers were using him to take over the city.[35]

On the surface and to outsiders, these observations look like ammunition for petty squabbles over style. These squabbles, however, mask an important conversation about candidates' congruence and cultural fluency. Richard Fenno observed that successful members of Congress have to translate their work for their constituents. Regardless of how smoothly they navigate the Beltway social scene, they must present themselves at home as men and women of the people.[36] Part of that self-presentation is being aware of local cultural conditions. If Booker has difficulty relating to his constituents or town notables, then it could hamper his reelection efforts or at least make it difficult for him to effectively communicate his successes to his constituents.

Mamie Bridgeforth intimated that Booker's lack of cultural fluency actually hampered his efforts to be an effective spokesman for the good things his administration actually was doing:

> I think he [Booker] is a really serious policy wonk, which is good because the city needs that. But I think he has . . . he has to watch himself, that he doesn't get so enmeshed in all of the little details of the policy that he is not able to convey the larger aim of the policy to the population.[37]

Booker's problems with his cultural fluency were not lost on his close advisers. Carl Sharif, Booker's 2006 campaign strategist, admitted that this was a challenge for Booker but argued that he worked on it and greatly improved from 2002 to 2006. He told me the following story:

> I [was] once in a kaffeeklatsch and he [Booker] told people that he can imagine how difficult it was to navigate "the byzantine labyrinth of City Hall." I just sort of dropped my head in the back of the room going like this, "What are [you] talking about, Cory?" . . . Ed Danzer was around

handling communications for us, [and] he would point those things out to Cory right away. Very quickly. His term was "cultural clues." Cory had to understand all these cultural clues. We did keep him aware of it, kept pushing him and just said to him, "Use other language, Cory. . . . There's nothing wrong with it, it's just not necessary. There's a more basic way, a cleaner way of communicating with people." We did help him on that. He got better at it.[38]

The Learning Curve

Booker's issues with cultural fluency continued to haunt him as his career moved into Newark's city hall. Political opponents (and even some allies) projected their already preconceived notions of Booker's hubris onto some of the decisions he made early in his tenure. This perceived arrogance certainly colored their assessments of Booker's leadership and the success of his administration.

The tensions between Booker and Sharpe James continued throughout the transition between administrations. Booker and James had only one brief meeting. The transition leader and former business administrator John "Bo" Kemp reported that despite his best efforts to reach out to members of the James administration, he had very little contact with them. He claimed that when he reported to work after Booker's inauguration, there were only a few boxes waiting for him from the old administration. Former business administrator Richard Monteilh disagreed, maintaining that Kemp did not reach out to him.[39]

In most of my conversations with Booker's opponents, they were very quick to condemn Booker's treatment of the old guard. In any transition from one mayor to the next, political appointees know that they also must leave when their mayor leaves office. Because Sharpe James's appointees had been working there for as long as twenty years, some of Booker's aides thought it best to remind them that their employment would end as soon as Cory Booker took the oath of office. Booker's chief of staff, Pablo Fonseca, sent termination notices to the political appointees in June 2006, a move that was widely criticized, even in the Booker camp, as heavy-handed. One of the people who received a notice was the wife of former mayor Kenneth Gibson.

This act reinforced the widely held belief among Booker's opponents that he was just power hungry. Moreover, it contributed to the impression, also widely held among his opponents, that Booker was arrogant and unwilling to learn from his predecessors' experience. Almost all of Booker's political opponents that I interviewed criticized him for purging officials from the previous administration. They contended that to his credit, Sharpe James kept on Kenneth Gibson's staffers, who gave him stability and needed institutional memory. Booker, in contrast, forced out workers from James's administration who had no civil service protection. In their minds, Booker was letting go valuable personnel who would be willing to help him make a smooth transition.[40]

Some of Booker's supporters saw only sour grapes. A conversation I had after an interview with a key Booker adviser was enlightening. I was preparing to leave, and my respondent, whose identity I will not reveal, saw me out as he headed to the restroom. He proceeded to give me unsolicited advice on my research design, suggesting that I arrange a debate between key aides of Booker and James. He promised me that the truth would come out immediately: the James camp was angry that Booker had power and they did not. On some level, this impression might be true, but the tone of this respondent's comments does evince a certain arrogance on the part of some Booker confidants, who really did view James's aides as competitors that needed to be vanquished.

Not all Booker allies saw sour grapes. Indeed, some acknowledged a tendency of Booker's aides to be cocky. Councilman Donald Payne Jr. sensed this attitude very early. On their first day at city hall, Payne recalled a Booker aide walking into city hall proclaiming that the "talented tenth" had just walked into the building. He cautioned that "no one is all good, and no one is all bad," exhorting the Booker administration to observe greater humility and a greater willingness to listen to old-timers.[41]

To many outsiders, these debates may appear to be distractions from the real business of improving the city of Newark. But the battle over turf is important because it indicates that the frame of Booker as being insincere, aloof, instrumental, and out of touch with regular Newarkers resonated in the city even after his election. If this frame remains relevant, it could be used against him in a moment of political weakness.

Booker on the Job

From a normative perspective, the most important metric by which to judge Booker should be his performance on the job. Voters will see Booker's public presentations and make their judgments accordingly. Elites will also view these events and try to shape public opinion of him in their role as opinion leaders.

The Booker administration began with what it perceived to be an unprecedented commitment to responsiveness and openness. Before Booker took office, his transition team held a series of town hall meetings to which they invited voters to provide feedback on what they thought the city's priorities should be. Each of the meetings addressed a particular theme: public safety, economic development, child and family well-being, and neighborhood development.

I attended two of the four meetings, and they appeared to portend a very responsive Booker administration. The gatherings were impressive. Instead of hosting citizens' grievance meetings at which the voters queued up and complained one by one at a centrally located microphone, Booker's transition team operated these meetings like a working group. A member of the transition team began the meeting with brief remarks, and then Booker said a few words. The attendees then broke up into small, randomly assigned, groups, in which a team leader guided a brainstorming session about how the issue at hand should be addressed. After about an hour, the residents appointed a spokesperson to write down the group's policy recommendations on easel paper and present them to all the meeting's participants. The transition team then used those sheets of paper to incorporate the ideas into their 100 Day Plan.

The citizens' meetings were designed to help set the tone for the new administration. To maintain his interaction with residents, Booker continued a tradition from his city council days and held regular office hours (first biweekly and then monthly). At these sessions, citizens could air their grievances to the mayor directly. In turn, Booker pledged that his staff would address their concerns as quickly as possible.

For a series of articles on his first year of office, *New York Times* journalist Andrew Jacobs followed Booker around. In one of his articles, Jacobs examined the impact of Booker's regular office hours and followed up with a sample of twenty-four citizens who came to the office hours to see how his administration had addressed those concerns. Jacobs found that most of the people he contacted were dissatisfied with the follow-up. The families complained that although Booker seemed concerned about their problems, they had not heard from his staffers after those initial meetings. While the Booker administration disputed some of those stories, they were forced to redouble their efforts to ensure that everyone who attended an office hours session received the proper follow-up.[42]

Budgetary Concerns

The Booker administration also faced unexpected financial hardship in the first two years of the term. Before Sharpe James left office, he announced that the city had a $30 million budget surplus, but according to the Booker administration, that was just not true. In fact, former business administrator Bo Kemp says that he found a $180 million budget deficit. Kemp tried to enact cost saving measures across the city, but he was left without many options and had to cut city jobs. The city offered some workers an early retirement package in the hopes that eight hundred would willingly relinquish their jobs. Only about two hundred actually took the buyouts, so the city was forced to cut four hundred jobs. To do this humanely and in accordance with state law, the city eliminated certain obsolete job titles and allowed workers to bid for other remaining jobs if they had the proper civil service credentials to do so.[43]

These layoffs occurred as the Booker administration was hiring political appointees and restructuring its own offices. For instance, under the James administration, deputy mayorships were largely ceremonial positions that paid less than $70,000 a year. The people who held those positions often held other jobs. For example, Ronald Rice Sr. continued to serve as a state senator, and Ras Baraka worked as a school administrator while holding this position. Even though the positions were ceremonial, these men did help the mayor with political duties such as legislative or youth outreach or, as in the case of Luis Quintana in the 1990s, Latino outreach. Booker revamped the offices to give the deputy mayors serious policy-making duties. One deputy mayor would oversee the administration's economic development efforts; another would oversee neighborhood engagement; and the third would oversee public safety initiatives. Because of their expanded responsibilities, the Booker administration nearly doubled their salaries.

Other political appointees also negotiated six-figure salaries, some of which exceeded the maximum prescribed by city ordinance. As a result, Booker had to issue executive orders to increase those salaries retroactively, as it took a few months for the salary increases to win the council's approval. To the uninitiated, the salary increases appeared to be raises given to political appointees after just three months on the job.[44]

The Booker administration defended these high salaries as the cost of doing business,[45] but most activists were outraged, especially in light of the pending layoffs. Amiri Baraka, for instance, thought that it was unjust for the city to fire city workers making $30,000 a year while at the same time hiring administrators making four times that amount. In his view, it seemed hypocritical and insensitive for the city to make such high-profile hires while claiming to have a budget deficit.[46]

One salary negotiation in particular was emblematic of the perception problem and highlighted the Booker administration's sensitivity to this issue. Newark's highest-paid official is its housing administrator, Keith Kinard. Kinard was brought in to take over the Newark Housing Authority after the former director, Harold Lucas, was accused of corruption. Kinard was recommended to Mayor Booker by the Department of Housing and Urban Development, and in a short time, he turned around the embattled authority, thereby earning the respect of both the Booker administration and the municipal council. Because Booker wanted to make sure that Kinard stayed in Newark, he charged the housing authority board with negotiating a five-year contract for him, which would keep him in Newark through 2012. The board offered Kinard a base $225,000 annual contract, plus generous incentives to tear down and replace dilapidated public housing units. With these incentives, Kinard's compensation package would amount to more than $2 million over five years.

Central Ward Councilwoman Dana Rone, who also was a member of the housing board, was furious at the exorbitant contract being offered to Kinard. She publicly revealed the private contract negotiations, thus derailing the generous contract offer. Kinard's final package did not include those generous bonuses that would nearly double his salary. I asked Modia Butler, then the chairperson of the housing board and later Booker's chief of staff, why the city would offer Kinard such a generous contract in the first place. Butler pointed out that the Department of Housing and Urban Development approved the initial contract offer because it recognized the need to use generous incentives to keep Kinard in Newark. But Butler also acknowledged that in hindsight, that offer was too generous and impolitic, given the city's layoff situation.[47]

The salary brouhaha reflected the political clash of business-oriented technocrats with the more grassroots-oriented activists. The technocrats, who had been socialized in a more corporate mindset, were sometimes oblivious to the political implications of their recruitment efforts. To them, it was worth paying competitive wages to recruit the best people to work for Cory Booker. One senior adviser even told me that the extra pay amounted to no more than $1 million to $2 million, a mere drop in the city's budget. To engage in such recruitment and salary negotiations during a budget crisis and layoff period was insensitive, however, and as I will show, Booker lost some credibility.

The Keith Kinard affair also revealed the growing political rifts between Booker and his municipal council running mates. From the beginning, critics of the Booker administration charged that the municipal council was nothing more than a rubber stamp for Booker. As such, council members felt a certain pressure to demonstrate their independence and occasionally to stand up to Booker.

Separation of Powers Concerns

Political missteps by the Booker administration gave municipal council members an opportunity to challenge the mayor, which cost the administration some political capital. For instance, the Law Department sought the council's approval to award legal contracts to local law firms who were helping the Law Department clear a backlog of cases left over from the James administration. These legal contracts had been a source of controversy because many of the lawyers who won these contracts were also contributors to Booker's campaign. The Booker administration defended the awards, noting that the campaign had received contributions from most of the major law firms in the state of New Jersey. Thus, the city would be extremely hard pressed to find a major law firm that had not made a contribution and that was willing to accept the extremely discounted, legally mandated, hourly rate.

In late May 2007, a particular set of legal contracts came up for a council vote. Included in this legislative package was $1.3 million worth of contracts for the firm of Schwartz, Simon, Edelstein, Celso and Kessler. Attorneys at this law firm were known Booker boosters. The Law Department thought it exigent to have these contracts approved immediately, but only six council members were present at this meeting—just over quorum. When the contracts came up for a vote, four council members voted to approve them, which was a majority of the members present but not a majority of the council members. As a result, a debate ensued about the meaning of the word *majority*. The council members believed that five council members —a majority of the council—would have to approve the contracts in order to award them.[48] The corporation counsel, Aney Chandy, disagreed, believing that based on legal interpretations of the provisions of New Jersey's Faulkner Act, which govern the structure of municipal government, only a majority of council members present at a council meeting were needed to pass legislation, as long as there was a quorum. Chandy argued that she had received the minimum votes needed to approve these contracts.[49]

This contract dispute caused a minor controversy and created a rift be-tween Newark's executive and legislative branches. The council members believed that they were being exploited. In addition, the local media began reporting the story. In the end, the administration retreated, reintroducing legislation approving the contracts and having those contracts approved by a majority of the full council.[50]

This controversy was one of the incidents that emboldened council members to assert their independence of Mayor Booker. I spoke with most of the council members in the fall of 2007, and at that time, they still were trying to maintain unity and claimed that the 2006 coalition was still intact. It was very clear even then, though, that the unity that had ushered them into office in July 2006 was disappearing. Booker could usually count on having the minimum five votes to get legislation passed, but former al-lies started publicly antagonizing the mayor in 2007. Councilman-at-Large Luis Quintana, for instance, ran against Booker's endorsed candidate in the Twenty-Ninth State Senate District race in 2007. Central Ward Coun-cilwoman Dana Rone became an outspoken critic of the mayor, and in early 2008, she announced that she would no longer run with Booker.[51] In June 2008, Booker angered Augusto Amador after he attempted to replace members of the East Ward Democratic Committee without consulting the councilman. Two more council members, Donald Payne Jr. and Aníbal Ra-mos, had tenuous political ties to Booker from the start. Payne Jr., the son of Congressman Donald Payne Sr., has his own following as the scion of a powerful political family, whom Booker challenged in local elections in 2007 and 2008. Ramos is connected with North Ward political boss Steve Adubato. That these two men have a political support base independent of Booker allows them to make maverick moves when they deem it appro-priate. For example, Ramos publicly challenged the Booker administration when he believed that it was diverting police away from neighborhoods to protect the new Prudential Center Arena.[52]

On the surface, these squabbles seem to have been minor political scuf-fles that any administration might experience in the early years of its term. But when considered in the context of the Booker administration's already having been portrayed as arrogant, these incidents become more impor-tant, as they reinforce an existing negative frame and divert attention from the Booker administration's strengths.

Who's in Charge, Anyway?

The intra–city hall squabbles also caused another public relations prob-lem for the Booker administration. In reality, Booker was only indirectly

involved in many of these controversies; a Booker appointee was usually
the point person and lightning rod for them. But they gave the entire administration the image of hubris, and they lent credence to the perception
that Booker was an absentee, ineffectual leader.

Booker's associates have always been a source of controversy. From
the beginning of his political career, his out-of-town friends, donors, and
campaign volunteers have fed suspicions that he was a tool of conservative
or neoliberal white interests who wanted a hostile takeover of the city. Although Booker's campaign blunted the impact of those charges in 2006 by
putting more Newark-born talent on his campaign staff, those suspicions
never went away entirely. So when Booker appointed out-of-towners to
high-profile positions—the original business administrator, police director, communications director, deputy mayor for economic development,
and press secretary all were from New York (although four of the five did
move to Newark)—the opposition railed against him for letting carpet-
baggers invade the city. Critics levied these charges even though the Gibson and James administrations had out-of-town appointees, and they were
unforgiving when these appointees made mistakes. Former mayor Kenneth Gibson, for instance, complained that some Booker hires made geographic mistakes. He declined to name names, but city hall insiders had
already confirmed to me that Booker's first press secretary did not know
ward geography well and called the wrong council members to participate
in press events for the wards. To an outsider, this mistake may seem minor;
one would hope that as a new official settled into her job, she would learn
the terrain and not make errors in the future. But to those who already
were suspicious of Booker, this mistake was unforgivable.

There also were suspicions that Booker was not completely in charge.
Both his schedule and his personality contributed to the perception that
he was an absentee mayor. Rahman Muhammad, president of Local 617
of the SEIU, expressed grave concerns about Booker just days before he
was inaugurated, even though he had endorsed him for mayor that year.
He maintained that Booker was too "Hollywood."[53] Given Booker's high-
profile friendships with people like Oprah Winfrey and Gayle King, Muhammad worried that Booker would cultivate his image as a celebrity
mayor at the expense of his duty to run the city.[54]

Some of Booker's actions confirmed Muhammad's fears. Booker maintained an active speaking schedule, and early in his tenure, he appeared
with Barack Obama on *The Oprah Winfrey Show*. And after Obama announced his candidacy for the presidency, Booker became his New Jersey

campaign cochair. His busy schedule took a toll on Booker's standing among city hall staff and his elective colleagues in New Jersey. On one trip to Newark, a city hall employee mentioned to me that "a Booker sighting at city hall was rare nowadays." Even elected officials found it difficult to get appointments with him. For instance, Assemblyman Thomas Giblin suggested that Booker was spending too much time campaigning for Obama and not enough time tending to the city's business.[55]

To be sure, not all of Booker's out-of-town junkets are for personal or extrapolitical activities. He does travel to lure business to Newark and participate in professional development activities such as the annual meeting of the U.S. Conference of Mayors. However, the notion of Booker's being an absentee mayor does have implications for how insiders assess his leadership. His absences have given credence to the idea that Booker is not completely abreast of everything going on in city hall.

Moreover, Booker's easygoing manner, albeit a rhetorical and fundraising asset, can be a liability to him as a manager. As former deputy chief of staff Jermaine James told me, "Cory, you know, takes . . . criticism hard . . . he's a very . . . passionate person . . . loving person . . . he wants to be liked . . . he's the type that he'd rather be loved than feared, you know, any day."[56] This suggests that Booker might be predisposed to delegate tough decisions to underlings instead of facing them head-on.

Moreover, there was definitely an impression among city hall workers that Booker's former chief of staff, Pablo Fonseca, wielded an inordinate amount of power in the administration. Fonseca served in Sharpe James's administration as the chief code enforcement officer, and he also was very active in James's political outreach to the Latino community. After James demoted him for unauthorized political activity, Fonseca successfully sued the administration for violating his civil service protection. He later joined Councilman Booker's staff to help him reach out to Latino residents in his ward. After that, Fonseca had a meteoric rise through Booker's staff. He oversaw the North and East Ward operations in both 2002 and 2006 and was named chief of staff after Booker's mayoral election in 2006. After stepping down as chief of staff in 2008 to work on Barack Obama's New Jersey campaign, Fonseca became Booker's 2010 campaign manager.[57]

Fonseca had a reputation for playing hardball that carried over from his days as a Sharpe James operative. Even Booker's council staffers were reluctant to welcome him to their staff because of his connection to the James administration.[58] Fonseca thus remained a polarizing figure, but to Booker, he has been a loyal adviser and trusted friend. Most of the Booker opponents I spoke to believed that Fonseca was a liability to Booker. I asked everyone—friend and foe—at the end of their interviews to give the mayor hypothetical advice. Firing Fonseca was a common refrain.

To many current and former city hall insiders, though, Fonseca was the real mayor during the first half of Booker's first term. Only a current and a former worker were willing to speak on the record. Both workers, who to the best of my knowledge are not friends with each other and are on opposite ends of the political spectrum, confirmed that Booker's reputation in city hall was that he was a hands-off mayor. They indicated that Pablo Fonseca was regarded as the real mayor of Newark, and they suggested that Booker's close aides did not always carry out his directives as ordered.[59]

The Booker administration also faced its own charges of cronyism and nepotism. For instance, critics questioned the appointment of Margarita Muñiz, the wife of Councilman Carlos Gonzalez, as deputy mayor for neighborhood engagement. Muñiz, who had impressed Booker with her extraordinary management of her husband's campaign and the Booker team's North Ward field operation, worked as a retail executive and law office manager before her government appointment. Critics also took issue with the appointment of David Giordano as fire director. Giordano had served as the firefighter's union president and was a longtime Booker supporter. However, he had not served in an upper-level management position in the Newark Fire Department. Naysayers argued that Booker passed over more qualified battalion chiefs in favor of a friend and donor.[60] Finally, there was an issue with Carl Sharif's son Ali winning more than $2 million in contracts to update the city's website. By 2008, the website was still not fully up-to-date and that links did not work. The city had to end up hiring another firm to manage the website, which attracted additional criticism.[61]

A recitation of these problems should not be construed to mean that Booker's administration is completely dysfunctional. Longtime city employees recognized that Booker changed Newark's corporate culture, and in many respects, this could be considered a success for the Booker administration, which campaigned in 2006 to improve customer service and to change the public perception of city hall as being "silly hall" with unresponsive workers. In June 2007, during the state legislative primary, I was assigned to canvass with a long-term city employee with decades of experience. As we walked our assigned district, I asked her to compare her work experiences in both the James and Booker administrations. Her response was quick and resolute: in her view, the Booker administration was clearly the more professional operation. Augusto Amador, who served in elective office for the last eight years of the James administration, echoed this sentiment. Speaking about the Booker team members who assumed office in 2006, Amador said,

> I think we're more professional, that much I have to say. Because I saw things in my eight years as a councilman that were appalling. And they were appalling for the fact that I came from the private sector, and those would never be tolerated in the private sector. Not being on time, not running through the agenda effectively, disrespectful to people who would travel for miles and miles to attend a meeting, and then come to the office, to city hall, and then to find out that the meeting is not going to take place because one politician decided not to come to city hall that day. That was absolutely appalling to me. . . . I haven't seen a meeting yet, because that person is not there, that councilman is not there, because there is no quorum in the city council . . . the meeting didn't start on time. So, that level of efficiency, that level of professionalism, exists today.[62]

Nonetheless, the idea that Booker is a hands-off mayor, despite the good that he has done, reinforces the notion that he may be using the city for personal or political gain and that he is a disengaged, disinterested outsider.

Stories and the Insider/Outsider Conundrum

Some of Booker's public statements also helped reinforce the frame of his being an ambitious, craven outsider. One of the ways that he tries to relate to audiences is by telling vivid stories. For instance, the first time I heard Booker speak at Yale Law School in September 2001, he told the story of T-Bone, a drug dealer who threatened Booker's life not long after he moved to Newark. As Booker told the story, he stood firm to T-Bone's threats and eventually befriended him. The last time he saw T-Bone, Booker says, the man broke down and started crying in his car about his tragic life.[63]

The story was definitely moving to someone like me, the product of a southern middle-class suburb studying at an elite institution. To Newark residents, even Booker allies, though, the story is apocryphal. Councilmen Ronald Rice Jr. and Aníbal Ramos both questioned the veracity of the story,[64] and their sentiments were echoed by Rodney Lewis, a prominent local blogger. He recommended that Booker stop telling the T-Bone story because he believed it was just not true.[65] For his part, Booker defended the veracity of this story to me,[66] insisting that T-Bone really existed, although he acknowledged that he had not seen him since he wept in his car more than a decade earlier.[67]

One of the reasons people expressed misgivings about the T-Bone story is that to them, the story sounds too stereotypical. First, "T-Bone" does not sound like an authentic name; it sounds like a name that a screenwriter would have chosen for a hip-hop movie character. Second, T-Bone's disappearance is too convenient. Many of the protagonists in Booker's stories are well known in Newark, so the fact that no one knows T-Bone is suspicious. Third, the resolution of the story (mean old T-Bone crying on do-gooder Booker's shoulders) is too neat. Finally, the story reinforces another problematic frame that Booker contends with: that he is the savior of Newark.

Booker's political opponents expressed concern with his storytelling, particularly that he deliberately casts Newark and Newarkers in a negative light to drum up support for his political efforts. Newark's less than stellar reputation in New Jersey and beyond has been a sore spot for many of the city's residents since the 1967 riots. A generation ago, Johnny Carson famously lampooned the city; more recently, Conan O'Brien[68] did the exact same thing.[69] Sharpe James won the respect of his constituents by challenging these aspersions. Many city potentates are sensitive to any public criticism of the city and its residents, so for Booker to tell stories that reinforced Newark's negative reputation was traitorous to them.[70]

Moreover, some of Booker's stories had very negative racial connotations. When I began interviewing his critics in 2007, two stories emerged that cast the mayor in a very negative light among blacks. Booker was invited to give a talk at his old high school in Bergen County. According to a *New York Times* report, Booker, who was facing a recall effort at the time, referred to political gadflies as "dark angels."[71] Although no one knew what "dark angel" meant, many assumed that it had racial connotations. For instance, when Booker appeared at the People's Organization for Progress march commemorating the fortieth anniversary of the Newark riots, hecklers asked who the dark angels were. Booker later told me that he was misquoted in the *New York Times*,[72] that he had been quoting Abraham Lincoln's First Inaugural Address:

> We are not enemies, but friends. We must not be enemies. Though passion may have strained it must not break our bonds of affection. The mystic chords of memory, stretching from every battle-field, and patriot grave, to every living heart and hearth-stone, all over this broad land, will yet well the chorus of the Union, when again touched, as surely they will be, by the better angels of our nature.[73]

Given the context of both Lincoln's comments and Booker's political situation, Booker may indeed have been misquoted.

For former assemblyman William Payne, the story fit a larger pattern of Booker's ridiculing blacks for his personal benefit. To him, Booker's quotation was symptomatic of his greater tone deafness on racial issues. For instance, Payne reported being especially offended by Booker's attempts to mimic his grandmother's accent. Payne was convinced that Booker was affecting a fake dialect that his presumably well-educated grandmother could not possibly have used.[74]

To be sure, Cory Booker does understand racism and prejudice from personal experience. In the newspaper columns he wrote as a college student at Stanford, he recalled the mildly racist comments that classmates would make when he was a child, and after the 1992 Los Angeles riots, he recounted his own experiences as a victim of racial profiling.[75] Nevertheless, Booker had to learn to be more racially sensitive to Newark residents, particularly black Newark residents.

Even more controversial comments surfaced in late July and early August 2007. At a Democratic fund-raiser for a friend in nearby Summit, New Jersey, a wealthy white enclave near the exclusive Short Hills Mall, Booker spoke of the people who had inspired him. He told the story of the late Judy Diggs, a former district leader with whom he had worked for years until her death months earlier. Booker painted a picture for his audience with the hopes of drawing them into his story. He described Mrs. Diggs as being "portly" and "toothless." He noted that "she used profanity the way we use punctuation." He then told a story of how Sharpe James attempted to bribe Mrs. Diggs to gain her support in 2002. According to Booker, although Mrs. Diggs affirmed her support of Booker, she told him that she was no fool and that she took James's money.[76]

Booker finished the story talking about Mrs. Diggs's tenacious spirit and noted that she died serving her community (she was reading to local schoolchildren when she had a heart attack). But at that point, the damage had been done. The speech was posted on YouTube, and *Star-Ledger* columnist Joan Whitlow wrote a scathing column criticizing the mayor, calling his comments

an Uncle Remus act before a mainly white audience in a wealthy suburb, performed by the mayor of a city with a majority of black and brown people who by and large are not so wealthy and did not elect the guy so he could entertain others with tales about them.[77]

Mrs. Diggs's family was outraged at the suggestion that their matriarch had accepted bribes. McKenzie Collins, a Diggs family member, noted that in 2008 many family members were still angry with the mayor for his comments—angry enough to not vote for the mayor and to mobilize friends and family to not vote for him either.[78]

The backlash from that speech was devastating for Booker. When the word of the speech went public, key political leaders refused to speak to him for a few days. Booker was clearly upset that he had hurt people. Reflecting on the speech, he acknowledged that he "had not spoken in love" when he made those comments, and he vowed to do better.[79]

Despite Booker's remorse, there was some discussion in his camp about the appropriateness of those stories. Some of his advisers were quick to defend their boss. Jermaine James, Booker's deputy chief of staff, had attended the Summit fund-raiser and contended that the mayor's comments had been taken out of context.[80] Elnardo Webster, Booker's former law partner and campaign treasurer, believed that people were unnecessarily hypersensitive to what people said in (racially) mixed company:

> I think that my frustration, you know, the last couple of weeks, with the whole Judy Diggs comment thing, was that . . . I've listened to that story. And I don't know if this is me . . . but I don't have a problem with that story. I know Judy Diggs. And Judy Diggs was fat; Judy Diggs had missing teeth; and Judy Diggs talks like a sailor. And Judy Diggs has taught Cory a lot of lessons about how to be effective in politics in Newark. And I think that his admiration [and] respect . . . is expressed to both white and black audiences. So I think to take that speech, at that time, and take it, almost, out of context, is fucked up.
>
> You know, I disagreed, that he should apologize . . . it's not like he's saying anything that's not true. And, was it . . . to explain, kind of, give a picture of what was going on here, and how this operated. . . . It was a judgment call, and he made a decision. And he decided to put it behind him.
>
> . . . He was criticized for making that speech . . . in a white setting. But he's made that speech in black settings. He's talked about Judy Diggs to people in Newark . . . the black people have heard that same story and never come and say, "That's a terrible story, don't talk about Judy" . . . that's where he gets in trouble . . . that he doesn't modify himself to his audience.[81]

I asked McKenzie Collins about this charge that Booker had described Judy Diggs similarly in black audiences without recrimination. Collins disputes this claim, contending that yes, Booker described Diggs as being feisty but never referred to her appearance and never talked about her taking bribes.[82]

Right or wrong, Newark elites of all races agreed that Booker's description of Diggs was completely tasteless and that it could damage Newark's reputation in the long term. I recall speaking to Steve Adubato to set up my official appointment to interview him. As soon as I got him on the phone, he began a tirade about the Judy Diggs comments: "How dare he go outside of Newark and tell stories like that!" he told me. He thought this was completely tasteless.

Augusto Amador had the following to say:

> The statements that Cory made outside of the city regarding an African American individual, I . . . I attribute that to a . . . lack of sensitivity on the part of Cory regarding this city and where he is the mayor. I'm not going to answer for him because he is going to have to respond to those issues and why he did what he did. And that's his responsibility. But I think that when you're in a position of responsibility, like he is, at that level to be, when you go outside of the city, and you talk about your city, where you come from, I think you have to be careful about who you talk to and who you talk about. . . . As we move forward and we attempt to build a new Newark, we can't forget sacrifices that were made by individuals of color and . . . and anybody who stood behind and said, "I'm going to take a stand," after 1967 because those individuals deserve all the credit in the world because they really are the motors of the renaissance of this city. So he should be more careful in the future, more sensitive. Not careful, sensitive.[83]

The Judy Diggs incident could have been an even bigger problem for Booker. Unfortunately, the tragic murder of three college students shifted attention away from his comments. On the night of August 3, 2007, four childhood friends, Iofemi Hightower, Natasha Aeriel, Terrance Aeriel, and Dashon Harvey, were listening to music on the playground of the Mount Vernon School in the city's West Ward. While they were listening to music, they were approached by five teenagers and young men. The males shot all four youths and slashed the faces of the two young women. Three of the four friends died; only Natasha Aeriel survived.[84]

The shooting captured national attention and served as a defining moment for the Booker administration. To most political observers, the shooting galvanized Newark's elite to temporarily put aside their differences, join forces, and try to apprehend the suspects. Booker was uniformly praised for his handling of the murders. To observers, he appeared mayoral, at the forefront of the coordinated effort between the city and county law enforcement. In his public appearances, he balanced righteous indignation with a resolve to solve the crime.[85] That the fugitives were apprehended quickly also contributed to the perception that Booker handled this crisis effectively.

The Press Paradox

After the Mount Vernon School shootings, many of the Booker administration's public safety policies had short-term positive effects. Six months later, Newark enjoyed the homicide drought that I mentioned at the beginning of this chapter, and the city's success in reducing homicides brought the administration very positive national attention. Even though Booker was able to use the media to help build his political base and his national profile, the positive press coverage has had a downside. Not only does an excessive amount of positive media coverage raise suspicions among black voters and elites, but Booker risks losing control of the positive media image he has worked so hard to cultivate.

Positive media coverage can catapult a black political entrepreneur into the media stratosphere and elective office, but it can undermine that entrepreneur's credibility in the black community. Adolph Reed noted this trend when he excoriated Jesse Jackson in *The Jesse Jackson Phenomenon*. He charged that Jackson behaved very much like a black political entrepreneur in 1984 by selling himself to the mainstream media before he put together a coherent campaign strategy and platform. Jackson manipulated the mainstream media's desire to anoint the next black spokesperson and presented himself as the perfect one. In doing so, both Jackson and the mainstream press overlooked the fact that he had significant opposition among black elected elites, and they ignored the fact that Jackson did not enjoy uniform support among black voters. The press in particular failed to acknowledge the fact that Jackson's presidential bid could have been a publicity stunt. Instead, Reed argued that the press was so eager to not appear racist that it bent over backward to cover Jackson positively and often, even though the election results suggested that he warranted far less attention than he received.[86]

Cory Booker's situation showed some, but not all, of the similarities to

Jackson's in 1984. There is little question that Booker's political career benefited from positive mainstream media coverage, which began before he
had had much chance to deliver on his policy initiatives. Part of the reason that Booker and his colleagues received so much attention also stems
from the mainstream media's fatigue with figures like Jesse Jackson and Al
Sharpton, who by the early 2000s, appeared to be more racially strident
and disagreeable to some mainstream news consumers.

Booker also more closely fits the mythology of Martin Luther King Jr.'s
"I Have a Dream" speech. To many non-Newark observers, he is evidence
of America's continuing racial progress, not of how far the country has yet
to go to be truly equal. Booker makes them feel good, not depressed. This
is the reason he earned such high esteem from columnists like George Will
and Ellis Cose, who saw Booker as the culmination (not the continuation)
of the civil rights movement.[87]

The positive media coverage of Booker also is problematic because it
ironically serves only to reinforce negative stereotypes about blacks. This
reinforcement happens on two fronts. The media often condense stories in
order to help readers keep track of key themes. This tactic works especially
well for long-term stories like political campaigns.[88] When a black political entrepreneur bursts onto the scene and contrasts himself with his black
establishment opponent in an attempt to attract media coverage, he often
feeds into this trope. He hopes that he is seen as the good guy, and his opponent as the bad guy.

The problem is that there are just as many insidious good stereotypes
of blacks as there are insidious bad stereotypes of blacks. Black political
entrepreneurs may, consciously or not, be helping reinforce these long-
standing, outrageous notions of blackness when they try to make the evening news. Paul Gilroy confronted this reality in his controversial book
Against Race. He provocatively opposed the continued use of racial catego-
rization because race was a social construct that was weighed down with
too much baggage. Blacks, in particular, were never allowed to be human.
Whether they were characterized as good or bad, blacks acquired an unbe-
lievable mythic quality. They were either superheroes (Gilroy uses Michael
Jordan as an example) or superpathological. But the racialized superhero is
just as problematic as the supervillain, for a number of reasons. To Gilroy,
the idea of the superblack can be as enslaving as the concept of the sub-
human or morally inferior black.[89] In a more explicitly political context,
the success of the superblack is not predicated on the uplift of all black
people. Rather, superheroes wind up serving as exceptions that prove the

rule of black inferiority and justify policies that disproportionately disadvantage black people.

Clearly, Cory Booker fits the mold of a superhero. He is tall and good looking. Even among elites, he has an exceptional résumé. He has a choir boy reputation, even turning down corporate job offers to dedicate himself to improving the plight of the urban poor. His story is the stuff of which movies are made.

Except that this is not a movie. As Gilroy points out, a fixation with black superheroes allows some people to absolve themselves of any responsibility to address their own prejudices against blacks. If we support Booker, then we can feel good that we are not racist. Moreover, if we support Booker, we can take pride in having contributed to the uplift of the poor, urban masses.

The notion of the black political entrepreneur may not be so bad (unrealistic expectations notwithstanding) if he could exist in a vacuum. But every superhero has to have a foil. In Booker's case, his foil is Sharpe James and the entire preexisting black establishment. If Booker is all good, then James must be all bad, and his style of leadership must represent everything that is wrong with black politicians and black people.

When Sharpe James is not the foil, the people of Newark become the foil. They do not know a good thing when they see it. They would rather wallow in the muck of what their city has become and be swayed by predatory politicians than follow a good man like Cory Booker into the Promised Land.

The problems with this construct are legion. It focuses too much attention on Cory Booker. He is always viewed as separate from the community he aspires to lead. Moreover, his positive portrayal comes at the expense of the community he is trying to join. Booker may sincerely intend to use his celebrity to help the community, but all the press that seems to emanate from this relationship seems mainly to help Cory Booker.

A 2008 *Esquire* profile of Booker epitomizes this point. The reporter, Scott Raab, shadowed Booker for four months in late 2007 and early 2008. In the resulting article, Raab used the plot of the movie *I Am Legend* as an analogy for Cory Booker's role in Newark. Booker is Will Smith's character, charged with saving the world (Newark) from annihilation by zombies.[90]

Outside Newark, the public response was positive. Both Raab and Booker aide Kevin Morris reported getting compliments for the article. Booker, however, was not pleased. In particular, he took issue with the apparent portrayal of Newark residents as zombies. In a lengthy rebuttal to the article, Booker wrote a scathing letter to *Esquire*'s executive editor, apparently a personal friend, criticizing Raab for maligning the character of Newark's residents and ignoring all the good that was happening in the city.[91]

Booker had clearly learned from the Judy Diggs incident. By issuing a swift rebuttal to *Esquire*, he was being careful to defend the portrayal of Newarkers in the mainstream media. As the subject of the article, he wanted it to make clear that he had never referred to his constituents as zombies. This move clearly showed that Booker was growing in office and learning from past mistakes.

That said, Booker still must take some of the responsibility for how Newark was portrayed in the article. I asked Scott Raab what he meant by referring to Newarkers as zombies. His response was enlightening. He said that he had no intention of portraying the citizens of Newark as zombies. Rather, the zombies were meant to be the drug dealers and criminals, not the vast majority of the city's residents. He told me that he got the idea to use the *I Am Legend* analogy because Booker actually took him to see the movie the first night he began following him. In Raab's estimation, Booker deliberately frames himself as the savior of Newark because it is politically advantageous for him to do so. Raab was admittedly skeptical of this frame, referring to Booker as a "bullshit artist."[92] His goal was not to malign the collective character of the citizens of Newark; instead, his target was Cory Booker's vaunted self-image.[93] Even though Booker may be learning from his past mistakes, he still had to make up for years of telling T-Bone and Judy Diggs stories.

Not long after I interviewed Cory Booker, Matt Bai published an article in the *New York Times Magazine* entitled "Is Obama the End of Black Politics?" Here Bai discusses how young black politicians differ stylistically from older black politicians, who were socialized during the civil rights movement. In the article, Bai interviews Booker as an example of the new, post-racial black politician and quotes him as saying:

> "I don't want to be pigeonholed," he said. "I don't want people to expect me to speak about *those* issues." By this, presumably, he meant issues that revolve around race: profiling by police, incarceration rates, flagging urban economies. "I want people to ask me about non-proliferation. I want them to run to me to speak about the situation in the Middle East." Since the mayor of Newark is rarely called upon to discuss such topics, I got the feeling that Booker does not see himself staying in his current job for

anything close to 20 years. "I don't want to be the person that's turned to when CNN talks about black leaders,' he said."[94]

Not long after the article was published, I received a text message from Booker:

"Soooo upset about n y times magazine," he wrote.

"Why?" I wrote back.

"My quotes butchered and he took what he wanted and left the substance of my points to him out," he responded.

It seemed that Booker was starting to realize that he did not have the control over the media that he thought he did. Bai apparently selected this particular quotation because he wanted to highlight the fact that young black politicians see themselves as more than race men and women. Instead, they are ambitious and see themselves as being capable of having a national and international reach.[95] Matt Bai was not the least concerned about how a quotation like the one he used would play at the intersection of Broad and Market Streets; all he saw was that Booker had the potential to be the second Barack Obama. What Bai failed to realize is that Booker has to pass through Newark if he ever wants to get to Washington, and quotations like the one Booker claims that Bai took out of context could make it difficult for him to get out of Newark with his political career intact.

Incidentally, even though I asked him more than once, Booker never told me what he actually said.

These incidents underscore the precarious relationship that even black political entrepreneurs have with the press. They may be media darlings, but they play a subordinate role to reporters in the framing of their image, even if they initiate the relationship. In addition to having to worry about being misinterpreted by the press, black political entrepreneurs also have to contend with potentially divergent expectations of their social "peers" who stand ready to warmly welcome them into the halls of power.

Black political entrepreneurs engage in elite displacement in part by presenting themselves as more collegial than their more combative predecessors. Because entrepreneurs claim to move more easily through mainstream social institutions because they have benefited from integration for their entire lives, they present themselves as being good middlemen, or good translators of black interests to the white establishment.[96]

What if the white establishment does not want good translators who can more effectively articulate the policy needs of the black poor? What if they, in the words of former New Jersey NAACP president Walter Fields, really only want to put more compliant people in power for the purpose of "Negro control?"[97] Or what if the purpose, as Fields lamented, was to set black America's best and brightest up for failure, to prove that nothing could be done to salvage the urban underclass?[98] Indeed, Fields's comments evince the very real possibility that black political entrepreneurs are expected to engage in the same type of secondary marginalization that their predecessors were required to perform in order to stay in power.[99]

Cory Booker: The View from the Citizenry

How do Newarkers view Cory Booker? The impression of voters—regular citizens—is paramount because they make up the vast majority of the electorate. How do they see Cory Booker? Have they noticed the policy changes he has instituted?

To answer this question, I present the qualitative findings from two focus groups. As I did in 2003, I thought it was important to include the voices of regular voters in this book, particularly voters of color. To that end, in July 2008 I conducted two focus groups of black and Latino Newark voters. I wanted to see whether voters from these two constituencies had different views of the mayor and different perceptions of the direction of the city under the Booker administration.

Methodology

Qualitative public opinion research has both strengths and weaknesses. Focus-group samples are not chosen randomly and thus must be considered convenience samples. Also, in a qualitative research design, researchers can talk to only a limited number of respondents. Unlike large-N survey data, though, focus groups and in-depth interviews allow researchers to explore issues thoroughly and to ask follow-up and probing questions for clarification. So even though qualitative designs sacrifice some representativeness, they compensate with the richness of the data that are produced.

Even though the focus-group sample is not representative, I did take care to be sensitive to Newark's demographics when putting this group together. I interviewed both black and Latino self-identified registered voters, who represent Newark's two largest racial and ethnic constituencies. I contracted out the recruiting to a professional focus group facility, who brought together diverse groups of respondents. Professional facilities recruit respondents in malls and public places and maintain lists of thousands of prospective respondents. Respondents gave their informed consent and were paid $100 to participate in the group, which was the standard rate that the focus-group facility paid.

The African American panel had eight respondents, three men and five women, ranging in age from very young adult (eighteen to twenty-nine) to advanced middle age (fifty-five to sixty-five). Half the respondents were thirty-five to forty-five years old; two other respondents were younger and two were older. The group included both lifelong Newarkers and recent transplants to the city. They lived in the Central, West, and South Wards of the city. Three of the respondents had bachelor's degrees; four reported having some college or an associate's degree. One respondent was a high school graduate. Most respondents reported voting in both the 2002 and 2006 municipal elections. Three respondents voted in 2006 but not in 2002. At least two of these respondents did not live in Newark in 2002, and one of them was too young to vote in 2002 anyway.

Nine respondents participated in the Latino focus group, which was conducted in English only. The respondents were overwhelmingly Puerto Rican, but there was Dominican representation as well. One respondent was Dominican, and another was both Dominican and Puerto Rican. The group included mostly lifelong residents of the city; all but one lived in the North Ward, and the other lived in the South Ward. This group also was younger. Two respondents were between eighteen and twenty-nine; four were between twenty-nine and thirty-five; and three were between thirty-five and forty-five. Five of the respondents were high school graduates, and four had some college or an associate's degree. Six of the nine respondents reported voting in both the 2002 and 2006 municipal elections, and the other three voted in 2006 but not in 2002.

Each session with the focus groups lasted for two hours, followed a semistructured format, and covered the same topics. This structure allowed me to compare answers across the groups but also gave me the flexibility to ask probing and clarifying questions when necessary. As part of my introduction to the group, I disclosed my personal connection with Booker and his family, and the response of both groups was interesting. They did not seem fazed by my friendship with the mayor. In fact, some people in both groups said that they did not know the mayor and hoped that I would offer some insight into him during the session. Although I did not reveal any information about the mayor, their comments revealed that Booker remains an enigma to many of his constituents.

I asked both groups to begin by giving an outsider an impression of their city. The black respondents emphasized the idea that the city was progressing. A couple of respondents wanted outsiders to know that the city was improving. In particular, one respondent wanted to give credit to previous mayors, particularly Kenneth Gibson, for laying the foundation for the city's improvement. In contrast, the Latino respondents were more muted in their assessment, noting merely that there were good things and bad things about the city. One woman observed that when people acted shocked or horrified to hear that she was from Newark, she explained that not all Newark is bad; one just had to know which sections to avoid. Another respondent saw "slow improvement."

Since most of these respondents were long-term residents of the city, I asked them to provide their assessment of Sharpe James. Black respondents saw both good and bad in James and felt that he had helped some people but not others. When one person called James "a crook," another agreed with the assessment. Latino respondents also gave a mixed assessment of James, with some believing that he had been a good mayor. One respondent credited him with bringing the Prudential Center arena to Newark. Nonetheless, the respondents were generally disappointed in his leadership. One respondent described James as "flashy," and many agreed that Sharpe James ignored the Latino community.

Both groups discussed various aspects of the 2002 campaign. I asked them to describe the campaign. Whereas the Latino respondents used *aggressive* and *confusing* to describe the 2002 election, the black respondents used *age*, *experience*, *crime*, *money*, and *education*. One Latina woman recalled that the debate during the 2002 race was heated and that people she knew were afraid to reveal their vote preferences for fear of retribution. When I asked the Latino respondents about their reaction to the "black enough" debate, they said that they had tried to ignore it. One man likened that whole scenario to "crabs in a barrel."

The black focus group discussed class and empathy. Booker's most ardent critic, a man, explained that Booker's higher class status was really the issue of that campaign. In his view, whether or not Booker was black enough was not the issue. Rather, it was whether he had ever been "poor enough" to understand the plight of residents in Newark, a comment with which other respondents disagreed. Booker's most ardent supporter in the room, a college-educated immigrant woman, contended that such a perspective was shortsighted. But others agreed with the critic. One woman had lived in the Stella Wright Homes, a now-demolished housing project that was located behind the Brick Towers, where Booker lived for a number of years. She said that because she never saw Booker around the neighborhood, she did not really believe that he had actually lived there.

I asked voters to explain the outcome of 2002. The Latino voters in particular attributed the results to inertia, believing that voters were comfortable with the status quo. One black respondent claimed that Sharpe James had bought votes.

In general, the Latino respondents, who perceived Sharpe James to be unresponsive to their interests, were impressed that Booker actually campaigned in their community and did not leave Newark after losing in 2002. He also earned high marks for speaking Spanish, even from one Anglophone respondent. One woman even suggested that her mother thought that Booker was Latino because of his language skills and fair complexion.

When I asked them about the 2006 election, the respondents made a number of interesting points. What stood out most is that none of the Latino respondents realized that Booker had a challenger in 2006. When I asked them to give their impression of Ronald Rice Sr., they asked, "Who?" I asked both groups whether or not the 2006 election was an endorsement of Booker personally and/or a referendum on change. Both groups agreed that in 2006, the voters wanted a change. Four of the black respondents indicated that they personally liked Booker, too. One voter in the Latino group said that she voted for Booker " 'cause he's smart." Another attributed his success to the power of the Latino vote.

I asked each of the groups to grade Mayor Booker and his administration on a standard A through F scale based on their performance during the first two years of the term. On average, the groups gave the mayor approximately the same rating (C+), but the distribution of the grades in the groups was markedly different. Booker earned one A, two B's, three C's, and two D's in the African American group. He earned praise for reducing crime and for being out in the community. Those who were critical of him were either predisposed against him (voting for Ronald Rice Sr. in 2006) or upset with his actions. One particularly angry respondent was upset that Booker had laid off city employees (he had a relative who had been fired). Another woman charged that the city's program to find jobs for felons returning from prison was not working, and a man said that he wished the Booker administration would focus more on promoting black entrepreneurship.

Booker earned two B's and seven C's in the Latino group. In their view, he had not delivered on many of his campaign promises. As one woman put it, she gave him an "A for effort, but not for the job." One respondent praised Booker for his visibility, but in general, these voters were very concerned about crime in their neighborhoods (though admittedly, one person brought up a recent crime that had happened in the next town). Although they saw changes in the downtown, there still were gangs in their neighborhoods. One was critical of Booker's employees who "ain't doing their job," and they thought their taxes were too high for the few services they received.

The Latino respondents had a particularly skeptical opinion of the police. On the one hand, they were very concerned about police officers being fired because they wanted a larger police presence in their neighborhoods. They were critical, however, of the services the police were currently providing. They accused those officers who, they believed, lived outside Newark of being disinterested. One woman maintained that the police were around to give residents tickets but not around when serious crimes were committed. A little later, a respondent also questioned the community-policing tactics. In her view, the police were befriending criminals and letting their relatives get away with breaking the law.

The subject of city hall salaries and the hiring of out-of-towners came up in both groups. Both sets of respondents understood that sometimes the best-qualified job candidates were indeed from outside Newark. The salary concerns were minimal, although the Latino respondents were more concerned about overtime than salaries over $100,000. One black woman was convinced that Booker had not cut his own salary (he had). Voters in both groups were critical of the city for not training its own residents to fill positions staffed by out-of-towners. A respondent in the black focus group credited Sharpe James with giving locals a chance and allowing them to grow into their jobs. Respondents in the black group also emphasized that they thought that judging a person's qualifications solely by his or her formal education was insufficient. In their view, some uneducated people had experience that qualified them for certain jobs as much if not more than someone with a degree. For instance, one person noted that Oscar Sidney James was far too young and inexperienced to have been a councilman.

I asked the respondents if they had followed the stories about Booker's verbal gaffes from the year before (i.e., the "dark angel" and Judy Diggs incidents). No one in the Latino groups had been aware of them, and the black respondents had not heard of the "dark angel" comments. When I explained what happened, they did not think that the comments were racial. Two black respondents had heard about the Judy Diggs incident.

When I recapped the story for the rest of the group, even Booker's most ardent supporter had to agree that that was a misstep (though she gave Booker the benefit of the doubt that he had any malicious intent).

The findings of these focus groups thus reveal the extent to which regular voters share the opinions of Newark's political elite. The qualitative findings indicate that elites and regular voters think about some, but not all, of the same things. Black voters, like black elites, seem to be concerned about how Newark is portrayed to the outside world. Although they were not incensed by the "dark angel" comments, there was some sensitivity to the Judy Diggs incident. And both black and Latino voters recognized Sharpe James's shortcomings and acknowledged that the election of Cory Booker marked a positive change for the city.

The discussion of Booker's racial authenticity was especially enlightening. The respondent who articulated this position the best made it very clear that racial authenticity was really a proxy for class authenticity and empathy. Because Booker had a more privileged upbringing, the respondent was not convinced that he really understood poverty enough to be an effective champion of improving it. Moreover, that discussion demonstrated that, six years after the 2002 race, some black voters still questioned Booker's residency status and sincerity.

The Latino respondents' somewhat lukewarm assessments of the Booker administration were surprising. While they praised Booker for actually engaging their communities, they clearly wanted to see more improvement in the city. Latinos have been one of Booker's most reliable and enthusiastic voting blocs in the last decade, so the conventional wisdom would suggest that they would be very supportive of the mayor. Instead, the focus-group data indicate that while Latino voters like Booker, they may be supporting him only because they do not see any viable political alternatives. In fact, most of the Latino respondents indicated that they voted for Booker in 2006 only because they thought he was the only person running.

Conclusion

Cory Booker is in the difficult position of maintaining a precarious political balance. He clearly ruffled some feathers when he assumed the mayoralty, and he has yet to earn the trust or respect of some city elders. He may never win over some of them. His tenuous relationship with some of the potentates contributed to his reputation of being a climber and a bit arrogant. Therefore, anytime he or his staff makes mistakes, people tend to hold him to a higher standard.

Booker still enjoys the admiration of outside audiences, particularly the mainstream media. The evidence suggests, however, that the media's fascination with Booker has its advantages and disadvantages. Yes, Booker has a positive national profile, but the city of Newark and its residents still are stigmatized. While Booker sees his role as helping empower residents to take charge of their own communities, outsiders look to him as the agent of change. As such, Booker's mesmerizing stories unwittingly helped perpetuate the myth that Newark is a derelict slum that only he can save.

To be sure, it is mostly elites who spend their days and nights parsing the meaning of every little thing Booker says and does. Voters just want the garbage picked up and police protection. While the Booker administration has made some improvements, some voters claim not to see the fruit of all those efforts. It is especially troubling that some of the loudest criticism comes from the Latino community, one of Booker's most reliable voting blocs. Voters may continue to vote for Booker now because he is the only viable political option. But if a reasonable alternative emerges to challenge Booker, his electoral coalition could fall apart.

7

The Politics of Perception

Cory Booker in Local and State Affairs

IN THE LAST chapter, I examined Cory Booker's standing among minority voters in Newark. They gave Booker middling grades halfway into his first term. Some voters credited Booker with reducing crime, while others did not see any progress in the city.

Voters' opinions are extremely important because citizens have the power to defeat incumbents at the ballot. Elected officials also are important stakeholders in any politician's career. As Jeffrey Pressman noted in the 1970s, a mayor's effectiveness is partially a function of being able to harness his jurisdiction's political organizational structure to gain support for his agenda.[1] Thus, the local politician must forge strong relationships with other local and state politicians if he expects to be an effective legislator or executive.

In this chapter, I look at Cory Booker's relationship with local, county, and state officials. Just as residents have decisive impressions of the mayor, Booker's colleagues in elective office also judge him and decide each day whether and how to cooperate with him. Any strain in the working relationship between Booker and his colleagues can obstruct the passage of local and state legislation that could direct resources to Newarkers, and it could rob Booker of needed support should he decide to run for higher office.

Booker's relationship with his political colleagues is not formed in a vacuum, as his interactions on the state and local levels also affect other political actors in the region. If Booker is respected, then his allies will have an easier time winning the support of elites and voters when they run for office. But if Booker is not highly regarded among local and state elites, his endorsement will carry little weight and his coattails will be short. In this chapter, I look at these working relationships and Booker's role in the local and state elections held after his own election in 2006.

Elite Displacement and Comity: Do Black Political Entrepreneurs Play Well with Others?

Black political entrepreneurs who engage in elite displacement both implicitly and explicitly claim to be more effective than their predecessors at delivering goods and services to their constituents. They use their credentials as evidence of having the proper training to fulfill campaign promises. They pledge to govern with integrity so as not to embarrass their constituents or waste the public's time addressing scandals. More important, black political entrepreneurs imply that given their upbringing and crossover style, they are better equipped to build bridges with other power bases in order to pass legislation and carry out a policy agenda.

This strategy is logical, even effective, for entrepreneurial candidates, but what is the fallout of this strategy once a black political entrepreneur has been elected? Is elite displacement a scorched-earth policy? Can black political entrepreneurs attack and beat establishment blacks and then work with the friends and colleagues of the vanquished once they assume office?

Incorporation, Comity, and Contentious Campaigns

The experiences of vanguard minority elected officials can reveal the problems that black political entrepreneurs might face once in office. Even though the first black elected officials came to office with high hopes of being able to use their positions to continue the march toward equality, they were largely thwarted in their efforts. In earlier chapters, I discussed the structural factors that prevented black elected officials from being able to deliver all their campaign promises. These first black elected officials entered office during a period of industrial decline and reduced federal aid. Thus, they had fewer resources to carry out an ambitious political agenda.[2]

In addition to facing structural impediments to implementing desired policies, these officials sometimes faced hostile political environments even after they were elected. Rufus Browning, Dale Marshall, and David Tabb explain that just because minorities can be elected, they may not be empowered to pass and implement legislation and policies that would benefit their constituencies. If these elected officials are unicorporated, or not part of the dominant legislative coalition, they will constantly be outvoted. Thus, minorities who are elected but are not part of an electoral coalition face the prospect of being constantly frustrated and thwarted throughout their term in office.[3]

Harold Washington's challenges as mayor of Chicago are exemplary of those that the first black elected officials faced. Washington became Chicago's first black mayor in 1983, in one of the most racially polarizing elections ever in the city's history. Blacks turned out in unprecedented numbers and voted overwhelmingly for him, giving him the margin of victory.[4]

The racial vitriol did not die after the election. Whites still had enough power in the city to thwart much of Washington's agenda in his first term. Chicago has a strong city council that shares power with the mayor. Consequently, if a faction opposed to the mayor controls a majority of the seats on the city council, it can block the mayor's proposed legislation. In 1983, Washington ran without having aligned himself with any city council candidates, even though some supported him. The majority of the city council was aligned with its president, Ed Vrdolak, and he was overwhelmingly opposed to Mayor Washington's agenda. Accordingly, Vrdolak used his power to thwart most of Washington's efforts. Washington learned the mistakes of his isolation, however, and ran with a slate of candidates in 1987. But even though he succeeded in placing allies in a majority of the council seats in 1987, he was never able to use his new majority to push legislation through the council. He died shortly after his reelection in November 1987.[5]

As a case study, Harold Washington highlights the importance of having a critical mass of sympathetic political allies to advance a legislative agenda. Any politician can be elected, but if he is in the governing minority, he will have little chance of getting anything passed. The takeaway lesson from Chicago is that it is important to cultivate allies in order to have laws passed and policies implemented. Minority politicians, who rarely comprise a descriptive majority of any legislative body, must cultivate relationships outside their racial or ethnic group in order to advance their legislative agenda.[6] Sharing ideological and policy preferences goes a long way to help politicians join forces for a particular issue, especially for nonpartisan legislative bodies like Newark's municipal council.

Black political entrepreneurs market themselves as being less threatening than their black political forefathers. Often this strategy is effective, especially with white voters. Ruth Ann Strickland and Marcia Lynn Whicker argue, for instance, that in 1989 the success of Doug Wilder, David Dinkins, and Norm Rice owed a great deal to their nonthreatening images.[7] David Canon, Matthew Schousen, and Patrick Sellers found empirically that given a choice between a racialized and a deracialized black candidate, white voters in majority-black districts with large white populations chose the less threatening, deracialized candidate.[8]

An important question to ask in light of such findings is whether the strategy of elite displacement can backfire on black political entrepreneurs once they assume office. By positioning himself as nonthreatening, the black political entrepreneur implies a certain deficiency in his opponent, an established incumbent. These charges can be strengthened if the black political entrepreneur also suggests that the opponent lacks the technical skills to do his job well, has participated in unethical behavior, or is otherwise difficult to engage on a professional or social level. Although this strategy may work in the short term, it may end up placing the black political entrepreneur at a disadvantage when he enters office and must work with the friends and former colleagues of the person he beat. These allies may be reluctant—even hostile—to work with him if they think their former colleague was unfairly attacked. Moreover, if the black political entrepreneur truly believes the hype of framing his election as a battle of good versus evil and smart versus incompetent, he may be reluctant to work with members of the old political regime, even if they are willing to work with the new administration.

If a black political entrepreneur enters office with a wave of other, new, like-minded colleagues, then there are few consequences for having characterized the opposition as scoundrels. But if he enters office without political allies or with only tentative allies, he will have difficulty getting anything done. Since black political entrepreneurs tout their training as evidence of their ability to deliver on policy promises, it is important for them to be able to work with their colleagues. Otherwise, they will have nothing to show for their term of office.

An Embarrassment of Riches: Mandates and Incorporation Possibilities at the Outset of the Booker Administration

Cory Booker clearly understood the legislative impact of not being incorporated; in fact, it influenced his decision to run for mayor in 2002. Before running for mayor, he served one term as Newark's Central Ward councilman, and during his term, Booker had numerous problems getting anything passed by the city council. One member, the late Donald Tucker, sometimes aligned with Booker, but most of the time, Booker was outvoted. Councilman Luis Quintana, who was first elected to Newark's municipal council in

1994, said of those times, "Well, he [Booker] was in the minority, which is very difficult. And when you are in the minority, it is hard to be heard."[9]

Booker's accomplishments as a legislator accordingly were sparse. He was able to pass one ordinance, which required speed strips around schools to encourage motorists to slow down on streets where children were likely to run. He also was the cosponsor of first-source legislation, which required that any company doing business in Newark try to hire Newark residents first before advertising outside the city. This legislation was a nonbinding resolution, not an ordinance, however, and according to Booker and Deputy Mayor Stefan Pryor, it was not enforced by the James administration.[10]

Booker's frustration with constantly being outvoted led him to challenge Sharpe James for mayor in 2002. Booker explained that he had learned very quickly on the city council that legislators had no power because of Newark's strong mayoral system. In his view, mayors had the ability to initiate and implement the transformative changes they wanted to enact in the city, so the only way he could be effective was to become mayor.[11]

Many of Booker's council colleagues and political opponents, though, believed that he was motivated more by opportunism than by frustration at not being incorporated. Furthermore, they believed that he stepped out of turn when he challenged Sharpe James for mayor. In their minds, candidates for Newark mayor had to meet two criteria before they could consider running. First, prospective candidates should serve as ward councilmen; only then could they run for an at-large council seat. At that point, they could consider running for mayor. Many cited Sharpe James's own trajectory: he first served two terms as a ward councilman (South Ward) and then two terms as an at-large representative.[12]

Kenneth Gibson, to be sure, did not serve on the municipal council before being elected mayor in 1970, so there is no hard and fast precedent for serving on the municipal council before becoming mayor. Nevertheless, this criticism did not seem unreasonable, so I asked Booker and his 2006 campaign strategist, Carl Sharif, whether they had considered running for an at-large council seat in 2002 instead of mayor. Both cited the lack of incorporation as the main reason that they did not consider it seriously. Booker could have demonstrated his citywide appeal with an at-large win, but he still would have been outvoted.[13]

According to Booker, he did not take any official steps to run for mayor until late 2001. Most of his opponents assert, however, that they knew he would be running for mayor the moment he won the Central Ward council seat.[14] Because I interviewed them eight to ten years after that 1998 election, I can never know for sure whether they were using 20–20 hindsight, but their comments do reveal a certain transparency consistent with other assessments of Booker. Even if these officials did not know for certain that Booker was going to run for mayor, they sensed that he might. For his part, Booker maintains that he did not seriously think about running for mayor until after he staged a hunger strike at the Garden Spires high-rise halfway through his term as a city councilman:

> Everyday was combat, and that was what was so frustrating because all you wanted to do is try to do the right thing . . . maybe after the hunger strike and Sharpe James made those promises I began to think, "I need to run for mayor." It didn't, that didn't really crystallize until, fully until two years in.[15]

On May 9, 2006, Cory Booker won Newark's mayoralty with 72% of the popular vote. Such a decisive victory certainly was evidence of a mandate. At his victory party, Booker proclaimed, "We have made a statement that will reverberate throughout this city that we demand change."[16] It would remain to be seen, though, if he indeed did have a mandate.

Newark residents also elected municipal council members on May 9. Because the city conducts nonpartisan elections, a candidate must win a clear majority of the vote in order to win outright. The municipal council has four at-large seats, and voters may select up to four candidates for those seats. Under the 2006 election rules, it was extremely difficult for at-large candidates to win a clear majority of the votes cast (i.e., a majority of voters must vote for them), so those four seats were almost always decided in a runoff election among the top eight candidates from the general election. Booker had three at-large running mates for the May election. Two of them, Mildred Crump and Luis Quintana, finished in the top two, and the third, Carlos Gonzalez, finished fourth, behind the incumbent Ras Baraka, son of the poet Amiri Baraka, who had been appointed by Sharpe James to replace the late Donald Tucker. Quintana almost succeeded in winning the support of the majority of voters on May 9.

Two of the Booker team's candidates won their ward council seats outright on the first ballot. Dana Rone, the Central Ward council candidate who had lost to Charles Bell in a runoff in 2002, beat him handily in 2006 with 56% of the vote in a four-person field. Incumbent Augusto Amador, also a member of the Booker team, beat his challenger, Fernando Linhares, by a 2-to-1 margin. In the West Ward, team member Ronald Rice Jr., the son of Booker's mayoral opponent, won a plurality of the vote in a four-person field but was about eighty votes shy of winning an outright majority, so he had to compete against incumbent Mamie Bridgeforth in the June runoff. In the South Ward, Oscar Sidney James, the son of Booker operative Oscar James Sr., received forty-one fewer votes than John James, the son of Sharpe James, in a three-person field. Thus the South Ward race was forced into a runoff as well.

Booker did not field a candidate in the North Ward council race, in which incumbent Hector Corchado faced school advisory board member Aníbal Ramos. Corchado had once been a Booker ally and a good friend of Booker's trusted aide Pablo Fonseca, and some of Booker's staff had maintained close relationships with members of Corchado's staff.[17] Ramos also had some ties to Booker. He had run successfully on the same Booker-backed school advisory board slate with Booker's longtime running mate and Central Ward council candidate Dana Rone in 2003. Moreover, Ramos had the support of Steve Adubato, the powerful boss of the North Ward Democratic machine. When Ramos won in a landslide on the first ballot, most people assumed that he, as a young up-and-comer in his own right, would align with Booker. Indeed, he appeared onstage at Booker's victory rally on the night of the May election.

After the election, Booker sought to add another at-large candidate to his slate of candidates, to make a clean sweep of the council seats. He interviewed Councilwomen Bessie Walker and Gayle Chaneyfield-Jenkins, who finished sixth and seventh, respectively, on the first ballot; Councilman Ras Baraka, who finished third; and Freeholder Donald Payne Jr., the son of Congressman Donald Payne, who finished fifth.[18] After his conversations with each of these potential candidates, Booker, on the advice of his strategists, named Donald Payne Jr. as his running mate.

In the June runoff, all four Booker team at-large candidate won decisively, as did Rice Jr. and James II in their ward races. Booker thus succeeded in sweeping both the mayoral and the council races. If his strong showing in the mayoral election did not convince observers that he had a mandate, surely the sweep of all the council seats was proof that he had the residents' overwhelming support to enact the changes he had been promising for four years. In June 2006, it seemed as though Cory Booker had long political coattails, that his endorsement would be necessary for any political aspirant.

The South Secedes: The 2007 State Assembly and State Senate Contests

Booker's first real electoral test came in 2007. In the 2000s, most of Newark was divided between two state legislative districts, the Twenty-Eighth and the Twenty-Ninth Districts. In New Jersey, each district has one state senator and two assembly members. In 2006, Sharpe James represented the Twenty-Ninth District in the New Jersey state senate,[19] and Ronald Rice Sr. represented the Twenty-Eighth District. Newark's mayors need to maintain excellent professional relationships with their state legislators, who funnel needed state funds to the city. In their capacity as state senators, both James and Rice had the potential to do great damage to Booker's political agenda. Booker's campaign staffers were concerned that neither James nor Rice could be trusted to be a forceful advocate for the city if being such an advocate would help Booker's political career, although during his talk with me, Ronald Rice Sr. disputed this.[20] To that end, many expected that Booker would recruit his own candidates to replace the incumbent state senators and state assembly members, in order to ensure that he had allies in Trenton who would push his legislation through the state legislature.

Sharpe James announced on April 9, 2007, that he would not seek reelection. Three serious candidates emerged to vie for his state senate seat. Assemblyman William Payne, the brother of Congressman Donald Payne Sr. and the uncle of Councilman Donald Payne Jr., wanted to move up from the state assembly to the state senate, believing that he was the best candidate for the seat. Not only was he a long-serving assemblyman, but he surmised that the district's demographics (the district was majority black) favored him as a black candidate.[21]

Newark Councilman Luis Quintana also was a contender for this seat. In 2003 Booker had backed him for the Democratic nomination for the state senate seat, although he did not win. Quintana ran in part because he wanted to challenge the power of the North Ward Democratic Party boss, Steve Adubato. In Quintana's view, Adubato, who is Italian American, wielded too much control in the Latino community, and he hoped that his election would demonstrate to Latinos that they did not need Adubato's blessing to win elective office.[22] The final prospective candidate was M. Teresa Ruiz, who had worked for years with Adubato.

The Payne family had had a good, long-standing relationship with Adubato for years, and they believed they could persuade Adubato to endorse Payne's candidacy. Adubato, however, wanted Ruiz to run as a candidate because there were no Latinos in the New Jersey State Senate, whereas there were five black state senators. In his estimation, it was time for Latinos to be represented.[23]

Payne did not disagree about the need for Latino representation; he just questioned why a black had to give up a seat in a majority-black district in order to make room for a Latino state senator. He maintained that if Adubato wanted to ensure Latino descriptive representation, he should push Passaic and Patterson, two heavily Latino cities, to elect Latino state senators.[24]

Adubato did not see it that way. Part of his motivation was personal. Two decades earlier, he had convinced his brother Michael to give up his state assembly seat to allow William Payne to run for office. Steve Adubato saw that blacks were the numerical majority of the district and were underrepresented at the state level. Consequently, he thought that it was time to ensure descriptive representation, even if it cost his brother his seat. Adubato saw the exact same situation in 2007, and he expected Payne to be just as charitable as Michael Adubato had been so many years before.[25]

Cory Booker appears to have been a minor player in the Twenty-Ninth District state senate fight. He and Adubato did have several private conversations about this contest. Booker agreed with Adubato to support Teresa Ruiz for the state senate seat, and he asked him to consider younger candidates for the assembly seats: local Portuguese American businessman Albert Coutinho, who had a friendly relationship with Adubato ally Joseph Parlavecchio, the chairman of the East Ward Democratic Committee; and African American attorney L. Grace Spencer, a longtime South Ward Democratic district leader and a Booker supporter.[26]

Payne and Quintana chose not to run against Ruiz in the June 2007 Democratic primary, so Ruiz had no opposition and won the primary easily. Instead, both Payne and Quintana decided to run as independent candidates in the general election, and many people believed that they actually coordinated their campaigns. To outsiders, it looked as though Quintana ran in an attempt to split the district's Latino vote, which theoretically would boost Payne's chances of victory, although there is no proof that Quintana and Payne ever had such an agreement. In addition to Quintana and Payne, Ruiz also had two more independents and one Republican challenger in the general election. Overall, Ruiz easily won her race, taking 56% of the vote; Luis Quintana won 20% of the vote; and William Payne won 17% of the vote.

A closer examination of the vote reveals some ward polarization. Table 7.1 shows that Ruiz dominated the race in Newark's North and East Wards, winning nearly two-thirds of the vote there. But William Payne won a plurality of votes in the South Ward, beating Ruiz by almost fifteen percentage points.

There was similar polarization in Twenty-Ninth District State Assembly race. In the primary, incumbent Wilfredo Caraballo faced the Booker-Adubato ticket of Grace Spencer and Albert Coutinho. Spencer and Coutinho beat Caraballo decisively to win the party nomination. In the general election, though, former Newark councilwoman-at-large Bessie Walker launched an independent bid for an assembly seat.

As in the state senate race, the contest was not even close. Table 7.2 records the election results by ward for the state assembly race. Grace Spencer and Albert Coutinho won more than twice the number of votes of their nearest competitor, Bessie Walker. But in the South Ward, Bessie Walker edged out Grace Spencer for a first-place finish.

It would be easy to overlook the importance of the South Ward results in the context of the overall electoral outcome of these elections. But

Table 7.1

Twenty-Ninth District State Senate Vote by Newark Ward, November 2007

	Teresa Ruiz	Luis Quintana	William Payne	Total number of ballots cast
North Ward	3,832 (64.4%)	1,511 (25.4%)	351 (5.9%)	5,948
South Ward	850 (30.3%)	509 (18.1%)	1,258 (44.8%)	2,805
East Ward	1,805 (65.9%)	468 (17.1%)	186 (6.8%)	2,738
Central Ward	1,914 (46.9%)	816 (20.0%)	1,085 (26.6%)	4,079

Source: Essex County clerk's office, author's compilation.
Notes: Ward totals do not include absentee and provisional ballots totals, which are not compiled by ward. Ruiz beat Quintana by two votes in the Twenty-Ninth District's one West Ward. Although there were six candidates in this race, the others were excluded from the table because they received only a few votes.

Table 7.2

Twenty-Ninth District State Assembly Vote by Newark Ward, November 2007

	Grace Spencer	Albert Coutinho	Bessie Walker	Carlotta Hall	Total number of ballots cast
North Ward	3,459 (58.2%)	3,467 (58.3%)	1,270 (21.4%)	1,131 (19.0%)	5,948
South Ward	1,303 (46.5%)	935 (33.3%)	1,345 (48.0%)	926 (33.0%)	2,805
East Ward	1,799 (65.7%)	1,986 (72.5%)	333 (12.2%)	273 (10.0%)	2,738
Central Ward	2,180 (53.4%)	1,938 (47.5%)	1,495 (36.7%)	924 (22.7%)	4,079
Total number of votes	10,022 (57.9%)	9,570 (55.3%)	4,687 (27.1%)	3,419 (19.8%)	17,296

Source: Essex County clerk's office, author's compilation.
Notes: The total includes the Twenty-Ninth Legislative District's one West Ward and the absentee and provisional ballots, which were not reported by the ward. Only the top four of the ten candidates in this race are listed in the table. Because voters could choose two candidates for this election, vote totals do not add up to 100%.

when considering the electoral results in light of the campaign's division of power, the weakness of the South Ward becomes more significant. Steve Adubato's machine was in charge of mobilizing voters in the North and East Wards. Parts of the Central Ward were once part of the North Ward before redistricting, so Adubato's machine had influence there as well. Booker's machine, led by Oscar James Sr., was responsible for turning out the vote in the South Ward. To insiders looking at these election results, Booker's operation seems to have been the weak link.

The South Ward has symbolic importance in the black political community. It is Newark's largest ward and also the home base of the city's black political community. Sharpe James lives in the South Ward; the Payne family lives in the South Ward; and the last three municipal council presidents were from the South Ward. When Booker's apartment complex in the Central Ward was condemned, he moved to the South Ward. Thus, the Booker-backed candidates' weak showing in state legislative races in the South Ward illustrated Booker's political weakness in the black community.

The Booker-Adubato slate was very sensitive to his weakness in the community, and the campaign tried to distance itself from Booker in the South Ward. Whereas campaign signs for Booker-backed candidates in the neighboring Twenty-Eighth Legislative Districts proudly proclaimed Booker's endorsement, signs in the South Ward did not mention Booker's name at all.

Booker's potential political weakness was even more apparent in the Twenty-Eighth District state senate race. This race had special symbolic importance because Ronald Rice Sr. was the targeted incumbent. A Rice victory in this election would be a partial vindication of his landslide loss to Booker in the 2006 mayoral election. Consequently, Booker would appear politically weak if he could not knock Ronald Rice Sr. out of his state senate seat.

A little more than a fourth of Newark's electoral districts were in the Twenty-Eighth Legislative District during the 2000s. (The Twenty-Ninth District was composed of only Newark districts; the Twenty-Seventh Legislative District included twelve West Ward districts). The rest of the district included the towns of Irvington, Bloomfield, and Belleville. Booker's foray into endorsement politics in this district, then, would test not only his political influence in Newark but also his influence beyond the city limits as well.

Booker and his team selected Bilal Beasley to run against Ronald Rice

Sr. Beasley, an Irvington city councilman, was a longtime friend of Carl Sharif, Booker's 2006 campaign strategist and political adviser. Booker also endorsed Cleopatra Tucker and Ralph Caputo to replace Assemblyman Craig Stanley and Assemblywoman Oadline Truitt. Caputo is from Belleville, which had never had any descriptive representation in the state legislature. Tucker is the widow of Donald Tucker, the long-term Newark councilman and assemblyman who sometimes supported Booker when they served together on the municipal council. Incumbent Craig Stanley is Donald Payne Sr.'s nephew and protégé. According to Steve Adubato, Booker did consult with him about the assembly races in this district. Before this meeting, Adubato had planned on endorsing Truitt in particular, but Booker persuaded him to change his mind.[27]

The assembly races were close, but Tucker and Caputo did manage to win the Democratic nominations. Table 7.3 shows the primary results. Stanley and Truitt posted strong showings in Newark's South and West Wards, which make up the majority of Newark's electoral districts in this district, while Tucker and Caputo won in the North and Central Wards. Not surprisingly, Caputo did very well in his native Belleville, followed by Tucker. Caputo won a majority of the voters' support in Bloomfield, while Tucker performed well in Irvington.

Table 7.3

Twenty-Eighth District Democratic State Assembly Vote by Jurisdiction, June 2007

	Cleopatra Tucker	Ralph Caputo	Craig Stanley	Oadline Truitt	Total number of ballots cast
Newark North Ward	209 (65.3%)	234 (73.1%)	69 (21.6%)	55 (17.2%)	320
Newark South Ward	795 (42.3%)	656 (34.9%)	1,026 (54.6%)	1,063 (56.6%)	1,879
Newark West Ward	786 (37.0%)	699 (32.9%)	1,247 (58.8%)	1,225 (57.7%)	2,122
Newark Central Ward	268 (53.1%)	251 (49.7%)	220 (43.6%)	214 (42.4%)	505
Belleville	791 (57.1%)	1,029 (74.3%)	364 (26.3%)	276 (19.9%)	1,385
Bloomfield	1,155 (44.4%)	1,357 (52.1%)	1,164 (44.7%)	1,053 (40.5%)	2,603
Irvington	1,901 (50.6%)	1,849 (49.2%)	1,686 (44.9%)	1,548 (41.2%)	3,759
Total number of votes	5,960 (47.0%)	6,112 (48.2%)	5,827 (45.9%)	5,478 (43.2%)	12,689

Source: Essex County clerk's office, author's compilation.
Notes: Although the Newark ward results do not include absentee and provisional ballots, which the wards did not report, those ballots are included in the total. The total number of ballots reflects all five Democratic candidates. Individual vote totals are for the four major candidates only. Because voters could choose two candidates for this election, vote totals do not add up to 100%.

The primary results for the Twenty-Eighth District in Newark's South and West Wards correspond to the South Ward showing in the Twenty-Ninth District races. The South Ward showed some weakness, as though its residents deliberately voted against Booker-backed candidates.

The state senate race further reinforced the perception of Booker's political weakness in the South Ward. As table 7.4 demonstrates, Rice decisively beat Beasley in this primary. Although Beasley posted strong showings in Newark's North Ward, that represents only a small portion of the district. While he won his native Irvington, many of his close friends thought that he underperformed there, especially compared with Ronald Rice's showing in Newark's West Ward, his home base. Rice won nearly 65% of the votes in that ward, as well as 59% in Newark's South Ward, whereas Beasley won only 55% of the votes in Irvington.

All three Democratic primary winners in the Twenty-Eighth Legislative District were well positioned to win in the November general election. Craig Stanley and Oadline Truitt did not mount independent challenges for their assembly seats, and both nominees posted strong victories against their Republican challengers in the general election. The Essex County clerk's records show that Tucker and Caputo defeated their challengers by 800 to 1,200 votes and that Rice beat his Republican opponent by a margin of more than three to one.

On the night of the June primary, Booker tried to place a good spin on the primary results. The Booker-Adubato team held their victory party at the Robert Treat Hotel. By the time I arrived at the hotel, very few people were there. Booker and some of his advisers, as well as key Adubato advisers remained. I went over to Booker to express my condolences for having lost. "Five out of six ain't bad," he said.

Five out of six was bad, though. It was a huge psychological blow to not defeat Ronald Rice Sr. One of the Booker team's workers spoke very candidly that night, telling me that the election results made Booker look like a "lightweight." He acknowledged that the only reason the Booker team won five out of six races was because he was aligned with Steve Adubato, who clearly had the better field operations in that election.

A Political Opening? Newark and the 2008 Democratic Presidential Primary

Booker redeemed himself in future elections, but he still had trouble. New Jersey held its Democratic presidential primary in February 2008. As cochair of New Jersey for Barack Obama, Cory Booker was expected to

Table 7.4

Twenty-Eighth District Democratic State Senate Vote by Jurisdiction, June 2007

	Bilal Beasley		Ronald Rice Sr.		Total number of ballots cast
Newark North Ward	224	(70.0%)	81	(25.3%)	320
Newark South Ward	737	(39.2%)	1,106	(58.9%)	1,879
Newark West Ward	711	(33.5%)	1,376	(64.8%)	2,122
Newark Central Ward	252	(49.9%)	243	(48.1%)	505
Belleville	742	(53.6%)	556	(40.1%)	1,385
Bloomfield	1,133	(43.5%)	1,306	(50.2%)	2,603
Irvington	2,059	(54.8%)	1,636	(43.5%)	3,759
Total number of votes	5,897	(46.5%)	6,372	(50.2%)	12,689

Source: Essex County clerk's office, author's compilation.
Notes: Although the Newark ward results do not include absentee and provisional ballots, which the wards did not report, those ballots are included in the total. Because the vote percentages do not include spoiled or blank ballots, vote totals do not add up to 100%.

mobilize as many voters as possible for him. Presumably, as mayor of Essex County's county seat, Booker could deliver the county to Obama.

Table 7.5 presents Essex County's primary results by town (Newark's results are broken down by ward). Overall, Booker did deliver the county to Obama, only one of two counties in New Jersey that he won. Hillary Clinton won the New Jersey primary by approximately ten percentage points.[28] Table 7.5 shows that Obama was able to win Essex County by posting decisive margins in the more densely populated (and heavily African American) urban centers such as Newark, Irvington, Orange, and East Orange, whereas Clinton won twelve of the county's twenty-two jurisdictions.

A deeper examination of Newark's results also indicates some geographic polarization in the primary contest. Hillary Clinton beat Barack Obama by more than two to one in the North Ward and by more than three to one in the East Ward. There are a couple of explanations for this outcome. Steve Adubato, who controls the North Ward Democratic machine and whose ally runs the East Ward Democratic operation, endorsed Hillary Clinton. I also asked my Latino focus-group respondents, nearly all North Ward residents, to explain their choice. All but one of them voted for Clinton. The group, which was largely female, said that they voted for her because they wanted to support a female candidate.

The Booker camp also disagreed on how much credit Booker could actually take for that primary victory. Jermaine James, then Booker's deputy chief of staff, noted at a fund-raiser that Booker would benefit politically

Table 7.5

Essex County's Democratic Presidential Primary Vote by Jurisdiction, February 2008

	Hillary Clinton		Barack Obama		Total number of ballots cast
Newark North Ward	5,642	(68.4%)	2,529	(30.7%)	8,246
Newark South Ward	2,504	(25.8%)	7,411	(76.4%)	9,694
Newark East Ward	3,293	(77.5%)	938	(22.1%)	4,249
Newark West Ward	2,398	(29.0%)	5,846	(70.6%)	8,281
Newark Central Ward	2,995	(40.8%)	5,471	(74.4%)	7,349
Belleville	2,836	(71.2%)	1,061	(26.6%)	3,985
Bloomfield	3,618	(53.5%)	3,021	(44.6%)	6,768
Caldwell	507	(49.8%)	468	(45.9%)	1,019
Cedar Grove	910	(61.7%)	525	(35.6%)	1,475
East Orange	3,183	(24.9%)	9,518	(74.5%)	12,769
Essex Fells	107	(47.8%)	109	(48.7%)	224
Fairfield	350	(74.9%)	149	(31.9%)	467
Glen Ridge	704	(43.6%)	872	(54.1%)	1,613
Irvington	2,677	(30.1%)	6,563	(73.7%)	8,904
Livingston	3,222	(62.9%)	1,780	(34.7%)	5,126
Maplewood	2,504	(36.6%)	4,213	(61.6%)	6,840
Millburn	1,800	(55.0%)	1,562	(47.7%)	3,273
Montclair	3,791	(33.8%)	7,290	(65.0%)	11,214
North Caldwell	433	(58.4%)	297	(40.1%)	741
Nutley	2,200	(62.7%)	1,202	(34.3%)	3,509
Orange	1,464	(27.7%)	3,777	(71.5%)	5,280
Roseland	513	(56.0%)	365	(39.8%)	916
South Orange	1,646	(33.5%)	3,075	(62.5%)	4,919
Verona	1,092	(52.5%)	936	(45.0%)	2,079
West Caldwell	787	(55.5%)	586	(41.4%)	1,417
West Orange	4,471	(48.8%)	4,487	(49.0%)	9,165
Total Votes	55,939	(42.9%)	74,570	(57.2%)	130,431

Source: Essex County clerk's office, author's compilation.

Notes: Although the Newark ward results do not include absentee and provisional ballots, which the wards did not report, those ballots are included in the total. The total number of ballots cast include spoiled votes and votes for candidates who dropped out before the primary, so percentages do not add up to 100%.

from the primary results, suggesting that he could take credit for having delivered a key voting bloc. But others had a less sanguine point of view. Bobby Marshall has more than twenty years of field mobilization experience and worked on the Obama mobilization effort in Newark. He told me that mobilizing for Obama on Super Tuesday was the easiest get-out-the-vote (GOTV) project he had ever had, so easy, in fact, that he did not even feel he could take credit for an Obama victory. He described voters as "literally skipping" to the polling place on the day of the primary. To him, black voters in particular were independently motivated to participate in this historic nomination process and did not need prodding from him or Cory Booker to get them out to the polls.

Hardened Retrenchment? The June 2008 Primaries

Booker had two more chances to flex his political muscle in 2008. In the June primaries, Democratic voters would select the nominees for Essex County freeholder as well as elect members of the ward's Democratic committees, the district leaders. District leaders are the lifeblood of Newark's Democratic Party organization. They are often the first line of defense in addressing constituents' concerns, so political candidates try to get their support, which is extremely valuable politically.

The Booker team's long-term goal was to get as many sympathetic district leaders on the ward committees as possible. Most of the existing district leaders had held office since the James administration and were loyal to the incumbent ward party chairs, who were not Booker acolytes. The South Ward committee was regarded as loyal to Congressman Donald Payne Sr.; Steve Adubato's wife headed the North Ward committee; Ronald Rice Sr. ran the West Ward committee; and Joseph Parlavecchio, a friend of Steve Adubato's, controlled the East Ward committee. Starting in 2006, the Booker campaign, led by Oscar James Sr., had begun grooming district leader candidates to run against incumbents. The goal was to win a majority of the district leader seats in the hope that these new leaders would elect a chair that was hand chosen by Booker.

Oscar James Sr. first attempted to transform the South Ward Democratic Committee in June 2006 but was unsuccessful, with Booker-backed candidates losing most of the races. The defeat could be attributed to hasty planning. The first district leader contest came right after the mayoral election and the week before the municipal council runoff election. With more important races left to decide, the majority of the Booker campaign's attention was focused on getting Oscar Sidney James elected as South Ward councilman.

The Booker team had two years to plan for the next district leader races. In 2008, they targeted not only the South Ward but also the Central and East Wards. Unfortunately, the two years of planning were for naught. The Booker-backed challengers lost more than 80% of the district leader races in the South Ward, and the Booker team's candidates won a little over 25% of the district leader races in the Central Ward. In the East Ward, Booker operatives supported those candidates who were denied the party line by the ward party chairman, Joseph Parlavecchio, but the Parlavecchio-backed candidates won. The local media interpreted such a decisive and overwhelming loss as a huge embarrassment and psychological blow for the administration.[29]

Two related incidents further embarrassed the mayor. Before the 2008 primary election, Booker and the party establishment had a dispute over the selection of potential freeholder nominees. In New Jersey's primary system, the parties are not completely neutral but are allowed to give their preferred candidates prime ballot space, or to put them on the ballot's "party line," usually line A. Other candidates are listed below the party line, so not being listed on the party line connotes outsider status. If an incumbent does not appear on the party line, that usually means that he or she is being disciplined or shunned by more influential members of the party.

Historically, the mayor of Newark has had some influence over the party's selection of freeholders, and at least one freeholder candidate is the mayor's handpicked nominee. Johnny Jones, for instance, was Sharpe James's selected freeholder during his administration.

Booker therefore expected that the Essex County Democratic Committee would be receptive to his recommendations for freeholder candidates,[30] and he chose Newark's director of constituent services Terrance Bankston to run for the Democratic nomination. Bankston, who was born in 1982, started working with Booker shortly after he graduated from Bloomfield College. He had been an active student leader who began his political life by running for a seat on Newark's school advisory board. After finishing college, Bankston started working for Booker's campaign, and in 2006 he served as the director of the Booker team's South Ward field operation.

Bankston's meteoric rise to the top of the Booker administration did not come without some controversy. Many regarded him as green, and a number of incidents confirmed this suspicion. During the 2006 campaign, for instance, Bankston's appointment was overshadowed by the fact that Oscar James Sr., the deputy campaign manager in charge of the South, Central, and West Ward campaigns, maintained an office in the South Ward campaign office. Although Bankston was the ward director, it was clear to anyone who walked in that office (as I did just about every other Saturday in the spring of 2006) that Oscar James Sr. was in charge. Moreover, Bankston was at the center of some of the Booker administration's public controversies. For example, his office was the one accused in a *New York Times* exposé of not following up on citizens' complaints made during Mayor Booker's office hours.[31]

The alternative to Bankston was Rufus Johnson, the chief of staff to State Senator Ronald Rice Sr. Johnson, who had worked with the senator for nearly a quarter century, was well known to party insiders. The party eventually decided to give the party line to Johnson instead of Bankston.

For the then Central Ward party chair Blonnie Watson, East Ward party chair Joseph Parlaveccho, and County party chair Phil Thigpen, the choice was easy. Bankston had no experience, whereas Johnson had paid his dues, worked his way up the ranks, and had been a party loyalist for more than two decades. They saw Booker's selection of Bankston—a neophyte—as an insult.[32]

Bankston's reaction to not being given the party line probably did not help, either. It is not unheard of for candidates, even incumbents, to not get the party line. When they do not get the party line, they often run off the line, and sometimes they win. Sharpe James allegedly had Ronald Rice Sr. removed from the party line when he ran for renomination to the state senate in 1999, the year after he unsuccessfully challenged James for Newark's mayoralty. Rice Sr. still won the nomination. Similarly, Montclair state senator Nia Gill fell out of grace with the party establishment in 2003 and still managed to win renomination.[33] A party rebuff, then, does not have to spell the end to a person's candidacy.

It did in this case, though. After not receiving the party line for freeholder, Bankston dropped out of the race entirely. He neither ran for the Democratic nomination nor made plans to run as an independent in the general election. He told me that he decided to run for office later, perhaps in another position.[34] By not staying in the race, Bankston reinforced party regulars' low estimation of him.

There were even greater implications for Booker's reputation. It already was embarrassing enough that Ronald Rice Sr.'s aide was selected as a candidate over his protégé. But for Bankston to not continue to run suggested that Booker was not confident of his ability to take on the county Democratic apparatus. If he were convinced that Bankston would make an excellent freeholder, then Booker could have used his substantial war chest to run him independent of the line. Not continuing to run thus was ammunition for critics who already thought that Booker was weak. In that context, the fight over the freeholder nomination was a game of chicken, and Booker gave in first.

Another fight focused on the chairmanship of the Central Ward Democratic Committee. Booker's deputy chief of staff, Jermaine James, challenged the incumbent chairwoman and freeholder Blonnie Watson for the job. Even though Watson had not been a consistent Booker supporter over the years, she occasionally did side with him. For instance, she endorsed Teresa Ruiz, Grace Spencer, and Albert Coutinho in the Twenty-Ninth District assembly and state senate races in 2007.[35] James, however, had worked for the mayor for nearly a decade and could be counted on to organize this crucial ward for Booker in future elections.

The fight between Booker/James and Watson allowed for a third candidate to emerge in this chairmanship battle. Dwight Brown,[36] a top deputy to Steve Adubato at the North Ward Cultural Center, entered the fray as an alternative to both James and Watson. After an intense debate among the ward committee members, Brown won the election.[37] Given his connection to Steve Adubato, it is easy to interpret his victory as a victory for Adubato vis-à-vis Booker.

The Central Ward again became an electoral battleground during the 2008 presidential election. In Newark, the legal troubles of former Councilwoman Dana Rone necessitated a special election to replace her on the municipal council. Rone had pleaded guilty to obstruction of justice after she got into an altercation with a Newark police officer who, she felt, had unfairly arrested her nephew. In accordance with a New Jersey statute, she was forced to resign her seat in July 2008. Booker did not name an interim council member to the seat but instead called for a special election, to be held on November 4. Sixteen candidates entered the race to succeed Rone, including her mother, Mary Rone; Charles Bell, the incumbent whom Dana Rone had defeated in 2006; planning board member Nakia White; and union leader Eddie Osborne. The race revealed a number of cleavages. There was disagreement about whether a young or an old person should represent the ward, given the ward's large senior citizen population. In addition, Rone's resignation from the municipal council left only one woman in that body, so some thought that a woman should replace her.[38]

Many political figures weighed in on the race. Mildred Crump backed Nakia White in order to support another female candidate. Steve Adubato supported Charles Bell. Even Sharpe James, who had gone to prison in September 2008 on a corruption conviction, endorsed Bell and sent a campaign donation. While Booker initially refused to endorse a candidate, in October he came out in support of Eddie Osborne, the union leader, who raised $115,000. Booker's efforts were to no avail, however; Bell came out of retirement to beat a crowded field of candidates on the first ballot.[39]

Implications

In late June 2008, not long after the Central Ward Democratic chair's race was settled, I spoke with Jermaine James at a fund-raiser for Cory Booker.

I asked for his interpretation of the results of the district leader races. He reminded me that although Booker had never had the support of the ward Democratic committees, that did not stop him from winning two elections in ten years. While James acknowledged that it would have been nice to have the support of the party apparatus, he said that Booker could survive politically without it. He was especially confident after Barack Obama was nominated for president. Because Booker was Obama's New Jersey cochair, James believed that Booker could bypass the local party apparatus. He pointed out that Obama's New Jersey campaign manager was at this particular fund-raiser, and he regarded this fact as proof of Booker's national cachet. James noted that the story might be different if Hillary Clinton had won the nomination, but with Obama at the top of the ticket, he predicted an easier ride for Booker. Jermaine James seems to have forgotten the age-old wisdom of Tip O'Neill: all politics is local.

The local election results in 2007 and 2008 demonstrated the limits of Cory Booker's political influence in the first part of his first term. His coattails shrank after the 2006 municipal runoff election. That he had difficulty extending his political reach beyond Newark City Hall demonstrates the resilience of the old political establishment in Newark and in Essex County in general.

Booker's actions in this series of elections could also have reverberations in future dealings with other political leaders. Many in the old political establishment saw Booker as picking unnecessary political fights with them. They claim that they were not predisposed to oppose him all the time but that it would be hard to forget his actions, particularly in the 2008 district leader races.[40] If Booker needed their support for anything later on, they might be difficult to win over.[41]

The election results also called into question the balance of power between Cory Booker and Steve Adubato, the legendary political boss. After the 2007 state legislative races, Adubato was widely rumored to have boasted that he was politically stronger than Cory Booker. He was very reserved in my interview with him, so I cannot confirm this, but many political insiders on the state and local levels agreed with him. After the 2007 elections, Luis Quintana believed that Steve Adubato, his nemesis, emerged politically stronger than Booker. Most insiders I interviewed in 2008, including pro-Booker people, shared Quintana's view, especially after the additional losses. They believed that the losses were a problem and represented a political vulnerability for Cory Booker.[42]

Political insiders from outside Newark also have been paying attention to the length of Booker's coattails, and they, too, noticed that they were short in 2007 and 2008. They may not go so far as to say that Steve Adubato is more powerful than Booker, but they do acknowledge that Booker was tarnished a little as a result of the 2007 elections.[43]

That said, the political troubles of Booker's first two and a half years of office did not completely dim his star in statewide politics. Although Assemblyman Thomas Giblin warned that Booker needed to tend to matters at home if he wanted a loftier political career,[44] Steve DeMicco, a veteran New Jersey political consultant and political strategist in Jon Corzine's 2005 and 2009 New Jersey gubernatorial campaigns, confided that Booker was on Corzine's short list as a potential running mate in his 2009 reelection bid.[45] Booker had long enjoyed a reasonably warm relationship with Corzine, even when Corzine could not publicly back Booker. DeMicco explained that Booker was still very popular within the state and that the lieutenant governor's office might have been a way to bypass the difficulties he had at the local level. He explained it as the difference between having a "constituency of one" (the governor) versus a constituency of 300,000 (the residents of Newark).[46]

DeMicco was not the only New Jersey political operative who believed that Booker's problems were temporary and confined to Newark. South Jersey political boss George Norcross contended as well that Booker's political problems were merely temporary. When asked about his problems with black voters, particularly those in the South Ward, Norcross commented, "I would say that they are a challenge he has while governing the city of Newark. Outside of that, it's irrelevant."[47] I encouraged Mr. Norcross to elaborate on his statement.

> I know from public opinion polling that Cory is enormously popular within the African American community, the Latino community, the white community. I believe that the difficulties that he experiences in Newark are political in nature and have a lot to do with legacy issues involving Newark. That's not the case outside of that pocket, if you will. And I think that become largely irrelevant outside of him serving as mayor.[48]

The Latino Question

What is probably most troubling about the political results of the 2007/2008 election cycle is that it calls into question Booker's rock-solid support in the Latino community. Booker's strongest performances in the last two mayoral elections were in Newark's North and East Wards, the heart of the city's Latino and Portuguese communities. Because these wards were assumed to be his base, Booker would have to shore up his support among blacks in order to win and stay in office. But the election results of 2007 and 2008 refute that popular wisdom, as Booker's allies carried those wards in 2007 and 2008 only when Booker was aligned with Steve Adubato. The implications for these results are far greater than serving to inflate Steve Adubato's ego or feed the impression that Adubato wields more power than Booker does. Rather, these findings suggest that Booker is not permanently guaranteed widespread electoral support in the Latino community.

In her study of interracial minority politics, Karen Kaufmann identifies New York and Los Angeles as models of two different forms of racial politics. New York's politics are explicitly racialized. Its old ethnic political machines socialized politicians, activists, and interest-group leaders into recognizing that different racial and ethnic groups are legitimate stakeholders in city government and need descriptive representation. As such, it is not unusual in New York and similar cities for elected and appointed officials to be very aware of proportionality when selecting political appointees and candidates for office. This makes New York politics seem inherently conflictual, as groups vie for the scarce resources of political seats. Los Angeles, in contrast, is a reformist city that never had a political machine. As such, racial and ethnic stakeholders cannot make the same type of descriptive demands for representation. Thus, while Los Angeles has racial politics and even racial tensions, it appears on the surface to be less conflictual, whereas there actually is no institutional mechanism to address descriptive concerns.[49]

Newark, with its long-standing political machines and history of ethnic politics stretching back well before 1970, fits the New York model much better than it does the Los Angeles model. As such, it should not come as a surprise that Latinos are demanding greater political power commensurate with their numbers. According to the U.S. Census Bureau's 2005 American Community Survey, 32% of the city's population is Latino.[50] In 2007, the Census Bureau reported that Newark has been the fastest-growing major city in the Northeast since 2000. Between 1990 and 2000, the Latino population in the Newark metropolitan area increased by 16%.[51]

I asked many of the political insiders to predict the growing Latino population's impact on Newark's politics. Many of the older establishment figures had difficulty accepting that Latinos would want political power. Kenneth Gibson, for instance, remained convinced that most of the new

Latinos were noncitizens and thus were not stakeholders in the political process.[52] But many Latinos were optimistic that blacks and Latinos could work together to share power.[53] Others, though, were convinced that a conflict between black and brown would soon commence. Pablo Fonseca believed that a political tug-of-war between blacks and Latinos was imminent, and in her role as a 2006 Booker team ward campaign manager, Marilyn Gaynor predicted that Newark's next mayor would be Latino.[54]

I wanted to get a sense of what ordinary citizens thought about the balance of power between blacks and Latinos in the city, so I made sure to ask both of my 2008 focus groups about the issue. One African American man was very dismissive of Latinos' claims for political power because in his view, they are not citizens and cannot vote. Most of the other panelists conceded, though, that it was fair for Latinos to have more political representation as their proportion of the population grew. One man even erroneously put forward the idea that Clifford Minor, Booker's 2010 challenger for mayor, had Latino ancestry, in the hopes that a Minor candidacy would reflect some kind of black-Latino coalition.

The members of the Latino focus group also believed in greater Latino representation, and they expressed the hope that blacks and Latinos would be able to share power. But they also were excited at the prospect of electing a Latino mayor. At one point in the session, I asked them to consider the prospect of a serious Latino mayoral candidate. Rather innocently, I used North Ward councilman Aníbal Ramos as an example of a potentially serious candidate. I could just as easily have used State Senator Teresa Ruiz or Councilman Carlos Gonzalez, but Ramos was the first person who came to my mind. The respondents instantly perked up. "Is Aníbal running for mayor?" they asked excitedly. Their reaction startled me a bit, and I had to tell them that Ramos had not announced any plans to run for mayor, although he is viewed as a rising star, and most people would not be surprised if he eventually did decide to run for mayor. Nevertheless, they all seemed excited at the prospect of a Ramos candidacy, despite the fact that earlier, some in the group had complained that they did not see him out in the community often enough. I asked the respondents to predict the candidates for the 2010 mayoral race. Four of the nine were convinced that Ramos would run for mayor in 2010. One man even went so far as to outline the proper strategy for him, with which his colleagues did not seem to disagree: Ramos should take a lesson from Booker's playbook by running for mayor in 2010, knowing that he likely would lose. Nonetheless, running for mayor would help build his profile and increase his name recognition outside the North Ward. Then, in 2014, a resurgent Ramos would be in a position to successfully challenge Booker for mayor.

Conclusion

Despite Booker's political troubles in Newark, he still has a bright political future and many political options. In 2008, he told me that he wanted to serve two to three terms as mayor and had not decided anything beyond that.[55] It was very clear to me, however, that others were at least eyeing him for a higher-profile office. Even before he ran for reelection in 2010, there were rumors that he might be a serious candidate for governor in 2013.[56]

The luxury of options could easily lull Booker and his advisers into a sense of complacency and embolden them to further risk Booker's working relationship with other elected officials by making bold political challenges. Such a step would be ill advised. Booker has enjoyed the support of a diverse set of constituents in his rise to political prominence, but that goodwill may not be permanent. Latino voters may be willing to support the right Latino candidate against Booker should one emerge. Furthermore, if Booker continues to antagonize the existing political establishment, particularly the black political establishment, he may not have a political base to call home.

8

2010

Electoral Politics Revisited

NEWARK—AND AMERICA—LOOKED VERY different in 2010 than it did in 2006. The sense of optimism and change that ushered Cory Booker into office had given way to the realities of governing an already distressed city during a severe recession. Like many of his peers and predecessors throughout the country, he learned that campaigning and governing are different, and in 2010, he found out whether voters would reward his learning curve.

In 2008, rumors started to swirl that Clifford Minor, the former Essex County prosecutor, was considering a run for mayor. Supporters were hoping that he would be the hometown version of Cory Booker, but with life experience. He had a law degree and had served in appointed positions at the state and local levels since Governor Jim Florio's administration. Minor lacked Sharpe James's flamboyance, but in 2008, this was viewed an asset (that year, James was convicted of profiting, along with his mistress, from the illegal sale of city property).[1]

Minor's sobriety aside, he would have to contend with the juggernaut that was Cory Booker's campaign apparatus. In addition to his incumbency advantage, Booker raised $7.5 million for the election (to be used by him and his city council running mates), compared with Minor's mere $265,000.[2] Moreover, Minor lost hope of a major endorsement when Steve Adubato chose to endorse Booker, who had spent years cultivating a political relationship with him. The two teamed up to endorse candidates for the Newark school advisory board and the state legislature in 2007. Finally, in late 2009, Adubato publicly buried the hatchet with Booker, paving the way for Adubato's endorsement of Booker in the 2010 mayoral election.[3]

Minor tried to assemble a slate of candidates, called "Newark's Choice," to run against the Booker team. Minor recruited John James (also known as J. Sharpe James), son of the former mayor, as an at-large council candidate, along with former mayoral candidate David Blount and two other

Fig. 8.1. Clifford Minor tried to invoke Barack Obama's campaign aesthetic in his 2010 bid for Newark's mayoralty.

candidates, Jean Perez and Carole Graves. He also recruited Charron Montayne, daughter of freeholder president Blonnie Watson, to run for the Central Ward council seat and Ras Baraka, the former deputy mayor and at-large councilman and son of the poet Amiri Baraka, to run for the South Ward council seat.

The goal of the Newark's Choice slate was twofold. First, they wanted to position themselves as experienced, native Newarkers who cared about the city's goals. The team's other aim was to call into question Booker's claims to have reduced crime. They hoped that as a former county prosecutor, Minor would have credibility on this issue and could reasonably

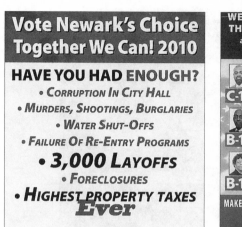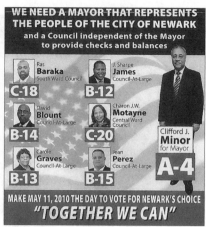

Fig. 8.2. The Newark's Choice ticket, led by Clifford Minor, attempted to unseat the
Booker administration by charging it with increased crime, corruption, and poor
city services.

promise to reduce crime. Minor indicated that he knew that he would lose
the North and the East Wards but hoped that he could rally the Central,
South, and West Wards to topple Booker.[4] Clearly, Minor hoped to beat
Booker by consolidating the black vote, just as Sharpe James had done
eight years earlier.

The Booker campaign chose a strategy of nonengagement. On my first
visit to the Central Ward during the campaign, Booker's deputy campaign
manager, Jermaine James, told me that the campaign had chosen to focus on Booker's record, not on Minor's allegations. James also indicated
that the Booker team was committed to running as a team. When I was
instructed how to canvass, for instance, James insisted that canvassers ask
voters to support the entire Booker team, not just the people they liked. It
was clear, however, that some voters might split their votes or oppose the
Booker team outright. In the upper Vailsburg neighborhood of the West
Ward, for instance, residents commonly displayed both Clifford Minor
and Ronald Rice Jr. (the Booker team candidate) signs in their yards.

Lawn signs do not vote. However, the eventual vote did reveal some interesting fissures, some of which were not surprising given the local election results in 2007. If turnout was any indication, this was a very low sa-
lience election. Only 28% of registered voters cast ballots, which was the
lowest turnout in a city municipal election in a generation (see table 8.1).

Proportionately, more people turned out to vote in 1990, when Sharpe James ran unopposed in his first mayoral reelection bid.

Although Booker won the election decisively, it was not by the margin by which he had won in 2006. Whereas he received 72% of the vote (compared with 24% for his closest competitor) in 2006, he won 59% in 2010. Minor, his closest competitor in a field of four candidates, won 35% of the vote.[5] Most notably, Booker did not carry all five of the city's wards, as he had done in 2006. Continuing their independent streak, the voters of the South Ward, the heart of Newark's black political community, repudiated Cory Booker by 939 votes (see table 8.2).

The South Ward voters' disapproval of Booker extended to some of the down-ticket races as well (see table 8.3). In the at-large council races, John James, son of the former mayor, finished among the top four finishers in

Table 8.1

Turnout in Newark Mayoral Elections, 1974–2010

Year	Turnout (%)[a]	Winner	Closest competitor	Margin
1974	68.59	Gibson	Imperiale	10.92
1978	46.79	Gibson	Donato	43.53
1982	50.73	Gibson	Harris	7.36
1986	49.01	James	Gibson[b]	15.5
1990	34.49	James	—	—
1994	41.89	James	Payne	43.77
1998	33.99	James	Rice Sr.	28.39
2002	43.93	James	Booker	6.41
2006	37.20	Booker	Rice Sr.	48.02
2010	28.42	Booker	Minor	23.84

Source: Newark city clerk's office.

[a] Turnout is the total number of ballots cast (including spoiled and unmarked ballots) divided by the total number of registered voters.

[b] Incumbent was unseated.

Table 8.2

Mayoral Vote by Ward, 2010 Newark Municipal Election

Ward	Booker vote		Minor vote		Other vote	
North Ward	6,095		1,224		419	
East Ward	3,868		687		263	
West Ward	3,794		3,132		406	
South Ward	4,338		5,277		544	
Central Ward	4,630		3,240		514	
Citywide	22,745	(59.1%)	13,132	(35.3%)	2,147	(5.6%)

Source: Newark city clerk's office.

Note: Citywide vote totals include emergency ballots not counted in the ward totals.

Table 8.3

Mayoral Vote Compared with At-Large Municipal Council Vote by Ward
(selected candidates), 2010 Newark Municipal Election

Ward	Booker	Booker Team Members				
		Payne	Crump	Quintana	Gonzalez	James
North Ward	6,095	3,923	3,930	5,192	4,482	1,327
East Ward	3,868	2,287	2,214	2,816	2,410	612
West Ward	3,794	4,214	3,714	2,810	2,694	2,711
South Ward	4,338	5,190	4,926	3,169	2,782	4,860
Central Ward	4,630	4,558	4,107	3,589	3,176	3,079
Citywide	22,745	20,358	18,918	17,576	15,547	12,589

Source: Newark city clerk's office.

the South Ward, ahead of Carlos Gonzalez, an incumbent at-large council-man and longtime member of the Booker team. Shockingly, Ras Baraka won the South Ward Council seat on the first ballot, thereby avoiding a runoff[6] and defeating Booker team member and incumbent Oscar Sidney James. The race was not even close. Baraka received 56% of the vote (compared with James's 37%) and beat James in all but two voting districts. Given that four other candidates were in the race, many people expected that Baraka and James would have to compete in a runoff. That Baraka won so decisively was a bit of a surprise.

Seven candidates ran for the Central Ward seat. In twelve years, this seat had had the greatest turnover of any ward seat in the city. Cory Booker held the seat from 1998 to 2002. Then when he gave up his seat to run for mayor in 2002, Charles Bell, a Sharpe James supporter, beat Booker team member Dana Rone in a runoff to succeed him. Rone then beat Bell in 2006, when the Booker team swept the Newark municipal council races. When an obstruction plea forced Dana Rone out of office in 2008, Charles Bell—with the help of a donation from the then-imprisoned Sharpe James —came out of retirement to beat a crowded field of candidates (including Booker-backed union representative Eddie Osborne).

Given Bell's former political alliances, it would be easy to assume that Councilman Bell would become the gadfly on the municipal council, serving as the opposition to the Booker regime. Bell, however, quickly began cooperating with the Booker team members on the council. As a result, by the end of 2009, Booker regarded viewed Bell as a trusted ally, not as an antagonist who represented old guard interests, and he asked Bell to join his ticket for the 2010 election. Booker's decision to align with Bell was largely strategic. As Deputy Campaign Manager Jermaine James told me on the first day I volunteered in the Central Ward, "If we [the Booker team] can't beat him, no one can." Given Bell's 2008 victory, Booker's campaign calculated that it would be futile to challenge him.

The ideological purists in Booker's camp were appalled at the decision to invite Bell to join the ticket, and this decision directly generated two Central Ward challengers: Richard Whitten, Dana Rone's former chief of staff and a Booker campaign operative since 1998, and Darrin Sharif, Booker's chief of staff from 1998 to 2000 and son of Carl Sharif, Booker's 2006 chief campaign strategist. Both Whitten and Carl Sharif have alleged that at various points in 2009, Booker's campaign officials tried to dissuade them from opposing the Booker team. Whitten contends that he was forced to resign his city job as a result of running against the Booker team, and Carl Sharif was so disgusted at Booker's request to ask his son to drop out of the race that he refused to help in Booker's reelection bid in 2010.[7]

Four other candidates (Newark's Choice candidate Charron Montayne, Gregory Good, Juanita Winslow, and Horace Brown) rounded out the field of Central Ward candidates. Given the number of candidates, it was reasonable to expect a June runoff. Bell finished the May election with 44% of the vote; Sharif finished second with 23% of the vote; and Charron Montayne finished third with 16% of the vote. According to election rules, Bell and Sharif would compete in the June 15 runoff.

At first glance, the 2010 runoff looks very similar to the 1998 runoff, in which a relatively unknown, twenty-nine-year-old newcomer named Cory Booker staged a come-from-behind victory to beat sixteen-year incumbent George Branch for the Central Ward council seat. However, on almost every dimension, Booker was better positioned in 1998 than Darrin Sharif was in 2010. Booker finished the municipal election only 340 votes behind the leader, whereas in the 2010 municipal election, Darrin Sharif was almost 1,400 votes behind Charles Bell. Whereas Booker earned the tacit support of Steve Adubato's machine in 1998, which helped him make inroads in the Latino parts of the Central Ward (Adubato's machine controls those sections politically),[8] Sharif had to run without Adubato's support because he was supporting Bell. Moreover, in 1998 Booker was running against a bit of a straw man. George Branch was well known and well liked in his community, but he was no intellectual heavyweight.[9] He was no match for Booker, the Rhodes Scholar with four degrees from elite institutions. In contrast, although the Sharif campaign alleged that Bell had falsified his credentials (claiming a college degree that he in fact did not have), they could not

John James y Clifford Minor quieren
continuar el legado de Sharpe James...
Barriendo el piso con los latinos !!!

Fig. 8.3. Surrogate elite displacement still played a role in the 2010 election. In this anonymous, independent ad directed toward Latinos, Clifford Minor and John James are linked to John's father, Sharpe James, who is depicted as a fool. The ad accused Minor and the younger James of continuing the elder James's "legacy of sweeping the floor with Latinos." The image of Sharpe James in this ad is the same image used by Citi Pac in one of its anti–Sharpe James ads in 2002 (see fig. 3.2).

claim that he was intellectually unfit for the job.[10] Finally, Bell had access to Booker's war chest. The Booker team allocated about $100,000 for the Central Ward runoff, with more than $1 million in cash reserves. Sharif raised only about $60,000.[11] Thus, his only advantage was that his father, Cory Booker's 1998 campaign strategist, was guiding his campaign.

To overcome his disadvantages, Sharif ran a grassroots campaign, relying on daily canvassing and phone banking. He secured the endorsement of some of Booker's natural antagonists. Richard Whitten endorsed Sharif and asked his supporters to vote for him in the runoff. Ras Baraka endorsed Sharif and lent him campaign volunteers. Finally, state senator and former acting governor Richard Codey endorsed Sharif. Although Codey claimed to have made his endorsement with no regard for politics, the previous fall Booker had supported a rival, State Senator Steve Sweeney, to replace Codey as New Jersey's state senate president. Sharif even secured the endorsement of hip-hop artist and former Newark resident Wyclef Jean.[12]

Going into Election Day, it was very difficult to predict who was going to win. The Booker team was confident, having suspended their canvassing operation before the last weekend of the campaign to focus on literature drops and sign visibility during the closing days of the campaign. I spent

Election Day embedded in the Bell campaign and was at Bell's campaign headquarters as the votes came in. District 39, the first district reporting, showed an initial count of 74 Sharif and 58 Bell, which was revised (twice) to 37 Sharif and 58 Bell.[13] As the other districts started reporting, it became clear that this race would be close. Sharif won some districts and Bell won some. With the exception of a few districts, the margins between the two candidates were razor thin. The tension in the room was palpable. Everyone was on edge, waiting to see what the final tally would be. A Booker campaign official even whispered in my ear, before all the results were in, "There's gonna be a fucking recount!"

Fig. 8.4. An example of elite displacement in the Municipal Council races, taken from a South Ward ad for underdog Oscar Sidney James. Note the facial expression of Ras Baraka, at top, in contrast to James, at bottom.

After all the districts came in, the internal tally was still close, but to Booker team members, it looked like Bell was leading Sharif by forty-seven votes. A senior campaign staffer declared victory, and the entire headquarters burst into applause and tears of joy. Reporters rushed Bell to get his statement. He thanked his workers and encouraged everyone to go down the street to the victory party. Most people, including Bell, left the headquarters to go to celebrate. About twenty to thirty people or so stayed behind to look at the numbers.

Within a few minutes, the mood at the headquarters shifted. The campaign received a call to revise District 39's tally to the original numbers (74 Sharif, 58 Bell), thereby shrinking Bell's margin to 12 votes. Next, the tally for District 29 was questioned. I later learned that someone had allegedly voted twice in that district, so the tally could not be made official without an investigation.[14] No one outside Booker's inner circle knew completely what was going on, but we spectators could tell by the changed atmosphere in the office and the somber looks on people's faces that something was wrong. We started to hear chatter that Bell had in fact lost the election.

Cory Booker walked into the office at about 9:25 that evening. Even though he was polite and spoke to people as he walked in, he was definitely all business. He went straight back to the huddle of senior campaign and administration officials to assess the situation. In a few minutes, he left the office to head over to the victory party. Jermaine James announced that Darrin Sharif was ahead by twenty votes, with fifty outstanding provisional ballots that would not be counted until the next day. We learned that Booker was about to break the news to the people gathered at the victory party.

I followed the crowd over to the victory party. When I got there, Booker was still outside with key members of his administration. They quickly moved inside, where they conferred with Bell in a huddle. I could not hear what they were saying, but it was clear they were preparing their remarks. Soon they went into the dining hall where the campaign workers were feasting on a buffet dinner. Booker addressed the crowd first, observing that had been a long day, and he thanked everyone for their time. He called it a "good fight" and gave the unofficial results: Darrin Sharif was up by twenty-five votes and there were sixty to ninety outstanding provisional ballots (which ended up being sixty-four). He said that the official results would not be ready until the next day. He told everyone to pray for victory tomorrow, and he expressed his "gratitude" to everyone for making sure that the Central Ward had the "best representation. I know in my core

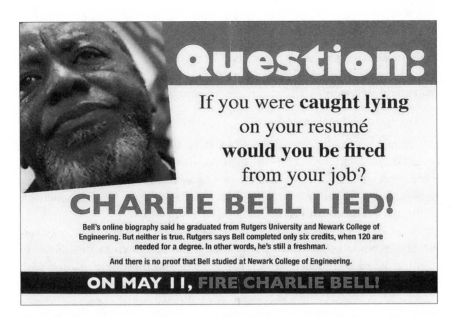

Fig. 8.5. Darrin Sharif's campaign used its own elite displacement tactics against Booker team member Charles Bell, warning voters that Bell had lied about having a college degree. On the opposite side of the mail piece (not shown here), Sharif confirms that he, however, had graduated from college. The mailer also includes a picture of him hugging his grandmother, a prominent local senior.

that the Central Ward has the best representation" [with Charlie Bell], and "I am proud of the battle we fought." He acknowledged the people who fought every night and weekend, expending "sweat equity" for this race. Finally he declared that "whatever the outcome, as mayor, you have my gratitude." He said that he had learned a lot in a short time from Bell, and he was still excited about how he would serve, regardless of the next day's outcome.

Bell spoke next. He acknowledged all the people who had participated in his campaign and said that he appreciated getting to know everyone. He declared that he had "no regrets about joining the Booker team, and I love you all." He then stated that he would be able to live with the outcome, no matter what it was. He thanked his wife of forty-six years and his daughters and grandchildren, observing that if he had to do it over, he again would take everyone into battle. He finished by noting that "it's not over until the fat lady sings, and the fat lady hasn't sung yet."

It took two days for the provisional votes to be counted. Although there were 64 provisional ballots, only 42 were actually counted, as the other 22 were invalidated for various reasons.[15] The Board of Elections opened and tallied the remaining ballots at a public meeting. Sharif won 14 additional votes, and Bell won 27. Ultimately, Sharif won by 11 votes: 2,388 to 2,377.

The 2010 Election in Context

Newark's 2010 municipal elections have both retrospective and prospective implications. Taken in isolation, no one can look down at winning eight out of ten races. But in the context of previous local elections, this outcome could be a barometer of Booker's future electoral chances. Although his future still is bright, he has weaknesses.

In 2007, it became evident that Booker's coattails were short. Booker-backed candidates fell short in their bids for offices from freeholder to Central Ward councilman to state senator unless they were aligned with Steve Adubato. Booker's short coattails were evident in this election, too. Not only did Booker lose two ward council seats, but there was evidence that in some parts of the city, the Booker team's municipal council candidates more than held their own against their team leader. An example is the West Ward. Earlier in this chapter, I mentioned that if the lawn signs were any indication, voters in upper Vailsburg were planning on splitting their vote, choosing Clifford Minor for mayor and Ronald Rice Jr. for the West Ward council seat. We can never be sure if voters split their vote or if some voters cast ballots in the mayoral race and not the council race, and vice versa. But the vote tallies in the West Ward do reveal some weaknesses in Booker's overall performance (see table 8.4). Overall in the ward, Rice actually won two more votes than Booker. It is highly unusual for a down-ticket candidate to earn as many votes as the top-of-the-ticket candidate, especially here when the West Ward voters cast nearly 2,300 fewer votes in the council race than they did in the mayoral race. As suspected, however, Rice actually outperformed Booker in fourteen out of thirty-five districts and tied him in two additional districts (Booker made up his margins in West Ward districts that formerly had been a part of the North Ward). Not surprisingly, most of the districts that Rice won were in Vailsburg, both in the lower (Districts 20 to 29) and upper (Districts 30 to 39) parts of the neighborhood.

Similarly, two of the Booker team's at-large candidates outperformed Booker in the city's historically black section. Donald Payne Jr. received only 2,332 fewer votes than the mayor did. Notably, Payne earned 400

Table 8.4
West Ward Vote Tallies for Cory Booker and
Ronald Rice Jr., 2010

West Ward District	Booker	Rice
6	95	91
7	118	143
9	89	65
10	151	156
13	91	87
15	98	86
17	100	96
19	98	130
20	62	65
21	54	55
22	91	109
23	112	112
24	79	74
25	86	108
26	107	105
27	103	104
28	93	100
29	75	71
30	102	84
31	153	147
32	139	173
33	113	133
34	115	150
35	164	152
36	156	156
37	125	131
38	152	149
39	93	96
40	177	150
41	100	80
43	48	47
44	105	62
45	68	58
46	104	65
47	47	62
Absentee votes	63	62
Provisional votes	68	81
Emergency votes	18	19
Total	3,812	3,814

Source: Newark city clerk's office.

more votes than Booker did in the West Ward and 1,000 more votes than
he did in the South Ward. Similarly, former municipal council president
Mildred Crump won 550 more votes than Booker did in the South Ward
(see table 8.3).

Because the 2010 census data had not been released by precinct at the time of this writing and because the city of Newark completely redrew the voting district lines in 2007, I cannot regress the districts' votes for Booker and his candidates by the districts' racial composition, as I was able to do in chapter 4, which I did using census data that I could divide using pre-2007 district lines. We still, however, see some of the same patterns found in 2007. Booker's political influence is weakest in the city's historically black wards, particularly those in which his allies do not control the Democratic Party ward machine. Congressman Donald Payne Sr. still controls the South Ward machine, and State Senator Ronald Rice Sr.—Ronald Rice Jr.'s father—controls the West Ward machine. In many ways, it seems that the younger Payne and Rice benefited from their fathers' political organizations. Thus, when we consider Steve Adubato's control of the Central and North Wards, and Joe Parlavecchio's control of the East Ward, we see that after four years in office, Cory Booker still does not control his city's political apparatus, in addition to continuing to have political trouble in the city's historically black sections.

What the implications of these findings are for Booker's political future is not clear. In 2008, when I interviewed Thomas Giblin and Steve DeMicco, they made it clear that these local losses had tarnished Booker's golden boy image in the state and could make a statewide run problematic. If Booker were going to dispel these concerns, not only did he have to win, but he would have to win decisively.

By any account, winning a second term by a twenty-four-point margin is a decisive win, but it was not as decisive as it could have been. The South Ward loss was particularly painful. While embedded with the Rice campaign on the afternoon of May 11 (Election Day), I heard a rumor that Booker was ahead two to one in the South Ward. Those who heard that rumor believed that such a decisive win guaranteed Booker's victory not just in the mayoral election but also in the 2013 Democratic gubernatorial nomination because it would dispel the rumors that Booker could not command the black vote. Booker's eventual loss thus only underscored his lack of control over that renegade ward.

There is another side of this story, though. Booker won the election despite losing the South Ward, which, Booker insiders argued, isolated itself by electing the combative Ras Baraka to be in the permanent minority on the municipal council. At the end of the day, some could contend that the South Ward—and, by implication, the black vote—is irrelevant to Booker's success. Indeed, a November 2009 Public Policy Institute poll taken just after Republican Governor Chris Christie's election revealed that Booker had a strong favorable-to-unfavorable rating statewide. Political analysts postulated that this could position him well should he choose to run for governor,[16] although they acknowledged that it was still too early to handicap a race that was nearly four years away.[17]

The Booker Victory in Comparative Relief

In 2010, many "post-racial" black politicians also tried to capitalize on the success of Barack Obama in 2008 to win or retain high-profile political offices. One of the highest-profile campaigns in the first half of 2010 was Congressman Artur Davis's bid to become Alabama's first black governor. Davis, like Booker, employed a strategy of elite displacement to weaken his predecessor's long-standing hold on political power. Even though he was unsuccessful in his first bid to unseat Congressman Earl Hilliard in 2000, Davis gained leverage in 2002 from a decennial redistricting process that brought new voters into the district. He also was able to attract outside financial support for his campaign by implying that Hilliard supported terrorists like Muammar Qaddafi, which was salient in a post-9/11 environment.

By all accounts, Davis won the Democratic nomination to his congressional seat (and, by default, the seat itself) without the support of Alabama's black political machines, all of which supported Hilliard.[18] Even though Davis beat them at the congressional level, his actions in 2002 had a significant impact on his ability to translate his congressional success into statewide success. In particular, he paid a price for not reconciling with the leaders of Alabama's three black political machines—Richard Arrington of the Jefferson County Citizens Coalition, Joe Reed of the Alabama Democratic Caucus, and Hank Sanders of the New South Coalition.

While it was never certain that he would actually win the general election, Artur Davis was an early favorite to win Alabama's 2010 Democratic gubernatorial nomination. He openly compared his improbable bid for governor with Barack Obama's 2008 presidential bid.[19] Given Alabama's large black Democratic population, we would naturally assume that African Americans would rally around him in his bid to become Alabama's first black governor.

Davis had reason to believe that because he had beaten the black political establishment earlier, he did not need to mend fences, even for a statewide race.[20] In a 2007 interview, Davis intimated that Alabama's black political machine was not as strong as it had once been; thus he really did not need them to become the congressman from the Seventh District. He figured that if he took his message directly to the people—without having to go through any gatekeepers—voters would be drawn to him.[21]

Unfortunately, Davis learned the hard way that the old-timers still had clout in the state. Infuriated that he had not made amends with them (and upset about his vote against President Obama's health care plan), the state's three major black political organizations endorsed Davis's white opponent, Agriculture Commissioner Ron Sparks. The voters took their cues from this endorsement. Black turnout was anemic, and Sparks had a strong showing among black voters. At the end of the day, Sparks beat Davis by nearly 25 percentage points.[22]

Davis's experience reveals that even in a post-Obama America, young, deracialized black politicians still must rely on black votes (in combination with nonblack support) to get elected. Just as their predecessors did, deracialized candidates have to balance making racially transcendent appeals with keeping black voters mobilized and engaged in their candidacies.[23] Artur Davis learned, just as Andrew Young had learned in Georgia in 1990 that it is possible for a black candidate to alienate his black constituents by failing to engage them and their issues of concern.[24] In Davis's case, part of this failure to address blacks' concerns stems from his failure to support an initiative (health care reform) widely perceived as benefiting blacks. The other part of addressing concerns is showing public respect to black political elders.[25] When Davis failed on both accounts, the black political establishment was able to reassert itself and chastise him in a very public way for ignoring his base constituency.

Davis's story suggests that the imperative for deracialized black candidates to maximize their share of the black vote when they run in majority nonblack jurisdictions is sometimes at cross-purposes with the elite displacement strategies that they employed to get elected to their first offices in majority black jurisdictions. Davis could afford to lose black votes when the majority of his constituency was black because he knew that he had a healthy advantage among white voters in his district. However, he needed every black vote to realize his gubernatorial goals. Unfortunately, the campaign and legislative decisions that Davis had made earlier in his career served to isolate him from parts of the black electorate when he needed them most.

Overall, 2010 was a rough year for many well-known, young, black politicians. Harold Ford Jr. abandoned a bid to unseat Kirsten Gillibrand as New York's junior U.S. senator. Ironically, he tried and failed to cast himself as

New York's version of Cory Booker.[26] Kendrick Meek, who once appeared to be a shoe-in for the Democratic nomination for Florida's open U.S. Senate seat, faced a tougher primary opponent than expected and eventually came in third in a three-way contest during the general election.[27] Deval Patrick won reelection as governor of Massachusetts with only a plurality of the vote.[28] Black political entrepreneurs fared just as badly. In addition to Artur Davis's loss, Adrian Fenty lost his mayoral primary to a old guard, establishment black challenger in Washington, DC.[29] And most notably, the optimism that catapulted Barack Obama into office in 2008 gave way to questions about his leadership skills and toughness, questions that contributed to his party's defeat in the 2010 midterm elections.[30] In the final analysis, some of these politicians will live to fight another day. Others will see the public phase of their careers end, either temporarily or some permanently. Time may eventually vindicate some black political entrepreneurs or their policy proposals.[31] In the short term, though, these cases provide a collective, cautionary tale about hubris, comeuppance, and the persistent racial terrain of American politics.

So what are we to learn from the story of Newark—or from any of these politicians? The biggest lesson to take from these cases is that the politics of winning elections by any means necessary is fraught with peril. Yes, elite displacement is a great strategy to break into politics, especially if a political aspirant lacks the political connections within the black community to ease his entry into the field. But it seems that black political entrepreneurs must heed the old adage, "Be careful whom you step on on your way up the ladder, as they will be the same people who look at you on your way down the ladder." Ignoring or deriding the old guard black leadership may help younger black candidates distinguish themselves from their predecessors, but they would do better to respectfully engage these older leaders and learn from their wisdom even while they challenge them for their seats.

To be sure, older black leaders have a responsibility in this relationship. They must make themselves available as mentors. They must accept that younger people will not share the same perspective on every issue. They must allow the younger generations to put their own spin on civil rights and urban policy. Most important, they must know when to gracefully shift to the role of elder statesmen and stateswomen.

In short, young and old black elected officials need each other more than they realize. The elders lend a sense of credibility to the young ones. And the young people still represent the legacy of the old leaders. Not everyone will agree on every policy, but they all should be working toward collaboration and not contestation.

Some politicians seem to be heeding the call to respect their elders and build coalitions. As early as 2010, a number of figures had emerged who could run to succeed Cory Booker as mayor of Newark in 2014 should he choose to not seek reelection. Not surprisingly, Councilman Anibal Ramos makes the short list, as does the school advisory board president Shavar Jeffries, who appears to be the homegrown version of Cory Booker. Born to a single, teenaged mother who died young, Jeffries was raised by his grandmother in Newark's South Ward. As a young child, Jeffries participated in after-school programs sponsored by philanthropist Raymond Chambers, a key behind-the-scenes player in Newark politics. Jeffries won scholarships to prep school, Duke University, and Columbia University Law School. He then practiced law for a decade, focusing on civil rights and education law. After a stint as counsel to Attorney General Anne Milgram, Jeffries formed an alliance with North Ward boss Steve Adubato, raised nearly $100,000 on his own, and won election to Newark's school advisory board. Jeffries espouses many of the same policy positions that Booker embraces, but as a native Newarker, he can more easily deflect the outsider criticisms that still occasionally dog the current mayor. Moreover, it was clear in my conversation with Jeffries that he was keenly observing Booker, learning from both his successes and his failures. For instance, when asked to critique Booker's performance in his first term, he mildly and circumspectly noted that perhaps Booker could spend more time in the community engaging residents and explaining his agenda. He also highlighted the fact that he, Jeffries, had had a decade of work experience before he ran for office.[32] Those answers demonstrate Jeffries's recognition of Booker's perceived weaknesses and his attempt to cultivate a different, perhaps more palatable, persona so that he does not receive the same type of criticism.

What about Booker? What does his future hold? What advice should he heed? Most people assume that he has his eye on a statewide office. In 2009, early polls suggested that Booker could make a viable candidate for governor in 2013. In 2011, Booker created a federal political action committee (PAC) to support candidates who supported urban issues. Many speculated that such a PAC could help Booker launch a U.S. Senate candidacy in the future. Booker ruled out a 2012 candidacy but did not rule out running in 2014.[33] While Booker is widely liked, he has to prepare for a street fight unlike anything he has ever experienced. The media that love him now will scrutinize him even more closely if he runs for statewide office. If he chooses to run against Governor Chris Christie, the former U.S. attorney responsible for putting Sharpe James in jail, he should expect that his opponents—both Democratic and Republican—will look for any whiff of scandal[34] in his life or that of his close advisers. Booker will have to prove that he can do more than just reduce crime for one year. Moreover, he will have to demonstrate that he has pushed Newark, which suburban New Jerseyans often view as a black hole for their tax dollars, to greater self-sufficiency. And he will have to prove to the entire state that he is more than just an energetic, pretty face who can give a good speech.

The first group of people that Booker will have to convince are black New Jerseyans, particularly black Newarkers, as they will likely be the critical swing vote in a primary election. While they may be naturally disposed to voting for him in a statewide contest[35]—for a lack of better options—if they are less than enthusiastic, they might not turn out in high enough numbers to make the difference in a close primary or general election. Moreover, Booker's problems in the black community make him appear weak to the party bosses who control the county Democratic organizations. If they back Booker, they may do so only because they think they can control him. Being beholden to party bosses would completely undermine the reformist image that Booker has worked so hard to create.

In closing, Newark has received a lot of attention in the past decade, mostly because of the force of Cory Booker's personality. How the city and its residents will benefit from that in the long term, however, is not clear. Do investment and philanthropic dollars pour into the city for the city's sake or for Booker's sake? I asked Raymond Chambers about this, and he was brutally candid: "I think that a lot of people have really fallen in love with Cory as a person, and so I think some will stay in Newark, but a lot's gonna go with Cory."[36] That realization is sobering, and it shifts the focus of our discussion from one of racial uplift to the contemplation of a potential cult of personality that really does not benefit the majority of Newark residents.

9

Uncle Julius's Cabin

Black Political Entrepreneurs and the Future of Black Politics

We must continue to produce intelligent, dedicated and courageous leaders. We need leaders who avoid the extremes of hotheadeness and "uncle-
tomism," leaders who, on the one hand, embrace wise restraint and calm
reasonableness and, on the other hand, reveal a courageous determination
to press on until the victory for justice is won. We need leaders not in love
with money, but in love with justice; leaders not in love with publicity,
but in love with humanity to paraphrase the great words of Holland: God
give us leaders; a time like this demands great leaders; leaders whom the
spoils of office cannot buy; leaders who have honor; leaders who will not
lie; leaders who possess opinions and a will; leaders who can stand before
a demagogue and damn his treacherous flatteries without winking; tall
leaders, sun-crowned in public duty an in private thinking.

—Martin Luther King Jr.

IN SEPTEMBER 1959, Martin Luther King gave a pep talk of sorts to
members of the Mississippi Southern Christian Ministers Conference. In
this speech, he prepared activists for the "season of suffering"[1] that they
were about to face. In doing so, he called for the emergence of a fearless
leadership cadre who was willing to risk everything to confront inequality.[2] While the locus of black leadership has shifted from the activist to the
electoral realm, there is still a robust debate about the archetypes and normative goals of effective black leaders. This debate has grown more acute
as the African American community has grown more economically diverse
and as blacks who are increasingly removed from the civil rights era come
of age.

Explaining how young, ambitious politicians with tons of energy and
great ideas integrate themselves into this larger black body politic has been

the subject of this book. Earlier I presented a theory to explain how black political entrepreneurs who lack the historic connections to established black political families and traditional organizations like the NAACP find a way to break into the insular world of black politics to become elected officials and launch national political careers. In the first chapter, I argued that young black political aspirants use their elite background and easy access to white political and social institutions to cultivate patrons outside the black community. In turn, these patrons can support them in their challenge for elective office against entrenched black elites, some of whom have worn out their welcome on the American political scene.

To illustrate this point, I presented a case study of generational political transition in Newark, New Jersey. I focused much of my attention on a black political entrepreneur, a telegenic ex–Rhodes Scholar named Cory Booker. He used his media contacts and the Yale and Stanford alumni directories to position himself to challenge Sharpe James, a stalwart of Newark politics for more than thirty years.

In many ways, James made it easy for Booker and the mainstream media to caricature him. He had a brash, flamboyant personality. When Booker challenged him for the mayoralty in 2002, James proclaimed on the *Today* show that Booker was a "tool of the Jews."[3] Then when James pretended to run for mayor in 2006, he showed up at city hall in late winter in exercise clothes and on a bike saddled with voters' petitions.[4] To any casual observer of Newark politics, these spectacles were farcical and served more to embarrass both James and the city than to demonstrate that Newark was a city on the make.

On the whole, then, given Sharpe James's behavior (and the fact that James later served nearly two years in prison for an illegal land deal), it is completely understandable that people black and white, rich and poor, Jewish and Gentile, rooted for Cory Booker. And because I count Booker as a friend and have grown to consider Newark as my second home, no one is rooting for his success more than I am.

That said, Booker's chosen path to power presented advantages and disadvantages. When the mainstream media embraced Booker for his pedigree and portrayed Sharpe James as a buffoon (no matter how much James helped them do it), they reified negative stereotypes of black masculinity and black leadership. Booker himself may have escaped such characterization and, in fact, benefited from James's negative press. But in going along with the media frame, Booker was complicit in perpetuating certain stereotypes about traditional black leaders instead of transcending them.

Eventually, Booker's complicity caught up with him. He himself got caught making what were perceived in Newark to be racially insensitive comments about poor black people. Were it not for a tragic stroke of luck, Booker's entire political coalition might have fallen apart in August 2007. And after a series of unflattering profiles in national press outlets, Booker himself began to realize that despite the talk of racial transcendence, his "friends" in the media really saw him as a caricature of a "safe" black man.

What is more, there is ample evidence from Booker's first term as mayor that his political exertions strained his working relationships with other elected officials, making it difficult to ensure the survival of his political coalition after he leaves local office. Some potential allies do not trust him, and some former allies are bitter. Moreover, in addition to still having to woo black voters, Booker must continue to cultivate relationships with one of his most reliable voting blocs (Latinos), lest another leader emerge who can win their support.

What larger lessons can we draw from the Newark case? Aspiring black politicians, elder statesmen, and interested third parties can all learn a tremendous amount from this study.

Advice for Black Political Entrepreneurs

Any aspiring young black politician needs to understand that while employing elite displacement has its rewards, there are also inherent risks. From a strategic standpoint, it makes perfect sense for black political entrepreneurs to use any leverage they have to gain an electoral advantage. However, they must be prepared to face the consequences of their strategy. Some incumbent politicians and black voters will be turned off by such bare-knuckle tactics. The establishment politicians may refuse to align with the entrepreneur on critical issues, and the voters may be disinclined to vote for the aspiring politician. If the likelihood of persuading those politicians or winning that voting bloc is small from the outset, then the black political entrepreneur may not mind losing potential allies and votes. However, if those officials share similar policy interests or if that voting bloc represents a base constituency, then it makes sense for black political aspirants to count the cost before alienating these groups with heavy-handed political tactics that achieve only short-term electoral goals.

One of the biggest findings of this study was that the discussion of Cory Booker's racial authenticity was really a discussion of class empathy. Newarkers, particularly black Newarkers, are suspicious of newcomers because of a belief that outsiders have exploited them. As a newcomer with a better socioeconomic pedigree, Booker bore the burden of making Newarkers feel at ease with him. Over time, residents have become more comfortable with him. However, every time Booker makes a misstep, his critics reignite the accusations that he is self-interested and that his background makes it impossible for him to really understand the plights of those he leads. And they remind him that he really is not from Newark.

Booker's story is instructive for those who seek to follow in his footsteps. Black political entrepreneurs, especially those who are not from the communities they seek to lead, must be proactive in assimilating into their adopted communities. A number of positive steps can help in this task. First, it is advisable to establish roots in a community before running for office. Booker had lived in Newark for only two years before he ran for his first elective office. Despite his protestations to the contrary, the timeline of Booker's political ascent makes him look instrumental, and some Newarkers respond negatively to that perceived instrumentality.

Related to the idea of rooting oneself in a community is the notion of experience. That Booker won his first elective office one year after finishing law school is also a disadvantage. More extensive work experience would have imparted additional gravitas to Booker. He could have diffused criticism that he was using public service to pad his résumé. He would have likely learned on-the-job skills that he could use in an executive capacity. Most important, he could have used his work experiences—particularly the interpersonal experience of having had long-term bosses and coworkers—to demonstrate empathy with working people.

In addition, black political aspirants must ask if the ends of elite displacement justify the means. Framing the black political entrepreneur as a superblack politician could have dire consequences for the advancement of a black political agenda that seeks to improve the economic and social well-being of all blacks, particularly poor blacks. Some black political entrepreneurs, Cory Booker included, enter politics with the sincere goal of addressing some of the intractable economic problems that black communities, particularly inner-city communities, face.[5] But by allowing themselves to be defined against traditional African American political foils who are cast in the role of buffoons and incompetents, these black political entrepreneurs end up assuming the role of secondary marginalizers, blacks who assume political power and are expected to maintain it by enforcing dominant norms and behavior on blacks (elite or otherwise) who are perceived to deviate from them.[6]

To the extent that black political entrepreneurs can empower their constituents to be their better selves or to resolve entrenched social problems, this may not be objectionable. However, this is a tall order. What happens if some problems remain unsolved? The fear of some, particularly in Newark, is that the failure of entrepreneurs like Booker may be justification for writing off the problems of the urban poor. The Great Society did not work. Descriptive representation in municipal government did not work, either. If newly elected post-racial black politicians cannot use their own brand of racially nonspecific and pragmatic politics to solve the problems facing poor communities of color, then some will undoubtedly blame the residents of these communities themselves and declare them unworthy of policy redress.[7]

It is this fear—that young black political entrepreneurs are unwittingly being set up to fail at ameliorating entrenched structural inequality—that animates concerns about the efficacy of black political entrepreneurs' holding positions of power and contributes to the very crude criticism that black political entrepreneurs lack the racial authenticity to hold office. So, while no one denies that the black political entrepreneur's more appealing political style may create opportunities for them to hold mainstream, high political offices, black political entrepreneurs cannot pretend that these concerns do not exist. They must be prepared to address these concerns when they choose to run for office.

Prospective black political entrepreneurs also need to assess their own resources before choosing a political strategy. Not everyone has the resources to engage in elite displacement. According to Grace Spencer, whom I cited in chapter 2, Cory Booker was uniquely positioned relative to his peers in Newark to challenge the black political establishment. There are politicians who may have similar aspirations but a dissimilar background. For instance, they may not have the same pedigree or lack the social or professional connections needed to circumvent the black political establishment. For aspiring black politicians who find themselves in this predicament, antagonizing the black political establishment may be a less desirable path to power.

Finally, black political entrepreneurs need to be unafraid to start their careers in majority nonblack enclaves. Given these politicians' inclination toward deracialized politics anyway, it may make sense for black political entrepreneurs to run in sympathetic multiracial and majority white districts, where they are likely to generate a high level of crossover appeal. In fact, winning office in these more diverse districts is another important way to increase black descriptive representation in elective office.[8]

Advice for the Black Political Establishment

The case study presented in this book shows that elite displacement can bring out the worst in both the challenger and the challenged. The challenger's self-assuredness may make older politicians less inclined to want to mentor him. In turn, the incumbent resorts to pleas of racial solidarity because he believes that the challenger is threatening his power. Both attitudes inhibit racial progress.

Highlighting the shortcomings of black political entrepreneurs should not be construed as an excuse to ignore the faults of older black elected officials, nor should it justify continuing to elect officials whose usefulness in elective office has long passed. The elder statesmen and stateswomen of black politics need to own up to their policy failures and determine why many goals around reducing black/white inequality remain unfulfilled. A circumspect examination of such policy failures allows elected officials of all ages to learn from past mistakes, and it provides a road map for future policy initiatives. To not afford younger politicians access to that type of institutional memory helps to set them up for failure, and at the end of the day, black communities—not the political entrepreneurs—suffer.

Advice for Third Parties

This study of Newark also lays bare the reality that interested third parties—activists, journalists, surrogates, and donors—play a critical role in helping shape the narrative of the generational clash within black political communities. Outside funding and media attention support the viability of black political entrepreneurs' challenges. Activist agitation can also help or hurt such candidacies. Whenever third parties take a side in electoral contests such as these, they would do well to make their agenda transparent and to make sure that they are fully informed about the political culture into which they are inserting themselves.

Cory Booker has had a lot of well-intentioned support over the years, from donors to surrogates who spoke out on his behalf to pundits who wrote sympathetic articles about him in the national and international press. These advocates did not always realize that their help was sometimes a hindrance to Booker within Newark. Whether they implied that Booker was a Republican in a Democratic city or portrayed everyday Newarkers in a stereotypical light, the advocacy of Booker's friends has often forced him into a defensive position within his own city limits. They really should consider the cultural context in which their advocacy is likely to be received before they act or make any pronouncements.

In addition, advocates, particularly those living outside Newark (or any city of interest), need to make the effort to gather information from as many sources as possible before drawing any conclusions about the city's politics. As I show in this book, Booker's reputation inside and outside Newark are not quite the same. While he is liked generally, journalists and politicians with closer connections to Newark are more critical. Any analysis of politics in Newark or any majority black city undergoing a generational transition in its leadership needs to understand this dynamic. The explanations for this dynamic may not change the overall conclusions, but they do serve to provide needed complexity and nuance to our understanding of the challenges facing black political entrepreneurs. And, I hope, they keep us from casting this generational struggle in overly simplistic, good-versus-evil terms.

Future Directions

Newark remains a ripe location for scholarly inquiry. Space and scheduling considerations demanded that I cover only the first four years and one month of Cory Booker's tenure as mayor. But developments since then warrant additional scholarly attention. For instance, Facebook founder Mark Zuckerberg's $100 million gift to the Newark public school system creates new opportunities to examine the relationship between public-private partnerships and educational outcomes. Assuming the cooperation of the city's Office of Prisoner Reentry, that program presents ideal conditions to conduct a randomized, natural experiment to test the effects of prisoner reentry programs on recidivism. The praise that Booker has garnered for his use of social media to communicate with residents could be used as a starting point to examine the relationship between modes of political contact and citizen satisfaction with government.

The evolution of Newark's politicians and its demographic makeup provides further avenues for additional work. For instance, as the city's Latino population grows and approaches parity with the black population, there will need to be more studies on interethnic cooperation and on balancing the descriptive representation needs of two large and powerful minority constituencies. Finally, as Cory Booker's political career progresses and as more young black politicians challenge elder black incumbents for power, there will be more opportunities (and more data points) to study the electoral prospects of deracialized black candidates at the statewide level and to explore the relationship between these candidates and the black voters who lived under their local leadership.

Finally, future work should explore the application of elite displacement beyond the African American community. There are other politically relevant groups in American society that contend with stereotypes. Political actors within these groups may also consider using elite displacement to best intragroup opponents. A logical next group to examine would be evangelical Christians who deemphasize social issues to try to engender crossover appeal. In addition, elite displacement could be an attractive strategy for ambitious politicians from ethnic minority groups, such as Latinos.

Conclusion

After the *New York Times Magazine* incident in the summer of 2008, Booker and I had an extended discussion about the story. In a series of text messages, I told him I was sorry that his words had been taken out of context, but I also explained to him that sometimes people embrace black leaders like him because they think they can project their own political agendas onto them.

After that conversation, I promised to send him some books that I hoped would sum up my view of the matter. I chose Joel Chandler Harris's *The Adventures of Br'er Rabbit* and Charles Chesnutt's *The Conjure Woman*. Although Harris and Chesnutt are contemporaries, in popular literary criticism they represent polar opposites in their perspectives on race relations. While Harris is widely credited with being a master of black folklore, many contend that his lens is racially insensitive and that his protagonist, Uncle Remus, is a shuffling, obsequious black person who is beloved because he would never upset the post-Reconstruction racial order or remind readers of the inherent indignities of the old slave system.[9]

Modern readings of Harris's work aside,[10] there is no denying the mainstream popularity of the plantation tale at the end of the nineteenth century. Because of that, black writer Charles Chesnutt found it difficult to publish anything about blacks that deviated from the dominant narrative. So to work around this, he turned the genre on its head and created a protagonist (Uncle Julius) who used his stories to gain material concessions from his boss and to expose the brutality of slavery. Julius was never militant in exposing the horrors of slavery, but in his own subtle way, he was very effective in disabusing readers of any fantasies they had about the goodness of slavery.[11]

In the note that I sent Booker with his books, I told him that many expected him to be Uncle Remus but that he was really Uncle Julius. I wanted to help him understand that some people embrace him because he is nonthreatening. I hoped, however, that he would use his entrée into mainstream circles to challenge popular assumptions about the urban underclass. In general, I think that is the charge of all black political entrepreneurs. Especially now that a black political entrepreneur has become president, it is abundantly clear that some blacks possess the charisma and the crossover appeal to be able to win the highest offices in our nation. In order to make sure that all blacks benefit from that kind of descriptive representation, black political entrepreneurs must be willing to risk their positions to speak truth to power, not just to trifling black people (on street corners or in elective office). Consequently, black political entrepreneurs bear the dual responsibility of providing uplift to the communities they serve without fueling classist misconceptions of some blacks that may advance their individual political careers but do little to provide permanent redress to underserved black communities.

In the final analysis, the story of Newark reveals that black political entrepreneurs have a pivotal role to play in improving black communities. They are going to have greater sustained access to more power than any other generation of black politicians in American history. They could be poised to provide more uplift to blacks than any other cohort. This all depends, though, on how they choose to work with and for black communities. If a black political entrepreneur retains his commitment to tearing down structural racism and consciously uses his crossover appeal as a means to that end, then his unique resources should be valued. If the black political entrepreneur's behavior conveys a sense of ambiguity about his motives, though, he should not be surprised if his agenda meets with resistance within a majority black jurisdiction.

Epilogue

INAUGURATION DAY 2010 was very different from its counterpart four years earlier. On a superficial level, the economic crisis demanded a scaled-down celebration. Although Booker had paid for his 2006 inaugural gala with donated funds, everyone knew that a splashy celebration in the midst of a recession and a massive city deficit would raise the ire of critics who already perceived Booker to be insensitive and gauche. Accordingly, his administration replaced the black-tie dinner with a dessert reception that immediately followed the noontime swearing-in ceremony.

Booker was very different this July 1. In 2006, fresh-faced optimism carried his rhetoric to new heights. In his first inaugural address as mayor, Booker eloquently paid homage to the ideals of common purpose and collective work. Rhetorically, it was the best I had ever heard him. He was brilliant. He was eloquent. He literally moved me to tears.

But 2010 was very different. As the incumbent, Booker no longer had the luxury of being able to make lofty promises and have constituents give him the benefit of the doubt as to whether or not he could deliver. He now had a four-year track record by which people could gauge their expectations and judge his rhetoric. And he had the burden of a massive budget deficit hanging over his head. Tough times called for tough measures, and Booker knew that massive layoffs and cuts in services were in the offing. No matter how prodigious one's rhetorical gifts are, there is no easy or eloquent way to fire someone. Not that he did not try. He attempted to frame the challenges as nothing new to Newarkers, but he contended that "we still have the power to choose our destiny." He urged his residents to be a model of optimism during tough economic times.

Despite the optimism that Booker tried to impart to his constituents, his second term would clearly be very different from the first, and not just because of economic uncertainties. The fact that two new councilmen—Darrin Sharif and Ras Baraka—were replacing allies of the mayor signaled a shift in tone. In 2006, everyone taking the oath of office had been on the same side. Inauguration Day for them was the beginning of a collective adventure, and together they would work to implement a transformative vision for the city. On July 1, 2010, in contrast, Booker could no longer guarantee nine votes. The question remained as to whether the addition of two ostensible opponents on the council would alter the balance of power enough to thwart Booker's second-term agenda.

Within fifteen minutes of Booker's inaugural address, it became clear that the change of two municipal council seats would dramatically alter the dynamic. In Newark, municipal council members are sworn into office immediately after the mayor's inaugural address. Once they have been sworn in, they, too, deliver their own brief inaugural speeches in alphabetical order by last name. Augusto Amador was the first to speak. Although Booker and Amador had had their differences over the years, Amador had been a loyal team member in 2010. His inaugural speech was uncontroversial.

Next, though, was Ras Baraka. As he strode to the podium to deliver his speech, his supporters gave him a rousing ovation. The applause and affirmations grew louder as Baraka delivered his speech. In the cadences of a spoken-word poet, Baraka delivered a fiery attack on unregulated capitalism and corporatist politics. He positioned himself as the champion of working-class Newarkers. And in an indirect jab at the mayor, he contended that the solution to economic inequality lay not in "multisyllabic words" or in people who "use their seat to gain privileges . . . there is no room for opportunism or opportunists. No personal ambition . . . we need personal ambitions that are so big it includes everyone." Baraka went on to assert his intrinsic Newark-ness and to chide the mayor for intemperate comments about Newark's pathology by declaring, "I am Newark. Born and raised here. I am not a junkie." He declared that he came in the tradition of famous Newarkers like Sarah Vaughn, as well as his own parents. And in another jab at Booker, he thanked everyone, even "those who didn't want to see me here." The applause was thunderous. Baraka received a three-minute standing ovation. Actually, he received two standing ovations, and the applause continued even after the clerk's office announced the next speaker.

Baraka's fiery critique of Newark's new status quo opened the floodgates for the rest of the municipal council. I heard from two independent sources who were either on or behind the stage that afternoon that after Baraka's speech, most of the remaining council members jettisoned their prepared comments. In their extemporaneous comments, they asserted their independence and made digs at Booker's expense. Mildred Crump, who just hours before had lost her reelection bid to be municipal council president (council members elect their own president), continued a theme from Ras Baraka's speech, noting that her son, a lawyer, had been born in Newark and was not a junkie. In a surprising move, she thanked the old guard, former politicians who had supported her council presidency reelection bid: Gayle Chaneyfield-Jenkins, Bessie Walker, Donald Bradley, and Sharpe James.[1]

The new council president, Donald Payne Jr., kept his comment briefs and cordial. While he pledged a spirit of cooperation, he did point out that one branch of city government should not dictate to the others. "The people elected all of us," he reminded his audience. Luis Quintana made it very clear that he was no rubber stamp for the mayor and promised that he would not be putting a "for sale" sign on Newark. Aníbal Ramos's remarks were very cordial, but even he reminded his listeners that his parents were living in Newark public housing when he was born.

Ronald Rice Jr. gave the wonkiest speech of all the council members. Armed with props, Rice revealed his one-hundred-day policy plan. He pledged progress on a variety of progressive initiatives, including pay-to-play reform and subpoena power for a citizen review board to monitor police activity. But he, too, asserted his Newark-ness, declaring himself a "third-generation Newarker, born in the South Ward, and raised in the West Ward."

Darrin Sharif was last. Before he even began to talk, he walked off the stage and down the aisle of the New Jersey Performing Arts Center. He walked up to his dad, Carl Sharif, and gave him a hug. The nearby audience cooed in support. When the younger Sharif returned to the stage, he thanked the rest of his family, but he explained that his father "has taken so many hits after helping so many people." He received applause for his comments. Although Sharif clearly included Booker in that number of betrayers, even Booker clapped at the remark. Sharif noted that his father had not put him up to running for office. His comments then became biting: "To everyone who threatened to ruin me and [ruin] people who supported me: elections have consequences. The people have spoken."

The installation ceremony for the mayor and municipal council set the tone for at least the first month of Booker's second term. During that period, the Booker administration faced an unprecedented challenge, but without assurance that they would have the full support of the legislative branch of city government.

Just before the inauguration, the mayor's office submitted its 2010 calendar budget, which included a structural deficit of $70 million. Usually, state aid filled in that gap, and in previous years, money from the $460 million

Port Authority settlement had supplemented state aid. The Port Authority money was gone by 2010, though, and the state of New Jersey had to cut municipal aid in light of its own budget crisis. Moreover, the city had reached its bonding capacity and could not borrow any more money.[2] Newark would have to make cuts and find a new revenue stream or raise property tax rates by at least 33%.[3] The structural deficit necessitated laying off city workers, but personnel cuts would not have any effect on the 2010 budget, although it would serve to reduce the structural deficit in the long term. To fill the short-term gap, Mayor Booker proposed creating a municipal utility authority (MUA) to replace the city's water department.

Contrary to popular belief, the municipal utility authority was not a privatization plan. The city would not sell its watershed. Instead, it would lease control of the watershed to the MUA, which for thirty years would be responsible for administering and distributing the city's water supply. As an entity separate from the city, the MUA would also have a separate bonding capacity, giving the city another needed credit line. Booker's plan was to use a new, $223 million bond to pay for federally mandated capital improvements to the city's water system. He also proposed taking $100 million ($70 million in 2010 and $30 million in 2011) to plug the structural deficit until cost-cutting measures like layoffs could take full effect.

Booker also touted the MUA as a way to promote the more efficient delivery of water services. In public hearings, Booker claimed that MUAs tended to have higher collection rates than the city water departments. The Newark Water Department's collection rate is around 80%, but other MUAs in the state have reported collection rates of more than 100% (they collected all current bills, plus some delinquent bills). He also noted that the capital improvements to the water and sewer system would prevent leaks and the loss of water, as well as provide a more accurate meter system so that water customers (municipal, corporate, and residential) could be accurately charged for their water usage. Finally, he contended that the capital improvements would bring Newark's water system into federal compliance. If those improvements were not made, the city would start to face expensive fines in 2011.

Booker had a hard time convincing both the municipal council and the people of Newark of the soundness of this plan. For years, Newarkers have opposed plans to create water authorities to generate revenue. Mayor Hugh Addonizio proposed and won passage of a water authority in 1968. The city engineer at the time, Kenneth Gibson, was a vocal critic of such a plan, and he sued the city to keep it from opening. After becoming mayor in 1970, he legally disbanded the authority. In 2001, Sharpe James proposed a nonprofit water authority as a revenue stream for the city. But members of the Booker team, including Cory Booker himself, were strong opponents of the plan.[4] I personally sat through an April 2003 municipal council meeting at which Ronald Rice Jr. decried the "water optimization scheme," as he called it, during the public comment portion of the meeting. The municipal council ended up voting against the plan, and two future members of the Booker team, Augusto Amador and Luis Quintana, were part of the opposition. Indeed, opposition to this idea had been so strong back in 2003 that when I first heard about the plan to introduce the idea of an MUA, I asked aloud, "Isn't that the same plan that Cory and company opposed in 2003? What made them change their mind?"[5]

While the public may have been naturally primed to oppose this plan, many people—both public officials and private citizens—questioned Booker's timing and motives for bringing the MUA to the table. He had first proposed the idea of creating an MUA to offset budget shortfalls in January 2009, but he did not formally propose the legislation for the MUA until June 2010—after his reelection. Booker then pushed for swift deliberation of the MUA deal. His administration claimed that if the MUA were not approved quickly, it would jeopardize the city's ability to attract bond buyers, thus making it impossible to pass a budget in a timely fashion. If the city did not pass a budget by December 2010, it would risk having the state put the city's governmental operations into receivership. Thus, to maintain the bond buyers' interest, Booker really wanted to pass the MUA by the end of July, at the latest.[6] Moreover, it was common knowledge that Booker's former law partner and confidant Elnardo Webster would become the lawyer for the MUA. To opponents of the plan, it looked like Booker was rushing through a plan that could enrich his friends.

The new members of the municipal council would not be rushed. Darrin Sharif alleged that he did not receive a copy of the city's budget until the day before his inauguration, and he wanted to be briefed on the issues before he made a decision. Returning council members also wanted to have public hearings before making a decision. So throughout the month of July, the municipal council voted to defer consideration of the MUA. These votes revealed the political tug-of-war going on behind the scenes and gave a glimpse into how Booker and the municipal council would wield procedure to achieve their legislative goals.

Newark has a strong mayor form of government. All legislation originates in the mayor's office, and the municipal council is responsible for passing those laws. Booker sent up the MUA legislation in June 2010. That month, the municipal council voted to ask the state to begin the investigatory process to allow for the creation of an MUA (the state has to submit a report about the feasibility of creating an MUA before a municipal legislature can vote to approve it). On July 15, 2010, the MUA came up for its first major procedural vote. The municipal council had to vote to permit the first reading of the bill that would allow for the creation of an MUA. If the bill passed the first reading, it then would have to pass the council again on a second reading and on a third, final, vote.

The municipal council did not pass the first reading of the MUA on July 15. Four council members (Augusto Amador, Carlos Gonzalez, Aníbal Ramos, and Ronald Rice Jr.) voted to pass the bill on first read. The other five council members (Ras Baraka, Mildred Crump, Donald Payne Jr., Luis Quintana, and Darrin Sharif) voted no. Sharif then successfully proposed deferring the issue to a later date. The council agreed that they would schedule public hearings to allow citizens to weigh in on the issue.

Claiming that time was of the essence, Booker tried to use his procedural power to reintroduce the issue the next week. He called a special meeting for Monday, July 19, at which he reintroduced the MUA bill that had just been defeated. Under Newark's charter, a mayor can reintroduce defeated legislation as often as he wants. As soon as I heard about the meeting, I assumed that Booker had convinced one of the five members who had voted against the MUA to change his vote. My gut feeling told me that if anyone would flip, it would likely be Donald Payne Jr. Payne is considered affable but not an intellectual heavyweight. Moreover, many people thought that Booker had quietly supported Payne's becoming municipal council president. Mildred Crump actually accused Booker of having withdrawn his support from her, but Booker maintains that he was neutral in the council presidency race. Payne corroborates that story.[7] Thus, people who believed that Booker had influenced the council presidency race also thought that Booker assumed Payne's easygoing nature would make him malleable to his agenda.

For a morning meeting that had been called on short notice, the municipal council chambers were packed. Opponents of the MUA came out in force, as well as senior Booker advisers who wanted to see the outcome of the vote. The meeting started about an hour later than scheduled, but it was over in five minutes. Council agreed to defer consideration of the MUA until July 27, the week that it was announced that public hearings would be held.

The outcome of that vote was shocking, to say the least. One would assume that if the mayor were calling a special meeting, he had counted votes and knew that he was assured of victory. It did not make sense that Booker had gone to all the trouble to call this meeting only to be rebuffed. Something was terribly amiss. I spoke with Aníbal Ramos outside the chamber soon after the meeting. He explained that the council members had conferred and realized that their votes had not changed. They decided to just defer the issue instead of bringing it up for a losing vote again.

That explanation still did not answer the question of whether and why the Booker administration was so confident going into this meeting, so I spoke with Councilman Payne about the events leading up to that vote. He acknowledged that Mayor Booker had tried to persuade him to vote to adopt the MUA on first reading, and going into the weekend, he was seriously considering voting for it. But over the next two days, he had many conversations and decided that he would remain steadfast in his opposition. I asked whether members of his family were part of those conversations. Payne's uncle and cousin, William Payne and Craig Stanley, two former state legislators who had been beaten by Booker and Steve Adubato in the 2007 elections, were very conspicuous at that July 19 council meeting. Payne acknowledged that his family was in the room during those discussions.[8]

Members of the Payne family remained silent when I asked whether politics played a role in Donald Payne Jr.'s decision to oppose the MUA. William Payne, Councilman Payne's uncle, told me at a public hearing that "Paynes vote on principle." In his interview with me, Payne Jr. alleged that the mayor's office had given them very few details about the MUA. He had seen only the legislation itself, which was a couple of pages long, and one PowerPoint presentation. In the very least, he wanted to see detailed, written assurances that the municipal council would have oversight authority over the MUA. He did not trust the mayor's statements that this would be so.[9]

Clearly rebuffed by the municipal council, Booker's budget plan was in jeopardy. In public comments, Booker started to blame the council for not having passed a budget. At a July 21 budget hearing on senior services, Booker faced an angry crowd of older residents who were worried that their programs would be cut. Really, the budget proposed taking advantage of existing county and private programs rather than assuming the expense of duplicating those services. Assuring the seniors that they would receive the same level of service, Booker calmly explained that the budget that they were protesting was moot anyway, because the budget he had proposed was untenable if the municipal council refused to pass his MUA. The mayor's comments incensed Mildred Crump, who publicly upbraided him and, from the dais, called him a liar. Booker stayed in the room for about fifteen or twenty minutes after Crump's tongue lashing while his director of child and family well-being, Maria Vizcarrondo, was questioned by the council. At one point during the questioning, Booker very clearly shifted his chair, turning his back on Mildred Crump.

Booker's July 22 press conference attracted national attention. That day, he declared that the municipal council's intransigence on the budget and the MUA would force draconian budget measures. He then announced a four-day workweek, which would slash municipal salaries by 20%. He said that the city would not spend money on holiday decorations later that year. He ordered city pools closed for the month of August, although a private donor later stepped in to keep the pools open. And in a move that made national headlines, he announced that city would stop purchasing office supplies, including toilet paper.[10] Most of the city employees I encountered in the days after that press conference were furious, although to be fair, I spoke mainly with council aides that week, so they may have been predisposed to disagree with the mayor. They thought that once again, Booker was making light of the city for national audiences. In response to Booker's announcement, four members of the municipal council (Crump, Payne, Baraka, and Sharif) held their own press conference, at which they refused to accept responsibility for the budget impasse.

The municipal council held budget hearings during the week of July 26. Each night, a different ward hosted the event. Booker and the current watershed manager, Linda Brashear, gave a brief presentation about the benefits of creating an MUA. In the first two hearings (in the West and Central Wards), they answered previously submitted questions before opening the floor to public comment. To provide an opposing viewpoint, the South Ward hearing featured a presentation by a member of a water advocacy group. By the end of the week, the public was allowed to comment as soon as the administration finished its presentation (all the hearings featured a public comment section).

I attended four of the five hearings (all but the one in the West Ward). Booker and Brashear gave the same presentation at each event. They noted the MUA's expanded bonding capacity, and they touted the capital improvements that the MUA could fund and how those improvements would spare the city federal fines. They argued that the delivery of service would improve, and they stressed that an MUA would not significantly raise water rates.

The residents' reaction was incredulous at best and hostile at worst. When Booker claimed that water rates would rise only $10 in the next ten years, audiences murmured in disbelief. In all the meetings I attended, residents were overwhelmingly opposed to the MUA (in the East Ward, voters seemed most opposed to tax increases). I was struck by the unity of opposition. Residents in every ward—of every race—expressed their opposition to Booker's plan. What was worse, the residents expressed a lack of confidence in Booker's leadership. For instance, at the North Ward hearing, an older white woman spoke. She talked about how she and her husband had stayed in the city after the riots. She waxed eloquent when she recalled how she supported Booker in 2006. Then she told Booker how much of a disappointment he had been. At the East Ward hearing, a younger white woman—a single mother—told the mayor that she had stopped believing in him. In her view, she was paying higher taxes for no services, and she was angry. She sat in the same row that I did that night, and when subsequent speakers alleged corruption and malfeasance, her face became even more downtrodden. She looked like she felt betrayed.

To be sure, Booker did have supporters at these hearings, and they spoke out in favor of the MUA. I knew most of the pro-MUA speakers, as the majority of them had been actively involved in the Booker campaign. I did not doubt their sincerity, but it was very clear that some were using talking points. Even though they personalized their speeches, the stilted language demonstrated their trying to work in certain points. Moreover, before one of the meetings, a personal friend asked me to help her friend craft pro-MUA remarks. I soon found out that my friend's friend had been asked speak in favor of the MUA. A city worker I met during the hearings also confirmed that young adults affiliated with Newark Now were also bused in to the hearings. At times during these hearings, they heckled opponents of the MUA. I watched these young people make outbursts at the North Ward hearing, and newspaper, message board, and eyewitness reports of the West Ward hearing alleged that members of the same group heckled the West Ward hearing.[11] To be fair, the MUA's opponents were sometimes less than civil. For instance, at the Central Ward hearing, an MUA opponent almost got into a physical altercation with Modia Butler, the mayor's chief of staff.

Booker tried to downplay the hostility. At the last hearing (in the East Ward), he praised the residents' passion on this issue, but he noted that the same 50 to 100 people had attended all the hearings, implying that the opposition was really a small group of organized people. Booker's observation was correct, but it needs a proper context. Yes, 50 to 100 people did attend all the meetings, and they were organized; but the attendance at those meetings far exceeded 100. In fact, newspaper accounts estimated the number in attendance at the West Ward hearing at 200.[12] Based on my own observation, I would estimate that were 200 to 300 people at the Central Ward hearing, 150 to 200 at the North Ward hearing, 500 at the South Ward hearing, and 200 people at the East Ward hearing. That would indicate that 1,050 to 1,150 people did not attend all five meetings. Moreover, I compared field notes with a friend who also recorded the public comments. Because I wanted to protect the residents' privacy as much as possible, I did not write speakers' names in my field notes unless I knew them. She, however, did write down the residents' first names, except for a couple she did not hear. I compared our lists. There generally were about five or six repeat speakers at each meeting, but approximately twenty to twenty-five residents who were allowed to speak at every gathering.

The public hearings did little to raise Booker's chances of getting the MUA passed in the municipal council. The council members deferred consideration of the measure one more time on July 27 because they had not completed all the public hearings. They then scheduled the vote for August 4, when, on a motion offered by Donald Payne Jr., they voted unanimously to table the issue.[13] Under Newark's procedural rules, mayors cannot reintroduce a tabled piece of legislation. Only the sponsor of the table motion can motion to un-table it. As Councilman Payne explained to the audience, he had no intention of raising this piece of legislation again.

Analysis

The outcome of the budget crisis has had long-reaching political and administrative consequences for both Cory Booker and Newark. From an administrative standpoint, removing the MUA from consideration left the city little room to fix the budget deficit. Significant tax increases were inevitable, and as Booker pointed out during the public hearings on the MUA, residents who were on the brink of foreclosure (he estimated the number to be about 25% of Newark's home owners), could ill afford a major tax increase. In an attempt to lessen the tax pain, Booker and the municipal council explored other revenue options, including leasing and selling city property. The city ended up settling on a 16% property tax increase and leased some city property to the Essex County Improvement Authority in exchange for revenue. In addition, in late 2010, Booker announced that since his administration and the police union could not reach a compromise on contracts, he would have to lay off 13% of the police force.[14]

Unfortunately, one piece of city-owned property will likely not be sold. Although Newark invested $210 million in the Prudential Center arena, a public asset, the city (as of 2010) has not made any money from it, and the New Jersey Devils' management has not paid rent on the building since 2008 (it opened in October 2007).[15] The issue of the Prudential Center's back rent is a recurring theme in citizens' public comments at municipal council meetings, but there seems to be no political will to force the Devils to pay their rent.

These dire economic straits put further fiscal strain on the city. In December 2009, Moody's downgraded its bond ratings for Woodbridge and Irvington, Newark's next-door neighbor.[16] Although Newark was spared a downgrading then, in December 2010, Moody's did lower Newark's bond rating to A3. Despite the cost-saving measures that the Booker administration and municipal council instituted, the city faced a projected $30 million to $42 million budget deficit for 2011.[17]

While the shrinking economy can easily bear a lot of the blame for Newark's budget woes, Newark's chief executive will necessarily have to shoulder some of the responsibility for the city's current situation. Booker's decision to delay consideration of the budget and the MUA until after the elections was a political calculation,[18] one that conflicted with a good-government ethos. Booker characterized the MUA as a crisis that warranted immediate attention, with little consideration for public sentiment, all while downplaying his role in creating this crisis in the first place. He also underestimated the political will and acumen of the municipal council members to counter his efforts.

Booker's defeat on the MUA further strengthens the perception that he is a good fund-raiser but a weak politician. Whereas insiders previously were concerned that Booker could not deliver black votes, they now had evidence that his management skills might be weaker than they once thought.

The debacle of the first month of Booker's second term also called into question his technocratic skills. Recall that black political entrepreneurs like Booker assert that they are more qualified to hold office than older generations of black elected officials are. They presume that their advanced training enables them to find pragmatic solutions to entrenched systemic problems that have beset black communities for decades. In the

case of Newark, Booker attacked Sharpe James and the previous municipal council for always turning in their budgets late. Once in office, though,
the Booker administration did exactly the same thing. Not only have they
turned in late budgets (the 2007 budget was passed in a timely fashion);
they also resurrected and retrofitted the previous administration's unpopu-
lar revenue schemes.

The problems that Booker faced in the summer of 2010 underscore the
observation of earlier scholars who noted that structural factors like recessions and reduced aid prevented the first wave of black mayors from being
able to provide the improved services that they had envisioned.[19] In the
face of similar constraints, the promise of technocratic competence seems
to have faltered. Certainly, some earlier politicians were derelict in their
duty or could have been better prepared to handle their jobs. But even the
best and brightest mayors now have difficulty improving the conditions of
their cities.

It is difficult to not place Booker's troubles in the context of other young
black politicians. Not long after Booker was reelected, Adrian Fenty lost
the Democratic primary for Washington, DC's mayoralty. Like Booker,
Fenty was elected in 2006 by promising energetic, engaged, technocratic
leadership.[20] Indeed, he told me that he expected the voters to judge him
by the quality of his achievements,[21] and the voters did recognize Fenty's
accomplishments as mayor. An August 2010 *Washington Post* poll showed,
for example, that about two-thirds of residents believed that the city was
better off in 2010 than it had been in 2006. This did not translate into reelection votes for Fenty, however. He lost his reelection bid to city council chairman Vincent Gray, a former bureaucrat with ties to former mayors Sharon Pratt and Marion Barry. Gray seized on black voters' concerns
about gentrification and their disapproval of School Chancellor Michelle
Rhee's imperious management style to stage an upset. If the polls were any
indication of the predicted split in the vote, black voters would support
Gray by a nearly two-to-one margin.[22]

Booker's predicament—and Fenty's loss—provide teachable moments
for those who study deracialization and for young black progressive racial
moderates who aspire to power. First, these cases demonstrate the importance of the black electorate to even the most deracialized black candidate's
political coalition. Black candidates need black votes to win, especially in
jurisdictions where blacks make up a majority or plurality of the population. Second, no amount of technocratic know-how can compensate for
a lack of empathy or perceptions of disrespect for institutional memory.

Fenty suffered greatly when the voters perceived him as arrogant and when he snubbed luminaries like Maya Angelou and Dorothy Height; the voters who opposed him thought that he catered to rich white residents and not to them.[23] Similarly, Newark residents were offended when Booker insulted their intelligence (e.g., promising an unbelievably low increase in water rates if the MUA plan passed). Finally, structural barriers affect the racialized and the deracialized alike. Perhaps some black political entrepreneurs should not be so quick to judge their predecessors until they have walked a mile in their management shoes.

In general, 2010 proved to be a rough year politically for black political entrepreneurs. Undoubtedly, this group of young politicians has a lot to offer, but, like their predecessors before them, they clearly still have a lot to learn.

Appendix A

Methodological Notes

The best research questions are often informed by unexpected observations that sidetrack a researcher from her original agenda. Sometimes she begins to explore one topic and finds data that lead to an entirely different project. I love it when that happens. However, I would be remiss to not note the challenges that come with such detours.

As will soon become clear, I did not come to Newark with the intention of writing a book on the city's racial politics. Long before I decided to write this book, I developed really close relationships with people who eventually became my research subjects. So when I came to the conclusion that I should write this book and that writing this book would require that I do research on my friends, I had to learn to manage my personal relationships in light of my new scholarly priorities.

I suspect that other people have found, or will find, themselves in a similar situation. I hope I can help provide insight into practical and ethical issues associated with doing long-term research among familiar people.

When I was a first-year graduate student, I took a class on social science approaches to African American studies, taught by Cathy Cohen. One week, she assigned Elliot Liebow's *Tally's Corner* and Carol Stack's *All Our Kin*, both classic ethnographic studies of poor black communities. To collect the data for the project, both Liebow and Stack moved into the communities they studied and became part of the cultural fabric. The day we discussed both books in class, one of my classmates asked whether researchers could live with their subjects. Cathy quickly pointed out that the question was simple yet profound. Scholars doing ethnographic research need to think carefully about proximity, objectivity, and professional distance.

Later, I took a class on participant observation with Joshua Gamson that similarly underscored the importance of the professional ethics involved with ethnographic research. In that class, students had to conduct their own participant observation studies while learning how to write field notes and to maintain professional boundaries. Joshua reiterated the importance of always remembering one's role as a researcher. That is, as much as a participant observer is a part of the action, she is always an outsider.[1]

There is no one way to manage the researcher-subject relationship in an ethnographic project. Different researchers have used different strategies. Some, like Richard Fenno, go to great lengths to maintain their distance from their subjects. For instance, in his book *Watching Politicians*, he recounts that he had a policy of not offering political advice to the officials he studied. The one time he did violate his rule, Fenno notes, he never used that politician for research purposes again.[2]

Other researchers have had no trouble being real participant observers, even stakeholders, in their research projects. Elijah Anderson, for example, offered to take minutes for the community meetings he attended as part of his research for *Streetwise*. Those notes helped him and the organizations he studied. Mary Patillo used a similar strategy, serving as the secretary for the organization at the heart of her work on intraracial conflict over gentrification in *Black on the Block*. What is perhaps most important to note about Patillo's study is that she actually lives in the neighborhood she studied for this project.[3]

My approach was somewhere in the middle, but closer to Patillo's and Anderson's method. I did not even realize I had a book project until four years into my study, after I had already developed personal relationships with many of the insiders. But because I have never officially lived in Newark, my involvement in the actual operation of city government was usually at the margins, so my influence was limited. This gave me the distance to be dispassionate while at the same time allowing me to use my personal relationships to maximize my ability to do research.

How This All Started

Both Cory Booker and I attended graduate school at Yale (he at the law school, and I in the graduate program in political science). While we have school acquaintances in common, he graduated two years before I arrived in New Haven. In 2001, at the beginning of my third year of graduate school, Booker returned to Yale Law School to deliver the annual Harper Address. At the time, I was writing my dissertation prospectus, in which I proposed to conduct a field experiment to test the effects of canvassing on minority-voter mobilization. I had not yet selected a research site. Much to my surprise, Booker talked about canvassing in his speech. At the reception after the talk, he and I struck up a conversation about canvassing, during which he told me of his plan to run for mayor of Newark in 2002. Immediately I asked if I could conduct my experiment in Newark on his campaign. Within about six months, I started to travel regularly to Newark to set up my experiment. The Booker campaign graciously allowed me to exclusively[4] canvass a group of West Ward districts for my project, which attempted to replicate Alan Gerber and Donald Green's 1998 study of the effects of canvassing, mailers, and phone banking on voter turnout.[5]

Because my research subjects at the time were voters, not the Booker campaign, I had no qualms about developing relationships with members of his family and staff or with helping his 2002 campaign. In my free time, I volunteered at the campaign office, canvassed other districts, and even became friendly with Booker's parents and his staff. Because it was his first major campaign and not nearly as professionalized as it is today, it was easy get to know key insiders and to be given actual responsibilities. I took advantage of this access, not because I thought I would write a book, but because I genuinely liked Booker and his team and wanted to help them out.

Because of the access I had in 2002, I was able to observe the intraracial, class, and even parochial dynamics of electoral politics in Newark and in the Booker campaign. They would have been hard to miss. Marshall Curry's *Street Fight* captured many of these elements,[6] but plenty of other things happened as well. I, like many others, was cursed out regularly for associating with Booker. In addition, residents often questioned my origins. Even though I am black, they would tell me that I "didn't look like I was from Newark." I was born in the nearby Oranges, so sometimes I would say that I was originally from the area and get a pass. However, on one canvassing excursion, a man harangued me for forty-five minutes and told me to "go back to the suburbs (he meant East Orange, where I lived as an infant) where you came from, and take Cory Booker with you." On another occasion, a man hung out of the side of an SUV that was driving past Booker's West Ward campaign office and yelled, "Cory Booker is the white man!" Ironically, from a skin tone standpoint, the heckler was actually as light, if not lighter, than Booker.

Because of those experiences, I started to realize that the more interesting story might be intraracial politics in Newark, not whether or not canvassing increases voter turnout. Nonetheless, I finished my dissertation, which required me to travel to Newark almost weekly for the next year to do archival work. Those regular visits helped me maintain the friendships that I developed in 2002. During that time, I did write one conference paper on racial politics in the 2002 election, parts of which were incorporated into chapter 3 of this book.

After I graduated and accepted a faculty position, I decided to revisit that conference paper. I figured I would write one journal article on the 2002 campaign and one journal article on the 2006 campaign. Naturally, I would have to go to Newark to observe the 2006 campaign, so I started traveling there almost biweekly once I received approval from my school's institutional review board to do so. Carl Sharif, on behalf of the Booker campaign, granted me permission to observe the Booker campaign. I started canvassing with the Booker team regularly, taking notes of the experiences I had on the campaign trail. I also helped with opposition research and voter targeting analysis. By the end of the election cycle, I realized that I had taken enough notes to write a full manuscript, and that is when the idea of writing a book started to crystallize. At first, I thought that I would write just about the campaigns, but as time went on, I had access to enough data to extend the periodization through Booker's first term as mayor.

Discovering that you are conducting an ethnographic project after you have been "in the field" for four years requires a bit of backtracking. I had not taken regular field notes, so I knew that I would have to supplement the notes I started taking in 2006 with in-depth interview data from key insiders in 2002. I did not want to rely on my memory to recreate the story of 2002. This helped me confirm my memories and corroborate events with more than one person. At this point, because these people had known me for years, convincing most of them to sit down with me was not difficult.

In general, I found that my preexisting personal relationships eased my transition into the book project. Because people knew me from the 2002 campaign and trusted me, they were more than happy to grant me permission to observe them and to conduct interviews. Familiarity brings its own set of issues, though.

On Going Native

For years, ethnographers have been warned of the dangers of "going native," or of becoming so much of an insider at their field site that they forget that their primary allegiance is to the good scholarship that they hope to produce.[7] As someone who conducted a multiyear participant observation project on people I know well, I was particularly susceptible to going native. On the one hand, getting close and involved does give one access to information that other people might not get. But if I were to get so close that I became the mouthpiece of my subjects, then my credibility would be completely compromised.

How did I manage to avoid the pitfalls of getting too close? A few other things also worked in my favor. First, Cory Booker and I are not that close (although I am close to his parents, who lived about twenty minutes away from me in Atlanta for a number of years). This made it easier for me to keep my distance.

The fact that I do not live in Newark also helped me maintain some distance. I initially looked at this as a disadvantage, but now I appreciate having lived in Atlanta during this project. Newark politics are interesting, so it is easy to get caught up in the drama. Having to go home allowed me to process my observations in ways that I would not have done if I had lived in Newark. In short, distance allowed me to see the big picture. Moreover, being a nonresident precluded my participation in certain governmental activities. I am the consummate outsider, and that was a boon for my research.

Most important, the duration of the project proved to be a blessing in disguise. A number of events took place over course of my field research. Having to put those events into context gave me greater perspective, and I hope that this has enriched my analysis.

By far, the biggest event during this time was the election of Barack Obama, to both the U.S. Senate and the presidency. I did not know who he was in 2002 when I first started working in Newark. But after I spent more time on this project, I was able to connect what I saw in Newark with what was happening in other places. I am particularly grateful to my colleagues at Emory for challenging me to think about the broader context.

Things happened in Newark, too. Spending a lot of time in one place for nearly a decade helped me paint a more complex picture than if I had completed this project in a few short years. Even five years ago, I had a very unidimensional view of some the figures and events in Newark. Today, as alliances have shifted, as I have gotten to know the other side of many stories, and as people and strategies have evolved, I recognize that things were always more complex than I originally realized. I appreciate having had the luxury to stick with the story because at the end, I think I have a better understanding of it and can convey that more clearly.

Altering the Research Environment

One of the other big questions that comes up during any participant observation project is determining how involved a participant observer should be. As social scientists, we should not manipulate the situations we are studying in order to get the outcomes we want. That said, when we enter a social environment to observe it, there is always the possibility that our respondents will change their behavior because they know that they are being observed.[8] Moreover, some research methodologies, like participant observation, are defined by the researcher's being a part of the action to some degree. How does a researcher manage her role and maintain the integrity of her observations, especially in a participant observation project?

Realizing my own lack of influence was an important consideration when trying to decide when and when not to intervene. Perhaps it is because I work with politicians, who are stubborn, wield a tremendous amount of power, and can sometimes have healthy egos. Perhaps it is also because I worked with people who knew me when I was a very young graduate student. When I realized that not everything I said would be heeded, I gained a little more latitude to be open, but I still had to be careful about not showing too many of my cards.

Perhaps the biggest issue when this came up was having to decide whether to offer advice or discuss my research findings before my project ended. This was especially difficult for me because of the length of time I spent in the field and because for the first four years, when I was not planning on writing a book on this subject, I had no qualms about sharing my opinions about the racial dynamics of Newark politics or management issues.[9] My respondents took a genuine interest in my research project, so it was not unusual for them to ask what I was finding. Since these people were gracious enough to share part of their lives with me, I thought it would have been rude to say nothing. So, I learned to share without sharing. I may have discussed the difficulty in reaching out to certain respondents. (Usually someone would help me make the necessary connections.) Or I might talk about where I was in the writing process. I might share minor findings or offer my opinion on minor episodes, but as much as possible, I tried to stay clear of discussing the overarching theories that I would use to organize the book. (Booker and I did discuss deracialization after I interviewed him.)

The bigger challenge was how to respond when people asked my opinion about certain issues related to Newark politics. I was in the unique position of being on speaking terms with people on opposite sides of Newark's political spectrum, many of whom were interested in learning more about their enemies. My response varied depending on the situation. In many instances, I would listen politely and ask follow-up questions to get information out of them. At other times, I would participate in the conversation by sharing inconsequential stuff that would satisfy their curiosity but not divulge important information.

Censoring oneself in front of friends is difficult. In normal friendships, people discuss their feelings and talk about ideas. In this circle of friends, it would not be unusual to talk about political strategy or political actors. This, of course, could be problematic for me as a researcher. I decided to approach the situation as naturally as possible. Usually, I did not mind talking about tangential issues that were not relevant to my research project. Talking strategy was a little trickier, but because I had no real opportunities to advise Booker, that was not much of an issue.

Sometimes when I did offer my opinion on salient issues. I would offer these insights after the event had taken place (so I had no say in the original event or the immediate response/aftermath), and I would offer my insights to people who were on the periphery. The biggest example that comes to mind is the Judy Diggs incident. At the time, I believed that Booker's lack of racial common sense in this instance warranted my saying something. Even though I knew he would not listen to me, I thought that his parents might. So I arranged to meet them at their home in Atlanta.[10] I framed my warning to them in the context of "I'm hearing things on the street." I was hearing things, but I was mainly expressing my own opinion on the matter. I made it very clear that I thought that Cory needed to stop telling stories and that voters needed to see him more in the community. The next time I saw them, Mrs. Booker made a point of telling me of her son's efforts to hang out with residents more. And, I must admit, I have not heard Booker tell many anecdotes in the past couple of years.

In the end, I decided to insert myself in this particular story because I believed that the moral gravity of the situation required that I not keep silent in a teachable moment. Telling somewhat unflattering stories about dead, poor, black people to rich, white people at a suburban political fundraiser in a time and place where there are heightened racial sensitivities is politically risky. If Booker did not know that by 2007, I did not feel it proper to wait until 2012 to tell him, for then he could dismiss the critique as ancient history.

In general, I had more latitude than most researchers in getting involved with my respondents because I did not have to deal with the same issues of hierarchy that other researchers do. In many instances, researchers occupy a higher social status than their research subjects. They are older and better educated and have very high-status (and sometimes relatively higher-paying) jobs. When the researcher and the subject are of different races, the researcher often comes from the majority group. When researchers are doing research in which they occupy a higher social status than their research subjects, they must take care to not exploit their status.[11] In my case, I was a social equal of or even a subordinate to most of my subjects. I am black, as were most of my research subjects. I am significantly younger than most of them. While I have a high-status job, I do not make as much money as many of them do, and I have no political power. Accordingly, I could be more forthcoming without worrying about my research subjects feeling the need to alter their behavior in an attempt to try to impress me.

On Taking Sides

Initially, the idea of taking sides by choosing to embed myself with one side of Newark's mayoral campaigns was self-evident and not a problem. I already knew Cory Booker, and my research question focused on how young black politicians approach politics and how that affects the achievement of policy goals that are of particular interest to blacks. It made perfect sense to observe the campaign of the young black politician in Newark who was raising money, winning elections, and setting himself up to be influential at the local, state, and national levels.

This initial strategy presented problems, however, when reaching out to allies of Sharpe James and when parts of the Booker coalition fell apart. Given my research interest in young black politicians, this book naturally focuses on Booker's campaigns. But in order to write a balanced analysis of black politics in Newark, I had to talk to opponents of Booker and his policies. Given my connections to Booker, I was initially concerned that his opponents would refuse to speak with me. As soon as I started reaching out them, though, I was pleasantly surprised to see that most people responded to me positively.[12]

I did have to devise a special plan when I interviewed Booker's opponents. First, I immediately disclosed my Booker connection, so that no one could accuse me of having deceived them. Most of James's allies initially mistook me for a journalist, and they assumed that all journalists were biased in Booker's favor anyway. Thus, being a friend of the family was no big deal for them. I would assure them that I would treat them fairly and that I would not be writing a pro-Booker puff piece. They would express their doubts but give me the interview anyway. When possible, I tried to establish a personal connection. Senator Ronald Rice Sr. and I bonded over our mutual connection to central Virginia (he was born there; I grew up there). In other cases, I could fall back on my own connections to Newark. For instance, a branch of my family settled in Newark during the Great Migration. It just so happened that some of my mother's first cousins were childhood friends of Amiri Baraka, and I did not hesitate to let him know who my relatives were. Sometimes it was just a matter of being nice.

I did have two interesting experiences with Booker's opponents when I needed to do more convincing. One respondent wanted to know whether I had donated money to Booker's campaign. I had decided years ago that as long as I was studying Booker, I would not contribute money to his personal campaign, in order to avoid the appearance of bias. He seemed to be satisfied with my response. In another incident, a James associate openly berated and insulted me during the interview. I yelled back at him. It got very tense, and I had to end the interview and erase my tape. In the end, though, he agreed to resume the interview. He later bragged to his wife about how he had given me a hard time. It seems as though he wanted to see how tough I was, and when I stood up to him, he cooperated.

The hardest thing I had to deal with in 2010 was managing the shift in alliances that took place within the Booker team. The development was fascinating to me as a researcher, but I knew that some would interpret my spending time with certain people as an indication of my loyalties. As a researcher, this might hurt my gaining future access to certain people or certain types of information. I was used to navigating between the Booker camp and the old Sharpe James camp, but dealing with the fracture in the Booker team between Booker and the Sharif family was a lot more complicated.

My biggest concern was not alienating either the Booker or the Sharif camps, so I had to make some tough choices about who to observe ethnographically. Since I was at the end of the project and knew that I still needed to collect data from the Booker administration, it made sense to focus my ethnographic attention on the Booker team. Because of my friendship with the Sharif family, I was able to explain my decision to them, and they understood and respected my choice. This allowed me to compensate in other ways for being unable to do participant observation research with the Sharif campaign. Darrin Sharif agreed to keep me apprised of campaign

developments, and we agreed to do an in-depth interview immediately after the campaign. I also knew people who were working on his campaign,
and I would get regular updates on what was going on from them. Thus,
having long-standing relationships with people allowed me to save face
and still continue to get information.

Because I was getting information from both sides, it was also very important for me from an ethical standpoint to maintain discretion during
the campaign. I did not find out any intimate campaign secrets from either
side, but I knew that I could not casually talk about the campaign details
I did know. I made a point of making it clear to my friends who were used
to hearing me talk about my research activities that I would be extremely
more reticent during this election cycle, and they respected that decision.

Discretion and Disclosure

Having to disclose unflattering information is hard for any ethnographer,
but it is particularly hard when one is friends with one's research subjects.
I could not let my personal feelings for respondents interfere with my professional responsibility to analyze data accurately and to present information objectively.

Many of the people I interviewed or observed have been implicated in
scandals through the years. A number of considerations influenced my decision to discuss them. With the exception of discussing scandals that directly
implicated previous mayors or therir administrations, I do not discuss improprieties that took place before 2006. Where possible, I try to discuss
scandals in endnotes so as not to distract from the overall narrative. And
unless they had a direct bearing on their professional performance, I do
not discuss the personal peccadilloes of the people I studied for this book.

Despite these painstaking efforts, I am sure that it will be difficult for
some people, especially friends, to read parts of this book. I wish that there
were something to say to assuage them, but at the end of the day, I had a
professional obligation to my readers and my discipline to present the data
—good and bad. I hope they understand.

Managing My Most Personal Relationships

Earlier in this appendix, I alluded to the fact that before I decided to write
this book, I had already developed close personal relationships with some

of my respondents. In an ideal world, I would have been able to complete this project without their assistance. Unfortunately, though, some of my friends were a little too well placed to exclude them from the analysis. I did use my personal relationships to gain access, but I also considered those friendships when deciding to limit the use of certain sources for this book.

I divided these relationships into three different types, each representing the close personal relationships I had to manage. My friendship with Councilman Ronald Rice Jr. was emblematic of many of my close personal relationships in Newark. We met in 2002 when I was assigned to the West Ward campaign office. Ron lives in the West Ward, so he used Booker's West Ward campaign office to stage his at-large council campaign. We became fast friends and have maintained our friendship over the years.[13] As a member of the Booker team, Rice has been an invaluable resource to me, but as my buddy, I am mindful of how I use him. He is a part of the fabric of black politics in Newark, so I cannot exclude him from the story, but I was especially careful to not rely on him too much as a source for this book. I spent a lot of time with Rice and his staff, and my conversations with them often ended up in my field notes. If I had relied on their perspectives only, I would have presented a biased viewpoint. So, with few exceptions, I cited only my interview with Rice, and I deliberately did not interview his staff, although I included some of my ethnographic observations of them. If Ron or his staff told me something that was interesting and relevant and someone else to whom I was not as close told me the same thing, I cited those other people instead.

My treatment of Rice Jr. as a source relates to how I used other sources. As General Stanley McChrystal and his staff learned the hard way, nothing is off the record unless one specifically asks that it be considered off the record. When subjects spend a considerable amount of time with a researcher, they can easily let their guard down and say things that they may not want revealed.[14] Academic researchers must balance their IRB-mandated responsibility to allow respondents the right to not disclose information they do not want to reveal with the need to make respondents as comfortable as possible so that they want to share as much information as possible. Working among friends for years should have maximized my respondents' comfort level, but it also made them particularly susceptible to being too comfortable and putting themselves in a position in which I could easily exploit them. Fortunately, my closest friends never forgot about my role as a researcher. If they said something confidential in front of me, they quickly let me know that the comment was off the record, and I honored their request (The last time someone made such a request was in 2010.) My research routine also served to create distance between me and the people I was studying. For instance, unlike Richard Fenno, I often carry a notebook with me to write field notes (I do not do this when I'm canvassing; I write those notes later in the day when I've returned from the field). I found out recently that people really did notice the notebook.[15] For instance, a volunteer saw me one day without my notebook and commented that I did not have it (I did, but it was in my bag). Now that I am aware that people were watching me, I am sure that the notebook signaled to people that I might be observing them for professional purposes.

I did decide to exclude some friends as much as possible. For instance, I have been really good friends for a number of years with a woman I will call Deborah, who works for the city. She has always been helpful when I needed to figure out whom to contact to obtain certain information or how to interpret certain facts on the margins. And as a city hall employee, she had a really good grasp of what was going on in the building. However, I did not want to put my friend in the position in which she felt like she was informing on colleagues. As such, I decided to not formally interview her, even though she would have been a great source.[16]

Booker's parents were a different story. I genuinely adore them. In the past ten years, they have become like surrogate parents to me. I would have loved to have kept them out of my research project entirely, but that was not possible. Aside from their being instrumental in helping me set up the interview with their son, they were a valuable source because they have been involved with their son's campaigns from the beginning. They also were able to provide valuable information about the environment in which their son formed his attitudes toward race and black uplift.

Given my relationship with Booker's parents, I was concerned about how they would feel about any criticism of their son. In particular, I was concerned about whether they would think that I had befriended them in order to get information about their son so I could criticize him. Although I knew that I had developed a friendship with them without any ulterior motives, I had to find a way to convey that I really liked them, even if the data did not always allow me to praise their son.

I decided that the best way to do this would be to occasionally criticize Booker in their presence. For instance, in February 2010, Mr. Booker started a nonpolitical conversation about Cory which allowed me to be candid and a little critical. I was brutally honest, and I let them know that some of my personal criticism emanated from professional observation. Again, in December 2010, I had a heated discussion with Mrs. Booker about Newark politics in which we had to agree to disagree about the interpretation of certain events. I hated having to have those conversations with the Bookers, but I needed to hint to them that I sometimes would be critical of their son in this book. I felt that given my personal relationship with them, I was obligated to prepare them for the fact that this book would not be completely flattering so that they could understand that my criticisms were professional and not personal.

Parting Thoughts

In the end, as long as researchers can properly balance their personal relationships with their research objectives—and as long as they disclose their personal relationships—I think the benefits of doing research among friends outweigh the disadvantages. Often, important stories are not told (or are told incorrectly) because writers do not have adequate access to data or because they are unfamiliar with the terrain they are studying and do not properly identify all the key stakeholders. People who are more familiar with the key actors have the advantage of already having done the legwork. As long as we take care to create distance between ourselves and our subjects, we should use those natural advantages instead of running away from them.

Appendix B

List of Formal Interviewees

Name	Role in Newark	Date of interview
Stephen Adubato Sr.	President, North Ward Cultural Center; chairman, North Ward Democratic Committee	11/3/2007
Augusto Amador	East Ward councilman, 1998–present	10/5/2007
Marjory Avant Cocco	At-large council candidate, 2002	6/16/2008
Terrance Bankston	Booker team's South Ward field director, 2006; West Ward field director, 2010; former director of constituent services; 2008 Essex County freeholder candidate	1/9/2008
Amina Baraka	Local community activist	7/18/2007
Imamu Amiri Baraka	Poet, playwright, and local activist	7/18/2007
Ras Baraka	At-large councilman, 2005–2006; South Ward councilman, 2010–present	9/16/2007
Charles Bell	Central Ward councilman, 2002–2006, 2008–2010	7/14/2007
Carolyn Booker	Cory Booker's mother	3/4/2008
Cary Booker Jr.	Cory Booker's brother	12/2008
Cary Booker Sr.	Cory Booker's father	3/15/2008
Cory Booker	Central Ward councilman, 1998–2002; mayor, 2006–present	8/3/2008
Mamie Bridgeforth	West Ward councilwoman, 1998–2006	7/16/2009
Modia Butler	Executive director of Newark Now, 2003–2008; chief of staff for Cory Booker, 2008–present	12/13/2007
Richard Cammarrieri	New Community Corporation	8/6/2008
Anthony Campos	Newark police chief, 2006–2008	8/7/2008
Raymond Chambers	Philanthropist and Newark booster	8/6/2010
Aney Chandy	Corporation counsel, 2006–2007	12/17/2007
Gayle Chaneyfield-Jenkins	At-large city councilwoman, 1995–2006	6/10/2008
McKenzie Collins[a]	Judy Diggs's relative	8/11/2008
Hector Corchado	North Ward councilman, 2002–2006	7/18/2007
William Crawley	Cory Booker for Councilman campaign manager, 1998	6/28/2008
Mildred Crump	At-large councilwoman, 1994–1998, 2006–present	12/14/2007
Joseph Del Grasso	President, Newark Teachers' Union	5/2/2008
Steven DeMicco	Media consultant for Sharpe James, 2002, and Cory Booker, 2006	6/12/2008
Walter Fields	Former director, New Jersey NAACP	12/18/2007
Pablo Fonseca	Aide and chief of staff for Cory Booker, 2006–2008	1/10/2008
Marilyn Gaynor	West Ward field director, 2006; director of public buildings, 2006–2008	6/28/2008
Thomas Giblin	State assemblyman	5/1//2008
Kenneth Gibson	Mayor of Newark, 1970–1986	12/18/2007
Darryl Godfrey	Campaign staffer 1998; West Ward field codirector, 2002	11/5/2007

Name	Role in Newark	Date of interview
Donna Jackson	Local community activist	5/3/2008
Jermaine James	Chief of staff for Cory Booker, 2000–2002; Central Ward field director, 2006, 2010; deputy chief of staff for Cory Booker 2006–2008	10/7/2007
John Sharpe James	Sharpe James's son; South Ward council candidate, 2006, and at-large council candidate, 2010	6/18/2010
Oscar James (Sr.)	Field director for Sharpe James, 2002; Central, South, and West Ward field director for Cory Booker, 2006	7/25/2006
Oscar Sidney James (Jr.)	South Ward councilman, 2006–present	10/8/2007
Shavar Jeffries	President, Newark Public Schools advisory board	7/21/2010
Virginia D. Jones	Local community activist	6/9/2008
John "Bo" Kemp	Director, Newark in Transition, 2006; business administrator, 2006–2007	12/17/2007
Alfred Koeppe	Former chairman, PSE&G; executive director, Newark Alliance	8/5/2008
Ron Lester	Sharpe James's pollster, 2002	8/13/2010
Rodney Lewis[a]	Local blogger	7/17/2008
Garry McCarthy	Police director, 2006–present	7/22/2008
Clifford Minor	Mayoral candidate, 2010	7/8/2010
David Mitchell[a]	Former city hall employee	8/10/2008
Richard Monteilh	Business administrator, 1997–2002, 2004–2006	1/3/2007
Kevin Morris[a]	Booker aide	7/28/2006
Rahman Muhammad	President, SEIU Local 617	6/24/2006
Margarita Muñiz	North Ward field director, 2002 and 2006; deputy mayor for Neighborhood Engagement, 2006–present	1/9/2008
George Norcross	Former chairman, Camden County Democratic Party	9/30/2010
Joseph Parlavecchio	Chairman, East Ward Democratic Committee	7/31/2008
Donald Payne Jr.	At-large councilman, 2006-present; council president, 2010–present	10/6/2007, 7/21/2010
William Payne	State assemblyman, 1999–2008	7/16/2007
Desiree Peterkin-Bell	Communications director, 2006–present	12/13/2007
Wendell Phillips[a]	City hall employee	8/8/2008
Byron Price	Former Rutgers–Newark professor; former director of Prisoner Reentry	10/8/2007
Clement Price	Professor of history, Rutgers–Newark	6/30/2008
Stefan Pryor	Deputy mayor for economic development	7/31/2008
Luis Quintana	At-large councilman, 1994–present	12/17/2007
Scott Raab	Feature writer, Vanity Fair	8/2/2008
Aníbal Ramos	North Ward councilman, 2006–present	12/19/2007
Ronald C. Rice (Jr.)	At-large council candidate, 2002; West Ward councilman, 2006–present	3/2/2007
Ronald L. Rice (Sr.)	West Ward councilman, 1982–1998; state senator, 1986–present; deputy mayor, 2002–2006; mayoral candidate, 2006	12/16/2007
Dana Rone	Central Ward councilwoman, 2006–2008	9/14/2007
Arthur Ryan	Former chairman of Prudential	7/23/2008
Carl Sharif	Senior campaign adviser for Cory Booker	7/22/2006, 7/26/2010
Darrin Sharif	Chief of staff for Cory Booker, 1998–2000; West Ward field codirector, 2002; Central Ward councilman, 2010–present	11/5/2007
L. Grace Spencer	South Ward district leader; state assemblywoman, 2007–present	7/31/2006

(continued)

Name	Role in Newark	Date of interview
Phillip Thigpen	Chairman, Essex County Democratic Party	6/16/2008
Omar Wasow	Cory Booker's college friend	1/9/2008
Blonnie Watson	Essex County freeholder	6/13/2008
Elnardo Webster	Booker team campaign treasurer; Cory Booker's former law partner	8/22/2007
Calvin West	Sharpe James's former chief of staff	6/10/2008, 8/13/2010
Richard Whitten	Booker campaign staffer, 1998, 2002, 2006; chief of staff for Councilwoman Dana Rone, 2006–2008; Central Ward council candidate 2010	8/8/2008

[a] Pseudonyms were used to protect the interview respondents' privacy.

Notes

Notes to the Introduction

1. Chanta L. Jackson, "Newark Panel to Examine Legacy of Ken Gibson," nj.com, October 5, 2009, available at http://www.nj.com/newark/index.ssf/2009/10/panel_examine_legacy_of_ken_gi.html, 27 (accessed June 27, 2010).

2. Simon Hall, "On the Trail of the Panther: Black Power and the 1967 Convention of the National Conference for New Politics," *Journal of American Studies* 37, no. 1 (2003): 66.

3. See Jackson, "Newark Panel."

4. See Matt Bai, "Is Obama the End of Black Politics?" *New York Times Magazine*, August 10, 2008.

5. U.S. Bureau of the Census, "State and County Quickfacts for Newark (City), New Jersey," available at http://quickfacts.census.gov/qfd/states/34/3451000.html (accessed August 18, 2009).

6. William E. Nelson, "Cleveland: The Evolution of Black Political Power," and Linda Williams, "Black Political Progress in the 1980's: The Electoral Arena," both in *The New Black Politics: The Search for Political Power*, 2nd ed., ed. Michael B. Preston, Lenneal J. Henderson Jr., and Paul Puryear (New York: Longman, 1987), 172–99 and 97–136.

7. Evelyn Brooks Higginbotham, *Righteous Discontent: The Women's Movement in the Black Baptist Church, 1880–1920* (Cambridge: Harvard University Press, 1993), 25–26; Katrina Bell McDonald, "Black Activist Mothering: A Historical Intersection of Race, Gender and Class," *Gender and Society* 11, no. 6 (1997): 773–95.

8. Cathy J. Cohen, *The Boundaries of Blackness* (Chicago: University of Chicago Press, 1999).

9. A good example of this type of secondary marginalization is then-candidate Barack Obama's dressing-down of absentee black fathers in a widely publicized Father's Day sermon in 2008. See Barack Obama, "Obama's Father's Day Speech," CNN.com, June 27, 2008, available at http://articles.cnn.com/2008-06-27/politics/obama.fathers.ay_1_foundation-black-children-rock?_s=PM:POLITICS (accessed October 12, 2010).

10. See Harold F. Gosnell, *Negro Politicians* (Chicago: University of Chicago Press, 1935).

11. Robert Dahl, *Who Governs?* (New Haven: Yale University Press, 1961); Clarence N. Stone, *Regime Politics: Governing Atlanta 1946–1988* (Lawrence: University of Kansas Press, 1989).

12. Todd C. Shaw, *Now Is the Time: Detroit Black Politics and Grass Roots Activism* (Durham: Duke University Press, 2009).

Notes to Chapter 1

1. Annette Gordon-Reed, *Thomas Jefferson and Sally Hemings: An American Controversy* (Charlottesville: University of Virginia Press, 1998), 1, chap. 2; Tali Mendelberg, *The Race Card* (Princeton: Princeton University Press, 2001), chap. 5; Sekou Franklin, "Situational Deracialization, Harold Ford and the 2006 Senate Race in Tennessee," in *Whose Black Politics? Cases in Post-racial Black Leadership*, ed. Andra Gillespie (New York: Routledge, 2010), 215–16.

2. Charlton McIlwain, "Perceptions of Leadership and the Challenge of Obama's Blackness," *Journal of Black Studies* 38, no. 1 (2007): 64–74; Charlton McIlwain, "Leadership, Legitimacy and Public Perceptions of Barack Obama," in *Whose Black Politics? Cases in Post-racial Black Leadership*, ed. Andra Gillespie (New York: Routledge, 2010), 155–72.

3. Robert E. Park, introduction to *Negro Politicians: The Rise of Negro Politics in Chicago*, by Harold F. Gosnell (Chicago: University of Chicago Press, 1935), xvii.

4. Ibid.

5. See Gwen Ifill, *The Breakthrough: Politics in the Age of Obama* (New York: Doubleday, 2009).

6. "The State of the Black Student: Freshman Enrollment at the Nation's Highest Ranked Colleges and Universities." *Journal of Blacks in Higher Education*, available at http://www.jbhe.com/features/61_enrollments.html (accessed June 26, 2010).

7. Editors of DiversityInc., "Fortune 500 Black, Latino and Asian CEO's," diversityinc.com, July 22, 2008, available at http://diversityinc.com/content/1757/article/3895/ (accessed June 26, 2010).

8. See Rachel L. Swarns, "Quiet Political Shifts As More Blacks Are Elected," *New York Times*, October 13, 2008.

9. David A. Bositis, *Black Elected Officials: A Statistical Summary* (Washington, DC: Joint Center for Political and Economic Studies, 2002), 26–27.

10. See Andra Gillespie, "Meet the New Class: Theorizing Young Black Leadership in a 'Postracial' Era," in *Whose Black Politics? Cases in Post-racial Black Leadership*, ed. Andra Gillespie (New York: Routledge, 2010), 14.

11. See Carol M. Swain, *Black Faces, Black Interests* (Cambridge: Harvard University Press, 1993).

12. Robert Dahl, *Who Governs?* (New Haven: Yale University Press, 1961), 85.

13. Ibid.

14. See Dianne Pinderhughes, *Race and Ethnicity in Chicago Politics* (Champaign: University of Illinois Press, 1987), chap. 2; Lucius J. Barker, Mack Jones, and Katherine Tate, *African Americans and the U.S. Political System*, 4th ed. (Englewood Cliffs, NJ: Prentice Hall, 1998), 6.

15. Barker, Jones, and Tate, *African Americans*, 20–26.

16. Dahl, *Who Governs?* 23–24.

17. Ibid., chaps. 4 and 5.

18. Gary Jacobsen and Samuel Kernell, *Strategy and Choice in Congressional Elections*, 2nd ed. (New Haven: Yale University Press, 1983).

19. Zoltan Hajnal, *Changing White Attitudes toward Black Political Leadership* (New York: Cambridge University Press, 2007).

20. Alan S. Gerber, "African Americans' Congressional Careers and the Democratic House Delegation," *Journal of Politics* 58 (1996): 831–45.

21. Andra Gillespie, "Community, Coordination and Context: A Black Politics Perspective on Voter Mobilization" (PhD diss., Yale University, 2005), 126.

22. Center for Responsive Politics, "Reelection Rates over the Years," opensecrets.org, available at www.opensecrets.org/bigpicture/reelect.php (accessed January 13, 2009).

23. One does not have to be young to be a black political entrepreneur. I focus on young black politicians only because much of the popular discussion of black political entrepreneurs is about young candidates. See Roland Martin, "Ready or Not. . . ." *Savoy*, March 2003, 52–56; Terrell K. Reed and Sonia T. Alleyne, "What It Takes to Win." *Black Enterprise*, November 2002, 82–95; Alexandra Starr, "We Shall Overcome, Too," *Business Week*, July 15, 2002.

24. Gillespie, "Meet the New Class," 22–25.

25. Gunnar Myrdal, *An American Dilemma* (New York: Harper Bros., 1944), 728–29.

26. Ronald Walters and Robert C. Smith, *African American Leadership* (Albany: SUNY Press, 1999), 38.

27. Katherine Tate, *Black Faces in the Mirror: African Americans and Their Representatives in the U.S. Congress* (Princeton: Princeton University Press, 2003), chap. 2.

28. "Scott, Robert Cortez" and "Washington, Harold," both in *Biographical Dictionary of the United States Congress, 1774–Present*, available at http:// bioguide.congress.gov/scripts/biodisplay.pl?index=s000185 and http://bioguide .congress.gov/scripts/biodisplay.pl?index=W000180 (accessed January 13, 2009); Bruce Ransom, "Black Independent Electoral Politics in Philadelphia and the Election of Mayor W. Wilson Goode," in *The New Black Politics: the Search for Political Power*, ed. Michael B. Preston, Lenneal J. Henderson Jr., and Paul Puryear (New York: Longman, 1987), 262.

29. Cathy J. Cohen, *The Boundaries of Blackness* (Chicago: University of Chicago Press, 1999).

30. Ibid., 37.

31. See Doug McAdam, *Political Process and the Development of Black Insurgency, 1930–1970* (Chicago: University of Chicago Press, 1982), 87.

32. Robert Putnam, *Bowling Alone: The Collapse and Revival of American Community* (New York: Touchstone Books, 2000), 76–77.

33. William E. Nelson, "Cleveland: The Rise and Fall of the New Black Politics," in *The New Black Politics: The Search for Political Power*, 1st ed., ed. Michael B. Preston, Lenneal J. Henderson Jr., and Paul Puryear (New York: Longman, 1982), 187–208.

34. Robert Catlin, "Organizational Effectiveness and Black Political Participation: The Case of Katie Hall," *Phylon* 46, no. 3 (1985): 179–92.

35. Andra Gillespie and Emma Tolbert, "Racial Authenticity and Redistricting: A Comparison of Artur Davis's 2000 and 2002 Congressional Campaigns," in *Whose Black Politics? Cases in Post-racial Black Leadership*, ed. Andra Gillespie (New York: Routledge, 2010), 52.

36. Marjorie Randon Hershey, "The Campaign and the Media," in *The Election of 2000*, ed. Gerald M. Pomper (New York: Chatham House, 2001), 46–72.

37. Morris Fiorina, *Retrospective Voting in American National Elections* (New Haven: Yale University Press, 1981).

38. David A. Bositis, *Black Elected Officials: A Statistical Summary* (Washington, DC: Joint Center for Political and Economic Studies, 2002), 5.

39. U.S. Bureau of Labor Statistics, "Databases, Tables and Calculators by Subject: Labor Force Statistics from the Current Population Survey," available at http://www.bls.gov/data/home.htm#historical-tables (accessed January 27, 2011); Jared Bernstein, "Weaker Job Market Re-Opens Racial Income Gap," Economic Policy Institute Snapshot, available at http://www.epi.org/economic_snapshots/entry/webfeatures_snapshots_20060705/ (accessed September 4, 2007); Rakesh Kochhar, Richard Fry, and Paul Taylor, "Wealth Gaps Rise to Record Highs between Whites, Blacks and Hispanics," July 26, 2011, available at http://pewresearch.org/pubs/2069/housing-bubble-subprime-mortgages-hispanics-blacks-household-wealth-disparity (accessed October 17, 2011); U.S. Department of Education, National Center for Education Statistics, *The Condition of Education 2010* (NCES 2010-028), Indicator 20, 2010, available at http://nces.ed.gov/pubs2010/2010028.pdf (accessed October 17, 2011); Rogelio Saenz, "The Growing Color Divide in U.S. Infant Mortality, *Population Reference Bureau*, available at http://www.prb.org/Articles/2007/ColorDivideinInfantMortality.aspx (accessed January 27, 2011); U.S. Bureau of the Census, *The 2011 Statistical Abstract: Births, Deaths, Marriages and Divorces*, available at http://www.census.gov/compendia/statab/cats/births_deaths_marriages_divorces/life_expectancy.html (accessed January 27, 2011); Isabel V. Sawhill, "Non-Marital Births and Child Poverty in the United States," testimony before the House Committee on Ways and Means, Subcommittee on Human Resources, June 29, 1999, available at www.brookings

.edu/testimony/1999/0629poverty_sawhill.asp (accessed January 13, 2009); Emily Yoffe, ". . . And Baby Makes Two," *Slate*, March 20, 2008, available at www.slate.com/toolbar.aspx?action=print&id=2185944 (accessed January 13, 2009).

40. Linda Williams, "Black Political Progress in the 1980's: The Electoral Arena," in *The New Black Politics: The Search for Political Power*, 2nd ed., ed. Michael B. Preston, Lenneal J. Henderson Jr., and Paul Puryear (New York: Longman, 1987), 97–136.

41. See Martin Gilens, *Why Americans Hate Welfare* (Chicago: University of Chicago Press, 2000), chap. 6.

42. Cohen, *The Boundaries of Blackness*, 79–90, 104–5.

43. Melissa V. Harris-Lacewell, *Barbershops, Bibles, and BET: Everyday Talk and Black Political Thought* (Princeton: Princeton University Press, 2004), 207–8.

44. See Shawn LaFraniere, "Barry Arrested on Cocaine Charges in Undercover FBI, Police Operation," *Washington Post*, January 19, 1990, A1; Linda Feldman, "Marion Barry's Return Reveals DC's Widening Racial Gulf," *Christian Science Monitor*, September 16, 1994, 2; Ronald Walters, "Why Barry Happened: For Many Black Voters, a Declaration of Independence," *Washington Post*, September 18, 1994, C1; Jonetta Rose Barras, "Old Face, New One Join Council: Marion Barry: Old Hand Returned to Politics," *Washington Post*, November 9, 1992, B1.

45. Maida Cassandra Odom, "FBI Probe Seen to Boost Philadelphia Mayor in Polls," *Boston Globe*, November 2, 2003, A6; Nancy Phillips and Maria Panaritis, "Federal Probe Leaves Street Chided, but Not Indicted," *Philadelphia Inquirer*, June 30, 2004, A16; James Dao, "Philadelphia's Ex-Treasurer Is Indicted in Graft Case," *New York Times*, June 30, 2004, A16; Marcia Gelbart, "Street's Response: 'Deeply Saddened,'" *Philadelphia Inquirer*, May 10, 2005, A11.

46. Louis Hartz, *The Liberal Tradition in America* (New York: Harcourt, Brace, 1955).

47. William G. Domhoff, *Who Rules America?* (Englewood Cliffs, NJ: Prentice Hall, 1967), 5.

48. Stanley Kramer, director, *Guess Who's Coming to Dinner?* (film), 1967.

49. The 2009 movie *Precious* would be a notable exception, but we must keep in mind that Perry signed on as an executive producer after it was made, for distribution purposes, but he had no say over the creative development of the film.

50. Alan Hughes, "Top 25 Hollywood Moneymakers," *Black Enterprise*, available at www.blackenterprise.com/magazine/2008/03/01/top-25-hollywood-moneymakers (accessed March 1, 2008); Lacey Rose, "Hollywood's Best-Paid Actors," *Forbes*, available at www.forbes.com/2008/07/22/actors-hollywood-movies-biz-m (accessed January 14, 2009); Matt Zoller Seitz, "A Very Busy Father," *New York Times*, February 15, 2007.

51. Adam Clayton Powell Jr., *Adam by Adam* (New York: Dafina Books, 1971), 71; Laura B. Randolph, "The First Black Elected Governor: L. Douglas Wilder Makes History with His Election to Virginia's Top Post," *Ebony*, February 1990.

52. David Bositis, 1997 *National Opinion Poll: Politics* (Washington, DC: Joint Center for Political and Economic Studies, 1997), available at www.jointcenter .org/databank/NOP/reports/1997_politics_report (accessed January 16, 2009).

53. David Bositis, *1999 National Opinion Poll: Politics* (Washington, DC: Joint Center for Political and Economic Studies, 1999), 20–21; David Bositis, *2004 National Opinion Poll: Politics* (Washington, DC: Joint Center for Political and Economic Studies, 2004), 6–7.

54. For a discussion of black mayors in particular, see Hajnal, *Changing White Attitudes.*

55. David T. Canon, Matthew M. Schousen, and Patrick J. Sellers, "The Supply Side of Congressional Redistricting: Race and Strategic Politicians, 1972–1992," *Journal of Politics* 58, no. 3 (1996): 846–62.

56. Joseph McCormick II and Charles E. Jones, "The Conceptualization of Deracialization: Thinking through the Dilemma," in *Dilemmas of Black Politics*, ed. Georgia A. Persons (New York: HarperCollins, 1993), 66–84.

57. Canon, Schousen, and Sellers, "The Supply Side."

58. Howard Schumann et al., *Racial Attitudes in America: Trends and Interpretations*, rev. ed. (Cambridge: Harvard University Press, 1997), 153–70.

59. Pew Research Center, *Optimism about Black Progress Declines*, monograph (Washington, DC: Pew Research Center, 2007).

60. Knowledge Networks, "The Associated Press–Yahoo Poll, Wave 6, in Partnership with Stanford University," interview dates: August 27, 2008–September 5, 2008 ($N = 2227$), 21.

61. Ibid., 22.

62. Ibid.

63. *The McLaughlin Group*, taped January 4, 2008, and aired January 5 and 6, 2008.

64. In a separate op-ed piece, George Will was even more explicit, although he eventually lost hope when Obama refused to endorse the appointment of a southern white to the Fifth Circuit Court of Appeals. Will wrote, "His [Obama's] candidacy kindled hope that he might bring down the curtain on the long-running and intensely boring melodrama 'Forever Selma,' starring Jesse Jackson and Al Sharpton." See George Will, "Obama Judges a Judge," *Washington Post*, August 12, 2007, B7.

65. Charles V. Hamilton, "De-Racialization: Examination of a Political Strategy," *First World*, March/April 1977, 3–5; "*First World* Interviews Julian Bond," *First World*, March/April 1977, 6.

66. McCormick and Jones, "The Conceptualization of Deracialization," 79.

67. Ibid.

68. "2007 Vote Ratings—House Ratings," *National Journal*, available at www .nationaljournal.com/njmagazine/print_friendly.php?ID=n (accessed January 16, 2009).

69. Leadership Conference on Civil Rights, *LCCR Voting Record: 110th United States Congress* (Washington, DC: Leadership Conference on Civil Rights, 2008), 18–35.

70. Sharon Collins, *Black Corporate Executives* (Philadelphia: Temple University Press, 1996).

71. Michael Powell and Jodi Kantor, "After Attacks, Michelle Obama Looks for a New Introduction," *New York Times*, June 18, 2008.

72. Joe Stephens, "Obama Camp Has Many Ties to Wife's Employer," *Washington Post*, August 22, 2008, A1.

73. Ms. Sher became Mrs. Obama's chief of staff after her husband became president.

74. Mary Patillo, *Black on the Block* (Chicago: University of Chicago Press, 2007).

75. Ibid., 113.

76. Ibid., 118.

77. Michael Dawson, *Behind the Mule* (Princeton: Princeton University Press, 1994).

78. Ibid.

79. Robert C. Smith, *We Have No Leaders* (Albany: SUNY Press, 1996), chap. 2.

80. Bositis compared black public support for vouchers with black elected official support for vouchers in 1999. Whereas 69% of black elected officials opposed vouchers, 60% of black respondents supported them. See David A. Bositis, *Changing the Guard: Generational Difference among Black Elected Officials* (Washington, DC: Joint Center for Political and Economic Studies, 2001), 29.

81. David A. Bositis, *2002 National Opinion Poll: Politics* (Washington, DC: Joint Center for Political and Economic Studies, 2002), 6–7.

82. Bositis, *Changing the Guard*, 21.

83. Roland Martin, "Ready or Not . . . ," *Savoy*, March 2003, 56.

84. Dawson, *Behind the Mule*, chaps. 1–3.

85. Martin, "Ready or Not . . . ," 56.

86. Tommie Shelby, *We Who Are Dark* (Cambridge: Belknap/Harvard University Press, 2005).

87. Ronald Walters, "Barack Obama and the Politics of Blackness," *Journal of Black Studies* 38, no. 1 (2007): 7–29.

88. Adolph Reed, *Class Notes* (New York: New Press, 2000), chap. 1.

89. Dawson, *Behind the Mule*, 210.

90. Douglas S. Massey and Nancy A. Denton, *American Apartheid* (Cambridge: Harvard University Press, 1993), 69. Karyn R. Lacy, *Blue-Chip Black: Race, Class and Status in the New Black Middle Class* (Berkeley: University of California Press/Russell Sage Foundation, 2007): 31-32, 42.

91. See Patillo, *Black on the Block.*

92. Adolph Reed Jr., *Class Notes* (New York: New Press, 2000), chap. 1.

93. For a discussion of black social isolation, see Massey and Denton, *American Apartheid*, 155–56. Since Massey and Denton's original study, the U.S. Bureau of the Census has continued to track residential segregation rates. While segregation improved from 1980 to 2000, blacks in the metropolitan areas studied still experienced high levels of residential segregation. In the census bureau's last report, published in 2002, Newark ranked as the fifth most segregated city for blacks and Latinos in the United States. See John Iceland and Daniel H. Weinberg, with Erika Steinmetz, "Racial and Ethnic Residential Segregation in the United States," paper presented at the annual meeting of the Population Association of America, Atlanta, May 9–11, 2002, available at http://www.census.gov/hhes/www/housing/resseg/pdf/paa_paper.pdf, accessed October 11, 2011, 64, 68–69, 86–87.

94. See Massey and Denton, *American Apartheid*, 158–60.

95. Ian Urbina, "Councilman Is Positioned to Become Washington's Youngest Mayor," *New York Times*, September 14, 2006.

96. Patillo, *Black on the Block*, 120.

97. "Democrats Name Harlem Lawyer," *New York Times*, September 18, 1966; "Legality Is Urged for Numbers Play," *New York Times*, December 18, 1966; "Harlem Seeks Separation," *New York Times*, October 5, 1968.

98. "Adam Clayton Powell Beaten by 205 Votes," *Chicago Tribune*, June 24, 1970, 4; "Miracles Never Cease," *Chicago Tribune*, June 25, 1970, 20.

99. Thomas A. Johnson, "Powell Absence Felt by His 'Real People,'" *New York Times*, August 13, 1967, 62.

100. Paul Good, "A Political Tour of Harlem," *New York Times Magazine*, October 29, 1967, 50.

101. Jesse H. Walker, "Rangel Ready to Say It," *New York Amsterdam News*, February 14, 1970; Jesse H. Walker, "The Candidates on the Attack," *New York Amsterdam News*, June 20, 1970, 1.

102. Jesse H. Walker, "Rangel Makes It Official," *New York Amsterdam News*, February 21, 1970, 1, 43.

103. "I'm a Part-Time Congressman," Advertisement paid for by the Rangel for Congress Committee, New York, *New York Amsterdam News*, April 11, 1970.

104. "Powell's Defeat Blamed on Absenteeism, Young Voters," *Los Angeles Times*, June 25, 1970.

105. Jesse H. Walker, "Honor Powell As Others Seek Seat," *New York Amsterdam News*, January 30, 1970.

106. Ibid., 42.

107. Jesse H. Walker, "The Name of the Game Is Politics," *New York Amsterdam News*, March 14, 1970, 42.

108. Thomas Johnson, "Powell Requests Ballot Recount," *New York Times*, June 25, 1970, 48.

109. Artur Davis, interview, September 12, 2007; Earl Hilliard Sr., interview, October 19, 2007.

110. Gillespie and Tolbert, "Racial Authenticity and Redistricting," 51–54.

111. Randolph Burnside and Antonio Rodriguez, "Like Father, Like Son? Jesse Jackson Jr.'s Tenure As a U.S. Congressman," in *Whose Black Politics? Cases in Postracial Black Leadership*, ed. Andra Gillespie (New York: Routledge, 2010), 89–90.

Notes to Chapter 2

1. Komozi Woodard, *A Nation within a Nation: Amiri Baraka (Leroi Jones) and Black Power Politics* (Chapel Hill: University of North Carolina Press, 1999).

2. Clement Price, interview, June 30, 2008.

3. See Peniel Joseph, *Waiting 'til the Midnight Hour* (New York: Henry Holt, 2006), 184–85; Woodard, *A Nation within a Nation*.

4. Woodard, *A Nation within a Nation*, 143, 151.

5. Zoltan Hajnal, *Changing White Attitudes toward Black Political Leadership* (New York: Cambridge University Press, 2007), 175.

6. Joseph, *Waiting 'til the Midnight Hour*, 259–60.

7. Amiri Baraka, interview, July 18, 2007.

8. Arthur Ryan, interview, July 23, 2008.

9. Kenneth Gibson, interview, December 18, 2007.

10. Arthur Ryan, interview, July 23, 2008; Alfred Koeppe, interview, August 5, 2008.

11. Calvin West, interview, June 10, 2008.

12. Ronald Smothers, "Mistrial for Ex-Mayor of Newark," *New York Times*, November 29, 2001.

13. Joseph F. Sullivan, "Gibson Loses Bid for a Fifth Term," *New York Times*, May 14, 1986, A1; Joseph F. Sullivan, "Gibson's Long Struggle Ends, Newark's Continues," *New York Times*, May 18, 1986, 4:7. Thomas J. Lueck, "Economic Hopes Rising amid Newark Troubles," *New York Times*, May 5, 1986, B1; Brad R. Tuttle, *How Newark Became Newark: The Rise, Fall, and Rebirth of an American City* (New Brunswick: Rutgers University Press, 2009), 214.

14. Amiri Baraka, interview, July 18, 2007.

15. Joseph F. Sullivan, "In Newark Mayor Race, Clashing Visions of City. *New York Times*, April 26, 1986. A30.

16. "Disappointing Choices for Newark," *New York Times*, May 9, 1986. A34.

17. Margo Hornblower, "Voters Tell Mayor Gibson He's Been Out of Touch; Newark Elects New Executive after 16 Years," *Washington Post*, May 15, 1986, A4; Brad R. Tuttle, *How Newark Became Newark: The Rise, Fall, and Rebirth of an American City* (New Brunswick: Rutgers University Press, 2009), 221.

18. Andra Gillespie, "Community, Coordination and Context: A Black Politics Perspective on Voter Mobilization" (PhD diss., Yale University, 2005), 131.

19. Marshall Curry, director, "Street Fight" (DVD), 2005.

20. Curry, "Street Fight"; Terry Pristin, "Ex-Newark Aide Is Sentenced for Bribery," *New York Times*, July 15, 1997.

21. Tuttle, *How Newark Became Newark*, 225.

22. Neil MacFarquhar, "Judge Orders a State Takeover of the Newark School District," *New York Times*, April 14, 1995; Neil MacFarquhar, "Newark School Takeover Is Seen As Early As July," *New York Times*, May 20, 1995.

23. Damien Cave, "HUD Demands $6.4 Million from Newark," *New York Times*, April 23, 2005; Damien Cave, "In Troubled Era, Housing Chief in Newark Sets His Retirement," *New York Times*, January 28, 2006.

24. Ras Baraka, interview, September 16, 2007.

25. Technically, the two Rices are not senior and junior. Rather, the elder Rice is named Ronald L. Rice, and his son is Ronald C. Rice. But the younger Rice does refer to himself as Ronald Rice Jr., and to avoid confusion, I use the Jr./Sr. designation to distinguish between the two. In the case of the two Oscar Jameses, I usually refer to the father as Oscar James (Sr.) and the son as Oscar Sidney James (II).

26. Marjory Avant Cocco, interview, June 16, 2008.

27. Modia Butler, interview, December 13, 2007.

28. Gayle Chaneyfield-Jenkins, interview, June 10, 2008.

29. Cory Booker, interview, August 3, 2008.

30. Modia Butler, interview, December 13, 2007.

31. L. Grace Spencer, interview, July 31, 2006.

32. Ibid.

33. Cory Booker, interview, August 3, 2008; Virginia D. Jones, interview, June 9, 2008.

34. Charles Bell, interview, July 14, 2007; Gayle Chaneyfield-Jenkins, interview, June 10, 2008.

35. Cory Booker, Harper Address, speech delivered at Yale Law School, New Haven, September 24, 2001.

36. William Crawley, interview, June 26, 2008.

37. Another young black person was interested in running for the Central Ward Council seat, banker Darryl Godfrey. Godfrey, a native Newarker, was persuaded not to run for the seat because Booker was believed to be better financed. See Darryl Godfrey, interview, November 5, 2007.

Notes to Chapter 3

1. Charles V. Hamilton, "De-Racialization: Examination of a Political Strategy," *First World*, March/April 1977, 3–5.

2. Jim Sleeper, "The End of the Rainbow," *New Republic*, November 1, 1993, 20.

3. Lenneal J. Henderson Jr., "The Governance of Kurt Schmoke As Mayor of Baltimore," in *Race, Politics and Governance in the United States*, ed. Huey L. Perry (Gainesville: University of Florida Press, 1996), 151–64.

4. Charles E. Jones and Michael Clemons, "A Model of Racial Crossover Voting: An Assessment of the Wilder Victory," in *Dilemmas of Black Politics*, ed. Georgia A. Persons (New York: HarperCollins, 1993), 128–46.

5. Joseph McCormick II and Charles E. Jones, "The Conceptualization of Deracialization: Thinking through the Dilemma," in *Dilemmas of Black Politics*, ed. Georgia A. Persons (New York: HarperCollins, 1993), 66, 68.

6. Carol A. Pieranuzzi and John D. Hutcheson, "Deracialization in the Deep South: Mayoral Politics in Atlanta," *Urban Affairs Quarterly* 27, no. 2 (1991): 197–98.

7. Saundra C. Ardrey and William E. Nelson, "The Maturation of Black Political Power: The Case of Cleveland," *PS: Political Science and Politics* 23, no. 2 (1990): 148–51.

8. David T. Canon, Matthew M. Schousen, and Patrick J. Sellers, "The Supply Side of Congressional Redistricting: Race and Strategic Politicians, 1972–1992," *Journal of Politics* 58, no. 3 (1996): 846–62.

9. Ibid., 849–51.

10. Ibid., 858.

11. See McCormick and Jones, "The Conceptualization of Deracialization"; Robert C. Smith, "Ideology As the Enduring Dilemma of Black Politics," in *Dilemmas of Black Politics*, ed. Georgia A. Persons (New York: HarperCollins, 1993), 66–84.

12. Richard F. Fenno Jr., *Home Style: House Members in Their Districts* (New York: HarperCollins, 1978), 60.

13. Ibid., 61.

14. Marjorie Randon Hershey, "The Campaign and the Media," in *The Election of 2000*, ed. Gerald M. Pomper (New York: Chatham House, 2001), 47–49, 67–70.

15. Ibid.

16. Ibid., 47.

17. Carolyn Martindale and Lillian Rae Dunlap, "The African Americans," in *U.S. News Coverage of Racial Minorities: A Sourcebook, 1934–1996*, ed. Beverly Ann Deepe Keever, Carolyn Martindale, and Mary Ann Weston (Westport, CT: Greenwood, 1997), 63–146, 98–102.

18. Ibid., 114.

19. Ibid., 114–15, 127.

20. Melissa V. Harris-Lacewell, *Barbershops, Bibles, and BET: Everyday Talk and Black Political Thought* (Princeton: Princeton University Press, 2004), 208.

21. Adolph Reed Jr., *The Jesse Jackson Phenomenon* (New Haven: Yale University Press, 1986), chap. 8.

22. Katherine Tate, *From Protest to Politics: The New Black Voters in American Elections* (New York: Russell Sage Foundation/Harvard University Press, 1994), 138–40.

23. Reed, *The Jesse Jackson Phenomenon*, chap. 8.

24. Ronald Walters and Robert C. Smith, *African American Leadership* (Albany: SUNY Press, 1999), 217.

25. Canon, Schousen, and Sellers, "The Supply Side"; "How Turnout Turned the Race," *Newark Star-Ledger*, May 15, 2002, 25.

26. Calvin West, interview, August 13, 2010; Ron Lester, interview, August 13, 2010.

27. Ron Lester, interview, August 13, 2010.

28. Jeffrey Krause concluded, for example, that Booker was too green to win the election. His findings, which are based on a secondary analysis of print media only, are overly simplistic. Taking Booker's candidacy seriously allows for a more nuanced analysis of the political dynamics at play in this election. See Jeffrey Krause, "Generational Conflict in Urban Politics: The 2002 Newark Mayoral Election," *The Forum* 2, no. 3 (2004), available at http://www.bepress.com/forum/vol2/iss3/art7 (accessed August 19, 2007).

29. See Gary Jacobsen and Samuel Kernell, *Strategy and Choice in Congressional Elections*, 2nd ed. (New Haven: Yale University Press, 1983); Tom Moran, "Booker's Challenge," *Newark Star-Ledger*, April 7, 2002; Owen Moritz, "Bloody Newark Mayoral Bout Goes to James," *New York Daily News*, May 15, 2002, 7.

30. Ron Lester, interview, August 13, 2010.

31. Steve DeMicco, interview, June 12, 2008.

32. Cory Booker for Mayor, untitled 2002 campaign video.

33. Moritz, "Bloody Newark Mayoral Bout."

34. See Marshall Curry, director, "Street Fight" (DVD), 2005.

35. I omitted articles that are clear duplicates of articles that appeared in other, usually national, versions of the same newspaper.

36. I found one more article just before this book went to press, which I added.

37. After a last-minute discovery of five online articles from 2002, I conducted a content analysis of the final four articles in the database.

38. The intercoder check was based on a sample of newspaper articles covering the mayoral race for all of 2002, a data set containing 283 articles, 30 of which I coded.

39. A third coder coded 25 articles (or about 9% of the articles in the 2003 data set before we found additional minority-press articles, but she graduated before she could code new articles), and approximately 82% of her coding decisions matched those of the outside coder.

40. Randy Hodson, *Analyzing Documentary Accounts* (Iowa City: Sage, 1999), 51; Ange-Marie Hancock, *The Politics of Disgust* (New York: NYU Press, 2004), 170.

41. As explained in subsequent notes, the coding process is somewhat subjective. Although it may be easy to distinguish editorials from news articles because editorials often appear in their own section of the newspaper, other classifications are less obvious. For instance, what may appear to one coder to be a general news story could look like a news analysis story to another coder if it contains numerous quotations from experts. Moreover, identifying discussions of certain themes is more subjective, and determining the tone of an article is even more so. As expected, we agreed far more on the more objective coding schemes and less

often on the more subjective coding decisions. We agreed 97% of the time about whether an article mentioned the candidates' educational credentials and 60% of the time on the tone of the article, which was our lowest agreement rate. Both these agreement rates are within acceptable ranges. See Hodson, *Analyzing Documentary Accounts*, 51; Hancock, *The Politics of Disgust*, 170.

42. One coding disagreement should be noted. I and the coders disagreed on the classification of an article appearing in *Wall Street Journal* ("Newark, Zimbabwe?" by John Fund), which appeared on May 8, 2002. Both outside coders classified it as a news analysis piece. But given the piece's placement in the newspaper and the fact that John Fund is listed as an opinion.com columnist, I decided to reclassify the article as an editorial. This was the only time I overruled the coders' classification decisions.

43. To determine the positive or negative spin of an article, we looked at the balance of positive and negative attention given to each candidate in an article. If an article gave equal attention to each candidate's strengths and weaknesses, we coded the article as neutral. If the article was more laudatory, we coded the article as positive, and vice versa.

44. The *Black Commentator* is an online newsmagazine that began in spring 2002. The magazine, which has a national following, was founded in New Jersey and devoted a considerable amount of space in its first editions to Newark's mayoral race. Because of the magazine's proximity to Newark in 2002 and because articles from the magazine were mailed anonymously into Newark by supporters of Sharpe James, I included it in the database and coded it as a New Jersey news outlet.

45. See Hershey, "The Campaign and the Media."

46. In this study, extreme multicollinearity is defined by tolerance values of less than .1.

47. See Tali Mendelberg, *The Race Card* (Princeton: Princeton University Press, 2001).

48. "Bill Clinton Was the 'Comeback' President," direct-mail leaflet, paid for by Citizens to Elect Sharpe James, Newark, NJ.

49. "From Newark For Newark . . . Love Newark," direct-mail leaflet for Sharpe James for Mayor, paid for by Citizens to Elect Sharpe James, Newark, NJ; "Do You Know Cory Booker's Real Newark City Council Record?" direct-mail leaflet, paid for by Citizens to Elect Sharpe James, Newark, NJ.

50. "Maybe if Cory Booker Came from Newark, He'd Understand," direct-mail leaflet, paid for by Citizens to Elect Sharpe James, Newark, NJ.

51. Martin Kilson, "A Letter from Harvard: How to Spot a Black Trojan Horse," personal letter to Lee Daniels, Blackcommentator.com, 3. To be fair, in a *New Yorker* article about Booker's first eighteen months in office, Kilson later praised Booker. See Peter Boyer, "The Color of Politics," *New Yorker*, February 4, 2008.

52. Kilson, "A Letter from Harvard," 1.

53. "Voter Intimidation," leaflet, paid for by CitiPac, Newark, NJ.

54. Komozi Woodard, *A Nation within a Nation: Amiri Baraka (Leroi Jones) and Black Power Politics* (Chapel Hill: University of North Carolina Press, 1999), 153.

55. Ibid., chaps. 4 and 5.

56. Ibid., 109.

57. "Cory Booker: Restoring Newark's Promise," direct-mail leaflet, paid for by Citizens for a Better Essex County, Montclair, NJ; "Cory Booker: Fiscal Responsibility for Newark," direct-mail leaflet, paid for by Citizens for a Better Essex County, Montclair, NJ.

58. Confidentiality requirements prevent further elaboration on the respondents' political activities. It is safe to say that none of the respondents was a member of Booker's or James's slate of municipal council candidates or senior campaign staff. I should note that I met my contact in this group of voters because of a connection to the Booker campaign.

59. William Finnegan, "The Candidate: How the Son of a Kenyan Economist Became an Illinois Everyman," *New Yorker*, May 31, 2004, 36.

60. Fenno, *Home Style*, 56.

Notes to Chapter 4

1. Andrea Anderson, "Booker Says Newark's Race Will Be No 'Street Fight,'" Associated Press and Wire, February 12, 2006.

2. Richard Lezin Jones, "Newark Hasn't Heard the Last of Booker," *New York Times*, May 16, 2002.

3. Luis Quintana, interview, December 17, 2007.

4. Carl Sharif, interview, July 22, 2006.

5. Ibid.

6. Oscar N. James, interview, July 25, 2006.

7. Certainly some of the people with whom I spoke during the ethnographic portion of this project believed that Oscar James Sr. obtained a position for his son on the ballot as a part of his agreement to work for Booker. Oscar James insists, however, that Sidney James himself asked Booker to be placed on the ballot; see Oscar N. James, interview, July 25, 2006. Carl Sharif did not give me any evidence to contradict Oscar James's version of events. In any case, it is important to note that Sidney James was not expected to win the South Ward seat anyway. That seat was previously held by Donald Bradley, the municipal council president. Bradley was perceived to be too powerful and too popular to be ousted, even by someone chosen by Cory Booker. But after being indicted in the spring of 2011 on corruption charges stemming from the scandal involving the University of Medicine and Dentistry in New Jersey, Bradley had to pull out of the race. (Bradley served on the board and was alleged to have illegally procured jobs for his friends and family.)

8. Oscar Sidney James, interview, October 8, 2007.

9. Carl Sharif, interview, July 22, 2006.

10. Ibid.

11. Arnold eventually reached a rapprochement with Booker and took a job in the city's business administrator's office.

12. Ibid.

13. Kevin Morris, interview, July 28, 2006.

14. Carl Sharif, interview, July 22, 2006; Oscar N. James, interview, July 25, 2006.

15. Carl Sharif, interview, July 22, 2006.

16. Cory Booker, interview, August 3, 2008.

17. L. Grace Spencer, interview, July 31, 2006.

18. The Scheme Machine leaflet attacked the Core/Downtown corporation only because Quintana and Amador initially voted for the neighborhood corporations. At the March 15 municipal council meeting, Quintana and Amador tried to rescind their vote but lost the motion to do so. The state enjoined the corporation until after the new council members took office on July 1, 2006. At their first regular council meeting, they voted to rescind the corporations.

19. "Scheme Machine," direct-mail leaflet, paid for by Booker Team for Newark, Newark, NJ.

20. Rahman Muhammad, interview, June 24, 2006.

21. Damien Cave and Josh Benson, "Newark Mayoral Candidate Tries to Escape Shadows," *New York Times*, May 5, 2006, B1.

22. Damien Cave, "On Second Try, Booker Glides in As Newark's Mayor," *New York Times*, May 10, 2006, A1.

23. "Good News for Newark Residents!" 2006, leaflet, paid for by Committee to Elect Ronald L. Rice, Newark, NJ.

24. "Why Are They Buying Your City," leaflet, paid for by Activists Concerned for Newark, Newark, NJ.

25. Carl Sharif, interview, July 22, 2006.

26. I ran models that included dummy variables for wards and Booker's 2002 performance as control variables, but because of collinearity issues, I removed them from the model.

27. Canon, Schousen, and Sellers, "The Supply Side."

Notes to Chapter 5

1. Adrian Fenty, interview, March 5, 2008.

2. I will not examine the Booker administration's impact on public education because it was not a priority of Cory Booker's first term in office, and Mark Zuckerberg's announcement of a $100 million donation to the Newark public school system took place after I ended the ethnographic portion of this project. Any

future project examining Booker's second term in office will no doubt examine his influence in public education.

3. Linda Williams, "Black Political Progress in the 1980's: The Electoral Arena," in *The New Black Politics: The Search for Political Power*, 2nd ed., ed. Michael B. Preston, Lenneal J. Henderson Jr., and Paul Puryear (New York: Longman, 1987), 128–29.

4. Robert C. Smith, "Recent Elections and Black Politics: The Maturation or Death of Black Politics? *PS: Political Science and Politics* 23, no. 2 (1990): 160–62.

5. Melvin G. Holli. *The American Mayor: The Best and Worst Big-City Leaders* (State College: Pennsylvania State University Press, 1999), 147.

6. Clarence N. Stone, "Political Leadership in Urban Politics," in *Theories of Urban Politics*, ed. David Judge, Gerry Stoker, and Harold Wolman (Thousand Oaks, CA: Sage, 1995), 96–116.

7. Clarence N. Stone, *Regime Politics: Governing Atlanta 1946–1988* (Lawrence: University of Kansas Press, 1989).

8. Richard M. Flanagan, *Mayors and the Challenge of Urban Leadership* (Lanham, MD: University Press of America, 2004), 151.

9. Ibid.

10. Ibid., chap. 5.

11. See Alexandra Starr, "We Shall Overcome, Too," *Business Week*, July 15, 2002.

12. Flanagan, *Mayors*, chap. 6.

13. Ibid., 190.

14. Roland G. Fryer Jr., Paul S. Heaton, Steven D. Levitt, and Kevin M. Murphy, *Measuring the Impact of Crack Cocaine*, NBER Working Paper Series 11318 (Washington, DC: National Bureau of Economic Research, 2005), 19.

15. Elnardo Webster, interview, August 22, 2007; Anthony Campos, interview, August 7, 2008.

16. Carla Fried, "America's Safest City: Amherst, N.Y.; The Most Dangerous: Newark, N.J.," *Money*, November 27, 1996.

17. State of New Jersey, Division of State Police, Uniform Crime Reporting Unit, *Uniform Crime Report, State of New Jersey 2005* (West Trenton: State of New Jersey, Division of State Police, 2006).

18. U.S. Bureau of the Census, "Crimes and Crime Rates by Type of Offense: 1980 to 2006" (Washington, DC: U.S. Bureau of the Census).

19. Carl Sharif, interview, July 22, 2006; Oscar N. James, interview, July 25, 2006.

20. William Payne, interview, July 16, 2007; Stephen Adubato Sr., interview, November 3, 2007.

21. Jonathan Schuppe, "Booker's Crime Campaign Falls Short," *Newark Star-Ledger*, September 6, 2006, 27.

22. Andrew Jacobs, "Booker Comes under Siege after Bloodshed," *New York Times*, August 7, 2007.

23. Stefan Pryor, interview, July 31, 2008.

24. Ironically, Kelling and Wilson developed this theory using Newark as a case study. See George L. Kelling and James Q. Wilson, "Broken Windows: The Police and Neighborhood Safety," *Atlantic Monthly*, March 1982.

25. Daniel Brook, "The Cracks in 'Broken Windows,'" *Boston Globe*, February 19, 2006; Kelling and Wilson, "Broken Windows."

26. Garry McCarthy, interview, July 22, 2008.

27. Although Campos is a native Newarker, his selection brought its own share of controversy. When compromising photos of the chief as a young police officer (he was off duty but in uniform) with scantily clad women at a Howard Stern party in Newark surfaced, Campos acknowledged the inappropriateness of the photos and chalked it up to his immaturity as a young police officer. There were also rumors that he had been photographed shaking the hands of the grand wizard of the Ku Klux Klan, but he denies that this ever happened (see Anthony Campos, interview, August 7, 2008). Despite this, Campos enjoyed a cordial relationship with members of the minority community, earning praise from Booker supporters and foes alike (see Augusto Amador, interview, October 5, 2007; Charles Bell, interview, July 14, 2007.

28. Charles Bell, interview, July 14, 2007.

29. Garry McCarthy, interview, July 22, 2008.

30. Anthony Campos, interview, August 7, 2008.

31. Ronald C. Rice, interview, March 2, 2007.

32. Calvin West, interview, June 10, 2008.

33. Luis Quintana, interview, December 17, 2007.

34. Anthony Campos, interview, August 7, 2008.

35. Garry McCarthy, interview, July 22, 2008.

36. Ibid.

37. Ibid.

38. See Peter J. Boyer, "The Color of Politics," *New Yorker*, February 4, 2008.

39. Garry McCarthy, interview, July 22, 2008.

40. Newark Police Department, "City Wide Crime Stats, Year Ending 12/31/2008," available at www.newarkpdonlne.org (accessed January 16, 2009).

41. I spoke about this with Donna Jackson, a prominent local activist and leader of the failed recall effort against Mayor Booker. She is a strong proponent of the idea that the Booker administration purposely underestimates the number of crimes taking place in the city. After talking with Director McCarthy, I began to get the sense that Ms. Jackson's allegations may stem from the old data collection system, which double-counted some crimes (e.g., the distinction between "shooting" and "shooting hits"). I asked McCarthy whether that could possibly explain Ms. Jackson's position. He was dismissive of her claim, but I think it may explain her assertion (Donna Jackson, interview, May 3, 2008; Garry McCarthy, interview, July 22, 2008). In any case, Mayor Booker stands behind the current

data collection practices and responds to those who claim that he underestimates the number of homicides in the city by saying that he "can't hide bodies."

42. The FBI reported in the summer of 2010 the actual crime rates for the United States through 2008. The 2009 report was still preliminary and may be corrected, but in it the FBI reported the percentage rates of change only from 2008 to 2009, which I used to manually calculate the crime rates for 2009.

43. This data set tabulates only the number of reported crimes, but it is very likely that some crimes (particularly rapes) are not reported. In this analysis, I must use the data available, even though I am aware of the limitations.

44. The Uniform Crime Reports (UCR) also collect data on arsons, which not all police departments consistently report. Accordingly, I excluded arson data from this analysis.

45. Keep in mind that Sharpe James was still mayor for the first half of 2006, so year-to-year comparisons from 2005 to 2007 cannot be attributed solely to either the Booker or the James administration.

46. Some cities are omitted from the UCR database. In order to qualify for the database, a city's population had to fall in the 100,000-to-500,000 range for the entire four-year period. Atlanta, for example, had a population below 500,000 in 2006, but it exceeded 500,000 in the years after that, so I excluded it from the database. I also excluded cities that changed their reporting standards during this four-year period because those changes make any year-to-year comparison meaningless. Finally, some cities inconsistently reported their crime rates to the FBI during this time period and so either never appear in the UCR database or appear only sporadically. I also excluded those cities (which include Durham, NC, New Haven, and most medium-sized cities in Illinois) from this analysis.

47. The 2009 UCR does not report crime rates for cities with populations smaller than 100,000 residents. Because all of New Jersey's other majority-black cities have populations below 100,000, their crime rates were not included in the 2009 UCR.

48. "Black Mayors of Cities with 50,000-Plus Population, 2007," Joint Center for Political and Economic Studies website, available at http://www.jointcenter .org/index.php/current_research_and_policy_activities/political_participation/black_ elected_officials_roster_introduction_and_overview/black_mayors/table_1f_ black_mayors_of_cities_with_50_000_plus_population_2007 (accessed September 14, 2010).

49. See Boyer, "The Color of Politics"; Lucy Kaylin, "Is Cory Booker the Greatest Mayor in America?" *O Magazine*, September 2010.

50. U.S. Department of Justice, Federal Bureau of Investigations, "Crime in the United States, Table 8: New Jersey Offenses Known to Law Enforcement by State by City, 2010," available at http://www.fbi.gov/about-us/cjis/ucr/crime-in-the -u.s/2010/crime-in-the-u.s.-2010/tables/table-8/10tbl08nj.xls(accessed   October 10, 2011).

51. Because New Jersey's other majority-black cities have populations of less than 100,000, their crime statistics were not reported in the 2009 UCR.

52. Note that the crime rates presented here are *reported* rates and may not reflect the true rate of victimization.

53. Calvin West, interview, June 10, 2008; Richard Monteilh, interview, January 2, 2008.

54. Richard Cammarrieri, interview, August 6, 2008.

55. Arthur Ryan, interview, July 23, 2008; Alfred Koeppe, interview, August 5, 2008.

56. See Gayle Chaneyfield-Jenkins, interview, June 10, 2008; Charles Bell, interview, July 14, 2007.

57. David Kociesniewski, "Former Mayor of Newark Is Indicted," *New York Times*, July 13, 2007; David Kociesniewski, "Newark Ex-Mayor's Deals Stirs Questions," *New York Times*, July 30, 2006.

58. Kociesniewski, "Former Mayor of Newark Is Indicted"; Jonathan Miller and Richard G. Jones, "Ex-Newark Mayor Convicted of Fraud," *New York Times*, April 17, 2008; Kociesniewski, "Former Mayor of Newark Is Indicted"; Kociesniewski, "Newark Ex-Mayor's Deals Stirs Questions." In September 2010, a federal judge overturned one of James's convictions. Earlier that year, the U.S. Supreme Court ruled that the federal statute outlawing "theft of honest services" (i.e., profiting from a conflict of interest) was too vague. The judge threw out James's theft of honest services conviction but upheld his other convictions. At the time of this ruling, James and Riley had already served their sentences. See Ted Sherman, "Federal Court Reverses One of Ex-Newark Mayor Sharpe James' Corruption Convictions," nj.com, September 16, 2010, available at http://www .nj.com/news/index.ssf/2010/09/federal_court_reverses_one_of.html (accessed January 27, 2011).

59. Stefan Pryor, interview, July 31, 2008.

60. The Nets will eventually settle in Brooklyn. Until their stadium is built, they are scheduled to play for two years at the Prudential Center, starting in 2011.

61. "Newark Bond Sale Advances an Arena," *New York Times*, June 12, 2004; Richard Lezin Jones, "Arena and Vote Are Not Linked, Governor Says," *New York Times*, January 23, 2002.

62. Supporters of big projects like NJPAC and the arena argue that these projects instill a sense of pride among community residents. Longtime Newark and Booker booster Raymond Chambers maintains, for instance, that in the years after NJPAC was built, Newark youngsters who attended sponsored summer programs took greater pride in their comportment because they were proud to have NJPAC in their town. He believed that the arena had the potential to create the same type of pride (Raymond Chambers, interview, August 6, 2010).

63. Stefan Pryor, interview, July 31, 2008.

64. Ibid.

65. Ras Baraka, interview, September 16, 2007.

66. Stefan Pryor, interview, July 31, 2008.

67. Ibid.

68. U.S. Bureau of the Census, "Fact Sheet: Newark City, New Jersey (American Community Survey 2005–2007)," available at http://factfinder.census.gov/qfd/sttes/34/3451000.html (accessed August 31, 2009).

69. Cory Booker, inaugural address, New Jersey Performing Arts Center, Newark, July 1, 2006.

70. Byron Price, interview, October 8, 2007.

71. Stefan Pryor, interview, July 31, 2008.

72. Ibid.

73. First-source legislation requires that when hiring, city contractors give priority consideration to Newark residents. Passing this resolution was one of Cory Booker's key legislative accomplishments as Central Ward councilman.

74. U.S. Bureau of the Census, "State and County Quickfacts for Newark (city), New Jersey," 2009, available at http://quickfacts.census.gov/qfd/states/34/3451000.html (accessed August 31, 2009).

75. Andra Gillespie, "The Third Wave: A Theoretical Introduction to the Post–Civil Rights Generation of African American Leadership," National Political Science Review 12, no. 1 (2009): 139–61.

76. U.S. Bureau of the Census, "State and County Quickfacts [for Newark (city), New Jersey, Atlanta (city), Georgia, Detroit (city), Michigan, Philadelphia (city), Pennsylvania]," 2009, available at http://quickfacts.census.gov (accessed August 17, 2010).

77. For example, the cigar, ice, and milk stores allow businesses to sell those products.

78. Stefan Pryor, interview, July 31, 2008.

79. David Mitchell, interview, August 10, 2008.

80. Alfred Koeppe, interview, August 5, 2008.

81. Cory Booker, interview, August 3, 2008.

82. Eddie S. Glaude Jr., In a Shade of Blue (Chicago: University of Chicago Press, 2007).

83. Roland Martin, "Ready or Not. . . ." Savoy, March 2003, 52–56.

Notes to Chapter 6

1. Peter J. Boyer, "The Color of Politics," New Yorker, February 4, 2008; Kareem Fahim, "In Calmer Newark, the Unease Persists," New York Times, February 16, 2008.

2. The Newark Teachers' Union paid for the sign on MacCarter Highway and a similar sign right next to city hall. Joseph Del Grasso, the union president, made a habit of purchasing billboard space to weigh in on salient issues in the

community. For example, before the pay-to-play billboards, he put up billboards regarding the city's high homicide rate, which angered both the Booker administration and local business and educational leaders who thought that the signs attracted negative attention. Del Grasso intended to use the pay-to-play billboards to draw attention to a general culture of corruption that had deep roots in Newark. But he made no specific allegations of corruption in the Booker administration (Del Grasso, interview, May 2, 2008).

3. Drew Westen, *The Political Brain* (New York: Public Affairs Press, 2007), xv.

4. Ibid., 16.

5. Ibid., 4–5.

6. Ibid., 7–8.

7. Ibid., 5.

8. Ibid., 9–10.

9. Ibid., 37.

10. Phillip Converse, "The Nature of Belief Systems in Mass Publics," in *Ideology and Discontent*, ed. David Apter (New York: Free Press, 1964), 206–62.

11. John H. Sullivan, John H. Aldrich, Eugene Borgida, and Wendy Rahn, "Candidate Appraisal and Human Nature: Man and Superman in the 1984 Election," *Political Psychology* 11, no. 3 (1990): 465.

12. Ibid., 459–84.

13. Ibid.

14. Ibid.

15. Carolyn Martindale and Lillian Rae Dunlap, "The African Americans," in *U.S. News Coverage of Racial Minorities: A Sourcebook, 1934–1996*, ed. Beverly Ann Deepe Keever, Carolyn Martindale, and Mary Ann Weston (Westport, CT: Greenwood, 1997), 98–102.

16. See Melissa V. Harris-Lacewell, *Barbershops, Bibles, and BET: Everyday Talk and Black Political Thought* (Princeton: Princeton University Press, 2004), 208.

17. Cory Booker, interview, August 3, 2008.

18. Ibid.

19. Ibid.

20. Gayle Chaneyfield-Jenkins, interview, June 10, 2008.

21. Clement Price, interview, June 30, 2008.

22. George Norcross, interview, September 30, 2010.

23. Alfred Koeppe, interview, August 5, 2008.

24. Cory Booker, interview, August 3, 2008; Carolyn Booker, interview, March 4, 2008; Cary Booker Sr., interview, March 15, 2008.

25. Virginia D. Jones, interview, June 9, 2008.

26. John James, interview, June 18, 2010.

27. Kenneth Gibson, interview, December 18, 2007.

28. Gayle Chaneyfield-Jenkins, interview, June 10, 2008; Clement Price, interview, June 30, 2008; David Mitchell, interview, August 10, 2008.

29. Ronald L. Rice, interview, December 16, 2007.

30. Ibid.

31. See Richard F. Fenno Jr., *Home Style: House Members in Their Districts* (New York: HarperCollins, 1978).

32. Mamie Bridgeforth, interview, July 16, 2007.

33. Ibid.

34. William Payne, interview, July 16, 2007.

35. William Payne, interview, July 16, 2007; Ronald L. Rice, interview, December 16, 2007.

36. Fenno, *Home Style*.

37. Mamie Bridgeforth, interview, July 16, 2007.

38. Carl Sharif, interview, July 22, 2006.

39. John "Bo" Kemp, interview, December 17, 2007; Richard Monteilh, interview, January 2, 2008.

40. See Kenneth Gibson, interview, December 18, 2007; Richard Monteilh, interview, January 2, 2008; Charles Bell, interview, July 14, 2007; Gayle Chaneyfield-Jenkins, interview, June 10, 2008; Amiri Baraka, interview, July 18, 2007; Ras Baraka, interview, September 16, 2007; Ronald L. Rice, interview, December 16, 2007; David Mitchell, interview, August 10, 2008.

41. Donald Payne Jr., interview, October 6, 2007. Note that Councilman Payne's father is Congressman Donald Payne, whose ties with mayor are tenuous.

42. Andrew Jacobs, "Access to Mayor Doesn't Solve All Problems," *New York Times*, March 8, 2007; Cory Booker, interview, August 3, 2008; Terrance Bankston, interview, January 9, 2008.

43. John "Bo" Kemp, interview, December 17, 2007.

44. Oscar Sidney James, interview, October 8, 2007. As a matter of full disclosure, I did point out to a future Booker administration official that compensation issues had prevented mayors in other cities from being able to attract top talent. I cannot be sure if my report had any effect on the administration's behavior.

45. Elnardo Webster, interview, August 22, 2007; Pablo Fonseca, interview, January 10, 2008; Jermaine James, interview, October 7, 2007.

46. Amiri Baraka, interview, July 18, 2007.

47. Modia Butler, interview, December 13, 2007.

48. Katie Wang, "Dispute Puts City Contracts in Limbo," *Newark Star-Ledger*, June 3, 2007.

49. Wang, "Dispute Puts City Contracts in Limbo"; New Jersey State League of Municipalities, "Types and Forms of New Jersey Municipal Government"; Aney Chandy, interview, December 17, 2007.

50. Aney Chandy, interview, December 17, 2007.

51. Councilwoman Rone had her own troubles. In December 2006, she was arrested for obstructing justice when she used her official position to defend her nephew, who was pulled over for a traffic violation. A New Jersey statute allows judges to remove elected officials from office if they are convicted for obstructing

justice. In 2008, the Essex County prosecutor, Paula Dow, did apply the statute in Rone's case and asked that she be removed from office. Dow later attempted to withdraw her request, but by then, it was too late. In July 2008, Councilwoman Rone lost her seat. See Jeffrey C. Mays and Katie Wang, "Ward Politics Again Get Better of Newark Mayor," *Newark Star-Ledger*, June 11, 2008.

52. Anibal Ramos, interview, December 19, 2007.

53. Rahman Muhammad, interview, June 24, 2006.

54. Ibid.

55. Thomas Giblin, interview, May 1, 2008.

56. Jermaine James, interview, October 7, 2007.

57. Pablo Fonseca, interview, January 10, 2008; Cory Booker, interview, August 3, 2008; Jeffery C. Mays, "Booker Sees Slate of District Leaders Fall Short," *Newark Star-Ledger*, June 5, 2008.

58. Pablo Fonseca, interview, January 10, 2008; Darrin Sharif, interview, November 5, 2007; Cory Booker, interview, August 3, 2008.

59. Wendell Phillips, interview, August 8, 2008; David Mitchell, interview, August 10, 2008.

60. Despite the early complaints, the municipal council voted in November 2010 to reappoint Giordano as fire director. The day after his reappointment, Giordano retired from the fire department. The next week, he started a job advising Booker on how to cut the city's budget. At the time of Giordano's retirement, he had just qualified for a significant increase in his pension. He would be eligible to collect his pension while earning a salary from the city as a member of the mayor's staff. Combined, Giordano would make more than $200,000 a year. In context, Giordano's situation is not unusual. For instance, a number of employees of the municipal council (this includes staff and council members) have second jobs, even though the council pays full-time salaries. This practice predates the start of the Booker administration. See David Giambusso, "Series of Career Changes for Former Newark Fire Director, Now Booker Aide, Nets Him 206K," nj.com, December 9, 2010, available at http://www.nj.com/news/index.ssf/2010/12/former_newark_fire_director_is.html (accessed October 22, 2011); Brad R. Tuttle, *How Newark Became Newark: The Rise, Fall, and Rebirth of an American City* (New Brunswick: Rutgers University Press, 2009), 227.

61. Jeffrey C. Mays, "Newark OKs Pact It Once Rejected to Fix Website," nj.com, October 22, 2008, available at http://www.nj.com/newark/index.ssf/2008/10/newark_oks_pact_it_once_reject.html (accessed October 22, 2011); Jeffrey C. Mays and Katie Wang, "Booker Fills More Top Jobs," *Newark Star-Ledger*, July 6, 2006.

62. Augusto Amador, interview, October 5, 2007.

63. Cory Booker, Harper Address, speech delivered at Yale Law School, New Haven, September 24, 2001.

64. Ronald C. Rice, interview, March 2, 2007; Anibal Ramos, interview, December 19, 2007.

65. Rodney Lewis, interview, July 17, 2007.

66. Former *Newark Star-Ledger* reporter Jeffrey Mays has his doubts about the story as well. In a recent article on theroot.com, he noted that he got Booker to admit that T-Bone is an "archetype" and that he embellished a story about a local crack house where children accompanied their drug-addicted parents to get high. Nikita Stewart and Jeffrey Mays, "A Tale of Two Post-racial Mayors," *The Root*, September 14, 2010, available at http://www.theroot.com/views/adrian-m-fenty -cory-booker (accessed September 14, 2010).

67. Cory Booker, interview, August 3, 2008.

68. In 2009, Booker and O'Brien engaged in a somewhat over-the-top You-Tube feud in which they both tried to ban the other from their respective towns and states. O'Brien invited Booker on *The Tonight Show* to end the feud. Booker left that interview with a $50,000 donation from O'Brien to his nonprofit organization Newark Now.

69. Andrew Jacobs, "A Political Neophyte in Newark Challenges a Shrewd Incumbent," *New York Times*, March 29, 2002; "This Morning," *The Hotline*, May 17, 2006, available at www.nationaljournal.com/hotline/ (accessed January 17, 2009).

70. Clement Price, interview, June 30, 2008; Mamie Bridgeforth, interview, July 16, 2007.

71. Andrew Jacobs, "Battling the Old Guard and the Rumor Mill," *New York Times*, July 3, 2007.

72. Cory Booker, interview, August 3, 2008.

73. Abraham Lincoln, first inaugural address, 1861.

74. William Payne, interview, July 16, 2007.

75. Cory Booker, " 'Spokesmodel' Speaks Out," *Stanford Daily News*, February 5, 1992;
Cory Booker, "Why Have I Lost Control?" *Stanford Daily News*, May 6, 1992.

76. Cory Booker's summit speech, youTube.com, posted by tvjersey, August 3, 2007, available at http://www.youtube.com/watch?v=vxOHVIaNXaY (accessed November 2, 2010); Joan Whitlow, "Mayor Gives Newarkers Cause to Doubt," *Newark Star-Ledger*, August 3, 2007.

77. Joan Whitlow, "Mayor Gives Newarkers Cause to Doubt," *Newark Star-Ledger*, August 3, 2007.

78. McKenzie Collins, interview, August 11, 2008.

79. Cory Booker, interview, August 3, 2008.

80. Jermaine James, interview, October 7, 2007.

81. Elnardo Webster, interview, August 22, 2007.

82. McKenzie Collins, interview, August 11, 2008.

83. Augusto Amador, interview, October 5, 2007.

84. Nate Schweber and Fernanda Santos, "Shooting of 4 College Friends Baffles Newark," *New York Times*, August 6, 2007.

85. Thomas Giblin, interview, May 1, 2008; Steve DeMicco, interview, June 12, 2008.

86. Adolph Reed Jr., *The Jesse Jackson Phenomenon* (New Haven: Yale University Press, 1986).

87. George Will, "Newark's Nasty Race," *Washington Post*, March 17, 2002; Ellis Cose, "What the Revolution Was For," *Newsweek*, May 13, 2002.

88. See Martindale and Dunlap, "The African Americans," 87, 98, 116.

89. Paul Gilroy, *Against Race: Imagining Political Culture beyond the Color Line* (Cambridge: Belknap / Harvard University Press, 2002), chap. 9.

90. Scott Raab, "The Battle of Newark, Starring Cory Booker," *Esquire*, July 2008.

91. Scott Raab, interview, August 2, 2008; Cory Booker, letter to Mark Warren, executive editor of *Esquire*, June 11, 2008.

92. Scott Raab, interview, August 2, 2008.

93. Ibid.

94. Matt Bai, "Is Obama the End of Black Politics?" *New York Times Magazine*, August 10, 2008.

95. Terrence Samuel, "Young, Black and Post–Civil Rights," *American Prospect*, September 4, 2007.

96. See Patillo, *Black on the Block*.

97. Walter Fields, interview, December 18, 2007.

98. Ibid.

99. See Cathy J. Cohen, *The Boundaries of Blackness* (Chicago: University of Chicago Press, 1999).

Notes to Chapter 7

1. Jeffrey Pressman, "Preconditions of Mayoral Leadership," *American Political Science Review* 66, no. 2 (1972): 512.

2. See Linda Williams, "Black Political Progress in the 1980's: The Electoral Arena," in *The New Black Politics: The Search for Political Power*, 2nd ed., ed. Michael B. Preston, Lenneal J. Henderson Jr., and Paul Puryear (New York: Longman, 1987), 97–136; Robert C. Smith, "Recent Elections and Black Politics: The Maturation or Death of Black Politics? *PS: Political Science and Politics* 23, no. 2 (1990): 160–62.

3. Rufus Browning, Dale Rogers Marshall, and David Tabb, *Protest Is Not Enough* (Berkeley: University of California Press, 1984), chap. 1.

4. Michael B. Preston, "The Election of Harold Washington: An Examination of the SES Model in the 1983 Chicago Mayoral Election," in *The New Black Politics: The Search for Political Power*, 2nd ed., ed. Michael B. Preston, Lenneal Henderson Jr., and Paul L. Puryear (New York: Longman, 1987), 139–71.

5. Preston, "The Election of Harold Washington"; See also Zoltan Hajnal, *Changing White Attitudes toward Black Political Leadership* (New York: Cambridge University Press, 2007).

6. Browning, Marshall, and Tabb, *Protest Is Not Enough*.

7. Ruth Ann Strickland and Marcia Lynn Whicker, "Comparing the Wilder and Gantt Campaigns: A Model for Black Candidate Success in Statewide Elections," *PS: Political Science and Politics* 25, no. 2 (1992): 204–12.

8. David T. Canon, Matthew M. Schousen, and Patrick J. Sellers, "The Supply Side of Congressional Redistricting: Race and Strategic Politicians, 1972–1992," *Journal of Politics* 58, no. 3 (1996): 846–62.

9. Luis Quintana, interview, December 17, 2007.

10. Cory Booker, interview, August 3, 2008; Stefan Pryor, interview, July 31, 2008.

11. Cory Booker, interview, August 3, 2008.

12. See Mamie Bridgeforth, interview, July 16, 2007.

13. Cory Booker, interview, August 3, 2008; Carl Sharif, interview, July 22, 2006.

14. Gayle Chaneyfield-Jenkins, interview, June 10, 2008.

15. Cory Booker, interview, August 3, 2008.

16. Katie Wang and Jeffrey Mays, "Booker Wins Big," *Newark Star-Ledger*, May 10, 2006.

17. Hector Corchado, interview, July 18, 2007; Carl Sharif, interview, July 22, 2006.

18. Carl Sharif, interview, July 22, 2006; Gayle Chaneyfield-Jenkins, interview, June 10, 2008; Ras Baraka, interview, September 16, 2007.

19. New Jersey allowed dual officeholding until 2008. Before then, many mayors simultaneously served in the state legislature. For example, the late Glenn Cunningham served in the legislature while he was mayor of Jersey City, and Congressman Albio Sires simultaneously served in the state assembly while he was mayor of West New York, NJ.

20. Ronald L. Rice, interview, December 16, 2007.

21. William Payne, interview, July 16, 2007.

22. Luis Quintana, interview, December 17, 2007.

23. Stephen Adubato Sr., interview, November 3, 2007.

24. William Payne, interview, July 16, 2007.

25. Stephen Adubato Sr., interview, November 3, 2007.

26. Ibid.

27. Ibid.

28. "Results: New Jersey," 2008, cnn.com, available at http://www.cnn.com/ELECTION/2008/primaries/results/state/#val=NJ (accessed January 26, 2011).

29. Jeffery C. Mays, "Booker Sees Slate of District Leaders Fall Short," *Newark Star-Ledger*, June 5, 2008; Joan Whitlow, "Worrisome Returns for the Mayor," *Newark Star-Ledger*, June 6, 2008; Joan Whitlow, interview, July 31, 2008.

30. Cory Booker, interview, August 3, 2008.

31. Andrew Jacobs, "Access to Mayor Doesn't Solve All Problems," *New York Times*, March 8, 2007.

32. Blonnie Watson, interview, June 13, 2008; Joseph Parlavecchio, interview, July 31, 2008; Phillip Thigpen, interview, June 16, 2008.

33. "District 34 Profile: 2008–2009 Legislative Delegation," available at www.njvoterinfo.org/d/34.php (accessed January 17, 2009).

34. Terrance Bankston, interview, January 9, 2008.

35. Blonnie Watson, interview, June 13, 2008.

36. Sadly, Brown passed away in 2009.

37. Jeffrey C. Mays and Katie Wang, "Ward Politics Again Get Better of Newark Mayor," *Newark Star-Ledger*, June 11, 2008.

38. Chanta L. Jackson, "Six Female Candidates among Those Vying for Newark Council Seat," *Newark Star-Ledger*, October 19, 2008, available at http://www.nj.com/newark/index.ssf/2008/10/six_female_candidates_among_th.html (accessed February 17, 2011).

39. Jeffrey C. Mays, "Charles Bell Wins Newark Central Ward Seat," *Newark Star-Ledger*, November 5, 2008, available at http://www.nj.com/news/index.ssf/2008/11/charles_bell_wins_newark_centr.html, (accessed February 17, 2011).

40. Blonnie Watson, interview, June 13, 2008; Joseph Parlavecchio, interview, July 31, 2008.

41. Max Pizarro, "Amador, East Ward Democrats, Feel Dissed by Booker on Election Day," Politickernj.com, June 3, 2008.

42. Luis Quintana, interview, December 17, 2007; Joseph Parlavecchio, interview, July 31, 2008; Phillip Thigpen, interview, June 16, 2008; Wendell Phillips, interview, August 8, 2008; Calvin West, interview, June 10, 2008.

43. Thomas Giblin, interview, May 1, 2008; Steve DeMicco, interview, June 12, 2008.

44. Thomas Giblin, interview, May 1, 2008.

45. New Jersey did not have a lieutenant governor, but after the resignations of governors Christie Whitman and James McGreevey, the voters opted to amend the state's constitution to elect a lieutenant governor starting in 2009, to ensure smoother transitions. See David W. Chen, "Corzine Prevails in a Nasty Governor's Campaign in New Jersey," *New York Times*, November 9, 2005.

46. Steve DeMicco, interview, June 12, 2008.

47. George Norcross, interview, September 30, 2010.

48. Ibid.

49. Karen Kaufmann, *The Urban Voter: Group Conflict and Mayoral Voting Behavior in American Cities* (Ann Arbor: University of Michigan Press, 2004), 43.

50. U.S. Bureau of the Census, "Fact Sheet: Newark City, New Jersey (American Community Survey 2005–2007)," available at http://factfinder.census.gov/qfd/sttes/34/3451000.html (accessed August 31, 2009).

51. Sam Roberts, "Biggest Urban Growth Is in South and West," *New York Times*, June 28, 2007; Roberto Suro and Audrey Singer, "Latino Growth in Metropolitan America: Changing Patterns, New Locations," working paper, Center on

Urban and Metropolitan Policy and the Pew Hispanic Center (Washington, DC: Brookings Institution, 2002), 18.

52. Kenneth Gibson, interview, December 18, 2007.

53. Luis Quintana, interview, December 17, 2007; Anibal Ramos, interview, December 19, 2007.

54. Pablo Fonseca, interview, January 10, 2008; Marilyn Gaynor, interview, June 28, 2006.

55. Cory Booker, interview, August 3, 2008.

56. David Giambusso, "Poll Finds Newark Mayor Cory Booker Would Be Strong NJ Gov Candidate," *Newark Star-Ledger*, November 12, 2009.

Notes to Chapter 8

1. Jonathan Miller and Richard G. Jones, "Ex-Newark Mayor Convicted of Fraud," *New York Times*, April 17, 2008.

2. David Giambusso, "Newark Mayor Cory Booker Has Raised $7.5M for Upcoming Election, Report Says," *Newark Star-Ledger*, May 5, 2010; Clifford Minor, interview, July 8, 2010.

3. Josh Margolin, "Stephen Adubato Sr. and Cory Booker Bury the Hatchet," nj.com, June 22, 2009.

4. Clifford Minor, interview, July 8, 2010.

5. In September 2010, Minor was indicted for allegedly being part of a scheme in which he was paid to serve as counsel for a client who falsely pleaded guilty to a weapons charge for a friend with a more extensive criminal record. The friend with the more extensive record was allegedly trying to avoid the extra penalties that would be levied against him. Both Minor and the friend making the false plea were allegedly paid for their services. See Joe Ryan, "Ex-Essex County Prosecutor Clifford Minor Is Charged with Bribery, Obstructing Justice," nj.com, September 23, 2010, available at http://www.nj.com/news/index.ssf/2010/09/former_essex _county_prosecutor.html (accessed February 17, 2011).

6. Newark elections are nonpartisan, so candidates must win a clear majority of the vote in order to win. If no candidate wins 50% plus one vote, the top two candidates must face each other in a runoff election about a month after the original election.

7. Joan Whitlow, "Mayor Cory Booker Still in a Political Street Fight in Newark," *Newark Star-Ledger*, February 12, 2010; Carl Sharif, interview, July 22, 2010.

8. Stephen Adubato Sr., interview, November 3, 2007.

9. Gayle Chaneyfield-Jenkins, interview, June 10, 2008.

10. "Question," campaign leaflet, paid for by the Committee to Elect Darrin Sharif, Brette Dawson, treasurer, Newark, NJ.

11. David Giambusso, "Central Ward Council Runoff between Bell, Sharif Is Too Close to Call," nj.com, June 15, 2010, available at http://www.nj.com/news/

index.ssf/2010/06/charles_bell_wins_against_chal.html (accessed November 4, 2010).

12. David Giambusso, "NJ Sen Codey Supports Newark Council Candidate Darrin Sharif with Automated Calls," nj.com, May 3, 2010, available at http://www.nj.com/news/index.ssf/2010/05/nj_sen_codey_robo-calls_newark.html (accessed June 17, 2010); Carl Sharif, interview, July 26, 2010; Chris Megarian, "Newark Mayor Rebuffs Codey, Throws Support to Sweeney for Senate Presidency," nj.com, October 1, 2009, available at http://www.nj.com/politics/index.ssf/2009/10/newark_mayor_rebuffs_codey_thr.html (accessed June 17, 2010).

13. The Booker campaign initially thought that this district count was incorrect, so they changed the tally in their offices. They eventually learned, however, that this was correct and amended their internal numbers accordingly.

14. Max Pizarro, "Unofficial Results in Newark's Central Ward: Sharif Beats Bell by 25 Votes," politickernj.com, June 15, 2009, available at http://www.politickernj.com/max/39754/unofficial-results-newarks-central-ward-sharif-beats-bell-20-votes (accessed November 4, 2010).

15. Some voters did not provide enough information to verify their identity or their address. A couple of them did not live in the Central Ward; two other voters were suspected of committing voter fraud; and a dozen provisional voters were not registered.

16. Just after his reelection in 2010, Booker made it clear that he did not want to seek a third term as mayor of Newark. According to Newark Star-Ledger reporter Tom Moran, Booker's exact words were, "I've asked my friends to get a weapon, preferably a gun or a knife, and shoot me" (see Joan Whitlow, "Off the Cuff Remark Weakened Mayor Cory Booker's Hand," Newark Star-Ledger, August 13, 2010). After Facebook founder Mark Zuckerberg made a $100 million gift to the Newark public schools on the condition that Booker play an active role in reforming the school system, Booker changed his position, noting that it would probably take more than one term in office to do this. See David Giambusso, "Newark Mayor Booker Likely to Seek Third Term on Heels of $100M Schools Grant," Newark Star-Ledger, September 26, 2010.

17. David Giambusso, "Poll Finds Newark Mayor Cory Booker Would Be Strong NJ Gov Candidate," Newark Star-Ledger, November 12, 2009.

18. Andra Gillespie and Emma Tolbert, "Racial Authenticity and Redistricting: A Comparison of Artur Davis's 2000 and 2002 Congressional Campaigns," in Whose Black Politics? Cases in Post-racial Black Leadership, ed. Andra Gillespie (New York: Routledge, 2010), 45–66.

19. Charles J. Dean, "Davis Set to Declare Governor's Race Bid: Would Be First Democrat to Announce," Birmingham News, February 1, 2009.

20. Such an effort would likely have been fruitless, as both Joe Reed and Richard Arrington declared their opposition to Davis's candidacy in 2009. See "Artur Davis Finds Opposition Coming from Black Leadership," Associated Press,

December 9, 2009, available at http://blog.al.com/live/2009/12/artur_davis_davis_finds_strongest_op.html (accessed January 29, 2011).

21. See Gillespie and Tolbert, "Racial Authenticity and Redistricting."

22. Chuck Dean, "Artur Davis' Loss in Alabama's Black Precincts 'Stunning,' " *Birmingham News*, June 3, 2010.

23. Robert Albritton et al., "Deracialization and the New Black Politics," in *Race, Politics and Governance in the United States*, ed. Huey L. Perry (Gainesville: University of Florida Press, 1996), 173–92; Charles E. Jones and Michael Clemons, "A Model of Racial Crossover Voting: An Assessment of the Wilder Victory," in *Dilemmas of Black Politics*, ed. Georgia A. Persons (New York: HarperCollins, 1993), 132.

24. Carol A. Pieranuzzi and John D. Hutcheson, "The Rise and Fall of Deracialization: Andrew Young As Mayor and Gubernatorial Candidate," in *Race, Politics and Governance in the United States*, ed. Huey L. Perry (Gainesville: University of Florida Press, 1996), 96–106.

25. See Mary Orndorff, "Outgoing Alabama Rep Artur Davis Shuts Door on State Politics," al.com, October 3, 2010, available at http://blog.al.com/sweethome/2010/10/outgoing_alabama_rep_artur_dav.html (accessed November 4, 2010); Thomas Spencer, "Artur Davis Says He Won't Run for Office Again after Loss in Alabama Governor's Race," al.com, June 3, 2010, available at http://blog.al.com/spotnews/2010/06/davis_wont_run_for_office_agai.html (accessed August 10, 2010).

26. Kenneth Lovett et al., "Harold Ford to Announce He Will Not Run for U.S. Senate Seat against Kirsten Gillibrand," *New York Daily News*, March 1, 2010; Harold Ford Jr., "Ford: I'm Gearing Up for Senate Race," *New York Post*, January 12, 2010.

27. "Florida Senate-Democratic Primary," Real Clear Politics, available at http://www.realclearpolitics.com/epolls/2010/senate/fl/florida_senate_democratic_primary-1096.html#polls (accessed November 4, 2010); Beth Reinhard and Adam C. Smith, "Kendrick Meek Calls Win 'a Victory for Everyday People,' " *Miami Herald*, August 25, 2010; Beth Reinhard, "Marco Rubio Defeats 2 Rivals for Florida Senate," *Miami Herald*, November 2, 2010.

28. Brian Mooney, "An Incumbent Defies Odds to the End," *Boston Globe*, November 3, 2010; Frank Phillips and Michael Levenson, "Patrick Roars to 2d Term," *Boston Globe*, November 3, 2010.

29. Tim Craig and Nikita Stewart, "Gray Defeats Fenty As Voters Choose Conciliatory Approach over Brash Tactics," *Washington Post*, September 15, 2010.

30. See Frank Rich, "Obama's Squandered Summer," *New York Times*, September 12, 2010; Mica Brevington, "Leadership Expert: Obama Is No 'A' Student," fortune.com, October 25, 2010, available at http://money.cnn.com/2010/10/25/news/economy/obama_leadership_review.fortune/index.htm (accessed November 4, 2010); Jim Rutenberg and Jeff Zeleny, "Democrats Outrun by a 2-Year GOP Comeback," *New York Times*, November 3, 2010.

31. In the summer of 2011, the U.S. attorney's office opened a criminal probe into allegations that Vincent Gray's campaign had paid a third candidate, Sulaimon Brown, to openly criticize Adrian Fenty in the 2010 Washington, DC, Democratic primary. Presumably, members of the Gray campaign would benefit from Brown's attacks without having to sully themselves or to fear that Brown, a longshot candidate, would actually win the race. Gray's favorability ratings fell during his first six months in office, during which allegations of nepotism and excessive staff salaries came to light. See Nikita Stewart, "Vincent Gray Campaign under Vigorous Federal Scrutiny," *Washington Post*, October 15, 2011, available at http://www.washingtonpost.com/local/dc-politics/vincent-gray-campaign-under-vigorous-federal-scrutiny/2011/10/13/gIQAfz0QnL_story.html (accessed October 20, 2011); Nikita Stewart, Jon Cohen, and Peyton Craighill, "Gray's Popularity Takes a Plunge, New Poll Shows," *Washington Post*, June 19, 2011, A1.

32. Raymond Chambers, interview, August 6, 2010; Shavar Jeffries, interview, July 21, 2010.

33. David Giambusso, "Poll Finds Newark Mayor Cory Booker Would Be Strong NJ Gov Candidate" and David Giambusso, "Newark Mayor Cory Booker Rules Out 2012 US Senate Run, Keeps 2014 Speculation Alive," both at nj.com, June 9, 2011, available at http://www.nj.com/news/index.ssf/2011/06/newark_mayor_cory_booker_rules.html (accessed October 22, 2011).

34. From 2006-2010, there were four notable scandals involving city officials. In 2009, Marilyn Gaynor, who served as buildings manager, pleaded guilty to falsifying time sheets for personal use. She hired workers from her department to do some home repairs. While Ms. Gaynor maintained that she paid a supervisor from her personal funds for the work (he was supposed to distribute the money to the workers), records indicated that the employees were paid overtime from the city for the job. The supervisor who served as the intermediary also pleaded guilty to falsifying the time sheets. Two municipal council employees were also caught in corruption scandals. Keith Reid, the former chief of staff to Council President Mildred Crump, pleaded guilty to bribery and extortion. In 2007, he was arrested in a statewide sting after accepting bribes from an undercover federal officer who posed as an insurance agent seeking access to local officials. Melvin Bittle, an aide to Councilman Ronald Rice Jr., was indicted in 2009 for offering to resolve a liquor license dispute for a bar owner for $1,000. Finally, the former deputy mayor, Ron Salahuddin, was indicted in 2010 for trying to use his office to steer city demolition subcontracts to a firm in which he had an ownership stake. He was convicted in 2011 of conspiracy to commit extortion. Cory Booker was not personally implicated in any of these scandals. In fact, when Salahuddin was indicted, Booker noted that his administration had helped secure the corruption convictions of nineteen people since becoming mayor. He later testified against Salahuddin. See Phillip Read, "Former Newark Building Officials Plead Guilty to Theft," nj.com, October 2, 2009, available at http://www.nj.com/news/index.ssf/2009/10/former_newark_building_officia_1.html

(accessed October 17, 2011); Katie Wang, "Ex-Newark Official Pleads Guilty to Attempted Extortion, Bribery," nj.com, November 24, 2008, available at http://www.nj.com/news/index.ssf/2008/11/exnewark_official_pleads_guilt. html (accessed October 17, 2011); Carmen Juri, "Former Aide to Newark City Councilman Indicted for Soliciting $1,000 from Bar Owner," nj.com, March 10, 2009, available at http://www.nj.com/news/index.ssf/2009/03/former_aide_to_ newark_city_cou.html (accessed October 17, 2011); David Giambusso, "Verdict in Newark Corruption Trial: Former Deputy Mayor Salahuddin Found Guilty of Conspiracy," nj.com, October 14, 2011, available at http://www.nj.com/news/ index.ssf/2011/10/verdict_in_newark_corruption_t.html (accessed October 20, 2011).

35. Lorrie Frasure, "The Burden of Jekyll and Hyde: Barack Obama, Racial Identity and Black Political Behavior," in *Whose Black Politics? Cases in Post-racial Black Leadership*, ed. Andra Gillespie (New York: Routledge, 2010), 133–54.

36. Raymond Chambers, interview, August 6, 2010.

Notes to Chapter 9

1. Martin Luther King Jr., "Address at Public Meeting of the Southern Christian Ministers Conference of Mississippi," in *The Papers of Martin Luther King Jr.*, ed. Clayborne Carson, vol. 5, *Threshold of a New Decade, January 1959 to December 1960* (Berkeley : University of California Press, 2005), 289.

2. Ibid., 281–90.

3. Marshall Curry, director, "Street Fight" (DVD), 2005.

4. Damien Cave, "The Bicycle Act, Revisited," nytimes.com, March 21, 2006.

5. See Alexandra Starr, "We Shall Overcome, Too," *Business Week*, July 15, 2002; Roland Martin, "Ready or Not . . . ," *Savoy*, March 2003, 52–56.

6. See Cathy J. Cohen, *The Boundaries of Blackness* (Chicago: University of Chicago Press, 1999).

7. Walter Fields, interview, December 18, 2007.

8. See Charles E. Jones and Michael Clemons, "A Model of Racial Crossover Voting: An Assessment of the Wilder Victory," in *Dilemmas of Black Politics*, ed. Georgia A. Persons (New York: HarperCollins, 1993), 128–46.

9. See Robert Cochran, "Black Father: The Subversive Achievement of Joel Chandler Harris," *African American Review* 38, no. 1 (2004): 21–34.

10. New scholars are giving Harris's work a more sympathetic look than it received in the latter part of the twentieth century. Remember, though, that when Joan Whitlow reported on Cory Booker's speech about Judy Diggs, she invoked the image of Uncle Remus to criticize Booker, thus demonstrating the staying power of negative feelings about that character. See Cochran, "Black Father," 21–34; Joan Whitlow, "Mayor Gives Newarkers Cause to Doubt," *Newark Star-Ledger*, August 3, 2007.

11. Robert M. Farnsworth, introduction to *The Conjure Woman*, by Charles W. Chesnutt (Ann Arbor: University of Michigan Press), v–xix.

Notes to the Epilogue

1. Keep in mind that Crump and James had been bitter political rivals. Crump ran against James for the mayoralty in 1998, and when James beat her and Ronald Rice Sr., he allegedly said that he "fried Rice and dumped Crump."

2. Booker mentioned in a July public hearing that the city had not issued any new bonds in two years. In August 2010, Newark's Standard and Poor's bond rating was AA, where it had been since it was downgraded in 2005. Moody's bond rating of Newark was Baa2, but in August 2010, Moody's noted that it would review the city's bond rating and warned of a potential downgrade in the future. See U.S. Bureau of the Census, "Table 434: Bond Ratings for City Governments by Largest Cities, 2008," available at http://www.census.gov/compendia/statab/2010/tables/10s0434.xls (accessed November 4, 2010); Jeffrey C. Mays, "Newark Retains Its Bond Rating," *Newark Star-Ledger*, April 27, 2007, 31; David Giambusso, "Newark Faces Possible Downgrade of Bond Rating," *Newark Star-Ledger*, August 13, 2010.

3. Some private estimates suggested a rate increase between 38% and 42%. Because Newark was already more than halfway through the budget year under consideration, any tax increases would be retroactive, which would mean that home owners would have to pay the entire tax increase in their last tax assessment of the year. Also, even though the New Jersey legislature passed a cap on property taxes in 2010, which would limit the extent to which cities and towns could raise property taxes in any given year, it was not scheduled to take effect until 2012.

4. See David Giambusso, "Municipal Utility Authority Could Bring Millions to Newark," *Newark Star-Ledger*, June 20, 2010.

5. In public hearings, Booker contended that his proposal was different from Sharpe James's 2001–2003 proposal. James had proposed creating a nonprofit organization to manage the city's water resources. In contrast, Booker's plan was to lease the city's water assets to municipal authority, which would manage the watershed and city's water department. Both mayors claimed that the city would retain control of its water assets under their plan. See Giambusso, "Municipal Utility Authority Could Bring Millions to Newark."

6. Some of this information was discovered during the ethnographic portion of this project. For more information, see David Giambusso, "In Pushback against Pressure from Mayor, Newark Council Delays Vote on Municipal Utility Authority," *Newark Star-Ledger*, July 15, 2010.

7. Donald Payne Jr., interview, July 21, 2010.

8. Ibid.

9. Ibid.

10. Phillip Read, "Newark Mayor Cory Booker Announces 4-Day Work Week for Non-Uniformed City Workers," *Newark Star-Ledger*, July 22, 2010; Bill Hutchinson, "Cory Booker, Newark Mayor, Won't Spend Public Funds on Toilet Paper for City Employees," *New York Daily News*, July 22, 2010; Steven Hoffer, "$70M Budget Gap Means Newark Mayor Can't Spare a Square," aolnews .com, July 22, 2010, available at http://www.aolnews.com/surge-desk/article/70m -budget-gap-means-newark-mayor-cant-spare-a-square/19566243 (accessed November 4, 2010).

11. Meredith Galante, "Hundreds of Newark Residents Attend Booker Municipal Authorities Hearing," nj.com, July 26, 2010, available at http://www.nj.com/ news/index.ssf/2010/07/hundreds_of_newark_residents_a.htm l (accessed July 27, 2010).

12. Ibid.

13. As a result of the public hearings, Booker actually lost support for the MUA among council members. Ronald Rice Jr., who had supported the MUA, told me that he had to change his vote in light of his constituents' overwhelming opposition to it. Note, though, that in fact he was late to the municipal council meeting on August 4 and voted to table the MUA after the official vote had been taken. (Newark allows tardy council members to vote on motions and legislation and have their votes counted in the official record.)

14. Kareem Fahim, "Fears of Regression and Newark Police Force Is Cut," *New York Times*, December 2, 2010.

15. The withholding of rent is related to an ongoing dispute between the Newark Housing Authority (NHA) (the official owner of the arena) and the New Jersey Devils about parking and original cost overruns, among other things. The Devils want to hold the city to a contract signed in the James administration in which the city agreed to pay the Devils $2.7 million in parking revenues, but the Booker administration and the NHA want to renegotiate that deal to share that revenue. See David Giambusso, "Parking Prolongs Prudential Center Rent Dispute between Newark, Devils," *Newark Star-Ledger*, May 26, 2010.

16. Star Ledger Wire Services / Bloomberg News, "NJ Towns See Their Bond Ratings Head South," *Newark Star-Ledger*, December 23, 2009.

17. Bloomberg News, "Moody's Downgrades Newark's Credit Rating As City Faces $30.5 Million Deficit," nj.com, available at http://www.nj.com/news/index .ssf/2010/12/moodys_downgrades_newarks_cred.html (accessed October 11, 2011).

18. David Giambusso, "Newark Council May Resist Booker's Push for Quick Approval of Utility Authority," *Newark Star-Ledger*, July 15, 2010.

19. William E. Nelson, "Cleveland: The Evolution of Black Political Power," and Linda Williams, "Black Political Progress in the 1980's: The Electoral Arena," both in *The New Black Politics: The Search for Political Power*, 2nd ed., ed. Michael B. Preston, Lenneal J. Henderson Jr., and Paul Puryear (New York: Longman, 1987), 172–99.

20. In contrast to the early Cory Booker, though, Fenty tended to be more gracious to his older black opponents, who were temperamentally less inclined to challenge Fenty's racial authenticity. See Rachel Yon, "The Declining Significance of Race: Adrian Fenty and the Smooth Electoral Transition," in *Whose Black Politics? Cases in Post-racial Black Leadership*, ed. Andra Gillespie (New York: Routledge, 2010), 195–213.

21. Adrian Fenty, interview, March 5, 2008.

22. Nikita Stewart and Jon Cohen, "Poll Shows DC Mayor Fenty Getting More Credit Than Support in Primary Race against Gray," *Washington Post*, August 28, 2010.

23. Nikita Stewart and Jeffrey Mays, "A Tale of Two Post-racial Mayors," *The Root*, September 14, 2010, available at http://www.theroot.com/views/adrian-m-fenty-cory-booker (accessed September 14, 2010).

Notes to Appendix A

1. See Michael Burawoy et al., *Ethnography Unbound: Power and Resistance in the Modern Metropolis* (Berkeley: University of California Press, 1991), 2, 272.

2. Richard F. Fenno Jr., *Watching Politicians* (Berkeley: IGS Press/University of California, 1990), 12–14.

3. Elijah Anderson, *Streetwise: Race, Class and Change in an Urban Community* (Chicago: University of Chicago Press); Mary Patillo, *Black on the Block* (Chicago: University of Chicago Press, 2007).

4. I use the term *exclusively* lightly. I was allowed to canvass those districts in part because they were perceived to be low-performing districts and in part because Booker's campaign had already canvassed that area in the months leading up to my arrival. They were confident that they had done all that they could in those districts and thus assumed that any additional votes that I could pick up would be a bonus.

5. Alan S. Gerber and Donald P. Green, "The Effects of Canvassing, Direct Mail and Telephone Contact on Voter Turnout: A Field Experiment," *American Political Science Review* 94, no. 3 (2000): 653–63; Andra Gillespie, "Community, Coordination and Context: A Black Politics Perspective on Voter Mobilization" (PhD diss., Yale University, 2005).

6. Marshall Curry, director, "Street Fight" (DVD), 2005.

7. Burawoy et al., *Ethnography Unbound*, 246.

8. See ibid., 2, 272.

9. I should note that before the launch of Booker's official transition (and before I decided to write this book), I prepared a memorandum for Bo Kemp in which I studied failed mayoralties for insight into how not to repeat their mistakes. The report did discuss staffing issues (including compensation) and handling budget crises. I do not know if anyone else saw the memo. At the time, I

looked at such advising as part of participant observation research, and I had no qualms about offering such support. As the scope of the project extended beyond studying campaigns to studying governance, it became clear that my research agenda would circumscribe my ability to offer Booker additional advice. It turned out to not be a problem, as no other official asked for counsel.

10. By the time we met, the Mount Vernon School murders had taken place, and everyone in Newark had to put their differences aside to address this crisis. Thus I really had no influence at all on Booker's initial response to this crisis.

11. Mary Waters, *Black Identities: West Indian Immigrant Dreams and American Realities* (Cambridge: Harvard University Press / Russell Sage Foundation, 1999).

12. Unfortunately, I was unable to meet with Sharpe James, although I was able to interview key aides and one of his sons. He was entangled in legal troubles and was incarcerated for more than eighteen months during much of my research project. After being released from prison, James was under house arrest and pursuing an appeal. Because of the appeal, James refused to talk to me because, as his son John explained, a gag order prevented him from giving interviews.

13. In fact, Rice Jr. is the only person to whom I have ever made a campaign donation, in 2004, before I officially started this project. I also made a non-research-related in-kind donation in 2010. I was supposed to be reimbursed, but I forgot to pursue it. As his friend, I have also offered Rice advice. I do not advise Councilman Rice about how to vote on specific issues.

14. See Michael Hastings, "The Runaway General," *Rolling Stone*, July 2010, 90–97, 120–21.

15. My IRB approval required that I gain permission from campaign higher-ups and anyone I directly observed for research purposes. In those instances, I could gain permission with a verbal assent. I encountered thousands of people over the course of this research project, most of whom are not explicitly mentioned in the book. Because I was not observing them specifically (or if I was observing them in a public meeting), I did not have to get permission to make observations in their presence. Those people were the most likely to see my notebook and ask what I was doing (or if I were a journalist). The high-ranking people already knew what I was doing.

16. Deborah did give me some ethnographic data that did make it into the book. Specifically, she was able to confirm some factual information, and because she was uniquely positioned to confirm those facts, I had no choice but to use her information.

Index

About the Author

Andra Gillespie is an associate professor in the Department of Political Science at Emory University.